THE CENTER FOR CHINESE STUDIES

at the University of California, Berkeley, supported by the Ford Foundation, the Institute of International Studies (University of California, Berkeley), and the State of California, is the unifying organization for social science and interdisciplinary research on contemporary China.

RECENT PUBLICATIONS

Lowell Dittmer
Liu Shao-ch'i and the Chinese Cultural Revolution: The Politics of Mass Criticism

Tetsuya Kataoka
Resistance and Revolution in China: The Communists and the Second United Front

Edward E. Rice
Mao's Way

Frederic Wakeman, Jr.
History and Will: Philosophical Perspectives of Mao Tse-tung's Thought

James L. Watson
Emigration and the Chinese Lineage: The Mans *in Hong Kong and London*

Conflict and Control

in

Late Imperial China

THIS VOLUME IS SPONSORED BY THE
CENTER FOR CHINESE STUDIES,
UNIVERSITY OF CALIFORNIA, BERKELEY

Conflict and Control
in
Late Imperial China

edited by

Frederic Wakeman, Jr.

and

Carolyn Grant

UNIVERSITY OF CALIFORNIA PRESS

BERKELEY · LOS ANGELES · LONDON

University of California Press
Berkeley and Los Angeles, California

University of California Press, Ltd.
London, England

Copyright © 1975, by
The Regents of the University of California

ISBN 0-520-02597-0
Library of Congress Catalog Card Number: 73–87247
Printed in the United States of America

To
John K. Fairbank

CONTENTS

MAPS

FOREWORD

In June 1971, the Center for Chinese Studies at the University of California, Berkeley, and the Committee on Studies of Chinese Civilization of the American Council of Learned Societies jointly sponsored a conference on local control and social protest during the Ch'ing period. The topic for the conference was first suggested by John K. Fairbank, who proposed that such a symposium probe beneath the surface of China's nineteenth-century political response to the West and explore the social history of the entire Ch'ing. Local control and social protest were chosen as governing themes because of their dialectical conjunction at the very point where polity and society converged. The shift of perspective from China's reactive "modernization" was thus designed to expose the endogenous social forces governing historical change long before the Opium War actually began.

Fourteen papers were presented at the conference, for which John Fairbank, Roy Hofheinz, and William Skinner served as discussants: Frederic Wakeman, Jr., "Localism and Loyalism during the Ch'ing Conquest of Kiangnan: The Siege of Chiang-yin"; Kanda Nobuo, "The Role of *San-fan* in the Local Politics of Early Ch'ing"; Jerry Dennerline, "Fiscal Reform and Local Control: A Tradition Survives the Conquest"; Silas Wu, "Trade, Intelligence, and Coastal Control: Li Wei in Chekiang, 1725–1732"; Ch'en Chieh-hsien, "Ch'ing Policies regarding the Maintenance of Manchu Traditions"; Muramatsu Yūji, "Banner Estates and Banner Lands in Eighteenth-Century China: Evidence from Two New Sources"; Fu-mei Chang Chen, "Local Control of Convicted Thieves in Ch'ing China Prior to 1800"; Randle Edwards, "Ch'ing Control of Aliens prior to the 'Treaty System' "; Ira Lapidus, "Hierarchies and Networks: A Comparison of Chinese and Islamic Societies"; Jonathan Spence, "Opium Smoking in Ch'ing China"; James Polachek, "Gentry and Local Control in Su-Sung-T'ai, 1830–1884"; Jerome Ch'en, "Modernization of Local Protest: A Study of the P'ing-Liu-Li Rebellion of 1906"; C. K. Yang, "Notes on Statistical Patterns of Mass Actions in Nineteenth-Century China"; Philip Kuhn, "Local Control and Local Self-Government."

The first eight papers analyzed the early Ch'ing local control system and its maintenance throughout the eighteenth century. Wakeman's and Dennerline's essays explored the Ming–Ch'ing transition in terms of loyalism and localism. Professor Kanda's paper then analyzed the social structure of the three feudatories (*san-fan*), to better explain the military and social mechanisms of the Manchu conquest. Ch'en Chieh-hsien and Muramatsu Yūji subsequently showed that, imperial efforts notwithstanding, the Manchu elite was in time culturally and economically absorbed by the society it ruled. The legal aspects of Ch'ing control were discussed in Fu-mei Chang Chen's paper on the probation of thieves and in Randle Edwards' careful analysis of the supervision of foreigners during the eighteenth century. The relationship between inner and outer control systems was more specifically delineated by Silas Wu's study of a crisis in Sino-Japanese relations during the Yung-cheng period.

As a midpoint consideration, Ira Lapidus compared the historiography of Islamic and Ch'ing societies. Lapidus' paper stimulated a fundamental reevaluation of the metaphors which inform our study of late imperial Chinese history, thereby clarifying its dichotomous nature: a highly stratified, regulated, and orderly world vision, on the one hand, and on the other a complicated, asymmetrical landscape of networks, disorderly cellular units, and competing interests.

The awareness naturally raised the conference's second theme—local disorder—which dominated the latter set of meetings. Spence's study of opium addiction demonstrated the breakdown of local control from the late eighteenth century onward. It also connected China's inner social process with the western intrusion, and thus served to introduce the last four discussions. First was James Polachek's account of the reestablishment of gentry control in Soochow just after the Taiping Rebellion. Polachek affirmed Muramatsu's thesis concerning the fusion between rent and tax collection, and further proposed that this merging so popularly identified the gentry with the state as to account for the radicalization of the peasantry in the twentieth century. An obvious corollary to this conclusion would be an increasing incidence of local protest, and this was verified by C.K. Yang's statistical study of all entries in the Ch'ing *Veritable Records* concerning mass movements during the nineteenth century. Yang's tentative discovery of a transformation in the tenor of local protest movements was specifically corroborated by Jerome Ch'en's paper on the 1906 revolt in Hunan. Finally, Philip Kuhn's study of the connections between statecraft (*ching-shih*) and the local self-government movement of the twentieth century demonstrated how the gentry continued to dominate rural administration long after the dynasty had fallen.

As the conference evolved, several themes became salient. First was a sense of the exceptional fragility of early Ch'ing rule, especially during the civil war of the 1670s. That in turn reinforced our appreciation of the stability of central power during the 1700s, with the legal system one of its most crucial components. Another important support of central power during the High

Ch'ing was the alien origin of the Manchu rulers. The Manchu language, for instance, served as an instrument of confidentiality which forwarded the development of both a palace memorial system and the Grand Council. Some participants also argued that the foreignness of Ch'ing emperors permitted a more flexible *Realpolitik* in foreign and domestic affairs than might have characterized a purely Han ruler.

On the other hand, a single dynastic rubric failed to embrace all of the social processes which ran through the Ch'ing and on into the republican period. However mnemonically convenient 1644—the year of the Manchu conquest—might be as a date, we came to feel that its significance should be reconsidered. Knowing the historian's illusion to be the perpetual continuum, we nonetheless found it impossible to discuss the fiscal policies of the 1880s without referring to the cadastral schemes of Ming ministers in the 1570s. Thus secular trends sometimes prevailed over dynastic epicycles, so that Ming, Ch'ing, and early republic came to be viewed as an entire late imperial period.

One example of this secular continuity was the ideology of statecraft (*ching-shih*). Statecraft represented the real interests which bridged the entire period, as the research of Dennerline and Polachek proved for both ends of the dynastic cycle. Just as gentry-statesmen protected their interests in the 1660s in the name of statecraft, so did a new urban-based landlord class ensconce itself in nearly identical terms at the end of the nineteenth century. The gentry's role during the Manchu conquest betrayed its social dependence upon central control, its natural tendency toward political collaboration, and its ambivalence toward local officialdom. Yet because this gentry determined local fiscal conditions and developed such a firm ideology of local elite control, it possessed a striking capacity for endurance over the centuries. Although this picture was complicated by the gentry's activities during the last half-century of the dynasty, when complex personal networks substituted for bureaucratic differentiations, one factor remained consistent. The lower-ranking gentry, whether Ming *sheng-yuan* or republican ward chiefs, crucially occupied the interstices between formal government and the society at large. Central political power shifted dramatically after 1911, but the role of the lower gentry changed more slowly. Evolving along lines which could be traced back to the Taiping Rebellion, these kinds of power brokers gradually continued to entrench themselves in rural China at the expense of the central government. They, the *t'u-hao* (local bullies) and *lieh-shen* (evil gentry) of the 1930s and 1940s, would ultimately be overthrown by Communist revolutionaries, but for a time they ruled supreme.

The articulation of all these themes was truly a collaborative effort. Local arrangements were entirely and gracefully handled by the staff of the East-West Center in Honolulu, where the meetings convened. Our rapporteur, Jonathan Grant, was formally commended by the conference for his excellent work. Planning before and after the conference was coordinated in the Center for Chinese Studies by Jane Kaneko and Josephine Pearson, who also helped with much of the final manuscript preparation, coordinated by Susan Alitto. The glossary was prepared with the help of Karl Slinkard, who also provided map information for our cartographer, Evelyn Prosser. During portions of the editorial time, Frederic Wakeman held fellowships from the American Council of Learned Societies, the Humanities Research Institute of the University of California, and the John Simon Guggenheim Memorial Foundation. Professors Joseph Fletcher, Irwin Scheiner, and John Wills provided critical advice for certain portions of the manuscript, while an editorial committee composed of Professors Fairbank, Kuhn, Spence, and Wakeman undertook the difficult task of choosing a few among so many excellent conference papers for inclusion in this volume. The final copy was scrupulously edited by Marjorie Hughes. The above deserve our deepest thanks, but this book owes its greatest debt to all those scholars whose discussions and deliberations during the symposium did so much to shape our concept of social process during the late imperial period of Chinese history.

F.W.
C.G.
Berkeley, 1975

CONTRIBUTORS

Fu-mei Chang Chen holds a doctorate in jurisprudence from Harvard University, where she wrote a dissertation on the Ch'ing legal system. Dr. Chen is now affiliated with the Society for the Humanities, Cornell University.

Jerry Dennerline is an assistant professor of history at Pomona College. His dissertation for Yale University is a study of Chia-ting in the seventeenth century.

Carolyn Grant is a doctoral candidate in the Department of English at Washington University. She has edited several books on China.

Philip A. Kuhn is professor of history at the University of Chicago. He is the author of *Rebellion and Its Enemies in Late Imperial China: Militarization and Social Structure, 1796–1864,* and has contributed a study of the Taiping Rebellion to *The Cambridge History of China.*

Ira M. Lapidus is professor of Islamic history at the University of California, Berkeley. The author of *Muslim Cities in the Late Middle Ages,* he is currently writing a biography of Ibn Khaldun.

James Polachek is an assistant professor of history at Columbia University. His dissertation for the University of California, Berkeley, concerns the social history of Soochow during the nineteenth century.

Jonathan Spence is professor of history at Yale University. He is the author of *Ts'ao Yin and the K'ang-hsi Emperor, To Change China,* and *Emperor of China: Self-Portrait of K'ang-hsi.*

Frederic Wakeman is professor of history and chairman of the Center for Chinese Studies at the University of California, Berkeley. He is the author of *Strangers at the Gate* and *History and Will.*

C. K. Yang is professor of sociology at the University of Pittsburgh. The author of numerous studies, he is perhaps best known for his *Religion and Chinese Society.*

ABBREVIATIONS
USED IN THE NOTES

Boulais

Gui Boulais, *Manuel du code chinois*, Variétés sino-
logiques, ser. 55 (Shanghai, 1924), reprint (Taipei:
Ch'eng-wen Publishing Co., 1966).

Ch'ing code

Ta-Ch'ing lü-li hui-t'ung hsin-tsuan [Comprehensive
new edition of the Ch'ing code] (Peking, 1873),
reprint (Taipei: Wen-hai ch'u-pan-she, 1964).

CL

Ch'ien-lung reign

CSL

Ta-Ch'ing shih-lu [Veritable records of the Ch'ing
dynasty] (Mukden, 1937), reprint (Taipei: Hua-
wen shu-chü, 1964).

CYHC

Teng Ch'uan-k'ai, comp., *Ying-yin Chiang-yin
hsien-chih* [Photoreprint of the Chiang-yin district
gazetteers], 1878 and 1919 editions, plus the
supplement, *Chiang-yin chin-shih lu* [Record of
recent events in Chiang-yin] (Taipei, 1968).

HAHL

Chu Ch'ing-ch'i, *Hsing-an hui-lan* [Conspectus of
penal cases], 1869 ed. (Taipei: Ch'eng-wen Publishing Co., 1968).

HAHLF

Chu Ch'ing-ch'i, Pao Shu-yun, and Hsu Chien-
ch'üan, *Hsing-an hui-lan, fu hsu-tseng Hsing-an hui-
lan, hsin-tseng Hsing-an hui-lan* [Conspectus of penal
cases, with two supplements], 1886 ed. (Taipei,
Ch'eng-wen Publishing Co., 1968).

HCCSWP

Ho Ch'ang-ling, comp., *Huang-ch'ao ching-shih
wen-pien* [Selected essays on statecraft of the Ch'ing

dynasty], 1821 ed. (Taipei: Shih-chieh shu-chü, 1964).

HCTC Feng Kuei-fen, *Hsien-chih-t'ang chi* [Collection from Hsien-chih hall] (Soochow, 1876).

HF Hsien-feng reign

HFC *Ch'ing-shih-kao hsing-fa-chih chu-chieh* [Legal treatise from the Ch'ing draft history with annotations] (Peking: Legal Research Division, Bureau of Legal Affairs, Council of State, 1957).

HMCSWP Ch'en Tzu-lung, comp., *Huang-Ming ching-shih wen-pien* [Selected essays on statecraft of the Ch'ing dynasty], 1638 ed. (Taipei: Kuo-lien ch'u-pan-she, 1964).

Hopei SCKP *Ho-pei sheng-cheng-fu kung-pao* [Hopei provincial government gazette].

HTSL *Ch'in-ting ta-Ch'ing hui-tien t'u shih-li* [Collected statutes of the Ch'ing dynasty, with cases supplemented], 1899 ed. (Taipei: Chung-wen Publishing Co., 1963).

IMC Imperial Maritime Customs

ITC *Chia-ch'ing ch'ung-hsiu i-t'ung-chih* [The Chia-ch'ing revision of the imperial gazetteer] (Taipei: Commercial Press, 1966).

KH K'ang-hsi reign

KHS Kuang-hsu reign

Kiangsu SCKP *Chiang-su sheng-cheng-fu kung-pao* [Kiangsu provincial government gazette).

NCIS Wen Jui-lin, *Nan-chiang i-shih* [Successive histories of the southern realm], 1830 ed. (Taipei: T'ai-wan wen-hsien ts'ung-k'an, 1959).

PAHP — Ch'üan Shih-ch'ao et al., comp., *Po-an hsin-pien, fu hsu-pien* [Collection of reversed cases, with supplements], 1784 ed. (Taipei: Ch'eng-wen Publishing Co., 1968).

PGT — *Translations of the Peking Gazette,* annual volumes (Shanghai, 1872–1890).

RoyCom — *The Minutes of Evidence and the Final Report of the Royal Commission on Opium,* 7 vols. (London, 1894–1895).

SC — Shun-chih reign

SPPY — *Ssu-pu pei yao* edition of 351 historical works (Shanghai, Chung-hua shu-chü, 1927–1935; western-style ed., 1937, 100 vols., reprint Taipei, 1966).

Staunton — *Ta Tsing Leu Lee, Being the Fundamental Laws of the Penal Code of China,* trans. George T. Staunton (London, 1810).

TC — T'ung-chih reign

TCHT — *Ta-Ch'ing hui-tien shih-li* [Compendium of Ch'ing institutional law and precedents] (Taipei: Ch'i-wen ch'u-pan-she, 1963).

TK — Tao-kuang reign

TLCA — Sun Lun, comp., *Ting-li ch'eng-an ho-chien* [Established regulations and precedents combined], original preface dated 1707.

TLHP — *Nieh-ssu ting li hui-pien* [Established regulations, as collected by the office of the provincial judicial commissioner] (Kiangsi, 1905).

TLTI — Hsueh Yun-sheng, *Tu-li ts'un-i* [Concentration on doubtful matters while perusing the special provisions of the code] (Peking, 1905).

WHC — Ts'ao Yun-yuan, comp., *Wu-hsien chih* [Wu district gazetteer] (Soochow, 1922).

YC   Yung-cheng reign

YPCC   Ch'i Ssu-ho, Lin Shu-hui, and Shou Chi-yü, eds., *Ya-p'ien chan-cheng* [The opium war], 6 vols. (Shanghai: Shen-chou kuo-kuang she, 1954).

MING AND CH'ING
REIGN TITLES

MING

Hung-wu	(1368–1398)
Chien-wen	(1399–1402)
Yung-lo	(1403–1424)
Hung-hsi	(1425)
Hsuan-te	(1426–1435)
Cheng-t'ung	(1436–1449)
Ching-t'ai	(1450–1456)
T'ien-shun	(1457–1464)
Ch'eng-hua	(1465–1487)
Hung-chih	(1488–1505)
Cheng-te	(1506–1521)
Chia-ching	(1522–1566)
Lung-ch'ing	(1567–1572)
Wan-li	(1573–1619)
T'ai-ch'ang	(1620)
T'ien-ch'i	(1621–1627)
Ch'ung-chen	(1628–1644)

CH'ING

Shun-chih	(1644–1661)
K'ang-hsi	(1662–1722)
Yung-cheng	(1723–1735)
Ch'ien-lung	(1736–1795)
Chia-ch'ing	(1796–1820)
Tao-kuang	(1821–1850)
Hsien-feng	(1851–1861)
T'ung-chih	(1862–1874)
Kuang-hsu	(1875–1907)
Hsuan-t'ung	(1908–1911)

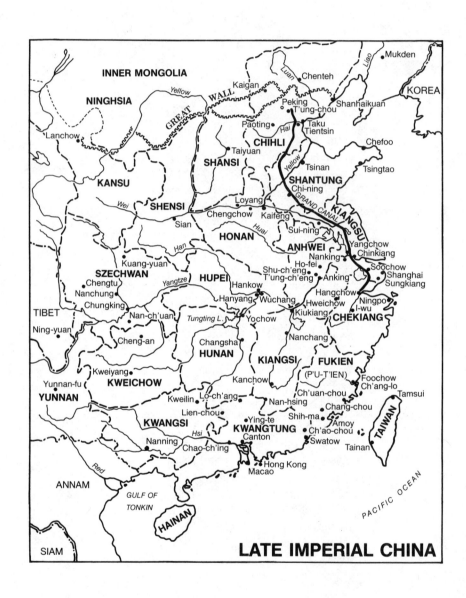

LATE IMPERIAL CHINA

Introduction:

THE EVOLUTION OF LOCAL CONTROL
IN LATE IMPERIAL CHINA

Frederic Wakeman, Jr.

Until recently Ch'ing historians have devoted most of their attention to the last century of imperial rule. What existed before the Opium War (1839–1842) was almost accepted as a given, a static world order which had so encyclopedically catalogued its past and so complacently frozen its institutions as to be incapable of reacting flexibly to the impact of imperialism. The Ch'ing was ruled by sinified Manchus, but that seemed to make its cultural conservatism all the more explicable. As a studied and self-conscious replica of earlier regimes, the Manchu dynasty rigidly encased the uniform persistence of Chinese culture. Some modern Chinese did, in the early 1900s, divorce the barbarian Ch'ing from the mainstream of their history. To radical nationalists like Chang Ping-lin (1868–1936), the Ch'ing emperors had usurped the past in 1644, adorning themselves with Confucian trappings to exploit the conquered Han race.[1] But once the Ch'ing fell in 1911 and cultural iconoclasts began to attack the patriarchal authority of Confucian monarchies in general, the Ch'ing was once more viewed as the embodiment of an entire, unchanging social and cultural order.

Marxist historiography carried that transformation a step further by identifying the Ch'ing with all the other feudal dynasties that had held progress in check. Chinese history then became "a lopsided story with a beginning and an end but hardly any middle. The vast stretch of some two thousand years from the formation of the Han states to the mid-nineteenth century constitutes a feudal embarrassment that seems safer left alone for the time being."[2] But the Marxist concern with "nodal points" of change also helped single out social changes ("sprouts of capitalism") during the late Ming and early

1. Chang Ping-lin, preface to Tsou Jung, *The Revolutionary Army*, trans. John Lust (The Hague: Mouton, 1968), p. 52.

2. Harold Kahn and Albert Feuerwerker, "The Ideology of Scholarship: China's New Historiography," in Albert Feuerwerker, ed., *History in Communist China* (Cambridge: M.I.T. Press, 1969), p. 10.

1

Ch'ing which lent the late imperial era of Chinese history a certain unique-ness.

Gradually, social historians began to realize that the entire period from the 1550s to the 1930s constituted a coherent whole. Instead of seeing the Ch'ing as a replication of the past, or 1644 and 1911 as critical terminals, scholars detected processes which stretched across the last four centuries of Chinese history into the republican period. The urbanization of the lower Yangtze region, the commutation of labor services into money payments, the develop-ment of certain kinds of regional trade, the growth of mass literacy and the increase in the size of the gentry, the commercialization of local managerial activities—all these phenomena of the late Ming set in motion administra-tive and political changes that continued to develop over the course of the Ch'ing and in some ways culminated in the social history of the early twen-tieth century.[3] One such process, visible in several of the essays collected in this volume, was the evolution of rural government and local control.

RURAL GOVERNMENT AND THE AMBIVALENT ROLE OF THE GENTRY

Because the vigor of rural government depended upon the wary colla-boration of formal administrators and members of the local elite, the develop-ment of local control was inseparable from the evolution of the Chinese gentry after the T'ang period. During the eleventh and twelfth centuries, the old military aristocracy was replaced by a new elite whose primary status derived from bureaucratic office.[4] By middle Ming times such rank was acquired by passing the civil service examinations. Competition for this honor was intense. Even though the quota of district degrees (*sheng-yuan*) was enlarged at least

3. The novelty of these developments has been contested by historians who argue for a fundamental social and economic "revolution" in the Sung period, and insist that the late Ming changes were merely quantitative increments to, not qualitative advances beyond, the Sung urban, technological, and commercial improvements. See Mark Elvin, *The Pattern of the Chinese Past* (London: Eyre Methuen, 1973). However, because of the late Ming changes from estate to family farming, from state to private production, and from regional marketing to an integrated national market, Ramon Myers believes that "one can argue convincingly that Ming and Ch'ing China experienced changes as profound and far-reaching as those of the Sung." Ramon H. Myers, "Transformation and Continuity in Chinese Economic and Social History," *Journal of Asian Studies* 33.2:274.

4. As far as local control was concerned, this was not yet the "gentry" of the Ming and Ch'ing periods.

> In the Sung there were men with official status, and there were various groups possessed of miscellaneous privileges, and there were the rich, but it seems fair to say that there were no gentry. The more aristocratic society of earlier times in which local political influence tended to remain in the hands of certain families for generation after generation was dead, and the gentry society of later times had not yet been born. As a result the local elite consisted, not of the hereditarily influential or of the indoctrinated gentry, but simply of the rich.

Brian E. McKnight, *Village and Bureaucracy in Southern Sung China* (Chicago: University of Chicago Press, 1971), p. 6.

tenfold between the fourteenth and nineteenth centuries,[5] an average of thirty aspirants continued to vie for each degree awarded. Yet a successful *sheng-yuan* still had to pass at least the provincial (*chü-jen*) and metropolitan (*chin-shih*) examinations in order to be eligible for office. As the lower ranks swelled without a corresponding increase in the quota of higher degrees, the hundreds of thousands of *sheng-yuan* who failed to climb the upper rungs constituted a literate body whose capacity for discontent alarmed sixteenth-century imperial authorities toward the end of the Ming period.[6] Prominently involved in the urban demonstrations and "party" movements of the late Ming,[7] *sheng-yuan* were also frequently associated with peasant rebellions.[8] However, most members of the lower gentry eschewed such extravagant forms of protest, preferring to secure a livelihood as tutors, secretaries, rural relief managers, and tax agents engaged in proxy remittance (*pao-lan*). In some ways, therefore, the *sheng-yuan* belonged less to the world of the upper gentry than to the realm of district clerks (*hsu-li*) and yamen underlings who lived off the petty corruption that characterized the local government of late imperial China.[9]

This distinction between lower and upper degree-holders helps explain the ambivalent role of the gentry in a civilization where local control meant imposing a systematic blueprint upon a complex and resistant society which did not always live up to its governors' orderly expectations. For, beneath the centrally-ordered pattern of local administration there existed another China—out of control, disorderly, and unruly. As Ira Lapidus points out in his essay, lineage wars, smuggling rings, and secret societies were as characteristic of the empire as the *pao-chia* (mutual responsibility) public-security apparatus and the ideally serene surface of upper-gentry society. Conse-

5. By the late nineteenth century there were approximately 600,000 regular *sheng-yuan*, along with another 600,000 lower degree-holders who purchased their rank.

6. See, for example, *Ming shih-lu* [Veritable records of the Ming dynasty], Lung-ch'ing reign, chüan 24, cited in Fu I-ling, *Ming-tai Chiang-nan shih-min ching-chi shih-t'an* [An investigation of bourgeois economy in Kiangnan in the Ming] (Shanghai: Jen-min ch'u-pan-she, 1963), p. 110.

7. One of the best known examples of this kind of activity was the 1593 riot at Sung-chiang when the city dwellers and gentry from the three surrounding districts united in major demonstrations to keep their prefect from being dismissed from office. "Not only were there those who came to the city as a mob to present to the military defense circuit [intendant] at the surveillance office [a demand] to retain [Li Hou as prefect]; there were also degree-holding gentry and young first-place examination winners who came as well." Fan Lien, *Yun-chien chü-mu ch'ao* [Copied from hearsaying eyewitnesses], cited in Fu I-ling, *Ming-tai*, pp. 115–116.

8. For an exposition of this thesis, see Muramatsu Yūji, "Some Themes in Chinese Rebel Ideologies," in A. F. Wright, ed., *The Confucian Persuasion* (Stanford: Stanford University Press, 1960), pp. 241–267.

9. Chung-li Chang, *The Income of the Chinese Gentry* (Seattle: University of Washington Press, 1962), pp. 43–73; Ping-ti Ho, *The Ladder of Success in Imperial China* (New York: John Wiley and Sons, 1964), pp. 34–35. Ho classifies *sheng-yuan* as "scholar-commoners." The real distinction between *sheng-yuan* who were "gentry" and those who were not was probably a matter of self-conception. Obviously, some members of the *sheng-yuan* group saw that status as a transitional ranking and early set their aims on an official career.

quently, those who favored methodical control were often infuriated by the
discrepancy between their neat administrative solutions and the cluttered
world beyond the yamen wall.

> If we take the district of Soochow as an example [one Ch'ing official
> noted], we see that the disposition of the people of Wu is weak and brittle.
> The well fed are few; the indigent, many. Those styled as "scholars" by
> and large teach outside the home, leaving two or three dependents alone.
> The poor work as servants or peddlers, leaving early and returning at
> dusk, and [still] find that their livelihood is insufficient. The wealthy are
> only attentive to their own security and do not become involved with
> outsiders. The marketplace people are confined to their own occupations,
> fearing the juvenile delinquents in their wards as if they were tigers. If
> you wish to restrain this sort of people, then you would have to investigate
> by day and patrol by night. They would assuredly be vocal in their dis-
> content.[10]

The gentry did not make the task of legislating order any easier. As C. K.
Yang's essay suggests, the local elite led much of the mass dissent of the nineteenth century. Like the yamen officials who dominated criminal activities,
the *sheng-yuan* protected a status quo which included both order and disorder,
control and conflict.

A similar paradox characterized the higher gentry. A gentryman might
well serve as an incorruptible magistrate outside his native place, but once
retired (the average tenure of office was remarkably brief),[11] that same person was likely to use his bureaucratic influence and social status to acquire
property, finagle favorable tax rates, and protect his kin's interests. The
gentry's public interest in waterworks, charity, and education also accompanied a private interest in corporate trusts and income. Local social organizations therefore embodied contrary principles: integration into the imperial
system and autonomy from it. The dynamic oscillation between these poles
created the unity of Chinese society, not by eliminating the contradictions
but by balancing them in such a way as to favor overall order. The balance
was expressed in ideal terms as a Confucian compromise between Legalist
intervention and complete laissez-faire. In political theory, this meant recognizing a self-regulating society whose private interests were tempered by
moral enlightenment. As an administrative guide, however, such a notion
actually set the local gentry and the district government somewhat at odds,
the one preventing the corruption or overweening power of the other.

10. Huang Chung-chien, "Pao-chia i" [A discussion of *pao-chia*], in *HCCSWP*, 14:2b.
11. John R. Watt, *The District Magistrate in Late Imperial China* (New York: Columbia
University Press, 1972), pp. 59–68.

COMMUNITY RESPONSIBILITY AND LOCAL ADMINISTRATION

During the Sung period the bureaucratic gentry's influence had not yet permeated rural society, and village government was formally in the hands of wealthy peasants who were appointed as regular service officers to manage tax collection, militia organization, and the *pao-chia* networks.[12] By the fourteenth century rural government was not so neatly dominated by any single group. Local gentry and the former service officers now shared responsibilities and influence in an elaborate control system (*hsiang-chia*) whose basic unit was the *shuai* (command): a group of 100 families registered in a covenant (*yueh*). Normally only commoners joined a *shuai*, but reliable degree-holders were asked to help supervise it.

The *shuai* combined control and indoctrination. Two officers led the unit. An elected *yueh-cheng* was charged with legal mediation and control, while an appointed *yueh-shih* (who had to be literate) was supposed to exhort (*ch'in*) the householders with Confucian texts. Because exhortation was viewed as a kind of collective moral reinforcement, the *shuai* was expected to be something between a voluntary and an involuntary association. The combination was not easy to maintain. When the officers became police functionaries, the group lost its solidarity and ceased being a true constituency. When the *shuai* grew too independent, on the other hand, its leaders vitiated the authority of the magistrate. Consequently, two safeguards were written into the system: householders were theoretically able to petition the magistrate if their *yueh-cheng* abused his privileges, and the *shuai* officers were forbidden to collude with the regular yamen sub-bureaucracy.[13]

The *shuai* was only the first of many different rural control mechanisms organized during the Ming period. Its successors—the *tsung-hsiao-chia* of the 1440s, the *shih-chia-p'ai-fa* of the early 1500s, and the regular *pao-chia* of the 1600s[14]—varied in name, but they continued to fuse ideally normative rural communities with coercive state control networks. Usually the latter prevailed over the *Gemeinschaften* they were supposed to supplement, so that *pao-chia* was eventually designed to ensure adequate public security[15] without

12. McKnight, *Village and Bureaucracy*, pp. 178–185.

13. Wen Chün-t'ien, *Chung-kuo pao-chia chih-tu* [The Chinese *pao-chia* system] (Shanghai: Commercial Press, 1935), pp. 171–185, 193–200.

14. Sakai Tadao, "Mindai zen-chūki no hokkōsei ni tsuite" [On the *pao-chia* system of the first half of the Ming period], in *Shimizu Hakushi tsuitō kinen: Meidaishi ronsō* [In memory of Dr. Shimizu Taiji: Studies on the Ming period] (Tokyo: Daian, 1962), pp. 577–610. The Ming did initiate a form of village service officer using elders to adjudicate minor offenses, but that system was abandoned by the 1440s. Wada Sei, *Shina chihō jichi hattatsu shi* [History of the development of Chinese local self-government] (Tokyo: Chūō Daigaku, 1939), pp. 113–117.

15. One European visitor to China during the late Ming period remarked in astonishment that "Nobody can leave the districts of his own city, even if it is for another place in the same province, without a written permit; and if he does so, he is forthwith flung into prison and

increasing government law-enforcement expenses. For, the aim of all these institutions was the rotational assignment of rural service and management duties to a populace which, by regulating itself, would reduce the number of regularly appointed civil administrators throughout the empire. The actual savings, however, were partly illusory. Though yamen expenses were formally low, the magistrate still had to employ policemen who lived off petty bribes, and clerks who peddled their influence to the highest bidder.

This kind of venality ironically inclined the government all the more toward the principle of conferring administrative responsibilities upon community leaders. The early Ming tax system was the best example of this practice.

> When the present dynasty first acquired the empire [a Ming writer explained], [the emperor] was disturbed by the officials' oppression of the common people. The high ministers then suggested that since the [local] officials were all natives of other provinces, they were ignorant of local conditions, and were surrounded by unscrupulous clerks and entrenched magnates. It was no wonder that the people were misgoverned. It would therefore be better to appoint as collectors those magnates who were trusted by the people and to make them responsible for the land taxes of the common people and for their delivery to the government. Thereupon the magnates were appointed tax collectors.[16]

In 1371, after an accurate cadastral survey, the Board of Revenue divided the cultivated areas of central China into tax-paying units of ten thousand piculs per annum and named the largest landowner in each unit a tax collector (*liang-chang*). It was the duty of these *liang-chang* to collect and deliver to the capital the more than one million tons of barley, wheat, and rice which were needed every year by the central government. In this way Ming T'ai-tsu hoped both "to use good people to rule good people"[17] and to secure the good will of local magnates by honoring them with a semi-official post.[18]

The magnates initially welcomed appointment as *liang-chang* because they were allowed to petition for tax remissions and routinely hand down the post from father to son. Indeed, they used these privileges to their own private profit by arbitrarily seizing property and assessing other households unfairly. The throne responded by abolishing the post of *liang-chang*. But

punished." C. R. Boxer, ed., *South China in the Sixteenth Century. Being the Narratives of Galeote Pereira; Fr. Gaspar da Cruz, O.P.; Fr. Martin de Rada, O.E.S.A. (1550–1575)* (London: Hakluyt Society, 1953), p. 303.

16. Translated in Liang Fang-chung, "Local Tax Collectors in the Ming Dynasty," in E-tu Zen Sun and John De Francis, eds., *Chinese Social History, Translations of Selected Studies* (Washington, D.C.: American Council of Learned Societies, 1956), p. 250.

17. Translated in ibid., p. 249.

18. Supported by one accountant, twenty treasurers, and one thousand transport coolies, each *liang-chang* had an opportunity to go to Nanking each year and receive his tally sheets and instructions from the emperor in person.

that left tax collection in the hands of irresponsible yamen clerks who were not even on the official payroll. The government therefore tried to replace the *liang-chang* of central China with the *li-chang* used elsewhere. In the *li-chia* system ten households formed a *chia* (tithing). Every year by rotation one of these households guaranteed the corvee and tax payment of the other nine units. Ten *chia* constituted a *li* (hamlet or canton), which was supervised by ten more households of the village's wealthiest families who were enrolled in the district land registers (Fish-scale Illustrated Books) that were supposed to be revised decennially. Each of the wealthy households, once again by rotation, served as a *li-chang* responsible for the corvee and land tax of the entire *li-chia* unit of 110 households. The *li-chia* system therefore reflected the same Ming reliance upon wealthy households that characterized the *liang-chang* system, but added to it the principle of rotational responsibility.

The merging of the *li-chia* and *liang-chang* systems curbed the power of the magnates at the expense of the entire tax collection system, by emphasizing coercive responsibility rather than the rewards of local office.[19] Because the *li-chang* was less a rural agent of the emperor than a tax hostage for his community, the magnates bolted from the system, using their influence to foist responsibility upon village headmen. The latter were not always even the wealthiest landowners of their *li-chia* unit. The land registers had failed to keep up with the rapid turnover of landed property in areas like Kiangnan, and no longer reflected the actual distribution of wealth. Modest commoner households designated as *li-chang* were thus saddled with the tax responsibility for their entire village, without either the social sway to collect payments from others or the financial means to stand good in their stead. The hapless *li-chang* therefore either fled the land or became the tenants of more influential families which had managed to have their holdings removed from the land registers. In the meantime, gentry households entitled to at least limited land-tax exemption had learned to fragment their holdings and place each piece of property in a different *li-chia* unit, thus paying no taxes at all. As these sorts of evasion became more common, the burden on the remaining commoner households grew heavier. District quotas increased while the actual tax base narrowed, rendering appointment to the post of *li-chang* tantamount to a sentence of bankruptcy.

TAX REFORM

By the 1580s the central government was running an annual tax deficit of approximately one million taels. Local officials therefore tried to reform the

19. The move of the capital to Peking in 1421 also damaged the position of *liang-chang*: first, by making it impossible for the tax collectors from Kiangnan to present themselves at court (though that custom had practically lapsed anyway); and second, by adding on the further costs of purveying tribute grain up the Grand Canal from central China. For a listing of some of these costs, see Ray Huang, "The Grand Canal during the Ming Dynasty" (Ph.D. thesis, University of Michigan, 1964), pp. 143–148.

tax system by combining corvee (*i*) and land tax (*fu*) obligations into a single payment. This new Single Whip Tax (*i-t'iao-pien*) divided the land in a given district into ten equal parts. Each year one of these parts was subject to both *i* and *fu*—a practice which hopefully would use the more reliable corvee or household registers (Yellow Books) to prevent tax dodging and apply the principle of rotational responsibility to the land itself.[20]

That hope was disappointed. The Single Whip Tax reform simply identified evasion all the more strongly with gentry tax exemptions. Under the old system, influential landowners had manipulated the land registers. Now land and service quotas were amalgamated by billing taxpayers registered in the corvee register.[21] Since the gentry was excused from corvee, its members were not liable in the Yellow Book and consequently escaped the amalgamated tax altogether. Other landowners therefore evaded payment by falsely registering (*kuei-chi*) their households under gentry names. The ultimate effect of the Single Whip Tax reform was to make gentry privilege seem the root cause of the government's fiscal difficulties.

Many historians are familiar with the late Ming practice of false registry, but Jerry Dennerline is the first to show that landlords frequently did this without the knowledge of the gentrymen whose names they used. According to his essay in this volume, the seventeenth-century rural crisis in China was not solely a matter of poor peasants being forced by a constantly increasing tax burden to turn their land over to the gentry (*t'ou-shen*) in exchange for protected tenant status. Rather, resourceful landlords without legal privilege manipulated the household registers behind the gentry's back.

Dennerline's research has important implications. First, there was a noticeable distinction between the social interests of landlords and gentry. At times of fiscal crisis, in fact, "statesmen" gentry felt morally obliged to collaborate with the state by attacking landlord tax evasion, even though the statesmen's ulterior motivation was undoubtedly the protection of gentry privilege. Second, landowners were as much a part of the historical model of dynastic decline as the gentry is sometimes taken to be. Historians broadly argue that the gentry wanted a government which was lax enough to allow the elite to line its own pockets, yet not so debilitated as to neglect the social and economic services which kept potential peasant rebels from arising. This middle ground was hard to hold. As the gentry loosened government controls, removing more and more of the land from the tax rolls, the fiscal burden was shifted to peasant freeholders. A "critical level of disparity," as James Polachek's paper notes, was thus eventually reached, at which point the farmers' misery reached such proportions as to threaten political control altogether, helping topple the reigning dynasty. What Dennerline's piece suggests is that had the gentry acted alone, it might have been able to hold that middle ground

20. Liang Fang-chung, "The 'Ten-Parts' Tax System of Ming," in Sun and De Francis, eds., *Chinese Social History*, pp. 271–280.

21. By then, of course, the corvee was actually commutated into silver payments.

indefinitely during the late imperial period. But the additional inroads of less
politically responsive landlord elements pushed the situation to an extreme,
setting the scene for the fall of the Ming in 1644.

THE 1661 TAX CASE

The brief interregnum of the Southern Ming in central China made the
literati all the more aware of their reliance upon central control. Political
insecurity and social disorder brought them face to face with other local
competitors for power, in a situation where strength of arms mattered more
than civil arts. Constitutionally unable to transform its informal local control
into regional political government, the seventeenth-century gentry finally
acknowledged that even an alien imperial government suited its social interests best.

The gentry's political submission to the Ch'ing was rewarded by the new
dynasty's spirit of compromise during the first fifteen years of its rule. First
Dorgon (1612–1650), then later the Shun-chih emperor, recognized the need
to come to agreeable terms with the local gentry. To be sure, the higher
gentry no longer possessed the great political power which it had held toward
the end of the Ming. That influential cluster of literati, which was symbolized
in contemporaries' eyes by the Kiangnan political club called the Fu-she, had
once been able to command the highest bureaucratic support for its policies,
as well as fill local posts with its official friends. All of that, including even the
right to form such literati associations, was swept away by the new rulers, who
made certain that Kiangnan's magistrates were strangers to the old-boy
circles so prominent in the late Ming.[22] But generally speaking, the court did
agree that its own long-term stability depended upon the support of the
gentry, which was gradually drawn back into the fold by the K'ang-hsi
emperor and permitted to reacquire political influence in the metropolis. The
one exception to this policy was the troubling decade of the 1660s when the
Oboi regency decided to attack the fiscal privileges of the gentry of Kiangnan.[23]

At that time the government was ostensibly concerned about covering the
military expenditures of its Yunnan campaigns. Three weeks after the Shun-
chih emperor's death on February 5, 1661, the regents ordered the boards of
civil appointments and revenue to make every effort to collect the great
amount of taxes then in arrears throughout China. Officials at all ranks would
be denied promotion until the tax quotas for which they were responsible had
been fulfilled; and if those officials had still not met their obligations within a
limit prescribed by the boards, they would be dismissed or reduced in rank.

22. Lawrence D. Kessler, "Chinese Scholars and the Early Manchu State," *Harvard Journal
of Asiatic Studies* 31:179–200.
23. The statutory basis for this attack after the cadastral surveys of 1659–1660 is described
in Dennerline's essay in this volume.

As long as the government devoted its primary effort to Chihli (the region around the capital), it continued to employ sanctions upon bureaucrats. But once its attention turned to Kiangnan, which represented both the empire's major source of grain tribute[24] and the most glaring example of *pao-lan* and false registry, the government shifted its attack to the taxpayers.[25] Since many of the latter were members of the gentry, the new policy was interpreted by contemporaries as an effort to humble and punish the scholar-officials of the lower Yangtze—some of whom had revealed their continuing loyalty to the Ming when Cheng Ch'eng-kung (Koxinga, 1624–1662) attacked Nanking in 1659. One scholar even likened the Manchu regents to the Mongols, and compared the Kiangnan tax case to the Yuan dynasty's deliberate debasement of southern *ju* (literati) four centuries earlier.[26]

The Manchu regents certainly did harbor animosities toward the Kiangnan gentry, but the indictment of that group was actually the work of the province's governor, Chu Kuo-chih (d. 1673), who had already urged the gentry to make up its arrears. Convinced that stronger measures were needed, Chu compiled a 13,757-name register of tax resisters (*k'ang-liang ts'e*) which included approximately ten thousand members of the gentry.[27] Chu's register did far more than simply name tardy taxpayers; it denounced those who had fallen behind in their payments as willful criminals. Consequently, public proclamation of the list created a panic throughout all of Kiangnan.

Some literati used their influence with local officials to play for time. The

24. By the late Ming the single prefecture of Soochow, which had 1 percent of the cultivated land of the empire, provided 10 percent of its revenue. Within that area Sung-chiang, which held 0.25 percent of the cultivated land of China, provided 5 percent of the national revenue. Roughly speaking, the Su-Sung-T'ai circuit, along with the northern part of Chekiang, provided about one-quarter of the normal tax quota of the entire country. Chou Liang-hsiao, "Ming-tai Su-Sung ti-ch'ü ti kuan-t'ien yü chung-fu wen-t'i" [The question of severe taxes and official land in the Su-Sung region during the Ming dynasty], *Li-shih yen-chiu* [Historical research] 10:64 ff.

25. Chou Shou-ch'ang, *Ssu-i t'ang jih cha* [Daily letters from the Ssu-i lodge], cited in Meng Sen, *Hsin-shih ts'ung-k'an* [Collected writings of Meng Sen] (Hong Kong: Chung-kuo ku-chi chen-pen kung-ying she, 1963), p. 9. My account is based almost entirely on Meng Sen's careful collection of materials about the tax case. As he himself has pointed out, the development of the tax case is traced in the official record (the *Shih-lu* and the *Tung-hua lu*) up through the implementation of the regents' proposals in Chihli. Once Governor Chu published the list, the official record becomes silent and one has to depend upon the many private (*pi-chi*) accounts, which Meng cites *in extenso* in his own compilation with commentary.

26. Tung Han, *San wang chih-lueh* [A summary record of the three nets], cited in Meng Sen, *Hsin-shih*, p. 9.

27. Ch'u Hua, *Hu-ch'eng pei-k'ao* [A complete investigation of Shanghai], in *Shang-hai na-ku ts'ung-shu* [A collection of reprints of snatches of the past of Shanghai] (Shanghai: Chung-hua shu-chü, 1936), 6:3b. Chu's action was incited by a demonstration on March 4, 1661, of Soochow gentry. The gentry marched into the Confucian temple during a funeral ceremony for the Shun-chih emperor and denounced the local magistrate for forcing them to pay taxes. All told, twenty-two of the demonstrators in the Temple Lament Incident (*k'u miao an*) were arrested. Since their leader, Chin Jen-jui, called to the spirits of the Ming emperors under torture, Ch'ing suspicions of loyalism were enhanced. Eighteen of the men were found guilty of tax resistance and rebellion, and executed. For an excellent account of this aspect of the affair, see Robert B. Oxnam, "Policies and Institutions of the Oboi Regency, 1661–1669," *Journal of Asian Studies* 32.2:279–280.

prefect of Ch'ang-chou, for instance, was persuaded by a noted local professor to delay posting the list for three days, so that several hundred of the "tax resisters" could mortgage or sell their land in order to make up their taxes.[28] Even that was a hardship, however, because land prices immediately dipped. Shao Ch'ang-heng (1637–1704), the famous poet of Wu-chin, had to unload half of his eight hundred *mou* of land at a great loss. "I simply handed it over to others," he explained, and added bitterly that it was rapacious officials who "shamefully took advantage of the rescript" to bilk their charges.[29]

Those who had neither time nor means to sell were usually arrested and thrown into cells so crowded that "there was no place for the scholars to put their feet."[30] Theoretically those on the list were to be uniformly punished. If they held office, they were to be demoted two ranks and transferred. Degree-holders would be stripped of rank. The 240 yamen employees who were indicted would be sentenced according to the amount of bribes taken. In fact, however, the severity of punishment depended upon the official in charge. Governor Chu was the harshest of all. Gentrymen arrested by his agents were trussed in his presence and roughly packed off to his yamen for interrogation by judicial officials. To many the treatment seemed quite arbitrary.

> At the time the gentlemen of Wu could not comprehend the laws of the realm. Some really were in arrears and had not yet remitted [their taxes]. Some had paid in full, but the chief clerk had not completely recorded the cancellation [of their debt]. Some were actually not in arrears but rather among households falsely accused by other people. Some were natives of one district without arrears who were falsely accused by others for deficits in the latter's district. Some were 100 percent paid in full, but were indicted by chief clerks because of resentment. One incrimination followed another—too numerous to be counted singly. The four prefectures of Su-Sung-Ch'ang-Chen, along with the district of P'iao-yang, had altogether 3,700 members of the gentry who were reported to the court. The ministers of the capital deliberated and reported. The Board of Civil Appointments first decided that since degree-holders received an official salary, they should not refuse to pay taxes. Those currently holding office would be demoted two ranks and transferred. Those on the [gentry] lists would be remanded to the capital and delivered to the Board of Justice for a severe deliberation of penalty.[31]

28. This is from the funeral eulogy of Kuo Shih-ying by Chang Yun-chang, cited in Meng Sen, *Hsin-shih*, p. 24.

29. There is a biography of Shao Ch'ang-heng in Arthur Hummel, *Eminent Chinese of the Ch'ing Period* (Washington, D.C.: U. S. Government Printing Office, 1944), p. 636. The tax case debarred him from taking any future examinations. He did finally become secretary to the influential grand secretary, Sung Lao, when the latter was governor of Kiangsu. The account is drawn from Shao Ch'ang-heng, *Ch'ing-men lü-kao* [Boxed drafts from the green gate], cited in Meng Sen, *Hsin-shih*, p. 22.

30. This is from the funeral eulogy of Huang Chen-lin by Chang Tuan-ying, cited in Meng Sen, *Hsin-shih*, pp. 25–26.

31. *Yen t'ang chien-wen tsa-chi* [Random records of things heard and seen in the Yen lodge],

Whether or not a debtor was actually remanded to Peking for punishment depended upon the energy with which his prefect pleaded for custody. But even though many gentrymen escaped final judgment and were released after payment, the experience of arrest was frightening and painful. The prisoners (one of whom happened to be a descendant of Confucius) were frequently flogged and humiliated by yamen underlings who felt that their own tenure depended upon the alacrity with which they carried out the arrests. Others were summarily cashiered or forced to wear the cangue. Eighteen were executed. As Shao Ch'ang-heng remarked later:

> As I view those two years, the new laws were like frost withering the autumn grass. The district magistrate was like a voracious tiger. The lictors were like rapacious dogs. Scholars were flogged with bamboo in order to make up the taxes. This became a constant occurrence in the capital. Yours truly could not endure to [see] his parents pass away [without proper mourning rites, but at that very time] the district police hauled me into the law court. Bent down before tyrannical yamen officers, my body was stripped naked and beaten. I escaped from this [disaster] resolved to avoid calamity [in the future].[32]

Ch'ü Ssu-ta, a student of Ch'ien Ch'ien-i (the famous defector to the Ch'ing), was actually driven mad by his interrogation, and shortly after his release slaughtered his entire family in a homicidal frenzy.[33]

The tax case may even have provoked a momentary aversion to land-holding among the gentry, who were soon to have their serf-owning privileges rescinded by imperial decree. A contemporary wrote that "After it [the tax case], the gentry of the rural areas regarded landed property as the greatest encumbrance. Thus it can be seen that the Ch'ing court used the land tax [issue] to terrify the Kiangnan gentry."[34] An entire generation was so affected —ranging from the Grand Secretary Ts'ao Ch'i to Ku Yen-wu's nephew, Hsu Yuan-wen (first in the metropolitan examinations of 1659).[35] Men like these remained under a cloud for years, until pardoned by the K'ang-hsi emperor in the 1670s. Others gave up an official career altogether, or even fled south to join Wu San-kuei's entourage when he later rebelled against the Ch'ing.[36]

The opinion of contemporaries notwithstanding, the 1661 tax case was not merely a matter of Manchu resentment of the Kiangnan literati; it repre-

---

which is apparently taken from the *Lo-tung tsa-chu* [Random writings from Lo-tung], preface dated 1839, cited in Meng Sen, *Hsin-shih*, p. 19.

32. Shao Ch'ang-heng, *Ch'ing-men*, p. 22.

33. This is from the *Chia-pien lu* [Record of household changes], supposedly compiled by Ch'ien Ch'ien-i's consort, Liu Ju-shih, after his death. It is cited in Meng Sen, *Hsin-shih*, pp. 21–22.

34. This is a comment by Shao's biographer (see note 29), Ch'en Yü-chi, cited in Meng Sen, *Hsin-shih*, p. 23.

35. Hummel, *Eminent Chinese*, p. 327.

36. Chou Shou-ch'ang, *Ssu-i t'ang*, p. 9.

[handwritten annotation at top of page: "Can ch'ing's late history be seen as a fluctuating balance (not a balance) between local & central control — this is Wakeman's thesis"]

sented a more extreme version of the familiar attack on gentry privileges by the central government. As Dennerline's study shows, similar measures had been proposed thirty years earlier under the Ming, when some of the gentry had responded to government pressure by allying with their local magistrates against the large landlords in order to change the tax system. Their reform, which was perfected by the statecraft (*ching-shih*) writer, Hsia Yun-i, was called *chün-t'ien chün-i* (equal field, equal service) because it equalized the tax burden by attaching the corvee portion to the land. While the former household registers were retained by the magistrate so that he could meet his tax quota, landowners were simultaneously urged to enroll in the new *chün-t'ien chün-i* system which absolved its members from being responsible for other taxpayers in their unit. The reform succeeded momentarily because, on the one hand, the magistrates realized that they had to find some way of restricting the privileges of the local elite without undermining it altogether and, on the other, because the gentry realized that if they would retain something, they must give a portion of their rights away by registering all land in standard units in order to share the tax burden more fairly.

The same kind of compromise prevailed after the 1661 tax case frightened the gentry into surrendering some of its economic leverage. The solution, which hearkened back to Hsia Yun-i's reform, did not solve the problem of proxy remittance and false registry, but it did for a time remove some of the inequities of the original *li-chia* system.

MANCHU CONTROL

The Manchus originally conquered China with the aid of Chinese defectors like Li Ch'eng-tung (d. 1649) and Wu San-kuei (1612–1678). These militarists also helped the throne overcome the conciliar power of the Manchu princes who opposed imperial sinification because it enhanced patrimonial power at their own aristocratic expense. But the nobles' Manchuness, the preservation of their identity among the Han Chinese, seemed crucial to the throne when those original Chinese defectors turned against the Ch'ing during the 1673–1681 revolt of the three feudatories (*san-fan*).[37] Then it seemed that as long as the Manchu banner troops remained an elite, poised apart from the Chinese, military control would hold. But the throne soon discovered how difficult it was to keep the Manchus in a favored and separate economic position. The land enclosures awarded to bannermen in north China between 1645 and 1647 gradually fell back into Chinese hands.[38] The Manchus

37. However, as Kanda Nobuo's Honolulu paper showed, the dynasty could not rely on Manchus alone to suppress the three feudatories. In a sense, the K'ang-hsi emperor had to relearn the lesson of his ancestor, Abahai; he would have to rely upon Chinese generals and viceroys to conquer the South. Kanda Nobuo, "The Role of *San-fan* in the Local Politics of Early Ch'ing."

38. Muramatsu Yūji, "Banner Estates and Banner Lands in Eighteenth-Century China: Evidence from Two New Sources," paper delivered at the Honolulu conference.

adopted the practice of letting out their manor lands for service money (*ch'ai-yin*), which soon became a form of regular leasing to tenants whose rents were collected by Chinese bailiffs. Over time the latter turned into intermediate landlords, while the original Manchu owners abandoned their estates to reside in Peking. Since the blandishments of the capital were expensive, the Manchus' rental incomes were supplemented by mortgaging land to their former estate managers. By 1745 half of all banner land was in Chinese hands.[39]

Cultural autonomy was just as difficult to maintain.[40] The Manchus' memories of the hunt, the life of the forest, did at first help keep them apart from the Han. But the attractions of *wen-jen* (literatus) culture soon overcame that pride of tribal separation. The more gifted Manchus competed with Chinese literati on the latter's terms, while others simply forgot their own language. In spite of being favored with special examination quotas and appointment to high office in order to check their Chinese counterparts, by the late 1700s the Manchu aristocracy was barely distinguishable from the scholar-official elite.

Yet Manchu provenance did help rulers like the Yung-cheng emperor strengthen the power of the throne. Certain devices—unorthodox rules of succession which prevented factional court struggles,[41] the use of bannermen or bondservants (*pao-i*) in place of eunuchs as guardians of the privy purse,[42] an imperial intelligence network which employed secret memorials written in Manchu[43]—were peculiar qualities of Ch'ing rule which carried imperial centralism several steps farther along during the eighteenth century, supplementing the more familiar Chinese forms of despotism. The evolution of local control similarly stemmed from dual sources, in that the Yung-cheng emperor (who is usually regarded as the harshest and strongest ruler of the last dynasty) relied both upon special agents like the bannerman T'ien Wen-ching (1662–1732), and upon a resurrection of Chinese institutions like the *pao-chia*.

LOCAL CONTROL UNDER YUNG-CHENG

The Oboi regency had punished gentry tax evasion. The Yung-cheng regime, on the other hand, tried to keep the lower gentry from committing *pao-lan*. Taxes were usually collected in silver, whereas peasants normally possessed only copper currency. Gentry engaging in proxy remittance there-

39. Ma Feng-ch'en, "Manchu–Chinese Social and Economic Conflicts in Early Ch'ing," in Sun and De Francis, *Chinese Social History*, p. 349.

40. Ch'en Chieh-hsien, "Ch'ing Policies Regarding the Maintenance of Manchu Tradition," paper delivered at the Honolulu conference.

41. Harold L. Kahn, *Monarchy in the Emperor's Eyes: Image and Reality in the Ch'ien-lung Reign* (Cambridge: Harvard University Press, 1971).

42. Jonathan D. Spence, *Ts'ao Yin and the K'ang-hsi Emperor: Bondservant and Master* (New Haven: Yale University Press, 1966).

43. Silas H. L. Wu, *Communication and Imperial Control in China: Evolution of the Palace Memorial System, 1693–1735* (Cambridge: Harvard University Press, 1970).

fore collected the farmers' taxes in copper and paid them over to the official collectors in silver. This service did convey taxes to the government, but it also increased the burden upon the peasants because the remitters charged customary fees or manipulated the exchange rates to their own advantage.[44] By the nineteenth century *pao-lan* charges sometimes amounted to 250 percent of the regular tax quota set in 1713, while the revenues actually reaching the central government remained more or less constant.

One way of avoiding this intermediary mulcting was to require that revenues be paid in kind.[45] Another solution was to attack the local influence of the lower gentry. The Yung-cheng emperor had recourse to both, but it was the latter curtailment of the gentry's petitionary privileges which especially stood out in contemporaries' eyes. In Wu-hsi district, Kiangnan, for instance, it was said that before his reign the lower gentry and elders often joined together to petition the yamen, freely entering its gates to curb the lictors' power. But "during Yung-cheng, public petitions were forbidden, so that the officials had nothing to fear and the yamen clerks were as vicious as tigers and wolves.[46]

The Yung-cheng emperor's well-known animus toward *sheng-yuan* thus likened him to the statecraft school, whose spiritual godfather, Ku Yen-wu, had written:

Abolish the empire's *sheng-yuan* and prefectural government will be purified. Abolish the empire's *sheng-yuan* and the peasants' misery will be alleviated. Abolish the empire's *sheng-yuan* and the evil habits of [contemporary scholars'] disciples will be eradicated. Abolish the empire's *sheng-yuan* and there will emerge talent of some use in the world. In the empire today those who move in and out of the yamen gates disturbing prefectural government are *sheng-yuan*. Those who have a deep affinity for clerks and turn themselves into clerks are *sheng-yuan*. Those who arise in flocks to struggle against any prefectural government which acts contrary to their wishes are *sheng-yuan*. Those who seize control and traffic in all the shady affairs of the prefectural government are *sheng-yuan*.[47]

---

44. It also eventually cut into the regular tax quota. The Yung-cheng emperor's campaign after 1725 to reform local tax collection was thus mainly inspired by growing arrears. Kiangnan, for instance, had accumulated a tax deficit of 8,810,000 taels. See Wang Yeh-chien, "Ch'ing Yung-cheng shih-ch'i (1723–1735) ti ts'ai-cheng kai-ko" [Financial reforms during the Yung-cheng period (1723–1735)], *Chung-yang yen-chiu yuan: Li-shih yü-yen yen-chiu so chi-k'an* [Bulletin of the Institute of History and Philology, Academia Sinica] 32:61.

45. See, for example, T'ien Wen-ching's memorial dated YC 2/7/21, in *Yung-cheng chu-p'i yü-chih* [The vermillion rescripts of the Yung-cheng emperor] (Taipei: Wen-yuan shu-chü, n.d.), 1:51.

46. Huang Ang, *Hsi Chin chih hsiao lu* [A modest record of (Wu-)hsi and Chin(-kuei)], photoreprint of 1896 edition (Taipei: Wu-hsi wen-hsien ts'ung-k'an, 1972), 1:14b. I am grateful to my student, Mr. Shih Chin, for bringing this passage to my attention.

47. Ku Yen-wu, "Sheng-yuan lun" [A discourse on *sheng-yuan*], in *T'ing-lin wen-chi* [Collected prose of (Ku) T'ing-lin] (Taipei: Chung-hua shu-chü, 1966), 1:17. I am grateful to

But Ku Yen-wu would hardly have approved of some of the other aspects of Yung-cheng's attack on gentry privilege. As the Wu-hsi example shows, clerks and lictors were the first to benefit from the debasement of the local elite, so that yamen corruption simply replaced gentry pettifoggery.[48] Moreover, the Yung-cheng emperor did not confine his campaign to the lower gentry. All of the established families of an area suffered once his agents tried to curtail the *sheng-yuan*. For, when the emperor ordered that customary procedures conform with centrally-designed laws, or when he relied upon a few trusted officials like T'ien Wen-ching or Li Wei (1687?–1738)[49] to carry out the executive wishes of the throne, many of the informal and decentralized characteristics of the K'ang-hsi bureaucratic–gentry alliance were temporarily abandoned.

Nevertheless, the Yung-cheng emperor's drive for central control ultimately failed to provide for the diversity of the realm. His powerful will notwithstanding, the monarch still had to rule his vast empire with local officials who continued to administer as much by general norms as by specific institutions. Even where so explicit a category as criminal law was concerned, local variations were the rule and uniform procedures the exception. Legal methods may have been elaborately framed at the center, but ministerial regulations only worked efficiently because provincial variations were permitted in practice. Knowing that they were really only expected to comply with the norms of the criminal code, officials felt reasonably free to execute the law flexibly. Bureaucratic unity made procedural consistency unnecessary.

CRIME AND PUNISHMENT

One reason for the reliance upon norms was the ambiguity of the moral–legal spectrum in the Ch'ing code. According to Fu-mei Chang Chen's essay, the tattooing of convicted thieves was designed both to prevent recidivism and to visibly stigmatize criminals in the belief that shame induced repentance. The infliction of shame thus expressed a nominal Confucian confidence in individual rehabilitation and the importance of community redemption of the criminal—two legal characteristics that have been carried over into contemporary China.

However, community redemption was only an ideal; preventive measures did not actually reintegrate the criminal with civil society. In fact, visible stigmas created internal exiles from the community. Tattoos, like the police blotters of a modern society, were marks not easily removed, virtually turning

---

my student, Mr. Ch'eng I-fan, for bringing this passage to my attention.

48. To be sure, the Yung-cheng emperor did single out clerks for attack as well. See, for example, Sasaki Masaya, "Etsu-kaikan no roki" [The illegal tariff of the Kwangtung Maritime Customs], *Tōyō Gakuho* [Oriental Journal] 34:135 ff.

49. Li Wei's role in controlling coastal commerce and overseas trade was carefully spelled out in another paper at the Honolulu conference: Silas H. L. Wu, "Trade, Intelligence, and Coastal Control: Li Wei in Chekiang, 1725–1732."

the criminal into a lifelong outcast. Eminent statecraftsmen like Ch'en Hung-mou (1699–1771) therefore realized that stigmatization actually prevented rehabilitation. There were ways to prevent transforming part-time felons into professional criminals, but Ch'en found that effective rehabilitation either entailed social welfare payments from the office income of district magistrates, or required that the community accept the risk of recidivism by inviting the criminal to rejoin it as an equal. Most authorities therefore thought it cheaper to control rather than reform exconvicts. Ch'en Hung-mou did try to give the parolee a place in society by making him a police aid, but this reform was ironically self-defeating, because it actually made pariahs of both law enforcers and law breakers. Indeed, the entire structure of crime and punishment was relegated to that other, disorderly world of "mean people" (*chien-min*), so that policemen, like thieves or professional actors, were even disqualified from taking the civil service examinations. One could argue that this segregation did thwart the development of a Napoleonic sort of prefectural police system, but by classifying the preventers of crime with its perpetrators, the Chinese were forced to tolerate a high degree of extortion and racketeering.[50]

The relegation of police and criminals to the same underworld is hardly foreign to other societies. What made the Chinese situation more extreme was the administrative *déclassement* of agents of local control who were thus denied access to the regular civil service by legitimate bureaucrats who often regarded policemen as though they were deviants. Of course, this treatment made corruption all the more likely in an administration which depended as much upon self-restraint (normative controls) as upon sanctions (institutional checks) to keep its bureaucrats honest. However, the government could afford unreliable policemen so long as community and lineage guaranteed the control system. Even though *pao-chia* headmen and kinsmen accepted responsibility for parolees with the greatest reluctance, social self-regulation worked well enough until the end of the eighteenth century, when local control began to collapse. Then, as C. K. Yang's paper demonstrates, the high number of mass action incidents associated with "predatory forces" proved how dependent the traditional control system had been upon such "effective agents of the traditional order" as kinship and neighborhood groups.

INTERNAL ANXIETY AND EXTERNAL CALAMITY

Historians disagree over the causes of Ch'ing political disintegration. Some argue that the impact of the West was the primary source. Others emphasize endogenous origins. Ping-ti Ho, for example, has shown how population

50. As Jerome Ch'en's Honolulu conference paper argued, once law enforcement did become more efficient at the end of the Ch'ing, secret society elements were forced to defend their criminal bailiwicks by supporting revolutionary political movements, thereby helping undo the system altogether. Jerome Ch'en, "Modernization of Local Protest: A Study of the P'ing-Liu-Li Rebellion of 1906." The spread of firearms after 1700 also affected this process.

growth placed extraordinary pressures upon natural resources after 1775,[51] while Philip Kuhn has gone on to assert that social resources were strained as well.[52] Because China's huge population required more local administrative services than the Ch'ing system of social self-regulation could provide, informal politico-military organizations (secret societies on the one side, gentry militia on the other) sprang up to govern rural China.

The political conditions for this local militarization would have been a weakening of imperial control. We have seen how much the K'ang-hsi and Yung-cheng emperors did to establish the regulative procedures which prevailed until the very end of the Ch'ing dynasty. The interventionist style of these two monarchs set a heavy burden upon their successors because so much then depended upon the ruler's personal ability to oversee the details of central and local administration. Since few men possessed the capacity to bear such an executive load, which grew heavier over the course of the eighteenth century, the throne faltered. The early Ch'ing emperors had functioned like switchboards, routing most important policy decisions. Partly because of the Ch'ien-lung succession crisis and partly because of the greater volume of information submitted, the switchboard was short-circuited around 1800.[53] From our perspective this meant that the control system lost its primary regulator and was taken over by the very kinds of leaders whom Yung-cheng had attacked in the 1720s.[54]

Simultaneously, of course, the foreign threat appeared. O'Drury's occupation of Macao in 1808 marked a new phase in Sino-Western relations which suggested to the Chinese that their nei-yu (internal anxiety) and wai-huan (external calamity) were mutually connected. This perception was neither peculiar to the nineteenth century nor far removed from the question of social control. When the Yung-cheng emperor had declared, eighty years earlier, that the best defense against external aggression was firm internal control, he was both repeating the assumption of earlier dynasts that the advanced "arts" of Chinese civilization must be kept out of the hands of covetous neighbors, and reflecting the particular sensitivity of a Manchu ruling house accustomed to the seventeenth-century nei-wai collusion between Ming loyalists and foreign traders. Now the Chia-ch'ing and Tao-kuang emperors were all the more alert to the importance of preventing native

51. Ping-ti Ho, *Studies on the Population of China, 1368–1953* (Cambridge: Harvard University Press, 1959).

52. Philip Kuhn, *Rebellion and Its Enemies in Late Imperial China: Militarization and Social Structure, 1796–1864* (Cambridge: Harvard University Press, 1970).

53. The "switchboard" analogy was suggested by Professor Silas Wu at the Honolulu conference.

54. This is not to say that imperial regulation of the control system suddenly ceased altogether. My own work (*Strangers at the Gate: Social Disorder in South China, 1839–1861* [Berkeley and Los Angeles: University of California Press, 1966]) certainly shows how concerned the throne was lest the development of local militia suddenly escape its control. But the compound effect of the internal crisis, the foreign question, and the "jammed switchboard" analogy used above, resulted in precisely that occurring.

traitors (*han-chien*) from arising by keeping barbarian visitors under careful surveillance and control.

One of the methods long perfected by the Chinese to make foreign merchants observe administrative regulations was to grant or withold trading privileges.[55] Although the throne disdainfully wielded this weapon against the "profit-seeking barbarians" as if it had no mercantilist motives of its own, the emperor profited greatly himself. In 1683, when the great debate over foreign trade had been opened, some physiocratic counsellors wished to seal the empire off from barbarian contact. The K'ang-hsi emperor, realizing that prohibition would simply put smuggling profits in the hands of provincial officials, pragmatically decided to legalize foreign trade.[56] At the same time, avid for his privy purse, K'ang-hsi also made certain that only the most trusted of his personal officials were appointed to supervise what was essentially designed to be a royal monopoly trade. His agent at Canton (the "hoppo") was supposed by English East India Company factors to be a functionary of the Board of Revenue; the official actually represented the Imperial Household (*nei-wu-fu*), and was charged both with controlling foreigners and with forwarding customs revenues directly to the palace in Peking.[57] Thus, when the Ch'ien-lung emperor restricted all Northern European trade to the port of Canton in 1760, the connection between control and the imperial fisc was simply tightened all the more. In fact, because the hoppo was usually a bannerman, foreign affairs became a Manchu specialty over the course of the eighteenth century. At the time of the Amherst mission (1816), however, diplomatic responsibilities were transferred from Imperial Household representatives to regular civil servants. Thereafter, imperial commissioners like Lin Tse-hsu (1785–1850) leavened the throne's interests with a high degree of Confucian moralism, so that the opium crisis of the 1830s defied the hardheaded K'ang-hsi solution of combining control with profit. One might even argue that the later Ch'ing emperors were too sinified, too overcome by their own Confucian rhetoric, to divorce profit from moral considerations by legalizing the drug traffic under Imperial Household control. However, such a *Realpolitik* was unlikely because the "foreign poison" was so visibly linked with inner decay. To the Tao-kuang emperor—whose impoverished and dispirited Manchu bannermen were so commonly addicts—opium was both symptom and abettor of the internal social crisis.

One of the many important questions raised by Jonathan Spence's study in this volume is whether opium addiction increased during the late eighteenth

55. This aspect of control was carefully surveyed by Randle Edwards in his paper at the Honolulu conference: "Ch'ing Control of Aliens prior to the 'Treaty System.'"

56. Chang Te-ch'ang, "The Economic Role of the Imperial Household (*Nei-wu-fu*) in the Ch'ing Dynasty," *Journal of Asian Studies* 31.2:243–274.

57. When K'ang-hsi was advised to delay opening trade in 1683, the emperor replied that "The high officials of the border provinces should keep the people's livelihood in mind. Even though we prohibited trade before, were we actually able to prevent smuggling and illicit commerce? The reason for certain governors and governor-generals suggesting trade not be

century because of growing availability of the drug or because of heightened demand from the consumer. If the latter, can opium smoking be viewed as a measure of anomie, accompanying the political and social control problems discussed earlier? Could one argue in turn that such an opiate was a psychological form of escape which may even have prevented a higher degree of aggressive disorder than actually prevailed?

Not if we examine the crisis from the point of view of control alone. The control system was so vulnerable to corruption that opium profits pushed criminality above tolerable limits. The drug traffic actually mobilized lawlessness, promoting the growth of secret societies which helped distribute opium, and hastened the decline of police and Green Standard forces which were already far from reliable. However much opium could have deadened physical protest, the conditions of its sale were such as to throw together criminals and police all the more intimately. Military defeats during and after the Opium War (1839–1842) simply increased the grounds for addiction by creating a public sense of humiliation over China's inability to defend itself.[58] By the end of the nineteenth century, approximately 10 percent of the population was addicted to a drug which was gradually becoming a major source of government income, grinding in that humiliation all the more deeply.

MASS PROTEST

The rise in opium addiction over the course of the nineteenth century was one expression of the *nei-wai* crisis of late Ch'ing China. Mass action movements were another. The growth of social disorder during this period has been given statistical shape by C. K. Yang's essay, which draws primarily upon data from the *Veritable Records* (Shih-lu) of the Ch'ing dynasty, a source which is useful but slanted. Because the *Shih-lu* reflected court concerns, urban and political forms of protest were more likely mentioned than rural *jacquerie* or social banditry. Then, too, social distinctions became blurred from the Olympian vantage point of Peking. Nevertheless, the perspective is broad enough to let us discern several important qualities of social disorder in the nineteenth century. One that immediately stands out is the political (i.e., policy-aimed) nature of mass protest. Another is the urban venue of dissent. One-third of all incidents did take place in badly policed border or frontier areas, but most occurred in administrative centers where they often involved members of the local elite. It would seem, therefore, that the majority of peasant movements in the nineteenth century were not led by farmers at all. In fact, the word "peasant" may be a misattribution altogether. The rank-

---

allowed is that they are only thinking of their own personal profit [through controlling an illegal trade]." *CSL*:KH, 116:4.

58. Another effect of the war was, eventually, imposed legalization of the drug and consequently easier modes of importation into China. Since this argument for increased addiction is so well known, I have exaggerated the demand side in order to emphasize other causes suggested by Spence's paper.

and-file often came from minority groups like the Hakka, or from professions marginal to farming: salt-smuggling, convoy protection, boxing, *routier* transportation, charcoal gathering, silver mining, and so forth. And when farmers did join, they left much of their peasant character behind them. The Taiping rebels, for instance, composed a military society which disciplined its cohorts into new roles. Later adherents—the peasants ingested by the Taiping forces as they advanced up the western hills of Hunan—were transformed into "brothers and sisters" within the ranks, drilled and molded into the cohorts of an army on the march.

As long as the Taiping movement rolled forward, its armies continued to enroll dislocated peasants and reshape them into followers. But once the Heavenly Kingdom was established at Nanking in 1853, the Taipings confronted a fixed rural society which defied assimilation. Their choice at that point was to impose their military blueprint upon the countryside by co-opting local magnates and making them *liang ssu-ma* (sergeants), who were actually just tax collectors for the regime.[59] Since this form of local government utterly failed to curb the lower gentry, the Taiping rule over Kiangnan helped turn *pao-lan* (proxy remittance) into unabashed tax-farming.

LOCAL CONTROL AFTER THE TAIPING REBELLION

The Taiping tax farmers were opportunists. When it became clear to them that the Ch'ing side would win, many switched their allegiance to the imperial forces, putting their managerial skills at the disposal of the higher gentry of cities like Soochow. It was often such defectors who actually restored gentry order to the Kiangnan countryside by serving as the functionaries of the upper gentry's relief bureaus, likin (transit tax) collection agencies, and militia offices. However, the establishment of these new kinds of organizations did not begin with the suppression of the Taipings. Rather, as James Polachek's essay argues, their prototypes could be found in that part of China several decades earlier, when the Kiangnan gentry had previously faced a mounting fiscal crisis.

The early Ch'ing fiscal compromise may have corrected some of the inequities of the *li-chia* system, but it did not altogether obliterate the distinction between *ta-hu* (grandee households) and *hsiao-hu* (commoner households). Nor did the Yung-cheng attack on gentry privilege prevent the gentry from recovering much of its influence by the late eighteenth century, when the *sheng-yuan* again prevailed upon magistrates to adjust tax-collection exchange rates for their benefit.[60] By the 1820s new disparities were once more forcing land off the commoner registries and onto gentry rolls.

59. Kawabata Genji, "Enforcement of *Hsiang-kuan chih-tu* System of Rural Officials in the *T'ai-p'ing T'ien-kuo* and Its Background," *Acta Asiatica* 12:42–69.

60. However, this may not even have been true for all of Kiangnan. In Wu-hsi, for example, the Yung-cheng reorganization of local government in 1724–1728 brought to office a new

There appeared at that time, as there had in the seventeenth century, a group of metropolitan gentry willing to cooperate with the provincial government in order to remedy the situation. According to Polachek, these careerists found during the 1830s that the *pao-lan* practices of the lower gentry were harming their own property interests. When the Soochow gentry's lands began declining in productivity because the local government was too insolvent to maintain irrigation works, and falling in value because the fiscal crisis had thrown so much other real estate upon the market, the upper gentry decided to help Governor-General Lin Tse-hsu reform the tax system. With their support Lin tried to break the alliance between corrupt *sheng-yuan* and *t'u-hao* (local bullies). At the same time he also persuaded the central government to allow him to send tribute rice north by sea (*hai-yun*) instead of up the Grand Canal where so much grain was stolen or wasted. Whether or not these tax savings directly benefited the province in the form of a reduced quota then depended upon the metropolitan gentry's political influence in the capital.

Despite momentary successes, both these efforts failed by the 1850s to alleviate Kiangnan's economic distress. Lin's wedge between gentry and landlord interests was blocked by local militia movements which cemented *sheng-yuan* and *t'u-hao* together in new kinds of managerial collaboration. In the meantime, maritime grain transport did generate tax savings, but the Soochow "lobby" in Peking did not have enough influence to engineer a reduced quota for Kiangnan. Consequently, statecraftsmen like Feng Kuei-fen (1809–1874) felt forced to devise more mechanical means of ensuring their participation in local government—a resolve which fostered gentry militia bureaus in Soochow by 1853. As this local retrenchment went on, gentry influence continued to wane in the capital, where a new corps of tough Hunanese bureaucrats, allied with tightfisted Manchus like Su-shun,[61] utterly rejected the Kiangnan elite's pleas for tax remission. Recalling the 1661 tax case, the metropolitan gentry now determined to protect their interests by allying with the somewhat unsavory militia specialists and tax

---

group of magistrates dedicated to defeating the proxy powers of the gentry. Then, in 1728, a vigorous gubernatorial campaign to collect back taxes impoverished many of the urban gentry, so that thereafter the division between wealthy and poor was not so extreme, while a new group of less flamboyant rural landlords emerged to prominence in the countryside. "Some years ago, the people in the city owned more rental lands than the people in the countryside. Therefore rent collection was centralized. Now the people in the rural areas own more rental lands than the urban populace, and rent collection is decentralized." Huang Ang, *Hsi Chin shih hsiao-lu*, p. 37. This account is cited in an unpublished seminar paper by Shih Chin, "The Gentry and Imperial Power in Wu-hsi, 1522–1759" (Berkeley, 1973).

61. Su-shun was noted for his harsh measures to curb inflation. See Frank H. H. King, *Money and Monetary Policy in China* (Cambridge: Harvard University Press, 1965). In fact, Su-shun in some ways resembled Oboi, so that one can conjecture that had the 1861 coup gone his way (rather than favoring Prince Kung and Yehonala), the Kiangnan gentry might well have faced the same kind of pressure they encountered in 1661.

farmers who had taken over so much local control during the Taiping troubles. Lacking Peking's support, in other words, the literati consolidated themselves on home ground, replacing metropolitan influence with provincial connections.

The hegemony of *sheng-yuan* managers within the local control system and the alliance between gentry and landlords were both concretized in Kiangnan's landlord bursaries (*tsu-chan*), which routinely used their own police and arrest warrants to dun tenants in arrears.[62] In Soochow this bureaucratization of rent collection can be traced back to the Yuan-ho Rent Bureau of 1863, which established the post-Taiping pattern of property management. As control fell almost entirely into the hands of the local elite, taxes and rents, public and private, fused together. The rural gentry had ostensibly become master of its own estate.

One possible consequence of this fusion was the intensification of class conflict. During the High Ch'ing, gentrymen, however venal, at least pretended to stand for local paternalism. But now urban *rentiers* were represented by rent bureau bailiffs, often moonlighting policemen, who destroyed the particularistic *kan-ch'ing* (rapport) which once united rural landlords and their tenants. By the late nineteenth century a Soochow gentryman could no longer think of himself as a bucolic squire defending his local clients' interests before the district yamen. To those distant tenants he was merely an absentee landlord, identified absolutely with a local government whose police forces were often his own private militia (*min-t'uan*). The stage was thus set for the peasant movement of the 1920s, when remnants of the former local political elite stood ready to be condemned for their economic interests as *t'u-hao lieh-shen* (local bullies and evil gentry).[63]

LOCAL BULLIES AND EVIL GENTRY

In the shorter term, such local oligarchies accompanied the devolution of power from the center to the provinces. The "provincialization" of late Ch'ing politics[64] was mainly based upon western doctrines of constitutional

62. Muramatsu Yūji, *Kindai Kōnan no sosan: Chūgoku jinushi seido no kenkyū* [Landlord bursaries of the lower Yangtze delta region in recent times: studies of the Chinese landlord system] (Tokyo: Kindai Chūgoku kenkyū iinkai, 1970).

63. Of course, regions like Kiangnan or Kwangtung, where the gentry gripped local control the most tightly, were not areas where the peasant movement was most likely to succeed. See Roy Hofheinz, "The Ecology of Chinese Communist Success: Rural Influence Patterns, 1923–1945," in A. Doak Barnett, ed., *Chinese Communist Politics in Action* (Seattle: University of Washington Press, 1969), pp. 3–77. Peasant resentments seem to have festered helplessly in such landlord-controlled regions until the Red Army arrived to dispute the gentry's local control.

64. John Fincher, "Political Provincialism and the National Revolution," in Mary C. Wright, ed., *China in Revolution: The First Phase, 1900–1913* (New Haven: Yale University Press, 1968), pp. 185–226.

sovereignty, but there were statecraft justifications as well.[65] As Philip Kuhn points out, Feng Kuei-fen was inspired by Ku Yen-wu's theory of localism to propose a new kind of village-level government run by popularly elected *pao-chia* leaders. Above them, but still below the yamen, Feng hoped to institute an administrative cadre of local *sheng-yuan* to assume some of the clerical and control functions of the existing yamen bureaucracy. By realistically recognizing the administrative power which the *sheng-yuan* had seized in the 1860s, Feng thought to do away with the informal gentry management system. He would, however, have retained the bursaries and rent bureaus because by collecting rents they enabled the landlords to pay their taxes, thereby preserving the agrarian system while serving the state. Faithful to the statecraft belief in enlightened self-interest, Feng saw no fundamental incompatibility between particular interests and the collective good.

Did the system of local self-government (*ti-fang tzu-chih*) which actually developed after 1909 finally live up to the hopes of reformers like Feng? As a slogan, *ti-fang tzu-chih* was supposed to mobilize popular participation in local government, creating a politically educated citizenry for the nation-state in order to strengthen it against imperialism. But in practice—according to Kuhn's account—*ti-fang tzu-chih* simply justified the unchecked control of the rural gentry. Once the dynasty fell, national politicians quickly realized that the lower gentry was still using its village bureaus to withhold taxes from republican magistrates. This was why President Yuan Shih-k'ai (1859–1916) abolished village-level offices in 1913, and why the Kuomintang (after initial enthusiasm for *ti-fang tzu-chih*) decided in 1934 to repudiate the "local self-governments" which Kiangsu magnates had turned into private economic preserves.

By then, however, it was too late to reverse the tendency of local control organizations to evolve into landlord governments. Counterbalanced by administrators since Sung times, the local gentry had always been restrainable in the past. But now the Ch'ing had fallen, finishing off a bureaucratic order which had given the local elite its ultimate status. No longer forced to turn to the center for certification, the gentry engineered a fundamental shift in the local balance of power, virtually excluding national government from many parts of rural China. Indeed, the *t'u-hao lieh-shen* of provinces like Kiangsu so infested sub-county posts as to create a sphere apart from the district capitals. At first drawn from the same pool of *sheng-yuan* who managed the post-Taiping control bureaus, these "local bullies and evil gentry" were eventually aban-

65. Here there is a remarkable connection between Dennerline's statesmen and Polachek's later metropolitan gentry. The revival of statecraft by men like Feng Kuei-fen (who authored the 1863 Soochow reforms) accompanied the same kind of local fiscal reforms in the same area and among the same kinds of people (who were occasionally blood descendants of the seventeenth-century reformers) as in 1661. Hsia Yun-i or Ch'en Tzu-lung were thus remarkably similar, in terms of social group, interests, and political position vis-à-vis the central government, to the statecraft writers of the late Ch'ing. One might even ask how equivalent the Hsuan-nan Poetry Club in Peking during the 1840s was to the Fu-she two centuries earlier.

doned as a social embarrassment by the sorts of urban patrons who had formerly constituted the Soochow scholar-elite.[66] Culturally divorced from the westernizing world of the cities, the *t'u-hao lieh-shen* were free to transform their proxy powers of foreclosure and arrest into concentrated rural landlordism and usury. The countryside was thus left to the least deserving; those who were now unchallenged from above would be in the end, so soon to come, all the more vulnerable from below.

66. In Hunan, for example, reformist gentry leaders like T'an Yen-k'ai sided with the left wing of the Kuomintang in 1926–1927 precisely because of their common opposition to *t'u-hao lieh-shen*. See Angus McDonald, "The Urban Origins of Rural Revolution in China" (Ph.D. thesis, University of California, Berkeley, 1974), chapter 9 *passim*.

Hierarchies and Networks:

A COMPARISON OF
CHINESE AND ISLAMIC SOCIETIES

Ira M. Lapidus

As a student of Islamic and Middle Eastern history presenting a paper for this volume on China, I feel the diffidence of an outsider commenting on affairs of which I have no professional knowledge. But as an historian interested in the craft of history, I am led to wonder what are the basic assumptions, the explicit or implicit paradigms by which historians of China conceive Chinese culture? How do their conceptions of China compare with those which inspire scholars of Islamic and Middle Eastern studies? By comparing the basic thought models of Chinese and Islamic studies, can we test the validity of these models and explore the implications of the prevailing paradigms for our understanding of each civilization?

The central motif in contemporary scholarship about traditional China seems to be the nature of order in Chinese conceptions of the universe, of empires and society, and of man. This prevailing vision emerges in Derk Bodde's description of the Chinese view of a permanent and unified universe comprised of unequal and even contradictory elements, which are harmoniously integrated to maintain the unity of the whole. "The universe . . . is a harmoniously functioning organism consisting of an orderly hierarchy of interrelated parts and forces, which, though unequal in their status, are all equally essential for the total process." The universe, in fact, is formed of antithetical principles whose cyclical movements or oscillations between polar opposites confirm the inherent order of existence. "The universe is in a constant state of flux, but . . . this flux follows a fixed and therefore predictable pattern consisting either of eternal oscillation between two poles or of cyclical movement within a closed circuit; in either case the change involved is relative rather than absolute, since all movement serves in the end only to bring the process back to its starting point."[1] Opposed forces are essential to the ultimate reconciliation.

1. Derk Bodde, "Harmony and Conflict in Chinese Philosophy," in Arthur F. Wright, ed., *Studies in Chinese Thought* (Chicago: University of Chicago Press, 1953), pp. 21, 67–68.

At other levels of analysis, this basic conception also informs the Chinese view of man and society and the views of students of Chinese society and history. The Chinese social order, in all its reaches, from emperor through bureaucracy through gentry elites to local communities, is taken to be an harmonious organism combining Confucian ideals, political organization, and social structure. I need merely, and briefly, illustrate the kind of thinking involved to recall the system you have in mind.

In the Chinese political and social system, the emperor is the key to order. Confucian doctrine provides that the emperor orders society to accord with cosmic norms through generalized legislation and personal moral example; but moral leadership is known to be ineffective. In the alternative "legalist" conception, an ordered society requires coercion, total control of resources, standardized administration, and Draconian enforcement of laws. The emperor thus functions both as moral exemplar and as tyrant. Although the moral and coercive aspects of the monarchy diametrically oppose each other, both remain essential to a unified moral and political order.

The bureaucrats, or rather the gentry-officials who serve the emperor, function in similar balanced tension. On the one hand, they represent the emperor and the state order, execute the emperor's will, and guarantee his authority. Contrarywise, gentry-officials also represent ideal values and special interests which conflict with imperial authority. Though serving the state, they also embody the claims of Confucian morality by whose standards they judge, criticize, and reform the political practices of the state. Similarly, the gentry officials oppose their lord, the emperor, in defense of private (clan, local, and factional) interests, using their office to defend and aggrandize personal concerns. Thus, official careers both implement imperial control of society and bind private interests to the service of the imperial regime. "It was the genius of Confucian bureaucracy (though not always its achievement) to be poised between the poles of local and central power, magnetized to both, and resisting in its values the final claims of either."[2] One body of officials encadred in a single institution at once represented the dichotomies of sovereignty and society, court and country, Confucian challenge and legalist support of the emperor. The implicit tension made the empire politically effective, yet infused with Confucian ideals. The tension of opposites connected state and society and integrated the emperor with his subjects. Without contradictions, the ordered whole was inconceivable.[3]

A similar mechanism bound the official-gentry to scholar-gentry and to nongentry elites. Degree-holders without official posts transmitted orders from above and negotiated on behalf of the people below. As potential

2. Joseph R. Levenson, *Confucian China and Its Modern Fate: The Problem of Monarchical Decay* (Berkeley and Los Angeles: University of California Press, 1964), p. 35.

3. See Levenson, *Confucian China;* and David S. Nivison, "Introduction," in David S. Nivison and Arthur F. Wright, eds., *Confucianism in Action* (Stanford: Stanford University Press, 1959), pp. 3–24.

officials, they assumed public functions, including tax collection and even military defense, in collaboration with the gentry-officials. Nongentry elites maintained a similar dialectic of communication with gentry elites. Powerful clan chiefs, landowners, rich merchants, and other elites opposed state control and authority, on the one hand, and identified with it on the other. Because of the mobility afforded by the examination system, purchase of degrees, and award of degrees for public services, all notables had an interest in collaborating with the gentry elites and the emperor. All elite persons were thus divided between opposing and collaborating with governmental authority. Potential rebels were potential officials; expectation of mobility maintained the hierarchy of society.

Both the tensions and the unity of state and society reappear in the soul of the sage. The Confucian ideal requires the fusion of thought and action, principles and personal behavior, words and deeds. Thought must be fused with life; the scholar must assume public responsibilities. Private morality and learning must fuse with state service, and practical politics must harmonize with classical teaching without dissipating the tension of opposites. Private life affords individuals self-fulfillment through the study of the classics for their own sake and through the cultivation of Confucian ethics, while public life beckons to efficiency and mastery of society through purely political and pragmatic actions. Literati value the active life, but are corrupted in public affairs. Officials compromise the realization of ideals in practice. In Platonic terms, the just order of society which harmonizes imperial and individual interests depends upon the harmony within the souls of the elite. The proper balance of public and private interests in public life corresponds to the balance of worldliness and otherworldliness, activity and quiescence, in the souls of the learned officials.

These ordered antinomies are well known in Chinese thought and in writings about Chinese thought. Joseph R. Levenson's work has extended this intellectual style into the appreciation of Chinese government, and into the relationship between emperor and bureaucracy and between political and intellectual life. When we turn from emperor and elites to the masses of Chinese society, we find an analogous pattern of conscious or unconscious appreciations. Implicit in the growing literature of local history is a conception of Chinese society in which imperial control, and rebellion and protest, are seen as mirror images of each other—indeed, as conflicting components of a functionally integrated system. Of the many possible conceptions of local control and social protest, a dialectical image prevails.

In Chinese society state control of the masses and popular movements of protest had a common source in community organization. The empires controlled their subjects by purely administrative means. Under the *pao-chia* system all households were registered for surveillance and military conscription. Each group of households was held collectively responsible for maintaining order, and commoners were appointed as headmen to obviate the influence of scholar-gentry with government officials. Taxes were collected by similar methods. A purely artificial social structure subordinated Chinese villages to the authority of the state.

Opposed to this artifical organization was the "natural" structure of Chinese society. The natural structure focused on the basic framework of society—family kinship, lineage, and clan organization. Local communities were based on lineage, and local gentry often represented lineages and their interests. In the nineteenth century the development of the militia movement provided order and defense through *t'uan-lien* (militia) units, which were basically lineages mobilized under gentry leadership. Though born of the natural society, the militia could, like the natural elites, be legitimized and incorporated into the government system by official recognition, appointment of the gentry to offices, and similar means. Lineages could be mobilized to support the state, but to rely on them excessively would increase the power and autonomy of local gentry and thus unbalance the state system. This happened when regional political machines developed which deprived the central government of military power, tax revenues, and control of the peasantry.

The natural organization of Chinese society extended beyond the lineage village or cluster of villages. Militias grouped into large units through extensive lineage and clan connections, and through gentry collaboration organized in market towns, schools, or bureaucratic factions. Indeed, integration of local militia units by gentry associations and by personal loyalties reached regional and multi-provincial proportions. The expansion of the militia devalued the empire's major benefit to the gentry—the capacity to assure large-scale order—and displaced the balance of gentry and state power in favor of the gentry. It is important to observe, however, that gentry militia confederations lacked legitimacy independent of the state: their organization was a variation in imperial configurations, not a departure from the imperial system.

Lineage and associations had an obverse side; the "natural" order of Chinese society was equally the basis of disorder, banditry, rebellion, and revolution. The disorder generated by lineage wars and competition for control of land, markets, and prestige became an endemic problem of Chinese society. Insofar as lineages generated military power, they might use that power against the state.[4] Lineages and village communities were also a source of bandits and rebels. Local "natural" leaders, perhaps disaffected scholars, could rally support among village youth or economically deprived villagers and form bandit gangs or secret society cells. In such cases, whole communities or lineages might eventually join the rebel leadership or secret

4. Philip A. Kuhn, *Rebellion and Its Enemies in Late Imperial China* (Cambridge: Harvard University Press, 1970).

society. Bandits and rebels, "inner strangers," were recruited in otherwise peaceful communities.[5]

Thus, t'uan-lien and secret lodges were alternative expressions of the politically indeterminate natural order of local Chinese society. The market-town nexes adumbrated by G. W. Skinner[6] are shown by Philip Kuhn to be two faces—the Odette and Odile—of the same person. As Kuhn shows, the organization of rebels was parallel in form to that of lineages and gentry in defending local and state interests.

I find the clearest illustration of this intimate relationship between order and rebellion in the case of the Nien (1851–1868). The Nien rebels built up their organization by exploiting lineage feuds, by recruiting disaffected villagers, and by using their initial supporters to compel or win the allegiance of chiefs in adjacent villages, until they had constructed a region-wide solidarity dedicated to the rebellion. Indeed, the regional gentry gave the Nien their capacity for large-scale marauding and determined defense.[7] Suppression of the rebellion depended on aligning the same chiefs and lineages with the government. Order was the obverse of disorder. To suppress the rebellion, state commissioners registered the populace, induced local leaders to cooperate, created cells of support to bring neighboring villages into the government network, and enrolled the peasants into the government armies—in effect reversing the procedure which had built up the Nien rebellion. Thus Chinese local society and local social organization are seen, as are all levels of society and culture, to embody two contrary principles—integration into the empire system and autonomy from it; these principles exist in dynamic oscillation, which produces the larger unity of Chinese society. Without the capacity for rebellion implicit in the natural organization of society, the gentry would be unable to maintain the relative autonomy which permitted their balanced participation in the state system. Control and protest were systemic parts of the Chinese order in the classic sense of opposites reconciled in a larger harmony.

The model of Chinese society which emerges from the historical literature I have surveyed has a number of features. One notices first that the roles and institutions which constituted Chinese society were shaped by calculation and well polished by time. Lineage structure, gentry status and roles, bureaucratic organization, and the emperor's court were clearly defined institutions with well articulated norms.

Each of the component elements embodied contradictory possibilities in action. Historically, the essential problem in ordering Chinese society was not to eliminate contradictions—for they were essential to the system—but

5. Frederic Wakeman, "The Secret Societies of Kwangtung, 1800–1856," in Frederic Wakeman, ed., "Nothing Concealed": Essays in Honor of Liu Yü-yun (Taipei: Chinese Materials and Research Aids Service, 1970), p. 138.

6. G. W. Skinner, "Marketing and Social Structure in Rural China," Journal of Asian Studies 24 (1964): 1–43, 195–228, 363–399.

7. Siang-tseh Chiang, The Nien Rebellion (Seattle: University of Washington Press, 1954).

rather to balance their oscillations or cycles in a manner which favored the overall order of the whole. Tension, contradiction, and deviance were not exceptions but parts of the system itself. The order of the whole, however, depended on the hierarchical integration of each level of contained antitheses. Lineage, gentry, bureaucracy, emperor, and world order formed a hierarchy of levels, the architectural backbone of the Chinese order.

The image of Chinese society which emerges in the historiography is not quite an architectural pile, but rather a mobile—one of Calder's mobiles with well fashioned pieces trembling in balance or swinging in circles. Each arm is linked to another above, such that the movement in any horizontal plane affects the movement of the other arms. Yet, though in constant movement, the mobile as a whole floats gracefully, a complete form, a harmonious totality, assuming innumerable variant configurations without loss of its inherent unity. It moves in eternity. This, I think, is the historian's implicit image of China. It may be China's image of itself.

Not all historians hold this view in every respect or in the same degree of complication or sophistication, but it is generally assumed that China is an integrated, well ordered, and fundamentally harmonious society. Historians of China emphasize such factors as the natural structure of subordination, administrative organization and the means of social control, and the indoctrination of the populace in a comprehensive and coherent moral system. Deviation and disorder are generally treated as anomalous, occasional, and isolated events, meaningless occurrences which must and will be reabsorbed in the functioning whole of Chinese civilization.

However, new research in Chinese social history, especially the work represented in this volume, reveals orderly and peaceful China to be the scene of quite extraordinary conflict. Class struggle, clan warfare, and rebellious secret societies were not only endemic, but banditry sometimes occurred on a scale so massive as to defy any conception of China as an organized society at all. Great sectors of the Chinese economy—including the actual operation of the salt and opium industries, the sale and distribution of imported products, and many aspects of taxation—were defined as illegal and were operated by vast smuggling networks or by conspiracies of officials and merchants, producing an alternate economy parallel to the counter-society. Inept administration, political and factional struggles, hypocrisy, and unfairness in the application of the law seem as much a part of Chinese political life as orderly government. Is this all simply a deviation, a polar tension in an orderly system? Or is it not an alternative reality, equally massive and substantial? May we not question the image of China as a fundamentally harmonious world? Is there not a counter-reality, an anti-matter, to the China which is so intricately and suspiciously well-ordered? Behind the mystique of system, what behemoth, or what new force of life, lies concealed?

To an outside observer there seem to be two Chinas—one integrated and controlled, the other violent and chaotic. Ordered China does not fully contain disorder, nor does disordered China destroy the persistent wholeness of Chinese society. How can we mediate these extremes and restore a coherent view of China? Perhaps by taking a look at another society—in this case, because of my experience, Islamic society—we can re-examine the metaphors which shape our views of history, and return re-equipped to the problem of analyzing China.

Students of Islamic and Middle Eastern civilization also come to their subject with implicit metaphors and conceptions about the basic form of Islamic societies. Islamic studies, however, contain two prevailing views. One resembles the hierarchical pattern applied in Chinese studies. Without the many special refinements of the Chinese model, the hierarchical conception seems an obvious way to approach the history of the Abbasid caliphate of the eighth to the tenth centuries, or the Ottoman sultanate of the fourteenth to the twentieth centuries. In Islamic terms the caliphate, and later the sultanate, represented God's vice-regent on earth, his prince appointed to govern, uphold Islam, give justice, and assure the proper ordering of the world. Yet in practice the caliphate embodies the same contradictions as the Confucian emperorship. Islamic governments ruled by force of slave armies and subservient bureaucracies, served only their own interests or the interests of the state elites, exploited their peoples, and gave no more than lip service to Islamic ideals. The holy *qur'an* stood to one side of the caliph's throne, the executioner to the other.

The parallels may be extended further. To govern, Islamic regimes depended on the collaboration of both secular and religious elites. Regional lords and princes, district or village headmen, tribal *shaykhs,* wealthy landlords, and learned Muslim scholars, teachers, and lawyers collaborated with central government. These classes supplied the cadres for central administration, cooperated in taxation, raised manpower, and defended caliphal or sultanal interests in their districts. Religious leaders validated, legitimized, and justified obedience to royal authority. But, as in the case of China, a deep reserve was intrinsic in this collaboration. Local elites resisted absorption and domination by the central authorities, and defended their own economic and status interests and their authority in the communities they represented. Religious leaders withheld complete confirmation of political authority, asserting the superiority of holy writ, whose teachings served to judge human government, and appealing to the holy law against the abuse of political power. As in China, governmental power depended upon elites who preserved a measure of autonomy.

The organization of the common people also involved situations which parallel those of Chinese society. Middle Eastern communities—families, lineages, clans, villages, neighborhoods, tribes, fraternities, and so on—were cohesive bodies capable of defying and resisting the authority of the government, though they also served to transmit the authority of the state to every individual. Quasi-independent communities held a treacherous balance between autonomy and submission. The study of local control and social protest in the Islamic world may also be formulated in terms of the shifting balances between susceptibility to external organization and control and the internal capacity for autonomy and self-determination.

This perspective has yielded important results in Islamic studies. It has clarified the nature of conflicts over caliphal authority, the operation of bureaucracies, the ambivalence of local notables, and the characteristics of social order and rebellion. However, while the hierarchical metaphor emphasizes the similarities between Chinese and Islamic societies, it neglects the differences between them.

Islamic institutions were not as precisely articulated as Chinese, nor were they as thoroughly integrated. For example, neither caliphate nor sultanate had a precise definition in Islamic thought, since Islamic political traditions were an eclectic summation of ancient Middle Eastern, Persian, and Roman traditions, blended with Muslim religious and Arab tribal conceptions. Also, Middle Eastern regimes were quite alien to the populations they governed. Their military power was commonly based upon nomadic conquests or the recruitment of foreign slave forces; administrative support came from ethnic or religious minorities. A Muslim regime might comprise slave military forces, a Christian administration, and Jewish bankers and financiers, with its declared principles and the mass of its subjects as its only Muslim features. Muslim regimes do not appear to have had the same integral relationship to the societies they ruled as did Confucian emperorships.

Moreover, underlying the apparent similarity in the functioning of elites were very significant differences. In the Islamic world elites were not encadred in a state machine, and elite status was not defined by position in an imperial hierarchy or by any uniform educational or cultural attainment. The examination system had no Islamic counterpart. Islamic elite status derived from fluid combinations of religious learning, certified by school diplomas and acquired reputation; from wealth derived from trade or landed investment; from family prestige; and from office-holding or political influence. In the eleventh century, however, religious learning became the crucial factor, and from that time Islamic elites were primarily religious elites. Nevertheless, the primacy of religious considerations did not obliterate the other factors; status was defined from many perspectives, and remained a quantity which could be known only when measured in social encounters.

Furthermore, by the eleventh and twelfth centuries the Islamic state elites had separated from the local and especially the religious elites. Indeed, each elite derived from different milieus and operated under separate institutions. State soldier and administrative elites were organized as armies or bureaucracies: religious, teaching, and judicial elites were grouped in schools of legal study and practice or in religious confraternities. In effect, state and church had become virtually distinct institutions in the Islamic world, though the church—that is, the groups of Muslim divines—did not have the organizational form of the Christian church. Whereas the single order of the Chinese state could contain the tension between Confucian values and the actuality of statecraft, as well as the ambiguous relationship between gentry and emperor, in Islam the conflict between religious and political requirements and between the government managers and local religious elites was resolved by separating the elites and evolving two distinct institutions to embody the purposes and values of each. In China the confrontation of state and Confucian values was an interior monologue with implicit moral judgments. In Islam it was a marriage dialogue between separate persons, carried on in the language of Islamic religious convictions. Whatever the substance of the dialogues, Islamic societies did not have the integral unity of Chinese society.

In one further respect the structure of Islamic society differed from the Chinese. In China the systematic or integral character of the society as a whole was based upon the coherent structure of lineage and village organization and the ubiquitous capacity for peasant, gentry, club, sect, and secret-society associations. Islamic societies, however, seem to have been much more segmented and inchoate. Instead of ramified lineages, one finds a vast mosaic of small groups with little unity or even similarity of type. Although families and clans were basic to society, neighborhood communities, religious fraternities, craft associations, youth gangs, groupings of religious notables, paramilitary corps, and other groups divided Muslim societies into numerous small and self-sufficient units. Coalitions, of course, played a large part in the structure of Islamic society, but only bedouin and mountain peoples had the capacity to organize large-scale rebellions. Coalitions involving urban groups were always quite limited in scale. In the Islamic world we find no equivalent to the lineage linkages, the market-town confederations, and the gentry associations which could build small Chinese communities into regional-scale rebel governments. Muslim communities, then, could not generate the same political power as their Chinese counterparts.

For these reasons, some students of Islamic history have begun to move away from hierarchical images of society and from efforts to define the "constitutional" organization of Islam toward images of diversity, discontinuity, and differences within Islamic societies. Using case studies, they attempt to construct a picture of Islamic societies from the bottom up, tracing the ad hoc relationships formed by individuals and small groups. The main questions for research involve the motives for these interactions, the ways in which they are conceived, their durability, and their extensiveness. Implicit in this approach is an image of society as a network of relationships between component groups rather than an image of society as an architectural or hierarchical structure.

This second basic approach to Islam brings into focus the differences, rather than the similarities, between China and Islam. It presents social institutions such as clans, elites, churches, and states as the summation of relatively durable networks, and yet as extremely fragile, against the basic disintegrative tendencies of Middle Eastern societies. If the wonder of Chinese history is the intricacy of its systematic organization, the marvel of Islamic history is the persistence of a civilization without apparent integration at all. To illustrate, let me give you two examples of the network model of Islamic society as applied to nineteenth-century Morocco and fourteenth-century Syria. I choose these cases to illustrate two important variations within the same framework of thought. They also pose, as did the Chinese case, some questions about the relationship between social organization and cultural concepts, and about the influence of images and metaphors on the appreciation of social reality.

Morocco has a long history of repeated tribal conquests and rapid formation and disintegration of empires. Ibn Khaldun's (1332–1406) dictum that bedouin empires last but four generations derives from the experience of Morocco. In a land of weak governments, armies and bureaucracies often amounted to little more than the household of the ruler. Governments depended on tribal groups for political support.

Morocco was also a land of social anomie. Pastoral populations were relatively powerful, peasants relatively weak. Towns were isolated from the countrysides except when they served as market centers for the bedouins. Then the main tie between town and country was an uncertain symbiosis between pastoralists and merchants, rather than the more stable domination of landlords over peasants.

The tribes which dominated Morocco elude definition. Conventional genealogical and political explanations fail to describe the actualities of group confederation. A Moroccan tribe was a shifting rather than a stable entity, sometimes actualized by temporary confederation, by government organization, by religious loyalites, by fictive genealogy, or even merely by imitation of famous names. Tribal membership was constantly redefined, depending on the fortunes of chiefs or the rise of saints or warrior leaders. Morocco was a society of small units without a permanent large-scale organization. In the words of Clifford Geertz:

> Structure after structure—family, village, clan, class, sect, army, party, elite, state—turns out, when more narrowly looked at, to be an *ad hoc* constellation of miniature systems of power, a cloud of unstable micropolitics, which compete, ally, gather strength, and very soon overextended, fragment again.
>
> The social order is a field of small, pragmatical cliques gathering around one or another dominant figure as he comes, more or less transiently, into view and dispersing again as, largely traceless, he disappears. The cliques are somewhat more stable in the Moroccan High Atlas or the Tunisian steppe than they are in Algiers, but the difference is only relative. The

social partitions of North Africa are everywhere movable and incessantly moved.[8]

To understand this society, we must begin with the small kinship groups which were its basic feature, and decipher the logic behind the *ad hoc* combinations of which all larger entities were really made. As Edmund Burke has put it in a review article on Moroccan society: "In the predominantly rural and tribal context of nineteenth-century Morocco, politics was conducted less in terms of imposed religious and administrative norms, and more in terms of a network of social linkages based upon Moroccan popular Islam."[9] The crucial factor in Moroccan society was the veneration of the basic kinship groups for Sufi saints, called marabouts. The saints were blessed with divine favor, their *baraka*, which enabled them to intercede with God and mediate between Him and man. Moreover, the saints also mediated between different clans and tribes and won their followers by a combination of religious charisma and political skill. "Living generally near the borders between major segments of tribes, the *murabit* helped make peace between warring groups, arranged the payment of *diya*, or blood money, and intervened on request in countless ways to ease transactions and provide assistance to merchants traveling through the region under his . . . protection."[10] A saint's *baraka* was entirely bound up with his social and political skill. Thousands of *murabit* came and went, unable to survive the delicate demands made upon them. Those that survived might stabilize their leadership, regularize the gifts and payments made in recognition of their virtue, and extend the sphere of their influence to neighboring peoples. Still, *baraka* was a personal gift which evaporated with the vicissitudes of time and the shortness of life.

An occasional marabout, however, was able to pass his *baraka* to a chosen son or follower, and perhaps was able to enlist his followers in a regular lodge or confraternity, a *tariqa*. His followers would formalize their relationship by swearing their allegiance to him and his religious teachings, and their loyalty to each other. Such religious fraternities might even unite in a Moroccan-wide order, based on devotion to a founding saint and the missionary zeal of his followers, and gain considerable religious and even political influence. Like the marabout himself, the *tariqas* performed the crucial function of cutting across local kinship ties to bring individuals and families into new, religiously sanctioned, social relationships. Still, whether formed by direct intervention of the marabout or in the form of brotherhoods, ties between local kinship groups remained unstable, subject to disintegration and reformulation in different groupings, all depending on the skill of the *marabout*, the conjunction of interests, and the persuasiveness of the *baraka*. In nine-

8. Clifford Geertz, comments in *New York Review of Books* (April 22, 1971), p. 20.

9. My account of Morocco is based on Edmund Burke, III, "Morocco and the Near East: Reflections on Some Basic Differences," *Archives européenes de sociologie* 10 (1969): 70–94; quotation p. 70.

10. Ibid., p. 78.

teenth-century Moroccan society, Islam provided the main rationale for social alliances but did not produce enduring institutions to encadre the basic kinship communities. Moroccan society was formed by veneration for religious figures with a largely personal charisma and was thus a society constantly in the process of being made, unmade, and remade. Confederations worked by miracles were not constant in this world.

Government was construed in an essentially analogous way. The sultan of Morocco was neither ruler, administrator, nor chief executive, but rather resembled a kind of super-marabout. Nineteenth-century sultans were descended from the family of the prophet Muhammad, and therefore possessed a religious prestige, a *baraka*, which merited still greater veneration than that of the average marabout. Like the marabouts, sultans ruled by endless bargaining with clans, tribes, and religious brotherhoods, using their religious prestige and political acumen to weave one more of those ephemeral coalitions which made the nexus of Moroccan society. The sultan was simply the largest interest-broker of all, the one who commanded the greatest prestige and could mobilize the greatest resources. The state, then, was not a fixed institution, but a coalition of kinship groups called tribes or, rather, a net which could be strengthened or weakened, cut into pieces or sewn into larger sections. In this society all the strands of the net were woven out of religious faith. The one Moroccan institution was Islam, personified by the marabouts and the sultan.

Our second example, Syria in the thirteenth to the fifteenth centuries under Mamluk rule, was similarly a network world, but one with more pronounced institutional regularities. Syrian society had many of the features of the hierarchical model—relatively institutionalized government, organized religious bodies, elites with some continuity of family history, and socially stable communities—but it still operated as a network. Its political and religious institutions operated through *ad hoc* group relations and networks of patronage–clientage ties.

Syria was a land with a quite incredible mosaic of small communities. Tribal, ethnic, and religious minorities inhabited its mountain regions and isolated valleys. In the mountains of Lebanon, for example, the population included Maronite Christians, Alawite Muslims, and Druzes. The steppes and desert regions were inhabited by bedouin tribes. In the mountain and steppe regions governments maintained themselves either by force, by balancing local rivals, or by abandoning the people to fight their own battles; in the latter case, the state shared the tribute exacted by the victor from the losing side.

Urban situations were more complex. Townspeople were divided into family and clientele groups, neighborhood quarters, religious fraternities, youth gangs, paramilitary organizations, occupational communities, groups of religious notables, Islamic sects, and religious minorities of Jews and Christians. Relationships between the various urban groups were mediated through the marketplace by negotiations of *shaykhs* or group headmen and, when necessary, through informal contacts between the notables of one community and those of another. For many purposes these notables were the *ulama*, the religiously learned elites. Public works, security, mosque or school affairs affecting several groups could be informally handled by the religious notables.

Contacts between religious notables, however, were not purely *ad hoc*. The *ulama* themselves were grouped in organizations called schools of law. A Muslim school of law was the body of scholars devoted to the preservation and study of the *qur'an*, to tradition, and especially to one of the several orthodox corpuses of Muslim law. In Islam, law was the core of the faith, and obedience to the law the essential religious virtue. Insofar as Muslim law applied to many aspects of civil society—to family, marriage, divorce, inheritance, property, commerce, and so on—the schools of law also had an important role in guiding the everyday lives of believers in ways consistent with Islamic principles. The *ulama* of the schools were the teachers, *muftis*, consultants on law and ritual, and judges for the community of believers. Conversely, the masses of uneducated Muslims were followers of the school *ulama* insofar as they looked to the schools for religiously authoritative guidance on the proper living of a Muslim life. Organization aside, a school of law may be considered a kind of church or sect within the body of Islam.

As organized bodies of the urban religious elites, the schools also served as centers for other social purposes. They were a convenient setting for discussion of common religious, educational, and philanthropic concerns, as well as other public affairs. The schools provided a meeting place where the *ulama* coordinated their interests and the interests of their parochial communities on a host of matters; but a school was not in any sense a municipal council or government. Although Syrian towns had up to four schools of law, they had no formal relationships between them, nor did they have any jurisdiction over territory, taxation, military power, or any of the other essential prerogatives of a government. Moreover, in public matters the schools did not function in any formal way. Apart from religious learning and teaching proper, the schools did not operate as a corporate group and did not represent local interests or directly administer community affairs. Schools provided no formal procedures, methods, or ground rules for the larger play of members' interests. Indeed, insofar as the *ulama* had multiple interests, such as land owning, office holding, lineage status, religious reputation, teaching jobs, control of school revenues, and judgeships, their political involvement was governed largely by complex circumstantial considerations. They were the elites of the society mobilized for specific interests by specific circumstances, finding in the schools a convenient meeting group for *ad hoc* consultations. Thus, on the one hand, unlike the Moroccan *tariqas*, the Syrian schools had a strong institutional aspect in their formal organization for religious study, teaching, and judicial administration, and in their historical "permanence." On the other hand, the schools, like the *tariqas*, were the locus of intersection for the various networks which could coordinate community interests in a broad range of civil and religious matters.

A similar analysis may be applied to the state regime. In this period Syria was ruled by the relatively durable Mamluk empire, whose main province was Egypt. A regime of slave soldiers, the Mamluks had their own norms for the recruitment, training, and organization of soldiers, as well as historically stable policies for selecting officers, administrators, and the ruling officer, the sultan. They also possessed an ethos which rationalized the obligations of loyalty and service within the state machine and the duties of the state to its subjects. Moreover, in Egypt the Mamluks adopted a long tradition of bureaucratic administration. All in all, the Mamluk sultanate had a much more pronounced institutional aspect than the Moroccan sultanate.

Yet in the Syrian cities the Mamluk regime did not govern by what we would call institutional means. Apart from a few supervisory officials, no bureaucratic apparatus governed the towns, and no state services, procedures, special personnel, or budgets were provided for town administration. A Mamluk governor operated not as a subordinate official of the central government, but as a quasi-independent satrap with authority to pursue whatever policies accorded with public order and the collection of tax revenues. A governor was responsible for the well-being of his district, but was free to choose which aspects of local government he would control. A Mamluk governor ruled, in fact, by consulting local notables, usually the religious elites and quarter headmen. Some notables might be appointed to offices, but in most cases relationships between the governor and the collaborating notables were informal. The notables would help maintain order, assist in taxation, advise and inform the governor, while the governor, in turn, would lend the notables the authority of the state in dealing with their people, contribute to the support of religious institutions, donate funds for public works, and give the notables opportunities for financial gain. Similar ties were forged between the Mamluk governors and non-elite elements of the population. Youth gangs and certain quarters of the towns became clients and supporters of the governors, through the mediation of non-*ulama* "commoner" chiefs. Although no formal procedures existed for incorporating religious notables and commoner factions into the state system, the government operated through patronage–clientage ties between the governors and the urban elites. The state might be an institution, but its subjects were not an integral part of it. They were governed, if the term applies, by patronage networks.

This system of government controls was fragile. Governors governed by keeping a balance of power among local interests. Force alone could not facilitate day to day administration, but urban populations did not hesitate to use force against the regime. Protests against excessive taxation or abuse of authority were frequent in the towns, as armed communities demonstrated or even rebelled to dramatize their demands. Notables and factions which collaborated with the governors might turn against them to defend their basic interests. Cooperation with the state, then, was only one side of a balance formed by willingness to resist Mamluk authority. By balancing collaboration with rebellion, the subject populations could arrive at a *modus vivendi* with their masters.

Fourteenth-century Syrian society was knit together by patronage–clientage and by *ad hoc* consultative ties formed at the local social level by devotion to Islam and respect for the notables who preserved and implemented it, and at the political and imperial level by common conceptions of legitimate authority. Syria differed from Morocco in that its networks were not woven of charismatic and circumstantial considerations, but of stable religious and political conceptions and practices which were partly institutionalized in the schools of law and the Mamluk state regime, but which retained network systems as the basis of social integration. Coalitions, alliances, and social cooperation motivated by common interests and fortified by religious and sometimes political norms were the crucial features of Syrian society. Elite persons fashioned agreements and alliances; institutions like state and church were the dense knots where many network lines crossed.[11] Institutions were forms in potential, to be actualized by intermittent coalitions.

Thus, in the study of Islamic society, two different approaches have been used. Through the hierarchical approach we can study the vertical integration of society. With the network metaphor we can best understand the nonhierarchical aspects of Islamic society—the prevalence of small units; the *ad hoc* quality of their relations with each other and with governments; the large role of consultation and mediation in reconciling differences, keeping order, and assuring cooperation; the fragility of institutions; and the basic importance of voluntary arrangements consecrated by religious conceptions and by prophetic and learned leadership. Without exhausting the reality or vitiating aspects which are better understood from the viewpoint of hierarchical organization, the network model fits the actualities of Islamic societies, and enables us to comprehend a society which has a coherent overall order without formal structure.

At this juncture we can return to our original question and ask how we can use the contrasting qualities of Islamic society and the different historiographical approaches to Islam to illuminate the study of Chinese society. To arrive at a realistic appraisal, we have to consider one further issue: the relationship between the metaphors employed by historians and the culture—as opposed to the social and political structure—of each civilization.

The hierarchical and dialectical view of Chinese society corresponds to one of the traditional Chinese ways of seeing the world. In a similar way, the network view accords with the conceptual world of Islamic culture. For

11. I. M. Lapidus, *Muslim Cities in the Late Middle Ages* (Cambridge: Harvard University Press, 1967).

example, the Islamic viewpoint does not conceive of history as an ordered whole. History has a beginning and it has essential themes—the history of peoples and of God's grace in sending prophets to guide them according to His will, culminating in Muhammad. It does not, as does Christian history, proceed to an apocalyptic last judgement which is the end of temporal history; nor does it progress, like liberal modern history, toward this-worldly fulfillment; nor, as in Greek or Chinese history, do the affairs of men recur in cycles. History is the record of important events and reports of the great teachers of the Muslim community, but its overall and inner meaning is known only to God, whose providence it manifests.

Similarly, one may observe that Islamic arts eschew form: sculpture is almost unknown in Islamic culture; religious arts avoid reproduction of human and animal figures; architecture generally subordinates building form to utility and decorative effect. Islamic arts are known for ever-flowing calligraphy and arabesque designs. Literature similarly stresses elegance of language and practical content, but rarely unity of composition. In poetry the well-turned line is more valued than a poem integrated by theme, mood, image, or sound.

Orthodox Islamic philosophy and theology see the universe as being without an overall pattern or even causal interconnectedness. The world is created *ex nihilo* and maintained by continuous creation and recreation. All occurrences are governed by God's will; their apparent regularity is His bounty to men, but no regularity is intrinsic in nature. Nature is not governed by immutable, rational laws, but exists only by virtue of God's will to keep it in existence and give it the qualities and relations He does. The whole is an unfathomable creation of the remote, unknowable God.

The human ideal cannot then be ontological or moral conformity with the inherent order of the world and the soul. Moral growth is rather the ever closer approximation to the fulfillment of God's will as revealed in the *qur'an*. It is submission and ultimately the merger of the human will in the divine. The Islamic mystic, like the Confucian sage, envisages an ultimate unity of the soul in thought and action, but it is a unity achieved only by faith in the teachings of the *qur'an*, unassuming love for the creator, and submission of one's own will to the divine command. Thus in Islam, history, art, cosmos, and human life itself have no coherent order but are movements and actions correctly performed at each given moment in accord with God's will; in the same way, society is an ever living, never completed network of actions.

Thus the preferred metaphors of Chinese and Islamic historians are not accidental. They correspond to the cultural style and the world view of each civilization—and in fact may derive from the historians' familiarity with the societies they study. The structures of Chinese and Islamic societies, which accompany characteristic ways of understanding and acting in the world, are appreciated and interpreted by historians in terms of the metaphors which each culture suggests to its students. The analytical metaphor becomes a dimension of historical experience. Social reality, cultural style, and analytical metaphor are intrinsically interrelated. Thus the different approaches used in the study of China and Islam expose radical differences in the two civilizations.

At the same time, however, the metaphors employed by historians may be deliberately selected or modified in order to clarify aspects of the civilizations which are neglected or distorted by the predominant points of view. Metaphors and reality are also entwined in that what we see and comprehend of a society depends on the sensitive and fitting selection of guiding imagery. Social realities, after all, are multidimensional, and they will appear to be different according to the light in which they are examined. Thus in the Chinese case the preferred metaphors stress formal hierarchy and order, and in the Islamic case the network metaphor emphasizes informal and unstructured interconnections. Consequently, the informal structure of society, out of focus from the hierarchical point of view, is readily visible in the Islamic case, whereas hierarchical aspects minimized in the Islamic case dominate in descriptions of China.

Yet we have seen that Islamic society may be considered from an hierarchical point of view as well. Could the network point of view be used to focus on hitherto anomalous aspects of the Chinese experience? Would it be possible to integrate studies of Chinese local history, which seem to parallel local politics in the Islamic world, into network rather than hierarchical models? Would China look different if it were studied as the outcome of individual choices and actions rather than from the perspective of a total system? What would China look like from an approach which emphasized the differences between localities and provinces, or a point of view which emphasized individual motives and situations, or the actions and interests of cliques and factions, or class relationships, or popular mores and culture? Could informal or illegal phenomena, which seem to "deviate" from the Confucian conception of society and from the systematic ordering of Chinese society, be considered substantial realities in their own right rather than variant aspects of the Chinese system? Instead of seeing Chinese institutions as given forms for the organization of Chinese society, could they be interpreted as the outcome of the informal dynamics of Chinese social life?

Comparison of Chinese and Islamic societies and of the approaches of historians to China and Islam reaffirms the basic validity of the dominant view. But at the same time, comparison suggests that alternative approaches may be of value in coping with new findings in Chinese history. As an outsider, I cannot carry out the studies to test alternative hypotheses; I can only hope that this momentary interchange between the exotic Far West and China comes at a time when it may encourage and contribute to the interpretation of the new studies of Chinese social and local history presented in this volume.

Localism and Loyalism
During The Ch'ing Conquest of Kiangnan:
THE TRAGEDY OF CHIANG-YIN

Frederic Wakeman, Jr.

Are glories so akin to dreams
That what is true is
Taken for the false,
And the feigned for real?

Don Pedro Calderón de la Barca,
La Vida es Sueño, Third Day, Scene X

The Ch'ing conquest of Kiangnan, that region between Shanghai and Nanking once known as Wu, was not a uniform occurrence. Government policies alternated from year to year between the conciliation of a Hung Ch'eng-ch'ou and the harshness of a Pa-shan, while the inhabitants' own reactions varied from docile acceptance of the new dynasty to bloody resistance. A city like Sung-chiang, close to the lairs of the T'ai-hu bandits, went through states of placidity and turmoil quite different from those of Chia-ting or Shanghai. Region-wide events—Dodo's march to Hangchow in 1645, the 1657 examination scandal, the 1659 naval raids, the tax case of 1661—were qualified by specific local conditions: the organizational cohesiveness of the gentry in one area, the land tenure system in another, and so forth. Thus it would be misleading to exhibit one district's history as that of Kiangnan as a whole.

I exaggerate the dangers of such a generalization because the Chiang-yin resistance to Ch'ing control was even then considered exceptional for the region. Chiang-yin's siege was the bloodiest, its struggle the most famous; but for all those killed there, millions of other inhabitants of Kiangnan were quick to write *shun-min* (surrendering people) upon their city gates. Chiang-yin's struggle was unusual even when compared to other centers of resistance like Chia-ting, where rural militia played a more prominent role,[1] and Sung-

---

1. See, for example, Chu Tzu-su, *Chia-ting hsien i-yu chi-shih* [A record of events at Chia-ting hsien in 1645], in *NCIS*, pp. 183–202, esp. pp. 186–187. Chu Tzu-su, *Chia-ting t'u ch'ang chi-lueh* [An outline of the butchering of the city of Chia-ting], in Hu Shan-yuan, *Chia-ting i-min pieh-chuan* [A collection of biographies of the righteous people of Chia-ting] (Shanghai: Shih-chieh shu-chü, 1938), pp. 203–221, contains a variant of that account, and is identical in most respects.

chiang, where the Chi-she literary society of Ch'en Tzu-lung provoked much of the protest to Ch'ing rule.[2] Yet—precisely because it was such an exaggeration of suicidal Ming loyalism—the tragic struggle at Chiang-yin revealed more clearly than the others the ambiguousness of local resistance to Ch'ing control.[3]

CHIANG-YIN CITY

Chiang-yin—a hundred miles upriver from Shanghai—was the capital of a fertile farming and trading district which ran for twenty-five miles along the south bank of the Yangtze. Some of the half-million inhabitants of the country were fishermen, but more engaged in agriculture and handicrafts.[4] The district's lands were lush with yellow and early-ripening white rice, cabbage, melons, fruit and mulberry orchards, flower gardens, and cotton crops. The latter, especially in the villages west of the capital, provided employment for weavers who sold their cloth, along with burlap bags and rush fans, to wholesalers from Chiang-yin city.[5] The district capital's commercial position thus depended upon the fertility of its farming lands, many of which were *sha-t'ien* (polder fields): reclaimed alluvial soil.[6] But what the

2. See, for example, Ch'en Tzu-lung, "Nien-p'u" [Chronological biography], in *Ch'en Chung-yü ch'üan-chi* [The complete works of Ch'en Tzu-lung] (1803), pt. 2, pp. 30–32; and Ch'u Hua, *Hu-ch'eng pei-k'ao* [A complete investigation of Shanghai], in *Shang-hai na-ku ts'ung-shu* [A collection of reprints of snatches of the past of Shanghai] (Shanghai: Chung-hua shu-chü, 1936), 3:2.

3. My account of the resistance is primarily based on Han T'an, *Chiang-yin ch'eng shou chi* [Annals of the defense of Chiang-yin] (Ch'ang-chou, 1715), reprinted as an appendix to Hu Shan-yuan, *Chiang-yin i-min pieh-chuan* [A collection of biographies of the righteous people of Chiang-yin] (Shanghai: Shih-chieh shu-chü, 1938), pp. 158–198; on the biography of Yen Ying-yuan in the *Ming-shih* [Dynastic history of the Ming], Kuo-fang yen-chiu yuan ed. (Taipei, 1961), 277:3114; on *NCIS*, pp. 373–380; and on Yen Ying-yuan's biography in *CYHC*, p. 437. There is also a short biographical account of Yen Ying-yuan in Arthur Hummel, *Eminent Chinese of the Ch'ing Period* (Washington, D.C.: U.S. Government Printing Office, 1943), p. 912, and a standard summary of the resistance in Su Hsueh-lin, *Nan-Ming chung lieh-chuan* [Exemplary biographies of Southern Ming loyalists] (Chungking: Kuo-min t'u-shu ch'u-pan-she, 1941), p. 47.

There are three short, popular accounts of the Chiang-yin resistance: Li T'ien-yu, *Ming-mo Chiang-yin, Chia-ting jen-min te k'ang-Ch'ing tou-cheng* [The anti-Ch'ing struggle of the people of Chiang-yin and Chia-ting at the end of the Ming] (Shanghai: Hsueh-hsi sheng-huo ch'u-pan-she, 1955); Wang Hung, *Chiang-yin jen-min te k'ang-Ch'ing tou-cheng* [The anti-Ch'ing struggle of the people of Chiang-yin] (Shanghai: T'ung-lien shu-chü, 1954); and Hsieh Ch'eng-jen, *I-ch'ien-liu-pai-ssu-shih-wu nien Chiang-yin jen-min shou-ch'eng ti ku-shih* [Tales of the people's defense of Chiang-yin in 1645] (Peking: Chung-kuo ch'ing-nien ch'u-pan-she, 1956). There is also an excellent summary in Hsieh Kuo-chen, *Nan-Ming shih-lueh* [Outline history of the Southern Ming] (Shanghai: Jen-min ch'u-pan-she, 1957), pp. 82–86.

4. This is a gross population estimate. According to the 1377 census, the district contained 29,128 taxable households. By 1633 this figure had increased to 51,740. The census of 1672, taken after the conquest when the district was presumably repopulated, showed roughly the same levels as during the late Ming: 51,145 households, with a *ting* quota of 399,674. *CYHC*, p. 142.

5. *CYHC*, pp. 243–245.

6. *Sha-t'ien* first appeared in Chiang-yin's land registers during the mid-thirteenth century.

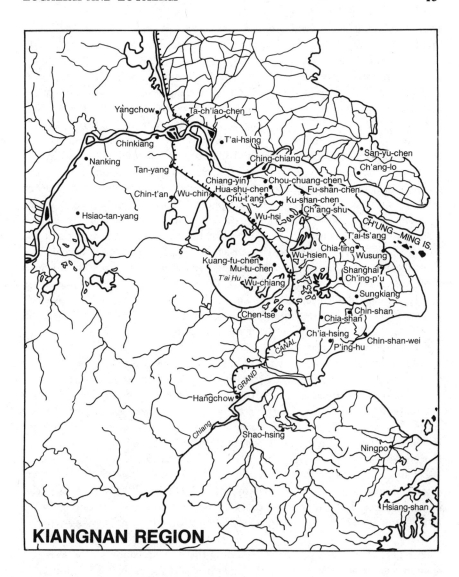

KIANGNAN REGION

river gave, it also took away. Changing water levels and tidal effects constantly threatened dikes and eroded fields, creating an economic paradox
which was later noted by the famous statecraftsman, Ku Yen-wu (1613–

The major increase in them really only took place during the last quarter of the sixteenth
century, when they reached a total of over 60,000 *mou. CYHC,* p. 156. They naturally presented a serious problem to successive district magistrates anxious to have them entered on the
land registers, since boundaries frequently shifted and it was extremely difficult to keep track
of ownership. Ku Yen-wu, "Ch'ang-chen," pp. 84–85b, in *T'ien-shia chün-kuo li-ping shu*
[Writings on the advantages and disadvantages of the prefectures of the empire] (Taipei:
Ssu-k'u shan-pen ts'ung-shu, n.d.), ts'e 7.

1682): "Chiang-yin is well known as a district of wealth which is heavily taxed by the state. Its lands often rise [in price] and its people are frequently in straitened circumstances."[7]

Ku Yen-wu did not connect this peasant impoverishment with land-lordism. Instead, he related it to irrigation difficulties stemming from earlier attempts to drain part of the T'ai-hu marshes to the south. The ditches linking that lake area with the Yangtze River ran right through Chiang-yin, but rather than draining lake water, their reversed currents admitted the Yangtze's flow. This initially profited Chiang-yin's farmers, because irrigation was intensified. Over time, though, the ditches silted up, causing the river to spill over tilled lands so that harvests were irregular and peasant freeholding insecure. "There was no place," claimed Ku, "where water control was as difficult as in Chiang-yin."[8] That in turn accounted for the district's public insecurity. Those who lost their lands to the river or to the moneylender frequently turned to smuggling or banditry as a way of life. Consequently, Ku Yen-wu believed that Chiang-yin was a perfect place to prove his theory that public order was a function of economic stability under gentry management. Local relief had to precede local control. Once the waterworks were repaired, the river would bring its profits again. Then the people of the district could settle down to agriculture, institute *pao-chia*, and extinguish social banditry.[9]

Ku's diagnosis of Chiang-yin's troubles physiocratically ignored the district's commercial interests. Chiang-yin's importance as a trading center seems to have declined by 1700 (perhaps because of the city's temporary destruction in 1645), but in pre-conquest years it was an affluent textile center.[10] Whether the busy trade there attracted urban toughs or not, Chiang-yin had at the time a notorious reputation for criminality. "Chiang-yin," Ku Yen-wu noted, "has long been known [as a place] of frequent disturbances by bandits and robbers, while it is furthermore said that there is an utter lack of effective policies to suppress the seditious."[11] Robbery was rife in the villages, but the gravest problem was riverine piracy conducted by large bands which plundered fearlessly. Yet at the same time Chiang-yin was not without public security organs. Since the tenth century the district had been regarded as a key point for defending the higher reaches of the Yangtze from naval attack. A major naval garrison in Sung times, Chiang-yin's military importance increased during and after the Wako raids of the six-

---

7. Ibid., p. 60b. In terms of the polished-rice tax on Chiang-yin's 1.1 million *mou* of registered fields, quotas remained constant from 1537 until the 1661 tax case. In 1537 the quota was 179,588 piculs; in 1582, 179,848 piculs; and in 1660, 179,849 piculs. However, there was an increase in the unpolished-rice quota (which by 1639 had reached a level of 72,912 piculs), as well as the additional levy of the three supplementary taxes of the late Ming. The latter equalled 89,798 *liang* of silver. *CYHC*, p. 161.

8. Ku Yen-wu, "Ch'ang-chen," p. 61.

9. Ibid., p. 61b.

10. *CYHC*, p. 245.

11. Ku Yen-wu, "Ch'ang-chen," p. 61.

teenth century. At that time the Yangtze Admiralty Office at Huang-t'ien-kang (the main port due north of the city) had built ramparts along the river, while the regular army garrison at Huang-shan-kang (the harbor northeast of the capital) had supervised the reinforcement of the county seat's thick walls.[12] The walls were further surrounded by a forty-foot moat which was connected to the Huang-t'ien River that meandered through the city between willow-draped banks. And beyond that moat stretched suburban wards (*fang*) as far as Huang-t'ien-cha (Yellow-field watergate), an area rimmed by the heavily wooded Chün and Huang hills from whose summits one could gain a spectacular view of the great river below.[13]

Chiang-yin's proximity to the Yangtze made the city a favorite resting place for travelers from Chekiang and Fukien preparing to cross the river and continue north to the capital. Of course, it also exposed Chiang-yin to pirate raids from Ch'ung-ming Island, but these at least served to sharpen the reflexes of local defense. Perhaps it was this militia tradition that made Chiang-yin's resistance to the Ch'ing so unusual, since—in the words of one collection of Southern Ming chronicles—"the southward advance of the heavenly troops was [relatively] bloodless."[14] In loyalist lore only two counties (Chin-shan in Chekiang and Kan-chou in Kiangsi) and a few cities had entirely refused to accept the new overlords. Chiang-yin was one of the latter.

THE FALL OF THE MING

News of the fall of Peking to Li Tzu-ch'eng reached Chiang-yin on the night of June 4, 1644. Fifteen days later the Prince of Fu would inaugurate the Hung-kuang reign in Nanking, announcing the accession of the first Southern Ming regime. But for the moment the death of the Ming emperor in Peking seemed to signal the end of a civil order. Chiang-yin did not explode into serf and tenant riots like some other parts of Kiangnan,[15] but there was enough plundering by marketplace mobs to spur the forces of order into action. Two key groups collaborated in this effort.

12. *CYHC*, pp. 37–62. The walls were more than twenty feet thick on the southern, northern, and eastern sides. *CYHC*, pp. 68–69. Even though the walls were destroyed in 1645, they were quickly rebuilt by the Ch'ing authorities. The city had completely regained its military prominence by the Tao-kuang era. *CYHC*, p. 197. During the twentieth century it was held to be one of the major defense points for the Kiangnan arsenal. In fact, young Chiang Kai-shek led an effort to take the fortress there during an anti-Yuan Shih-k'ai uprising in 1916. See Pichon P. Y. Loh, *The Early Chiang Kai-shek: A Study of His Personality and Politics, 1887–1924* (New York: Columbia University Press, 1971), p. 29.

13. *CYHC*, p. 92; Hsieh Ch'eng-jen, *I-ch'ien-liu-pai-ssu-shih-wu nien*, p. 3.

14. *NCIS*, p. 373.

15. The possibility of tenant riots must certainly have been in their minds, though rural discontent was apparently not as intense in Chiang-yin as in districts like T'ai-ts'ang where the famous serf revolts of 1644–1645 broke out. See Hsieh Kuo-chen's analysis of serf and tenant uprisings included at the end of Hsieh-Kuo-chen, *Ming-Ch'ing chih chi tang-she yun-tung k'ao* [Examination of the factional movement from Ming to Ch'ing] (Shanghai, 1934; Taipei reprint, Commercial Press, 1966); and Mark Elvin, *The Pattern of the Chinese Past* (London: Eyre Methuen, 1973), pp. 239–245.

First was the local notability: urban and rural-dwelling gentry who were led by the subdirector of studies (*hsun-tao*), Feng Hou-tun.[16] These men quickly formed a district-wide committee which sent degree-holders into the countryside to reassure village elders and other "good elements" that though dynasties might fall, the social fabric would hold.[17]

Second was the local military and police apparatus. The Chiang-yin district warden, Ch'en Ming-yü, and the local garrison commander, Chou Jui-lung, asked Feng Hou-tun to assemble the gentry around the city altars at T'ien-ch'ing gate. There all took an oath before the Ming's ancestral tablets to raise an army to "succor the emperor" (*ch'in-wang*).[18] The meeting-place itself was significant, since the altars (*she-chi*) designated the ritual interface between state and local religious worship.[19] As *she* (the earth spirit), the altar represented local identity, extending beyond the gentry to include all the city's residents. As *chi* (the god of grain), however, the altar symbolized duty to the imperial ancestors. This duty supposedly extended to all the people of the empire "fathered" by the royal family, but it was actually sensed as an obligation only by members of the gentry. For they, in contrast to the commoners of Chiang-yin, really were the social progeny of the throne —a status elite created by the emperor's degree-granting potency. This particular meeting was therefore much more a gentry than commoners' assembly. Yet interestingly enough, it was not the magistrate but the warden (*tien-shih*), Ch'en Ming-yü, who conducted it.

During the Ming, "the *tien-shih* [or warden] controlled the exchange of documents and [the records of] income and expenditures. If there was no assistant magistrate or no registrar (*chu-pu*), then he shared the duties of both."[20] Formally appointed at the chief officer level, the warden began by

16. Feng Hou-tun (T. P'ei-ch'ing) was from Chin-t'an (Chen-chiang prefecture, Kiangsu). A *kung-sheng*, he was made subdirector of studies (*hsun-tao*) in Chiang-yin in 1641, and in 1644 helped gather contributions for military supplies in Fukien for the Prince of Fu. When Chiang-yin fell, he hanged himself in the Confucian temple. His wife and concubine threw themselves into a well along with thirteen of his students. Like Ch'en Ming-yü and Yen Ying-yuan, he was honored by a tablet to his memory in the shrine of loyalty and righteousness (*chung-i tz'u*) by imperial order in 1776. See *ITC*, ts'e 92, 78:17b; and *CYHC*, p. 437.

17. The area northeast of the city, bordering the river, was visited by Hsu Chin, the local director of studies, and his friend, Ch'en Ming-shih, a *hsiu-ts'ai*.

18. Han T'an, *Chiang-yin ch'eng*, p. 163. Ch'en Ming-yü was from Chekiang and was appointed warden in 1642. *CYHC*, p. 437.

19. The use of these places of religious worship as centers of gentry control is well known. See, for example, Hsiao Kung-ch'üan, *Rural China: Imperial Control in the Nineteenth Century* (Seattle: University of Washington Press, 1967), pp. 277–279, 571–572. During most of the Ming, tax collectors (*liang-chang*) were periodically enjoined to gather together their district's inhabitants in order to explain the purposes of the *she-chi*. See Liang Fang-chung, "Local Tax Collectors in the Ming Dynasty," in E-tu Zen Sun and John De Francis, eds., *Chinese Social History, Translations of Selected Studies* (Washington, D.C.: American Council of Learned Societies, 1956), p. 254.

20. "Chih-kuan chih" [Treatise on officials], *Ming-shih*, cited in Morahashi Tetsuji, *Dai Kanwa jiten* [The great Chinese-Japanese dictionary] (Tokyo: Taishūkan Shoten, 1958), p. 1184.

supervising the clerical staff.[21] During the sixteenth century, however, his responsibilities came to include the organization of local defense. The rising influence of the warden was therefore related to the decline of the regular *ching-ying* and *wei-so* military system. As the registration of regular hereditary military families (*chün-kuo ping*) lapsed, local defense came to depend more and more upon a second and distinct military apparatus of *hsiang-ping* (village troops), which had been in existence since the early Ming.[22]

In its heyday the original *wei-so* system had represented the triumph of central military control and the culmination of the ideal *fu-ping* (divisional militia) of Wei and T'ang times. But the cumbersome enrollment of so many into an hereditary military caste was by the Wan-li period more effective as a corvee than as a military organization. To meet the Mongol challenge in the north and counter Wako invasions along the coast, the military system was allowed to evolve in two directions. First, generals like Li Ch'eng-liang and Ch'i Chi-kuang were permitted to train and form their own armies. Second, the formation of *hsiang-ping* was expanded. Although neither of these developments was allowed then to culminate in regional warlordism or local militar-

21. The office itself was established during the Yuan dynasty for eight northern districts near the capital. The appointments (one *tien-shih* and one *ssu-shih*, probably reflecting a civil-military distinction) were seconded to local magistrates. In the Ch'ing the term was often interchangeable with *lien-pu* (to detect and arrest). The police function was merely formal, however. As Ch'ü T'ung-tsu points out: "An assistant magistrate or a jail warden could also be assigned to conduct an inquest or on-the-spot investigation of a robbery when the magistrate was absent. However, many magistrates were reluctant to delegate investigations to a subordinate official on the grounds that he might accept a bribe or that his prestige was insufficient to command the respect of the people and their willingness to accept his judgment. Even a subordinate official with a specific assignment, such as *li-mu* or *tien-shih* (jail warden), might not actually discharge the duties indicated by his title. The jail wardens, although designated as officers in charge of police bureaus, actually had no voice in police affairs." See T'ung-tsu Ch'ü, *Local Government in China under the Ch'ing* (Cambridge: Harvard University Press, 1962), p. 13.

According to John Watt's figures, the jail wardens were ubiquitous throughout the Ch'ing. For example, in 1785 there were 65 independent department magistrates with 58 jail wardens; 146 department magistrates with 200 jail wardens; and 1297 district magistrates with 1292 jail wardens. The jail warden's total salary was 91.5 taels, as compared with 100 taels for an assistant magistrate and 1245 taels for a district magistrate in one given district. District salaries tended to differ for magistrates, but they seem to have been fairly constant for jail wardens. The jail warden was unranked, whereas the registrar was 9a, the assistant magistrate 8a, and the magistrate 7a. See John Robertson Watt, "Theory and Practice in Chinese District Administration: The Role of the Ch'ing District Magistrate in the Historical Setting" (Ph.D. thesis, Columbia University, 1967), p. 35.

22. There were three kinds of *hsiang-ping*. The first appeared in the Hu-kuang area in 1384, when local magistrates appointed local notables as deputy magistrates to recruit village males, establish police patrols, and form local defense units (*pao-chang*). The second was created four years later in Szechwan where aboriginal *hsiang-ping* were formed under official control. Finally, in 1393, the government began appointing regular assistant magistrates to recruit troops (suggesting that the original *hsiang-ping* were pre-existing "natural" and communal defense organizations incorporated into an official structure). The assistant magistrate was given the authority to designate by rotation certain households to provide supplies and men. These families were not registered as military families but remained on the regular or artisan lists under the purview of the Board of Revenue. Wen Chün-t'ien, *Chung-kuo pao-chia chih-tu* [The Chinese *pao-chia* system] (Shanghai: Commercial Press, 1935), pp. 172–173.

ization, they did eventually produce the prototypes of the Chiang-yin struggle.

In the first instance, the central government naturally feared the revival of what might loosely be termed "An Lu-shanism," recalling the T'ang commander of the marches who built a private military machine that eventually challenged the dynasty in 755 B.C. Thus the initial decision permitting Ch'i Chi-kuang to develop and finance his own frontier army was reversed when his capital sponsor, Chang Chü-cheng, died in 1582.[23] The price paid for this cautious reversal was military inefficiency: lackluster troops and garrisons staffed sometimes at only 10 percent of their full roster. Because battles did after all have to be fought, especially during the years of the great peasant rebellions in the 1630s, a compromise solution was worked out. *Condottieri* like Tso Liang-yü or Mao Wen-lung were enrolled in the imperial armies under regular bureaucratic high command. The virtue of this arrangement was that it kept *wu* (military) and *wen* (civil) somewhat apart to reduce the possibility of a single dynastic rival. Its disadvantage was that the secondary militarists were not incorporated sufficiently to guarantee their loyalty, as the high defection rates of Liaotung and Shensi officers to the Manchus later demonstrated.[24] By the time Liu Liang-tso besieged Chiang-yin, he would have successively served the rebel Li Tzu-ch'eng, the Ming general Huang Te-kung, the Prince of Fu, and Dodo of the Ch'ing.[25]

In the instance of *hsiang-ping*, the throne was concerned lest village defense forces be transformed into gentry-dominated militia, disturbing the balance of local power. This was why the original *hsiang-ping* of the fourteenth century were placed under the control of assistant district magistrates, while the later village troop contingents were supposed to be controlled by the extraprovincial warden. In the case of Chiang-yin, this meant the development of a district military system under the civil, rather than military, yamen. Chiang-yin's original *wei-so* garrison had numbered 1,000 regular troops. To supplement this contingent, a form of true local militia (*min-chuang*) was recruited in the late fifteenth century, but its roster of 1,460 men had been dissolved by the 1630s. In the meantime a new system of *mu-ping* (levied troops) had been instituted at the urging of Governor Wu T'ing in 1532. Reducing the number of *wei-so* troops in Chiang-yin to 200 in order to save government funds, he forced the district to pay for its additional military needs against pirate raids with a tax assessment based upon the *ting* registries. The revenues so gathered

23. Li Kuang-pi, *Ming-ch'ao shih-lueh* [An historical outline of the Ming dynasty] (Wuhan: Hu-pei jen-min ch'u-pan-she, 1957), pp. 126–130.

24. According to my preliminary and as yet unpublished analysis of biographies in the *Erh-ch'en chuan* [Biographies of twice-serving ministers], compiled by imperial order in 1776, the largest single contingent of defectors were professional military men. Of the forty-nine who defected, fifteen were from Tung-pei and eleven from Shensi.

25. Liu Liang-tso, from Ta-t'ung in Shansi, was defending Hsu-chou for the Nanking regime when Dodo arrived outside its walls. He promptly surrendered, bringing his army of 100,000 over to the Ch'ing side. There is a brief biography in English of Liu in Hummel, *Eminent Chinese*, p. 534.

were then used to hire professional soldiers, called *t'u-ping* (local troops), who were supposed to cooperate with the local garrison and with the volunteer militiamen (*min-chuang*). But by the end of the Ming, the former had virtually replaced the latter, so that the military defenses of the district depended almost entirely upon mercenaries commanded by the public security authority.[26] Normally the latter would have been an assistant magistrate, but because there had been no such official appointed to Chiang-yin since 1638, control at the time of the conquest was entirely in the hands of the warden, Ch'en Ming-yü.[27]

The existence of mercenary *t'u-ping* under official control did not alone prevent the enrollment of genuine local militia, peasant-staffed and gentry-run. But the throne was reluctant to sanction gentry defense efforts during the 1630s and 1640s, preferring whenever possible to keep local forces under the control of the district yamen despite the growing mystique that the statecraft school[28] attached to local self-defense by *t'uan-lien* (militia).[29] Given the sorry condition of regular garrison forces, however, the only alternative (which was tried at Lo-yang) was to hire bandits to fight bandits. This so disturbed the emperor that he finally did agree, on June 7, 1643, to order the enrollment of *t'uan-lien* in the Hu-kuang and Chiang-pei areas.[30] But he insisted that these

26. *CYHC*, pp. 198–200.

27. *CYHC*, pp. 287–288.

28. Here I am referring directly to Ch'en Tzu-lung and the Chi-she literary society in Sung-chiang. It was they who inspired Ho Kang's February 27th memorial. Their fiscal policies are covered in detail in Jerry Dennerline's article in this volume.

29. Hope in the efficacy of genuine local self-defense had been aroused by several examples of spirited local resistance to the rebel armies of Li Tzu-ch'eng and Chang Hsien-chung. In 1643, when Li was trying to consolidate his control over Shensi, he bribed the regional commander stationed at Yü-lin to surrender. When the populace learned of this they rebelled, the commander fled, and a retired military officer was publicly selected as his replacement. The townsmen and women (who actually participated in the fighting) held out for a thirteen-day siege until rebels finally bored through the walls on January 6, 1644, but street fighting continued for days. Another example occurred on May 1, 1642, when Chang Hsien-chung's armies attacked Shu-ch'eng in Anhwei. The local magistrate, garrison commander, and educational officials formed a people's army which defended the city for over seven months. In fact, they were even more effective than the regular garrison, which turned to looting when food supplies ran low and which eventually betrayed the city to Chang. The civil officials and gentry (one of whom, Hu Shou-heng, had been a Hanlin compiler) refused to submit and were all killed. See James Bunyan Parsons, *The Peasant Rebellions of the Late Ming Dynasty* (Tucson: University of Arizona Press, 1970), and P'eng Sun-i, *P'ing-k'ou chih* [On the pacification of the bandits] (Peiking: National Library Edition, 1931), 5:2. Nevertheless, when Szechuanese militia decisively defeated the notorious Liang Mountain bandit army, and the provincial governor, Liu Han-ju, asked that local notables be appointed military leaders, his advice was rejected and he himself was dismissed. *Erh-ch'en chuan*, 8:22–23.

30. Below the official level, leaders within the militia who captured bandit chiefs or recovered cities were to be rewarded with official posts, while their followers would be given monetary rewards, settled on reclaimed lands, provided with seeds and oxen, and pardoned from corvee. This policy was carried out almost immediately, especially in the Wuhan area where the gentry had to campaign for funds because the Wuchang treasury was completely empty. There were funds available in the privy purse of one of the resident Ming princes, Ch'u-wang, whose personal fortune included "several million ounces of silver." When the local officials asked him for some hundred thousand to pay for military rations, he refused—

troops were to be kept strictly under official control—a policy spelled out even more clearly on February 10, 1644, when the emperor ordered the Board of War to re-enlist disabled petty officers in order to supervise village braves (*i-yung*).[31] Yet though the throne remained reluctant to sanction gentry control, adherents of local defense continued to press for such a move. The very next day the president of the Board of Revenue, Ni Yuan-lu, proposed that such famous members of the Chekiang gentry as Hsu Shih-ch'i, Ch'ien Chi-teng, Liu Tsung-chou, and Chiang Ying-chia be invited to form their own militia troops (*t'uan-lien hsiang-ping*).[32] As the emperor wavered, still more pressure was directed at him by the statecraftsmen of Kiangnan.[33] On February 27 their spokesman, a secretary in the Board of War named Ho Kang, memorialized:

> If there are loyal, righteous, wise, and brave scholars in Chekiang, then they are in Tung-yang and I-wu [districts, about fifty miles south of Hangchow]. In former times many famous generals and able-bodied soldiers came from this area. I myself am an intimate friend of the Tung-yang *sheng-yuan*, Hsu Tu, who is by his very nature loyal and filial. The minute you lay eyes on him you realize that he is the kind of man who is capable of sharing both the good and the bad with the troops under his command. So I would like to use him [as an exemplar] to advocate training militia in order to gather together the extraordinary [human] talent of this area.[34] I myself would combine the gentry with Ch'i Chi-kuang's method of expelling [bandits]. Guiding the loyal and righteous [behind us], we will thereby be able to approach the roiling flood and tread lightly over its waters. I feel that the two *chin-shih*, Yao Ch'i-yin and Hsia Kung-yu, as well as [others elsewhere like] T'ung-ch'eng's *sheng-yuan* Chou Ch'i, Shensi's *sheng-yuan* Liui Hsang-k'o, and Shansi's *chü-jen* Han Lin—all of

---

perhaps because he feared that he would be accused of illegally raising his own army (though troops were later recruited under his command). Other officials did contribute, though, and the local defense policy succeeded admirably. P'eng Sun-i, *P'ing-k'ou chih*, 6:6.

31. *Ming shih-lu* [Veritable records of the Ming dynasty] (Kiangsu: Chiang-su kuo-hsüeh t'u-shu-kuan ch'uan ch'ao pen, 1940), Ch'ung-chen reign, 17:1.

32. Ibid. Ni was also in favor of an ambitious scheme to create a second line of defense south of the Yangtze by hiring an elite force of well-paid mercenaries. This would be accompanied by an attempt to build up the economy of the South and establish a governor-generalship over the four strategic provinces of Kwangtung, Fukien, Chekiang, and South Chihli—all of which he believed should be organized as a single territorial unit. Ray Huang, "Ni Yuan-lu; 'Realism' in a Neo-Confucian Scholar-Statesman," in Wm. Theodore de Bary, ed., *Self and Society in Ming Thought* (New York: Columbia University Press, 1970), p. 422.

33. Primarily the Chi-she circle of Sung-chiang around Ch'en Tzu-lung. For his views on militia, see Ch'en Tzu-lung, *Ch'en Chung-yü*, 22:17–18.

34. As matters turned out, Hsu Tu did not prove to be a very good exemplar. Indeed, he became an embarrassment for the pro-militia statecraftsmen. Having organized a private army in northern Chekiang (which was then regarded as a prime source of military talent for the empire), Hsu rebelled after some of his kinsmen were killed by the local authorities. Ch'en Tzu-lung himself had to have Hsu and his liegemen massacred in order to keep the rebellion from spreading. This information was kindly provided to me by Jerry Dennerline, who has been working on the Hsu Tu incident for another study.

whom are full of zeal in this time of grief—should be ordered to recruit the empire's courageous knights (*hao-hsieh*) so that the loyal, righteous, brave, and wise can rise together to aid our emperor above in accomplishing his great mission.[35]

Two days later the Ch'ung-chen emperor gave qualified approval. Ho Kang was himself ordered to Tung-yang to "help exterminate the bandits" according to his plan, while the boards of war, justice and civil appointments were asked to "exhaustively" consider the implications of carrying out this policy elsewhere.[36] It was thus only after the most careful speculation and at the very last moment that the throne issued its famous appeal on April 5, 1644, to "summon the troops of the empire to succor the monarch!"[37] Consequently, in many parts of the South control of the *hsiang-ping* remained in the hands of the district warden—not for want of gentry fervor in support of the loyalist cause, but because the wardens had for so long monopolized the organization of militia. This had two major implications for the loyalist movement. It meant in general that if Ch'ing administrators could persuade the local yamen bureaucracy to submit, then militia had often to be painfully (if at all) raised *de novo*; and in particular for Chiang-yin it meant that the primary military leaders of the resistance were not natives of the city.

THE MAGISTRACY OF FANG HENG

The meeting before Chiang-yin's altars had sealed the momentary alliance of two groups that normally related ambivalently to each other. The gentry cooperated with the district bureaucracy, to be sure, but it also often opposed it in matters of taxation and local political control. The bureaucracy—and especially its military-police wing represented by Warden Ch'en Ming-yü—expected that cooperation, but frequently worked without it, making alliances and recruiting personnel from another social sphere altogether. Indeed, the warden's specialty was dealing with members of the district's underworld: swords-for-hire, yamen policemen, salt-smugglers, and rural toughs. One would therefore expect the gentry to have dealt more readily with the civil side of the local yamen, but the registrar (*chu-pu*)—a Kweichow man named Mo Shih-ying—had preferred not to attend a Ming loyalist ceremony. He did remain in office under a Nanking-appointed magistrate, Lin Chih-chi,[38] but evidently for opportunistic not ideological reasons.

---

35. P'eng Sun-i, *P'ing-k'ou chih*, 8:5b. The memorial is mentioned but not reproduced in *Ming shih-lu*, Ch'ung-chen reign, 17:1b. Also see Ch'u Hua, *Hu-ch'eng*, 4.11; and *ITC*, p. 958. Ho Kang, a *chü-jen* from Shanghai, would die later when Yangchow fell. His biography can be found in the K'ai-ming edition of the *Ming-shih* (Taipei: K'ai-ming Book Company, 1962), 7758:4.

36. P'eng Sun-i, *P'ing-k'ou chih*, 8:5b–6.

37. Ibid., 8:12; *Ming shih-lu*, Ch'ung-chen reign, 17:6b.

38. Lin was a member of the famous P'u-t'ien (Fukien) lineage, and did not speak the Wu dialect. This exposed him to some ridicule (the townspeople referred to him as "Papaya"

It was Mo, however, who was left in charge of the yamen when Magistrate Lin abandoned his post on June 18, 1645, after the fall of Nanking.[39] This was, incidentally, a common enough pattern throughout central and south China during the days just after the Prince of Fu was defeated. In the North, which had not experienced a Southern Ming interregnum, magistrates as often as not remained at their posts when Ch'ing troops arrived. In the areas south of the Yangtze, many magistrates had received loyalist appointments even if they held office before Peking's fall. Fearing indictment for treason, they often abandoned their posts altogether, leaving district administration in the hands of local gentry or assistants like the registrar.

In the meantime, the Ch'ing authorities newly ensconced in Nanking were taking steps to extend their control over Kiangnan. The region was of crucial importance to them as a source of supplies for the further conquest of the South.[40] This meant that what mattered most at the moment was gaining access to the tax revenues of the area, even if it meant compromising with former Ming officials. Since there was an immediate shortage of administrative cadres, the first step in each case was to send a trusted official (usually Chinese, and often a native of the area) to the prefectural capital. From there, orders were despatched to the various district capitals requesting that the tax and population registers (ts'e) be turned over to them. Such a demand perfectly symbolized this phase of the Ch'ing conquest: first, an assumption of the former administrative system without supplanting local elites, altering taxation methods, or plunging directly into local control; and second, a progression down through the traditional urban points of contact (provincial, prefectural, and finally district capitals) between rulers and ruled. If the hair-cutting order which came slightly later represented the determination of the Manchus to impress an image of their own upon the Chinese, then the acquisition of the registers signified the other side of the dyarchic coin.

As far as Chiang-yin was concerned, securing the registers seemed at first to pose little difficulty. Liu Kuang-tou,[41] the civil official charged with the pacification of Ch'ang-chou (the prefecture governing Chiang-yin), promptly

---

Lin), but his own dialect proved extremely useful just after Nanking fell. Over a thousand demobilized troops, now wearing red turbans and commanded by a former Ming officer named Cheng, began to loot the district. Lin discovered that he and Cheng were natives of the same village, in time to persuade him to spare the city. *Ming-chi nan-lueh* [A sketch of the southern (regimes) of the Ming dynasty] (1671), reprinted in *T'ai-wan wen-hsien ts'ung-k'an* [Collectanea of Taiwanese documentary materials] (Taipei: Bank of Taiwan, 1959), p. 254.

39. The rest of the local administration departed in Lin's wake: Chang Su, the garrison commander; Ch'eng, the Yangtze admiralty representative; and Hu T'ing-tung, the assistant magistrate. This, at least, is the roster given in Hsieh Ch'eng-jen, *I-ch'ien-liu-pai-ssu-shih-wu nien*, pp. 3–4. However, the gazetteer roster differs, naming Lin as assistant magistrate, Ch'en Ming-yü as warden, and Mo Shih-ying as registrar. *CYHC*, p. 288.

40. Hung Ch'eng-ch'ou's memorial of October 8, in *Ming-Ch'ing shih-liao* [Historical documents of the Ming and Ch'ing] (Peking: Palace Museum, 1930), pt. 1, 2:170.

41. Liu was a former Ming censor from nearby Wu-chin. He was also a disciple of Ch'ien Ch'ien-i (1582–1664), the influential scholar who defected and urged a policy of amnesty upon the Ch'ing.

received a letter from the registrar and acting magistrate, Mo Shih-ying, who promised to turn over the local registers whenever needed.[42] Consequently, Liu had no reason to suppose that Fang Heng, the man he now sent to collect the tax documents, would encounter any difficulty in taking over as the new Ch'ing magistrate. Fang, a native of Honan, reached Chiang-yin on July 17, 1645, accompanied only by a small retinue of servants and his old tutor from Wu-hsi. Quite young, his official robes still bearing Ming designs, Fang quickly discovered that Mo Shih-ying (who was now reappointed registrar) did not actually have the tax books in hand. Fang therefore peremptorily called together the city's elders and demanded that they hand over their registers. The notables insisted that the books would first have to be brought up to date, but their attitude was so cooperative that Fang assumed it would only be a matter of days before that task was completed and taxes were transmitted to general army headquarters in Nanking.[43]

Whatever his original chances for success, Fang's plans were suddenly jeopardized by a new development in the Ch'ing policy of conquest. On July 8, 1645, the Board of Rites in Peking had received the following imperial command:

Hitherto the regulations on hair-cutting have not been explicitly ordered, and we have leniently awaited [the people's doing it] at their own convenience, forbearing from enforcing it until the regime was largely pacified. Now both the Central [kingdom] and Outer [marches] are one family; the ruler is like a father and the people are like sons. Since father and son share their physical essence, how can they be different or distant [from each other]?

If this is not made explicit and if in the end [father and son] are of two different minds, can we not expect to be [regarded as] people of a foreign state? This matter [should] not have [had] to await our [imperial] words. We believe that the people and the officials of the empire must also realize [the danger] themselves.

Within ten days after this proclamation has been issued in the capital, and within ten days after the board's dispatch has reached each province respectively, let the hair-cutting order be completely carried out. Those who refuse will be the same as bandits rebelling against our orders and must be punished severely. If any hide in order to spare their hair and

42. A slightly different impression is given by another contemporary account. "The district magistrate of Chiang-yin, Lin Chih-chi, and the lieutenant-colonel, Chang Su, handed over their seals. Ch'eng, in charge of maritime defense, and the assistant magistrate, Mr. Hu, simply fled in turn at the first opportunity. The censor, Liu Kuang-tou, also surrendered, and was charged with the pacification of Ch'ang-chou. The registrar, Mo Shih-ying, turned over his seals and records, and presented Liu with a fine horse. Thereafter, he cooperated by assuming charge of the district capital." Shen T'ao, *Chiang-shang i-wen* [Hearsay on the river], in Hu Shan-yuan, *Chiang-yin i-min*, p. 199.

43. Chi Liu-ch'i, *Ming-chi nan-lueh* [An outline of the Southern Ming] (Taipei: T'ai-wan wen-hsien ts'ung-k'an, 1959), p. 254. Fang accordingly appointed Mo registrar of the yamen.

cleverly refuse to dispute us [by pleading ignorance], above all do not let them off lightly. Let each of the officials of every region rigorously investigate these matters.[44]

It is difficult to think of any policy better conceived to force the issue of acceptance or rejection of the new regime upon the Chinese. Dorgon, the Manchu regent, would have the entire population of China practically overnight adopt what was to them the barbaric custom of shaving the front of the head and growing a pigtailed queue. Why he chose to impose such an order at this time, though, remains a puzzle. Perhaps he was giving in to the nativist sentiments of other Manchu princes who believed that the conquerors had already leaned too far in the direction of assimilation.[45] Perhaps Dorgon merely miscalculated the success of the pacification to date, and believed that the regime had garnered enough loyalty to guarantee only token resistance. If so, his was a tactical blunder, for the hair-cutting order, more than any other act, engendered the Kiangnan resistance of 1645.

Chiang-yin offers a perfect example of this effect. Fang Heng, already close to acquiring the local registers, now found himself under pressure from the less tolerant Ch'ing military establishment in Ch'ang-chou. Tsung Hao, the military commander there, gave Fang only three days to carry out the order; and, to ensure compliance, dispatched four bannermen to Chiang-yin. Under their scrutiny, Fang had no choice but to order on July 21 that the district's inhabitants commence shaving their heads. The popular response was immediate. By the following morning a delegation of elders from the Huang-t'ien-cha villages was at the gates of his yamen, respectfully petitioning to retain their hair. This placed Fang in a critically embarrassing position. To confess that he was being forced to follow non-Chinese commands from above would have jeopardized his magisterial dignity. But neither could he accede to the request without risking dismissal or worse. Frustrated, he let his anger overwhelm him and reviled the elders for their effrontery until one of the village representatives ended the audience by boldly shouting: "You are a Ming dynasty *chin-shih*. On your head you wear a silk cap, on your torso an oval collar. [Yet] you have come to act as a Ch'ing dynasty magistrate. Shameful! Disgraceful!"[46]

44. *CSL*:SC, 17:7b–8.

45. That in turn implies a structural divergence between the centralizing tendencies of a patrimonial Chinese form of rule (emperor and single regent with Dorgon able to rise to power by developing a monopoly over Chinese defectors) and a feudal Manchu aristocracy. "Manchu-ness" thus would be associated with the ideal of a council of peers, so that we would expect to find it expressed most vividly at times when the *beile* challenged Chinese-inspired despotism, or when a group of regents ruled. This complicated matter is analyzed in Robert Bromley Oxnam "Politics and Factionalism in the Oboi Regency, 1661–1669" (Ph. D. thesis, Yale University, 1969).

46. I would like to be able to believe that this conversation, reported verbatim by the twentieth-century historian Hu Shan-yuan (in Hu Shan-yuan, *Chiang-yin i-min*, p. 165) is accurate. Since his account is based upon his reading of earlier chronicles (many of which are unavailable outside of the People's Republic), that is impossible to verify. Though I do

The following day, July 23, Fang Heng tried to recover his authority by paying a ceremonial visit to the city gods. As his retinue wound toward the Confucian temple, a crowd of over one hundred gentry, elders, and commoners joined its wake. When the entire procession reached the temple, Fang descended from his sedan-chair to find himself face-to-face with some of the city's most prominent citizens. Again the confrontation began quietly enough as the elders insisted that Chiang-yin had already done its best to comply with the new dynasty's requirements by accepting its magistrate and preparing to hand over its registers. Why now insist upon this hair-cutting matter? Fang tried to explain that this was not a matter of local option. "This is a law (*lü*) of the great Ch'ing. It cannot be disregarded."[47] Besides, he now went on to admit, the four soldiers recently arrived in town were specifically sent to see that the law was executed. For a moment the balance tilted in Fang's favor, until a prominent local scholar named Hsu Yung[48] pressed forward and intoned: "We are all the people (*pai-hsing*) of the Ming. We only recognize T'ai-tsu, the Emperor on High, as our ancestor. How can these Tartar Mongols (*Ta-tzu Hu-erh*) so presumptuously dare to enter and dominate the central plain?"[49] Then, as he held up a portrait of Ming T'ai-tsu, all of the degree-holders fell to their knees, loudly lamenting the fall of their dynasty.

Fang left the demonstration at the Confucian temple with as much dignity as he could muster. Determined to preserve his authority, he returned to the

---

realize that Hu imaginatively embellishes his narrative, one would at least have to admit that his elaborations uncannily correspond to what one might expect was said. This, of course, raises the question of the reliability of many of these local chronicles. As Jerry Dennerline has pointed out in a careful study of *yeh-shih* (lit., "wild histories") historiography (Jerry Dennerline, "A Preliminary Analysis of a Limited Form of Narrative History with a View to Establishing Its Value as Historical Evidence," seminar paper, Yale University, 1967), Han T'an (author of the *Chiang-yin ch'eng-shou chi*) would only have been eight years old when the city fell; and since the preface is dated 1715, eleven years after his death, there is considerable reason to doubt its authenticity. Remembering H. L. Kahn's *caveat* as to *yeh-shih* and *i-shih* ("The characteristics of this literature seem to be those of all historical fiction: thematic truth encrusted with imaginative, often fabulous details"), I have tried whenever possible to verify these more fanciful accounts with other sources. See Harold L. Kahn, "Some Mid-Ch'ing Views of the Monarchy," *Journal of Asian Studies* 24.2:236.

47. *Ming-chi nan-lueh*, p. 255.

48. His name is given as Hsu Yung-te in *NCIS*. This seems to be an error, although Hsieh Kuo-chen accepts it. See Hsieh Kuo-chen, *Nan-ming shih-lueh*, p. 82. The *Ming-shih* accepts Hsu Yung. Many of Hsu's ancestors were well known local scholars. As a young student, he placed first in the district exams, but decided to abandon a bureaucratic career in favor of philosophical studies. He enjoyed a great reputation among the literati of the district, and led a demonstration in the Confucian temple when Nanking fell. After this incident it was he who urged Ch'en Ming-yü to lead the defense of the city. Later, he composed a famous song which was played for the moon festival. When he committed suicide, burning himself with his entire family, he was thirty-six years old. *CYHC*, p. 472.

49. Hu Shan-yuan, *Chiang-yin i-min*, p. 165. According to *ITC*, 88:226, "Nanking was lost, and the cities all fell one after the other. [Hsu] Yung spoke in favor of defending the city [of Chiang-yin]. Several tens of thousands of people responded from near and far." The same wording is found in the *Ming-shih*, 277:3114.

yamen and ordered that the clerks prepare laconic Chinese versions of the imperial proclamation: *Liu t'ou, pu liu fa; liu fa, pu liu t'ou* (Keep your head, lose your hair; keep your hair, lose your head). But disaffection had now spread to his staff. Several secretaries refused to write the characters, and one of the clerks even threw his writing brush to the floor in disgust. Fang furiously ordered the man flogged in the public hall of the yamen, then nervously rescinded the command when the usual crowd of onlookers began to mutter ominously.

By now there were three sources of opposition to the undermined magistrate. The first, symbolized here by the recalcitrant yamen clerk, was the sub-bureaucracy. The second, present most vividly at the temple, was the urban gentry, whose dissent may have been exaggerated by contemporary chroniclers because it centered on the idealized and distant figure of the Ming founder and on the righteousness of the degree-holders themselves. The third, represented by the delegation of elders from the northern villages, stemmed from a popular reaction to the hair-cutting order, bridging the gap between gentry and commoners who could not otherwise share the same social obligation to a single dynasty. Ming loyalism as such would not have united these three groups. Clerks could serve new regimes; peasants saw no reason to fear one set of rulers replacing the previous ones. But now interference with popular customs outraged even the illiterate, creating the basis for a wider ethnic opposition to Ch'ing rule and supporting the more refined Confucian loyalism of the gentry.

News of the temple incident reached the Huang-t'ien-cha villages by mid-afternoon. Fang Heng had already found this riverside area troublesome. Four days earlier, on July 19, he had learned that the villagers there were buying guns from loyalist naval vessels. Only a token number of these arms were surrendered when he ordered them confiscated. Now, inspired by young village boxers, the villagers brought out their weapons, selected leaders,[50] and began to march on the city. Beating gongs to attract a larger following along the way, they numbered ten thousand by the time they reached the yamen gates. There they flaunted Fang's prohibition against the possession of arms by firing off their muskets. The magistrate—sitting in formal judicial session—angrily commanded his lictors to collect the guns, but when the order was gingerly passed on outside, the peasants yelled back: "We are making military preparations to resist the enemy. To surrender [the arms] would be to return them for the use of the enemy. We would rather die than surrender!"[51] Their insubordination outraged Fang Heng's former tutor. But when the old gentleman indignantly left the protection of the yamen to harangue the villagers, the mob savagely turned on him. Fang tried desperately to save his teacher, but the old man was beaten to death and his corpse set afire.

50. Chi Shih-mei, Chi Ts'ung-hsiao, Wang Shih, Ho Ch'ang, and Ho T'ai.
51. Han T'an, *Chiang-yin ch'eng*, p. 166.

In spite of the murder, the magistrate's quarters and person were still inviolate. The crowd had held back from actually invading the yamen and had confined its attack upon Fang to his proxy. In fact, Fang retained enough authority to disperse the rioters by promising that he would not enforce the hair-cutting order. But this was only to buy time, for by now the magistrate was in an untenable position. If it had been solely a matter of securing the tax registers, then Fang could have administered the district without recourse to Ch'ing troops—a prospect which must have allayed his own misgivings as a collaborator by casting him in the role of a protector against Hunnish raids. However, once the hair-cutting order was issued, he had no choice ultimately but to call in the army. At the wider prefectural level this meant that control now passed from the hands of former Ming civil officials committed to amnesty (Liu Kuang-tou) to impatient Ch'ing military commanders used to harsher methods of control (Tsung Hao). As soon as the mob dissolved, therefore, Fang dispatched one of his aides with an urgent plea to Tsung Hao for a force to pacify the district. Ch'ang-chou was only twenty miles to the southwest, but before help could arrive one of Fang's clerks betrayed the secret to a contingent of village braves who had camped for the night outside the yamen. The magistrate's own treachery now cost him whatever authority he still possessed. Infuriated, the braves broke into the yamen, seized Fang, and wound a garrotte around his neck. At the last moment, though, one of the most prestigious notables of the city intervened to save Fang's life. Hsia Wei-hsin, a *chü-jen* of 1633, persuaded the villagers to put the magistrate under arrest in his—Hsia's—house.[52]

Hsia Wei-hsin's intervention was designed to avert the irrevocable murder of a Ch'ing magistrate. Once that happened, the city was doomed to attack. The very same evening, therefore, members of the urban gentry met to discuss alternatives at the home of a *hsiu-ts'ai* named Shen Yüeh-ching. The gentry's dilemma was obvious. On the one hand, they could not afford to anger the village braves by backing the magistrate altogether. But at the same time, they wished to avoid precipitating a movement involving non-townsmen, who were obviously much less concerned to preserve the city from destruction. Consequently, the gentry felt it essential to mediate between both sides, leaving room for themselves to negotiate with the Ch'ing authorities at Ch'ang-chou. But neither one of the opposing sides was willing to cooperate sufficiently. In fact, there had already developed a rift between the more moderate city and the aroused countryside. That same night of July 23, wild rumors (*yao-yen*) of betrayal by the urban gentry threw the villages on all sides of Chiang-yin into turmoil. The chronicles speak of "several hundreds of thousands" (many of whom were young boys armed only with knives) hastily forming banner ranks to beat the traditional gongs

---

52. Hsia Wei-hsin, who later became one of the men in charge of supplies for the resistance and was possibly beheaded for embezzlement, was originally from Ch'ang-chou. *CYHC*, pp. 373, 472.

of alarum and gather in the courtyards of local schools to plan defense measures against what they assumed to be imminent Manchu invasion. Roads were barricaded and produce trade was even curtailed with the city, closing down the urban market.[53]

Fang Heng, on the other hand, merely feigned cooperation with the gentry to secure his release from arrest. He did insist that the dispatch had been mistakenly sent by one of his clerks, publicly pledged with members of the gentry to resist any invaders, and agreed to let the peasant braves use the city's forges to cast weapons. But even while promising limited support of the resistance, he was also secretly writing to Ch'ang-chou that Chiang-yin was now in a state of open rebellion.

Fang's messenger got no further than the militia barricade outside Chiang-yin. When guards found the letter, they dismembered the courier and rushed the evidence back to the city's gentry-led defense committee. Once again the notables tried to appease the extremists by taking the magistrate back into custody, but this time the braves found other officials to attack. "Since we have already committed ourselves," one man yelled, "let's kill the four Manchu soldiers in the police station who came to have us cut our hair."[54] The defense committee restrained the mob by ordering the formal arrest of the four bannermen. After a brief struggle, the soldiers were captured and brought to the yamen for interrogation. At first the prisoners appeared unable to understand Chinese, and responded entirely in what seemed to be Manchu. But when a search of their luggage revealed Chinese belongings, one of the bannermen switched into Soochow dialect. If he had thought his local provenance would save their lives, he was greatly mistaken. The prisoners were savagely torn limb from limb. To the loyalists, cultural betrayal was more heinous than barbarian ancestry.

DEFENSE MEASURES

The execution of the bannermen permitted no turning back. Chiang-yin was formally in revolt—a state immediately characterized by four developments. First, leadership within the city passed almost instantly from the gentry to the warden, Ch'en Ming-yü, who was elected by the resistants to

---

53. These banners were probably remnants of the original *hsiang-ping* system. The barricading of the roads was characteristic of resistance in other parts of Kiangnan as well, since local defenders tried to parcel the canal-linked countryside into units where the enemy could be isolated and surrounded. It is difficult to determine whether or not these village troops were commanded by rural-dwelling gentry. The Chia-ting chronicles are much clearer in this regard. There the local gentry appears to have played a more prominent part in local militia organization. See Wu Wei-yeh, *Wu-shih chi-lan* [Collected readings of the poetry of Wu], *SPPY* ed. (Taipei, 1966), Vol. 15, pt. 2, p. 10; and Hung Chih-chün, comp., *Chiang-nan t'ung-chih* [Kiangnan provincial gazetteer], 1737 edition (Taipei: Ching-hua Book Co., 1967), 199:38b.

54. Han T'an, *Chiang-yin ch'eng*, p. 167. This is corroborated by *Ming-chi nan-lueh*, pp. 255–256.

organize and delegate urban defense.[55] Although the urban notables were not entirely displaced, their intimate defense committee meetings in the homes of degree-holders were now overshadowed by Ch'en Ming-yü's public gatherings. These daily convocations of the marketplace crowds served not so much to plan traditional militia measures, in the spirit of the statecraft school, as to ratify Ch'en's own preparations. For, rather than turn control over to neighborhood leaders, Ch'en preferred to rely upon the private contributions of a shadowy Anhwei salt merchant named Ch'eng Pi.[56] Ch'eng's contributions (which came to more than 175,000 taels) and mercantile connections with the underworld helped Ch'en Ming-yü recruit the kinds of professional soldiers hired before as t'u-ping. In a sense, therefore, the Ming altars' alliance now gave way to competition between the urban gentry and the warden, as power slipped from the former's hands into the grasp of a man surrounded by adventurers.

This did not mean that Ch'en Ming-yü could afford to ignore the village braves, whose fervor had given him authority in the first place. As a second development, standing hsiang-ping units for ten miles around were invited into the city to participate in its defense under the command of Ch'en's military aide, Chi Shih-mei. Even though armed resistance had begun in the villages, the city now became the symbolic center of opposition to Ch'ing control. Because the district capital brought great numbers of peasants together, it enlarged the scope of conflict. However, the city also focused the struggle more intensely, exposing the resistance to the conquerors at a single vulnerable point.

A third development was the recruitment of new rural militia units according to the statecraft model. Gentry-led, they closely resembled the loyalist groups of Sung-chiang or Chia-ting. The best-known Chiang-yin coterie were students of a Buddhist philosopher named Huang Yü-ch'i.[57] Huang

55. Tseng Hua-lung and Chang Tiao-ting, for example, were appointed to prepare weapons and build up supplies for an extended siege.

56. Ming-shih, Kuo-fang yen-chiu-yuan ed., 277:3114.

57. T. Chieh-chih. Huang was a kung-sheng who attracted students from all over the prefecture. After Huang and his insurgents were defeated at Chiang-yin, Huang himself fled to Huai-nan, and thence to T'ai-chou. There he was arrested when letters stamped with the seals of the Prince of Lu were found upon his person by the authorities in the spring of 1649. He was shipped back to the main jail in Nanking. Teng Ta-lin (see note 58) visited him in jail and smuggled out his teacher's collected writings. There is a biography of Huang in the Ming-shih, 277:3115; and in Ming-chi nan-lueh, pp. 269–271. Huang's biography in the local gazetteer mentions that he was a kung-sheng of 1621, and that his brother was a well-known poet. CYHC, pp. 472–473. Some contemporary accounts by scholars in the People's Republic of China, who have access to collections which I have not seen, claim that Huang tried to recover Chiang-yin by coup de main in 1646, and that he also led a revolt at Chusan, mounting a fleet to retake Ch'ang-chou. The fleet was supposedly sunk by a gale. See, for example, Hsieh Ch'eng-jen, I-ch'ien-liu-pai-ssu-shih-wu nien, p. 58. But according to NCIS, p. 380, Huang was arrested for signing letters with Ming seals. He poignantly confessed to his jailers that:

The Way commands the respect of gentlemen, teaching us of previous generations' loyalty and filial piety. Ah, I've been so long away from self-repose, how could I

himself organized militia at the village of Hsing-t'ang, while many of his
students—especially Hsu Ch'ü and Teng Ta-lin—actively continued to
oppose the Ch'ing after Chiang-yin's defenses were crushed.[58] But such
t'uan-lien were relatively insignificant in comparison with those of the *hsiang-
ping* and *t'u-ping* types.

Finally, Chiang-yin's defenders became obsessed with the task of ferreting
out potential traitors within the city. Tales of *nei-ying*[59]—someone who be-
trays a besieged city or encampment to the enemy—abound in Chinese
military lore, and fears of turncoats opening Chiang-yin's gates to the Ch'ing
inspired a reign of terror which gave Ch'en Ming-yü an opportunity to
strengthen his own position against the city's gentry leadership. For four
days, from July 25 to July 28, hardly anything but *nei-ying* was on people's
lips, so that the defenders devoted all their attention to a series of real or
imagined plots.[60] Many suspicions of treachery were confirmed when Ch'en
Ming-yü publicly interrogated an alleged spy captured on the morning of
July 27. Under torture the man confessed that the Ch'ang-chou prefectural
commander, Tsung Hao, had bribed seventy residents to revolt three days
hence.[61] Ch'en promptly executed the spy along with some of the residents he

---

have any desire for life now? It is difficult to retain your composure in the thralls
of righteousness, ardor, and zeal. The Ming lord [i.e., the Prince of Lu] was
indeed sincere, and sent an envoy to press a post on me, as he summoned other
worthies and selected them as officials, allotting to them that which had to be done.
Then grief distracted me from officialdom, struck me with guilt for all the dead.
I held on to my [official loyalist] seal while waiting for death to overtake me,
and signed a letter with it out of reverence for them.

58. Hsu Ch'ü participated in the 1645 uprising and in the winter of 1646–1647 led a suicidal attack along with fourteen other *chuang-shih* (heroic scholars) on Chiang-yin. All died.
CYHC, p. 473. Teng Ta-lin (T. Ch'i-hsi) was an orphan from Ch'ang-shou (actually part of
Soochow prefecture) who traveled to Chiang-yin to study with Huang Yü-ch'i. He recruited
soldiers around Ch'ung-ming at the time of the Chiang-yin revolt. After his teacher was arrested, Teng also came under suspicion, finding himself—in Huang Tsung-hsi's colorful
words—"on the blade's edge." But he "paid enough to keep his head on his neck." Released
by the authorities, he spent the rest of his life traveling through central China in search of
skilled sword-fighters to help plot a Ming restoration. He died in disappointment. Huang
Tsung-hsi, *Nan-lei wen-ting* [Literary fixations from the Nan-lei studio], *SPPY* ed. (Taipei,
1966), *hou chi*, 2:5–6.

59. The phrase goes back at least to the time of Ssu-ma Ch'ien, when he wrote in the
biography of Li Sheng in the *Shih-chi*: "You, sir, raise your troops and assault while I respond
within."

60. The first was supposedly discovered on July 25, just as the city buzzed with unsub-
stantiated rumors that Manchu forces had broken through the outer perimeter of barricades.
Townsfolk guarding the east gate suddenly decided that one of the regular garrison captains
was about to flee with their defense funds. In the confused melee which followed, the captain's
pennant-bearer was killed and he himself was wounded. He had managed to ride through the
crowd, though, and spent the night in a beanfield just outside the city. The next morning he
surrendered passively to militiamen and was thrown in jail along with his family.

61. Each man had supposedly been given four catties of gunpowder and had been paid four
taels of silver and 120 copper cash. Once the explosions were heard outside the city, the
Ch'ing troops were to attack from the outside. It must be remembered, of course, that such

had named, then promised a fifty-tael reward for any other information concerning the plot.

The next day tradesmen reported a suspicious loiterer in the market place. Seized and searched, he was found in possession of a map which detailed the location of the militia barricades. His public interrogation revealed that he was the clerk on Fang Heng's staff who had originally been sent to ask Tsung Hao for troops. Not only that; under torture he confessed that he and several other yamen clerks had attended several clandestine meetings with the scholar Shen Yueh-ching, plotting together to massacre the entire population of Chiang-yin. However fanciful the conspiracy, the clerk's revelation finally gave Ch'en Ming-yü all he needed to discredit his rivals among the gentry, and justify the execution two days later of magistrate Fang Heng and registrar Mo Shih-ying.

THE SEARCH FOR REINFORCEMENTS

On July 29 one thousand Ch'ing cavalry and half as many marines were reported only a few miles southwest of the city moat. Chi Shih-mei feverishly arranged for drum and gun signals to coordinate the disparate *hsiang-ping* units, and left to engage the enemy at noon. Their first encounter—at a place called Yü-men—was brief and bloody; the well-trained cavalry routed the disorganized militia units and killed Chi Shih-mei. The Ch'ing advance would halt the following day when they finally reached the Huang-t'ien River, where the main Chiang-yin lines were said to number as many as 100,000 braves.[62] But for the moment the Yu-men defeat had cost Ch'en Ming-yü both his major military aide and his psychological advantage. He did have a small corps of gentry aides,[63] but he obviously preferred to turn to professional *t'u-ping*. Shao K'ang-kung—a retainer and bodyguard of the Anhwei salt merchant, Ch'eng Pi—was therefore invited to assume command of the village defense forces (*pao-hsiang ping*) which daily continued to flock to the city.[64] Although Shao's forces did manage on August 2 to drive the exploratory Ch'ing force back to its major encampment at Ma-p'i-ch'iao,

---

plots as these might well have been the chroniclers' fancies.

62. The Ch'ing naval commander, a former pirate, did allow himself to get engulfed by portions of this force, losing over half of his men when his vessels grounded in mud.

63. For example, Ch'i Hsun (T. Po-p'ing), a native of Chiang-yin who had been a student in the National Academy and was then made a board secretary. Later he was appointed by the emperor to supervise the collection of military rations in Fukien. When Chiang-yin finally fell to the Manchus on October 9, he set fire to his house, burning himself and twenty-one members of his family and household. (*Chiang-nan t'ung-chih*, 153:30b.) He was imperially honored for his loyalty in 1776, along with many of the other Chiang-yin resistants. *ITC*, ts'e 92, 88:22b.

64. Shao K'ang-kung was a famous sword and lance fighter from Hui-chou (Anhwei) who commanded a private corps of fifty convoy specialists for the merchant Ch'eng Pi. He lived in Ch'eng's compound, and may well have been a salt smuggler. He has a brief biography in *CYHC*, p. 473.

Ch'en Ming-yü was under no illusion as to the real fighting strength of the rural braves. Whenever the Ch'ing could spare reinforcements for Tsung Hao, the peasant militia would be hopelessly outmatched. But rather than re-organize the different village units into a coherent force, Ch'en once more turned for help to external professionals.

Some of these were bandits who fought for either side. Others, perhaps not quite so distinct as we imagine, were former Ming military forces which were identical in most respects to the Ch'ing forces now before Chiang-yin: *condottieri* accustomed to the repeating crossbow, double sword, halberd, and firearm. Now privately financed or living off the land, these forces needed funds and food to survive. News of Chiang-yin's resistance filled such men with hope of reward or spoils. The first to appear was Chou Jui-lung, the loyalist regional military commissioner (*tu-ssu*) who commanded a small fleet under the famous general Wu Chih-k'uei (now supporting the resistance at Sung-chiang).[65] Ch'en Ming-yü's envoys persuaded Chou to land at Huang-t'ien-kang with a promise of future bounties and an immediate pay-ment of one thousand taels. Shao K'ang-kung was to attack the Ch'ing camp from the east gate while Chou Jui-lung came down from the north, but Chou's men fought listlessly and retreated as soon as possible to their ships.

On August 6 a second group of adventurers appeared: eight hundred sand troops (*sha-ping*) from the T'ai-ts'ang seacoast who were specially trained to fight off the pitching decks of flat-bottomed, two-masted coastal junks that operated in those waters. Their commander, Hsia Ch'i-lung, had been a member of Kao Chieh's warlord army, and now grandly announced by messenger that he had come to relieve Chiang-yin. Of course, his men would need a few supplies in return: wine, rice, gunpowder, oil, meat, and four thousand taels. Ch'en Ming-yü made the mistake of giving Hsia his bounty in advance. His rivermen promptly consumed most of the supplies and stag-gered off to battle half-drunk. After losing five hundred men, Hsia and the remnants drifted back to the coast, plundering along the way.

Other such mercenaries continued to appear from time to time,[66] but what was really needed was a larger, more formally organized force, like Wu Chih-k'uei's navy or Huang Fei's marines.[67] It would take more than rice wine to attract their soldiers, so that Ch'en Ming-yü's salt merchant, Ch'eng Pi, was entrusted with 140,000 taels to hire either one of these commanders. Perhaps because they already felt the struggle at Chiang-yin to be hopeless,

65. Wu Chih-k'uei was the former *fu-tsung-ping* of Kiangnan. His loyalist naval force head-quartered at Ch'ung-ming Island was supporting the Sung-chiang resistance. He was de-feated in early September. See Ch'u Hua, *Hu-ch'eng pei-k'ao*, 3:2; and *NCIS*, pp. 240–244, 365–366.

66. For example, a professional cudgel fighter from T'ai-hsing named Chang Ta, whose force of three hundred, including a famous fighting monk, was promptly wiped out when it tried to destroy the Ch'ing army's livestock.

67. Huang Fei (T. Wen-lu) had served under the famous general Huang Lung when the latter garrisoned Liao-yang. Adopted by Huang Lung, Fei inherited his stepfather's army in 1633 when the elder was killed by the Manchus. Ch'en Tzu-lung, "Nien-p'u," pt., 2 p. 31b.

Wu and Huang refused the offer. Ch'eng Pi did travel on into Anhwei to plead with Chin Sheng for help, but by the time he returned empty-handed, Chiang-yin had fallen.[68]

The beginning of that end came on August 12, when Ch'ing reinforcements commanded by Liu Liang-tso closed the ring around the city. Chiang-yin had refused the hand of amnesty (*chao-fu*); now it would face the prospect of *chiao* (pacification by means of military extermination). For, once these vanguard troops were loosed upon a region, they usually devastated it. Thus, after casually driving Shao K'ang-kung's sallying force back into the city, the invaders began sending Manchu cavalry units of bannermen through the surrounding villages to extirpate *hsiang-ping* and plunder wealthy households. Soon the attacks became socially indiscriminate. By August 14, dwellings had been burned in most of the villages northeast of the city, and that evening the weaving centers west of Chiang-yin were raided. Worst hit were Ta-ch'iao and Chou-chuang where entire villages were razed, their women raped and menfolk murdered.

Ch'ing pillaging was succeeded by local looting as erstwhile militiamen like the Huang-shan-kang salt smugglers slipped easily back into a more familiar role. "Government orders could not leave the city, and the distant villages burst into revolt."[69] Gangs of tenant farmers and day laborers burst into landlord villas, and those of the great families (*ta-chia*) who could escape now fled to the relative safety of Chiang-yin. Against this backdrop of burning farms and roving bands, the Ch'ing commander appealed for the surrender of the gentry.

LOCALISM

On August 15, 1645, a letter reached the city gates bearing the signature of Liu Liang-tso. It read:

> Let the local scholars, gentry, and commoners all know that I have been ordered to pacify this area. All [the people of] Chihli and Chih-nan, Szechwan and Shensi, Honan and Shantung have already cut their hair. Yet your district of Chiang-yin persists in disregarding the state's command. How can you have no regard for your persons, your families, your lives? Since receiving an imperial edict ordering us to pacify Chiang-yin, our great armies have been arriving over the last two days. To protect your persons and your families, cut your hair and submit immediately!
>
> I have discovered that Ch'eng Pi could easily finance the bonding [i.e.,

68. Chin Sheng (T. Cheng-hsi) was a *chin-shih* of 1628. He was noted for his skill at organizing militia in Shantung in 1635 during the White Lotus revolt. He refused an appointment under the Prince of Fu, but conducted the major Anhwei resistance movement against the Ch'ing forces. *An-hui t'ung-chih* [The gazetteer of Anhwei province] (Taipei: Hua-wen shu-shü, 1967), 204:10.

69. Han T'an, *Chiang-yin ch'eng*, p. 175.

ransom of the city]. As soon as all your peasants sign bonds (*chü-pao*) [to guarantee good behavior], I will arrange for the governing of your district. If there are civil and military officials, then they can keep their commissions so that arrangements will be made to [govern according to] the former administrative scheme.

I cannot bear to kill your peasants. You are all progeny of the Ch'ing dynasty, [yet you] regard money and provisions as a very small affair, while cutting your hair is a great matter. It is now the season of autumn harvests. In the villages you will be able to facilitate agricultural affairs, and in the city both trade and commerce. If you submit as soon as possible, I absolutely will not disturb a thread or kernel of yours.

A special proclamation.[70]

Liu's offer was addressed to the entire population of Chiang-yin, but it was couched in such a way as to assure the local elite that the new dynasty did not intend to disturb the gentry's social control of the region. Whether by design or not, the Ch'ing cavalry raids had already aroused enough tenant protest to remind the great families of their dependence upon imperial law and order. Let the resistants pay Liu's ransom, comply with the Ch'ing hair-cutting order, and file bonds (i.e., prepare population registers and institute *pao-chia*). Then the normal collaboration between government and gentry would resume so that life could go on as before: merchants thronging the marketplace, peasants tilling the cotton fields, and landlords living off their *sha-t'ien* rents.[71]

However fragile the gentry's private control of the district, Liu's letter was

70. Ibid.

71. The Chiang-yin gentry would have good reason to suspect this offer by remembering the punishments Kiangnan suffered at the time of the Ming establishment. After the Ming founder selected Nanking as his imperial seat, at least 59,000 "wealthy families" of Kiangnan and Chekiang were moved to the capital and their lands converted to "official fields," which the government rented to tenants. The most generally accepted interpretation of this decision was that Chu Yuan-chang (Ming T'ai-tsu) was taking revenge upon this social stratum because it had supported his rival, Chang Shih-ch'eng. See Albert Chan, "The Decline and Fall of the Ming Dynasty: A Study of the Internal Factors" (Ph.D. thesis, Harvard University, 1953), pp. 167–170; and Liang Fang-chung, "Local Tax Collectors."

Frederick Mote has shown how intimately connected this move of wealthy households was with the establishment of the capital. Perhaps fearing resistance from the original inhabitants of Nanking, Chu Yuan-chang had moved many of the city's residents out of the city, sending some along with expeditionary forces to Yunnan. To replace them, 45,000 elite households (*shang-hu*) were imported from Soochow and Chekiang—the adult males registered as craftsmen and assigned to factories, the others made commoners and settled around the city. Fourteen thousand more wealthy households (*fu-hu*) were put in charge of tax collection and lower-level administration. See Frederick W. Mote, "The Transformation of Nanking—1350-1400," Conference on Urban Society in Traditional China (Wentworth-by-the-Sea, N.H., 1968), pp. 58–62.

The animus argument is still not entirely settled, simply because there appeared to be a dual policy of resettling and executing the wealthy of Soochow on the one hand, while on the other, they were conciliated by being given official positions. In 1385 the Board of Civil Appointments was ordered to send the sons of the wealthy to the capital for appointment. See Robert Bruce Crawford, "The Life and Thought of Chang Chü-cheng, 1525–1582" (Ph.D. thesis, University of Washington, 1961), p. 22. The resettlement policy was clearly associated

—as one Chiang-yin scholar then put it—too vulgar. Its recognition of self-interest was too crass for notables who preferred to think of themselves in nobler terms. Until this moment, many of the county's gentlemen had been disengaged from the movement, leaving leadership to Ch'en Ming-yü and his cohorts. Those who did compete with the warden were more involved in intrigue than in heroic sacrifice. But the scenario had suddenly shifted. For the first time there were stirrings of historical grandeur; a moral passion play was in the making. An armored Ch'ing general stood at the gates demanding immediate surrender, and real interests had to be sacrificed to righteous duty. In that sense, Liu's letter brought the gentry back on stage. Ch'en Ming-yü had already been forced to make Shao K'ang-kung—who languished in prison—the scapegoat for defeat, in order to keep his own office. Now he instinctively turned back to the gentry for the kind of dramatic self-conscious-ness they had all displayed a year earlier at the Ming altars. After meeting in the yamen with the gentry defense committee, Ch'en Ming-yü authorized the scholar Wang Hua to draft a rejection of Liu's offer.

Chiang-yin is a land (*pang*) of rites and music and has always demon-strated its loyalty and righteousness. The biggest reason [which you give for surrender] is that [the mandate of heaven] has changed and that we should expediently follow vulgar (*ts'ung-su*) [self-interest]. But it has been said that even though we do experience dynastic changes, still we do not change our former clothes or tculure. Why, then, so strongly thwart the people's wishes by ordering us to cut our hair?

For this reason, old and young of town and village have sworn with unswerving persistence to die rather than submit. Soldiers have several times approached our borders and defeated [us]. When we received word of this, we took the righteous troops of each village and *chen* which support the [Ming] emperor, and rushed into battle. Thus if the great mass (*ta-chü*) within the city has exhausted itself strengthening our defenses, then it is precisely because it has not regarded the enemy frivolously.

---

with the reclamation of war-devastated areas. At the beginning of the Ming, four thousand landless households of Soochow, Sung-chiang, Chia-hsing, Hu-chou, and Hangchow were transported to Lin-hao where they were given oxen, seed, carts, and three years of freedom from taxation.

Later, in 1370, after General Hsu Ta had defeated Hung Pao-pao, the Mongol commander in Ning-hsia, 35,800 households were moved from Peking (then Peiping) and settled in the Northwest. In exchange, 32,800 Mongol remnants were moved into the Peiping area. Al-though they were made farmers, the Mongols apparently did not do well enough at agricul-ture to satisfy the Board of Revenue, which persuaded the emperor to move 140,000 Kiang-nan commoners to Hopei as well. This was the manner in which most of the area around Ta-t'ung was settled during the 1390s. That this was conceived as a way of relieving the more densely populated areas can be seen in the decision in 1382 to move 24,400 people from P'an-yü, Tung-kuan, and Tseng-ch'eng counties in the Canton delta to the Huai River area. See *Ming-shih*, 17:818; and Li Kuang-pi, *Ming-ch'ao shih-lueh* [An historical outline of the Ming dynasty] (Wuhan: Hu-pei jen-min ch'u-pan-she, 1957), pp. 23–28. For the Yung-lo em-peror's decision to so settle his new capital in Peking, see *Ming shih-lu*, Ying-tsung reign, 15:9b.

Since the struggle that is now extended across the empire is not confined to a single city, but rather the entire Su[chow]-Hang[chow] region and has no fixed headquarters, how can you so covet this area as to send in troops without respite? Besides, since this is a righteous uprising—which has made it possible for those who love and cherish the peasantry to gather together the people's feelings—how can you slaughter so treacherously, burn and plunder, enraging heaven and sorrowing the peasants, distressing the eyes and sickening the heart?

As for your present strategy, you should quickly recall your troops and quietly listen to reactions through the great prefecture of Su-Hang. If Su-Hang stirs, then what about the single city of Chiang-yin? If you do loose a million troops on this city, you may cut off the defenders' determination after they are dead, but you will never force them to beg demeaningly for life! Heed the following rule: always take Su-Hang as the leader. If these orders are not issued, then there is nothing more to say.[72]

Wang's manifesto celebrated the *pang* (land) of Chiang-yin, even though the gentry were not really political rulers or local satraps. Their region's boundaries were entirely cultural: the Su-Hang area's reputation for "rites and music." However, their provincialism was still quite cosmopolitan. The rites of Kiangnan were legitimate because they epitomized Confucianism's universal values. The area's popular customs (*feng-su*) alone were vulgar (that same *su*), and therefore not distinguished enough for a local elite which was defined by its connection with a higher *Kultur* rather than by an attachment to a particular anthropological culture of the region. Because that higher culture could not be monopolized by any single locale, the gentry of Su-Hang could not legitimately defend the area's popular customs against the new government; their loyalism had to be directed to a dying dynasty rather than to the local roots of a race. This made the resistance movement ideologically vulnerable. For Su-Hang merely epitomized Confucian rites which were equally available to conquerors who—despite the hair-cutting order—were already appropriating imperial ceremonies in the palaces of Peking.

Chiang-yin's ideological weakness was not a matter of cultural dependence alone. This entire generation of Ming loyalists was also hard-put to conceive of provincial political autonomy without the binding ties of central dynastic authority. Contemporaries of the Chiang-yin defenders, like the statecraftsmen of Sung-chiang, were used to thinking of local government in terms of two classical archetypes. These archetypes—the feudal (*feng-chien*) system of the Chou and the prefectural (*chün-hsien*) system of the Ch'in—had been elaborated over the previous millennium of Chinese history into systematic descriptions of two different ideals of imperial rule.[73] The prefectural model was used to justify a powerful emperor, a highly centralized administration,

72. Han T'an, *Chiang-yin ch'eng*, pp. 175–176.
73. For an excellent discussion of this tradition, see Yang Lien-sheng, "Ming Local Ad-

and bureaucratic intervention in social affairs. The feudal archetype was developed in reaction to these actual qualities of imperial government during the Han and T'ang periods, and soon became a means of arguing for the defense of local government against official encroachment and monarchic despotism. By the mid-T'ang, however, many political commentators had come to realize that feudalism was a system of the distant past which could not be practically revived. Liu Tsung-yuan (773–819), for instance, argued that feudalism must not be mistaken for an invented or sagely legislated institution. Rather, it necessarily accompanied particular historical developments which his own age, with its intricate bureaucratic structures, had superseded.[74]

Liu's institutional historicism was later used by Sung opponents of Wang An-shih's reforms to deplore the futility of restoring long-gone (if not ideal) Chou institutions which cut deeply into local society. But their other defense against central power continued to be the ideal of feudal autonomy, even though many realized that feudalism as such was just as impossible to recover from time as Chou bureaucracy. The same contradiction between historicism and the feudal ideal continued to bother seventeenth-century political thinkers who shared many of the Sung philosophers' opinions about overcentralization (e.g., Huang Tsung-hsi's *Ming-i tai-fang lu*) and historicism (e.g., Wang Fu-chih's force of circumstances, or *shih*). Their concern about these issues was heightened by memories of the Tung-lin and Fu-she struggles, by an awareness of the continuing though inefficient growth of state power since the Yuan,[75] and by the loyalist experience itself. No thinkers of stature among the Chiang-yin defenders expressed this concern theoretically, but some of their implicit ambivalences appeared in more explicit form as contemporaries like Ku Yen-wu struggled with the problem of local political control.

Ku Yen-wu repeatedly stressed the harmful effects of concentrating too much power in the hands of a nonresponsive state.[76] The ultimate consequence of centralizing authority in the single hands of the ruler was either legal depersonalization or clerical delegation.[77]

> In later ages there appeared inept rulers who gathered all authority into their own hands, but the countless exigencies of government are so broad that it is quite impossible for one man to handle them all, so the authority

ministration," in Charles O. Hucker, ed., *Chinese Government in Ming Times: Seven Studies* (New York: Columbia University Press, 1969), pp. 1–21. The theories are partly exposited in Hsiao Kung-ch'üan, *Chung-kuo cheng-chih ssu-hsiang shih* [A history of Chinese political thought], pp. 408–409, 461–469.

74. Liu Tsung-yuan, "Discourse on Enfeoffment," trans. Michael S. Duke in *Phi Theta Papers* 11:36–64.

75. J. Gray, "Historical Writing in Twentieth-century China: Notes on Its Background and Development," in W. G. Beasley and E. G. Pulleyblank, eds., *Historians of China and Japan* (London: Oxford University Press, 1961), pp. 186–212.

76. Etienne Balazs, *Political Theory and Administrative Reality in Traditional China* (London: School of Oriental and African Studies, 1965), p. 33.

77. Yang Lien-sheng, "Ming Local Administration," p. 3.

then shifted to the laws. With this a great many laws were promulgated to prevent crimes and violations, so that even the greatest criminals could not get around them nor the cleverest officials accomplish anything evading them. People thereupon expended all their efforts in merely following the laws and trying to stay out of difficulty. Thus the authority of the son of heaven came to reside not in the officials appointed by the government but in the clerks and assistants. Now what the world needs most urgently are local officials who personally look after the people, and yet today the men who possess least authority are precisely those local officials. If local officials possess no authority and the grievances of the people are not made known to the higher authorities, how can we hope to achieve peace and prosperity and prolong the life of the nation?[78]

As a moral philosopher, Ku Yen-wu condemned the increasing selfishness of later rulers who wished to make a territory their own; and thus viewed the prefectural model, the growth of clerks, as the institutional expression of human (i.e., despotic) will. Yet as an historian, Ku appreciated the inevitability of a gradual process of change which was beyond the power of a single man to affect. If one, for instance, examined the classical sources carefully enough, one could easily show that the *chün-hsien* (prefectural) system was not the invention of the centralizing emperor Ch'in Shih–huang (221–210 B.C.), but rather evolved gradually during the preceding centuries.[79] But while this historicism denied Ku the hope that a restored feudal system might be an antidote to centralization, it did assure him that the prefectural system itself would just as surely evolve in the future; and if "some sage were to appear who could invest the prefectural system with the essential meaning of feudalism, then the world would attain order."[80]

78. Ku Yen-wu, *Jih-chih lu* [Record of daily learning], 9:15–16, cited in Wm. Theodore de Bary, *Sources of Chinese Tradition* (New York: Columbia University Press, 1960), p. 611.

79. By treating the *Spring and Autumn* (and especially the Tso commentary) as an historical source, Ku Yen-wu was able to show many instances during the seventh and sixth centuries B.C. of *hsien* nomenclature describing the incorporation of smaller family-states into the expanding Warring States, e.g., Duke Hsuan of Chin bestowing a *hsien* upon one of his followers in 626 B.C., or the Viscount of Ch'u transforming a conquered area into a district in 597 B.C. The *Spring and Autumn* references cited by Ku usually demonstrated the establishment of *hsien* to incorporate conquered territory. For example, when the state of Ch'u invaded Cheng in 596 B.C., the latter's earl surrendered with the words: "So that I may change my course and serve your lordship equally with the governors of the nine [new] districts [which you have established]." (As translated in James Legge, *The Chinese Classics* [Taipei: Wenhsing shu-chü, 1966], 5:316.) The *Chan-kuo ts'e* and the *Shih-chi* also portrayed the *hsien* as a unit created more autonomously by cities which "formed" (*ch'eng*) a district. As for the *chün* (commanderies), of which the Ch'in supposedly created thirty-six to oversee the *hsien* of the empire, Ku applies the same research techniques to show: first, that there are many references to *chün* as an original sub-unit of the *hsien*; second, that at the beginning of the Warring States period, *chün* were established as military colonies and defense points against the barbarians; and third, that they were used before the Ch'in by other warring states to oversee their *hsien*. Ku Yen-wu, *Jih-chih lu* [Record of daily learning], Kuo-hsueh chi-pen ts'ung-shu ed. (Taipei: Commercial Press, 1956), Vol. 4, pt. 1, pp. 94–98.

80. Cited in Yang Lien-sheng, "Ming Local Administration," p. 3.

What was the institutional expression of this "essential meaning of feudalism"? Ku's dislike for centralization was colored by his observation of the
continuing development—originating with the Yuan regional censorate and
carried on by the Ming *hsun-an* system—of provincial administrations which
interposed a layer of supervisory officials between what had been the old Han
chün and the central government. This structure had, to be sure, strengthened
the position of the gentry because as the provincial administration after 1574
stripped district yamens of their office land and nonallocated revenues, funds
for construction and irrigation works were increasingly managed by the
notability.[81] But at least until the late nineteenth century, this was to be only
an accrual of influence instead of real political power—feudalization perhaps,
but hardly feudalism. What Ku wished to do was both to legitimize this
development by allowing members of the local elite to serve as yamen officials,
and to restore feudal dignity to the magistracy by abolishing the supervisory
posts above it, making the office itself hereditary, and allowing the official to
choose his own assistants.[82]

Ku Yen-wu's proposal, which was of course denied by the imperial laws of
avoidance, would become an important part of the repertoire of nineteenth-
century statecraftsmen like Feng Kuei-fen who argued for gentry political
power as a representation of the wishes of the locale, and for a restoration of
the original unity between ruler and ruled that had prevailed in earlier,
genuinely feudal times.[83] Local autonomy and patrimonialism thus appeared
to satisfy the Confucianist impulse toward face-to-face relationships by removing the bureaucratic intermediaries between higher and lower, polity and
society. In the end, however, Ku Yen-wu's yearning for an ideal harmony of
interest between ruler and ruled kept him and his later admirers from legiti-
mizing political association free of the state.

Let me try to clarify this by paraphrasing Ku's own scholarly analysis of
the *she* (which originally designated the altar to the god of the soil, and later
came to mean village or society). By studying the *Shih-chi* and *Li-chi* Ku was
able to show how in Chou times each feudal lord used earth from the emper-
or's central altar to establish his own local *she* for harvest ceremonies. As time
went on the state began to use the *she* as a form of social enrollment by
instructing the residents of each unit to keep a local population registry.
Since Ku was aware that in this way the *she* represented both the state's articulation of local identity and imperial religious subordination of aristocratic
lineages, he praised it for embodying the ideal combination of local association and central unity. For, the *she* was as well a natural (mechanic) social
unit: the collective representation of neighborhood or village membership.

81. Ibid., pp. 20–21.
82. Ibid., p. 4.
83. Feng Kuei-fen, "Fu hsiang-chih i" [A proposal for reinstituting a system of local
offices], in Chien Po-tsan, comp., *Wu-hsu pien-fa* [The reform movement of 1898] (Shanghai:
Shen-chou kuo-kuang-she, 1955), 1:8.

This meant, though, that it must be distinguished from unnatural or spurious *she*, i.e., voluntary associations.

> Later, people assembled followers and formed groups (*hui*). These are also [called] *she*. At the end of the Wan-li period (1573–1619), literati banded together to discuss literature. Each [band] would establish a name, to be called such and such a *she*. In the Ch'ung-chen (1628–1644) period Lu Wen-sheng memorialized with an accusation concerning the affairs of the Fu-she of Chang P'u and others, so that an edict was received ordering a complete investigation. Many of the officials who were involved in this matter were degraded or dismissed. In the biography of Hsueh Yen in the *Sung-shih*, [it is said] there was a member of the powerful local Li clan of Yao-chou who gathered together several tens of people as his retainers (*k'o*). They called themselves the *she* of daredevils (*mo-ming*). In the biography of Tseng Kung it is said that the people of Ch'ang-chou gathered village gangs (*tang*) called the *she* of hegemons (*pa-wang*). In the biography of Shih Kung-pi, it is said that the reckless masses of Yang-chou played the bravo (*hsia*) among rural villages. They were called the *she* of diehards (*wang-ming*). Furthermore, at the end of the Sui there were black *she*'s and white *she*'s by name in the city of Ch'iao-chün. In the basic annals of the T'ai-ting emperor (reigned 1324–1327) in the *Yuan-shih*, [it is recorded that] the starving people were forbidden to form a *she* of cudgel-men (*pien-tan*); for, one hundred people were wounded by sticks. I do not know how the various scholars of today can use such a name as this. After the T'ien-ch'i period (1621–1627), scholars wrote lampoons back and forth. The various *she* acted as though they were guardposts and spoke of oaths or of club pledges (*she-meng*). This is what the *Liao-shih* called "needling friends" (*tz'u-hsueh yu*). Today people's feelings [properly incline toward] associating four ways, by year [of examination], by *she* (altar), by village, and by clan; and that is all. Anyone doing away with these four would seriously [risk] losing the empire.[84]

By condemning all voluntary *she*—whether bandit gangs or late-Ming scholarly clubs—Ku rejected the one relatively autonomous political development of his time which could conceivably have expressed local rule. For, just as he denied the organizational legitimacy of corporations, so did his distaste for laws (viewed as expression of depersonalized rule rather than as principles of rational authority) deprive his favored local elite of protective guarantees against political absorption by the state. To be sure, that elite was not necessarily prevented from appropriating local political power; but until the very end of the Ch'ing period that was to lie within the interstices of a highly centralized administration, prefectural to the core. Indeed, such a system ultimately served the gentry of this period best. Their social interests—

---

84. Ku Yen-wu, *Jih-chih lu*, Vol. 4, pt. 1, pp. 106–107.

enhanced by limited autonomy—would be jeopardized by a complete divorce from central authority. Even with peasant militia behind them, as at Chiang-yin, the civil gentry of Kiangnan could not hope by itself to confront and control seventeenth-century militarists.

Had Chinese cities of that region possessed an articulated municipal identity, they might have secured more relative autonomy under a superimposed elite of foreign conquerors, like the communal separateness of thirteenth-century Islamic cities under Mamluk rule.[85] But Chinese political theory did not envisage a network of communities or cells (cities, religious orders, foreign peoples) which were each separately connected to the central bureaucracy above and jointly linked in the total and universally relevant community of the Koran. The only universal relevance to be found in China stretched across and above such putative cells in the form of that culturally cosmopolitan elite of gentlemanly public servants drawn out of society. Despite strong foci of local identity, a city like Chiang-yin could not alone gratify the political ambitions of its notables.

From the point of view of Ku Yen-wu, therefore, it was ironic that he who argued most eloquently for local political expression must in the end reject the true base of that power. All that remained was a much vaguer pride of place and an appreciation for locality as such. One would consequently have to be content with describing local conditions (e.g., the 120 chüan of Ku's T'ien-hsia chün-kuo li-ping shu) as though a love of locale, an elucidation of regional conditions, was evidence enough of the "essential meaning of feudalism." This emphasis on the ti-fang, the local region, characterized other writers as well—not only because they deplored centralized power for the same reasons as Ku, but because they felt that localism was China's best defense against the barbarians. There is much of this in Wang Fu-chih's writings, and there is no reason to doubt that it was derived from the observation of areas like Chiang-yin where pang sentiments were the strongest source of resistance. The mystique of locale was, in other words, as important as that of the righteous uprising of the people. Comparing these sources with similar ones for the Taiping period, one even finds the former outweighing popular fervor.[86]

---

85. By this I do not necessarily mean a commune. As Ira Lapidus has shown, there does not have to exist an absolute distinction between European self-governing communes and Asian bureaucratically administered cities. See Ira M. Lapidus, *Muslim Cities in the Late Middle Ages* (Cambridge: Harvard University Press, 1967), pp. 1–7.

86. After the conquest, the Ch'ing did make a conscious effort to eradicate loyalty to locale by forbidding the use of dialects among its officials. See Ho Ping-ti, *Chung-kuo hui-kuan shih-lun* [An historical study of *Landsmannschaften* in China] (Taipei: Hsueh-sheng shu-chü, 1966), pp. 1–9. However, it would be wrong to claim that the Chinese had lost their "localism" by the nineteenth century. The historiographic interest in local chronicles by such eighteenth-century historians as Chang Hsueh-ch'eng, or the locale-oriented writings of the statecraft scholars then and later, suggest both the influence of Ku Yen-wu himself and the continuing interest in local government. This is corroborated by the Polachek and Kuhn papers in this volume.

Wang Hua's call for continued local resistance depended upon rallying the village militiamen. Liu Liang-tso's plans for a successful siege in turn necessitated defending his rear from peasant harassment. On August 19 his military commanders were ordered to loot all the district's villages and kill any peasants who tried to flee. By August 21 Liu felt his rear safe enough to venture an all-out assault upon the city walls. He found them better defended than he had expected. Arrows "fell like rain" from above throughout the daylight hours. By nightfall it was clear to both sides that the siege would be a long one.

Four days later Ch'en Ming-yü lost his last professional military expert, Ku Yuan-pi, who had replaced Shao K'ang-kung as coordinator of the *hsiang-ping*. After townsmen claimed that Ku had deliberately let his arrows fall short of the enemy, he was arrested and his house searched. Certain compromising letters to the Ch'ing prefect were discovered, leading to his execution. Ch'en now had to find another military commander, and especially someone who could do more than recruit mercenaries. This time, following the recommendation of a former grain transport official, he turned for help to his predecessor as warden, Yen Ying-yuan.[87]

Yen—a tall, fierce-looking man—held a military *hsiu-ts'ai* degree from T'ung-chou (Chihli), where his family had moved from Shao-hsing (Chekiang). After competent service in one of the capital granaries, he had been appointed *tien-shih* of Chiang-yin in 1641, just as the district was attacked by a famous Ch'ung-ming pirate named Ku San-ma-tzu. Yen, of course, had his own *t'u-ping* to muster against Ku, but—unlike Ch'en Ming-yü—he made great efforts to organize the regular *hsiang-ping* of the riverside villages into a disciplined force. His strategy succeeded, and Yen was quickly able to expel the pirates from Huang-t'ien-kang and subdue the salt smugglers of the district. His superiors cited these victories to recommend Yen for the post of registrar in Ying-te (Kwangtung). But because the roads south were already cut by bandits Yen was permitted to remain in Chiang-yin district, where he moved his entire family (including his ailing mother) to a well-defended villa in the hills east of the city walls. Now Ch'en Ming-yü dispatched a special squad of sixteen men by night to the villa with a letter of appointment. Remembering the fate of earlier commanders, Yen refused to accept until assured that his orders would be obeyed unquestioningly. That same night he returned to the district capital with forty of his own liegemen (*chia-ting*) and assumed command.[88]

Yen Ying-yuan's defense measures were designed to reorganize existing militia units, recruit new village braves, guarantee an adequate source of supplies, and strengthen the city walls against siege warfare. An unruly mob

87. *NCIS*, p. 374. Yen's *tzu* was Li-hsiang. See *CYHC*, p. 287.
88. *Ming-shih*, 277:3114; *ITC*, ts'e 92, chüan 78; Han T'an, *Chiang-yin ch'eng*, p. 177.

of adventurers was weeded out from the currently enrolled forces, while the regular householders of the city were registered in a conscript system to provide decimally organized banners. Individual peasants (not bandit groups or clumsily trained militia units) were encouraged to slip through the enemy's lines and join the defenders—now, of course, commanded by a man respected by villagers for his past bravery.[89] And, just as Yen had helped heal the rift between the countryside and the city, so did he try to reconcile Ch'en Ming-yü with the gentry by having Shao K'ang-kung released from jail to supervise a committee of urban notables in charge of gathering supplies.[90] Once the walls themselves had been strengthened and weapons gathered on the parapets,[91] Yen proceeded to assign the defense of the east gate to a military *chü-jen* named Wang Kung-lueh, the south gate to a Sergeant Wang, and the western approaches to Ch'en Ming-yü. Yen himself formed a special elite corps (probably former *t'u-ping*) of one thousand expert archers to man the north gate. All entrances to the city were then blocked with timbers, and special torch-carrying patrols organized to man the battlements at night. The latter, as inconsequential as they seem, probably did more to prolong Chiang-yin's resistance than any other measure.[92]

By late August—the rainy season—daily downpours had swelled the river and moat, making assault more difficult but also dampening gunpowder

89. The chronicles particularly praised Yen Ying-yuan for overcoming the suspicion between villagers and city dwellers, and for bringing "inner and outer" together. Certainly his accomplishments were exaggerated. According to one account (Hsu Ch'ung-hsi, *Chiang-yin ch'eng shou hou-chi* [A later account of the the defense of Chiang-yin], in Hu Shan-yuan, *Chiang-yin i-min*, pp. 195–196), there were only one thousand armed and trained soldiers inside the city when Yen took command. The enemy, of course, was supposed by this time to have as many as one hundred thousand outside the city, organized into "several hundred" encampments. Supposedly, because of the respect in which Yen was held by rural military leaders, as many as two hundred thousand braves rallied to his banner. Despite the exaggeration, he probably did draw large numbers of peasants to the city's defense.

90. Carpenters and artisans were formed into work crews to make weapons, prepare watchtowers, and repair the city walls. Every household was required to contribute goods in order to reward the troops, along with any armor and weapons it had. These levies were collected and tallied under the supervision of the degree-holders Chang Ching-shih, Hsia Wei-hsin, and Wang Hua, who specified quotas of grain, salt, oil, and so forth. Though the populace was put on half-rations, salt and oil were soon discovered to be in short supply. Salt was therefore smuggled in from Huang-shan-kang by pirates, while boys too young to fight mashed oil from beans in requisitioned carts. A general inventory of the city's supplies showed that there was ample gunpowder and lead shot for the large Portuguese (*Fo-lan-chi*) cannons, but arrows were in very short supply and special squads were detailed to sneak out of the city at night and pick up used arrows on the battlefield. At other times, Yen had drums and gongs sounded in mock attack in the dark to invite a reusable hail of Ch'ing arrows. Yen also had a crossbow expert named Huang Ming-chiang manage a forge that eventually turned out over a thousand crossbows. The bolts they used were dipped in a gunpowder paste in order to increase the likelihood of infectious wounds.

91. The south wall, shorter than the rest, was reinforced and built up an additional three *ch'ih*. Tiles and bricks to be used as missiles were arranged in piles on the battlements, and the "barbarian cannons" were placed at strategic points.

92. One reason Chia-ting fell so quickly was because all its defenders stayed awake for nights on end until they were too exhausted to fight.

and weakening walls. On September 1, therefore, Liu Liang-tso had to use pontoon bridges to convey a spearhead equipped with scaling ladders across the moat. A few heavily armored soldiers did climb to the top of the battlement at the north gate; but the city's crossfire from cannons on both ends of the walls, plus the torrent of debris, tiles, and bricks which the townsmen hurled down, drove off the rest of the attackers with heavy casualties.

Nevertheless, the Ch'ing assault did so weaken the defenders' resolution that some began to talk openly of surrender. Yen therefore decided on an offensive maneuver to raise morale. Initiating discussions with the enemy, he promised Liu a preliminary gift of four *yuan-pao* (fifty-ounce silver ingots) which would be carried over the walls by a delegation of elders on September 3. But the caskets they bore actually contained gunpowder. Admitted into the Ch'ing encampment, the elders blew up themselves and several enemy officers.[93] However, they had failed to assassinate Liu Liang-tso, who retaliated by throwing his main force against the north gate the next day. Once again his men were driven back with *ballista* and tiles.

CH'ING REINFORCEMENTS

The city continued to hope for aid from the outside. Because nothing had been heard from envoys sent to contact other loyalist groups in Kiangnan, several hundred braves tried unsuccessfully to slip through the Ch'ing lines and reach the Southern Ming forces at Ch'ung-ming Island. Another group did reach a fleet of several hundred erstwhile loyalist junks, but their commander turned out to be Yen's former adversary, the pirate Ku San-ma-tzu.[94] Thus the defenders of Chiang-yin were entirely on their own when Liu Liang-tso attacked again on September 5. This time Liu moved his

93. A general named Hsueh Wang was supposedly killed. Hsieh Kuo-chen believed that Hsueh Wang was actually killed in a military engagement. See Hsieh Kuo-chen, *Nan-ming shih-lueh*, p. 84. Other defenders of Chiang-yin were also praised for devising similar tricks to confuse the enemy. Ch'i Fan (*chin-shih*, 1643), a former secretary in the Office of Scrutiny of the Board of Civil Appointments, was one of the members of the gentry placed in charge of rations. He once had a raiding party carrying hundreds of lanterns slip between two lines of Ch'ing troops at night, causing them to fire on each other. Ch'i Fan was also one of the figures associated with the many supernatural omens that filled the chronicles of the city's defense and fall. When the city was taken, he barricaded himself and his entire household of servants and relatives in the inner portion of his home, which was then set on fire. The wall upon which he wrote in large characters that he was committing suicide because he was a Ming servant was supposed to have remained standing, the characters etched out in white relief. At night they gave off a ghostly glow; and when it rained the droplets of water would not pass over the characters. See Ch'a Chi-tso, *Kuo shou lu* [Record of the state's longevity], *Wan-ming shih-liao ts'ung-shu* [A compendium of historical materials of the late Ming] (Shanghai: Chung-hua shu-chü, 1959), p. 160.

94. Historians of the time usually pinpointed lack of outside help as the major cause of the ultimate fall of Chiang-yin. These chroniclers bitterly condemned Wu Chih-k'uei and his ilk for failing to unite behind the city's defense. It is almost as though even the compilers of the *Ming-shih* believed that this might have been the one chance for the Southeast to effect a restoration or at least hold the line at the Yangtze (though that, of course, was long since lost at Yangchow). As a result even the *Ming-shih* compilers slightly distorted events to make it appear that Ch'en Ming-yü and Yen Ying-yuan stepped in only after loyalists outside the city

artillery closer, methodically smashing the northern wall of the city and sending assault troops across the moat under leather carapaces. But by pouring hot oil down on the armored Ch'ing soldiers, the loyalists turned the attack into a rout, pursuing the enemy back to their lines and destroying the rest of the pontoon bridges. On the heels of his victory, Yen Ying-yuan sent a midnight raiding party to infiltrate the Ch'ing headquarters at Shih-fang monastery, but even though his retinue suffered heavy casualties, Liu Liang-tso survived the raid.

On September 7 General Liu personally appeared before the north gate and called respectfully for Yen's surrender. Why resist, he asked, when the rest of Kiangnan had already been subdued? Yen answered:

> The literati and people of this river city, someone once said, have walked this land and eaten its fruits for three hundred years. Deeply honored by the [Ming] state's benevolence, we are incapable of watching [the way] the wind [is blowing] and surrendering. [Yen] Ying-yuan is a warden of the Ming dynasty. Righteousness will not let him serve two lords. [You,] general, hold a noble rank, and yet you rush reinforcements [against us]; but by advancing you will not be able to recover the central plain, and by retreating not be able to defend the left bank of the river. How can your countenance look upon the loyal and righteous literati and people of Chiang-yin?[95]

By extending the obligation of gratitude for the dynasty's social favor to the city itself, Yen Ying-yuan rhetorically combined gentry and *pang* sentiments into a single appeal which was probably designed more for his followers' ears than for the enemy's. Liu listened quietly, then turned his horse and rode away. Time, after all, was on his side. Each passing day reduced Chiang-yin's provisions and brought more troops for the siege.[96] These reinforcements now completely sealed off the approaches to Chiang-yin and trained new artillery on the walls that were steadily barraged after September 14.[97]

Cut off from the outside world, the loyalists began to seek supernatural allies. Five divine statues were placed on the ramparts: one of Kuan-ti, the god of war; one of the guardian city god (*ch'eng-huang ti*); two of Tung-p'ing

---

refused to rescue it. "Ch'eng Pi distributed all of his family's wealth (175,000 taels) to provide military rations. Then he presented himself before the *tsung-ping* of Wu-sung, Wu Chih-k'uei, to beg for an army. Chih-k'uei was adamant [in his refusal]. Pi consequently did not return [to Chiang-yin]. [Shao] K'ang-kung battled unsuccessfully. [Chou] Jui-lung's navy was also defeated and left. Then, [Ch'en] Ming-yü and [Yen] Ying-yuan came into the city." *Ming-shih*, 277:3114. Also see *NCIS*, p. 374.

95. Han T'an, *Chiang-yin ch'eng*, p. 184.

96. Wu Wei-yeh, *Nan-kuo yü-chung* [The loyal simpletons of the south land], in Hu Shan-yuan, *Chiang-yin i-min*, p. 209.

97. Of course, the fresh troops had to find food, and pillaging began again—often through areas that had already been looted: Ta-ch'iao, Chou-chuang, Hua-yeh, T'ao-ch'eng, San-kuan, Chu-t'ang (which resisted and was burned to the ground), and as far south as Ch'ing-yang, where the villagers had practiced close-order drill for a long time and were able to keep raiding parties out.

wang,[98] and one of Sui-yang wang.[99] Yen Ying-yuan was a stranger to Chiang-yin and consequently could not share the magic of the city god. But he did deliberately encourage the belief that he was divinely protected by Sui-yang wang as he strode boldly along the city wall, sword-bearing attendant in tow. The identification was even extended to Ch'en Ming-yü by contemporary observers:

> Long ago, Chang [Hsun] and Hsu [Yuan] (i.e., the co-defenders of Sui-yang); today, Yen and Ch'en. Circumstances are not the same, yet I fear that the prospect of surrounding the city is alike. The honors conferred for loyal service are not the same, yet the emotion of giving one's all are not unlike. . . . Some call Yen a stern father, Ch'en a soothing mother. Thus they unashamedly act as the people's parents.[100]

Yen even concealed lodestones in the whiskers pasted onto the gods' wooden faces, so that when armored soldiers scaled the walls the beards suddenly bristled, supposedly terrifying Ch'ing attackers.[101]

The gods may have momentarily inspired the desperate resisters who killed and drove off thousands of assailants at both the north and south gates on September 18 and 19, but morale quickly flagged during the next few days, as supplies ran out. Grass was harvested for want of other comestibles, tempers grew short, and whispers of surrender became bolder, less hushed. Couriers who managed to slip through the enemy lines told of hundreds of villagers voluntarily shearing their heads before the major Ch'ing encampment at Chün mountain. The rural militiamen were willing enough to fight at first—bitterly commented some of the city elders—but now it was the townsmen who had to pay the price. Then on September 22, 1645, came the bleakest news of all. Sung-chiang had fallen to Li Ch'eng-tung, the butcher of Chia-ting.[102] Chiang-yin not only stood alone; Li's fearsome army was

98. Tung-p'ing wang (named Ts'ang) was the eighth son of Kuang Wu Ti (reigned 25–57 A.D.), noted for his role in marking the restoration of the Han dynastic line by reviving the proper system of rites and music. Given the rhetoric of both a Ming restoration and the "rites" of the *pang* of Wu, he represented a perfect symbol of the aspirations of the resistance.

99. Sui-yang wang represented Chang Hsun, the T'ang official who led the famous defense of Sui-yang against the long siege mounted by the ninth-century rebel, An Lu-shan. Though the defense failed—appropriately enough—because reinforcements under Ho-lan Chin-ming failed to arrive in time, Chang Hsun was a popular image of military excellence and righteous resistance. Because he was from nearby Wu-hsi (where a major shrine had been built in his honor), he was also taken to be the chief of all the city gods of the northern Kiangnan region, and thus represented as well the *pang* sentiment of localism. Huang Ang, *Hsi Chin shih hsiao-lu* [A modest record of (Wu-)hsi and Chin(-kuei)], photoreprint of 1896 edition (Taipei: Wu-hsi wen-hsien ts'ung-k'an, 1962), pp. 42, 145–147. I am grateful to Professor Hsu Cho-yun for supplying this reference.

100. From the *Mu-lu shih*, cited in Han T'an, *Chiang-yin ch'eng*, p. 187.

101. Han T'an even insists that when Liu Liang-tso's son reached that portion of the wall where Sui-yang wang "reigned," the god's beard jerked, gunners fired at the appropriate moment, and the son fell dead. Liu is said to have decapitated the idol when he later took the city.

102. Li Ch'eng-tung, who had been one of Shih K'o-fa's officers, surrendered to Prince Bolo

now free to join Liu Liang-tso's siege. To prove how hopeless resistance was, Liu even had the loyalist commander and hoped-for rescuer, Wu Chih-k'uei, paraded before the walls in chains to urge Chiang-yin's surrender before it was too late.[103]

Under this strain the alliance which Yen Ying-yuan had arranged between the gentry and Ch'en Ming-yü began to break up, as the city's notables tried to seek a settlement with the enemy. Yen reacted harshly. Surrender-mongers were seized and killed on the spot, while two prominent members of the defense committee—Hsia Wei-hsin and Wang Hua[104]—were accused of embezzling the communal war chest and decapitated.[105] But others in the city managed to drop hair cuttings over the wall to tell the Ch'ing troops below that they were prepared to submit. It was in this manner that General Liu became aware of the split and decided to pit the gentry against the two wardens to his own advantage. First, he sent an emissary who promised no reprisals if the inhabitants replaced their Ming banners with Ch'ing flags and piked their leaders' heads along the city walls. Yen Ying-yuan naturally refused to entertain these demands, which he tried to keep secret from the citizenry. Liu therefore made his gestures public, pulling back his troops with a great show so that the peace party within the city could safely lower four men down to negotiate. After feting the delegates in his headquarters, Liu declared that within three days he wished to send a squad of officials into the city to conduct an investigation of the uprising and punish its major leaders. He then sent the envoys back to the city. Warden Yen promptly accused the four men of having been bribed by the enemy to submit, and—in a gesture of his own—had them decapitated in the public square. On September 26, when Ch'ing soldiers rode up to the north gate for the city's answer, they were told that General Liu's demand was unacceptable. Chiang-yin would continue to resist.

A curious switch had taken place. Righteous loyalism—normally the prerogative of the gentry because of status obligation—was being monopolized by the warden. This was partly because Yen Ying-yuan did not share the predicament of the gentry, who saw their city threatened with destruction. For, those most deeply imbued with the Confucian ideal of *chung* (loyalty) were also the ones who had the greatest interest in accom-

---

before being commanded to pacify large portions of Kiangnan. It was he who slaughtered the inhabitants of Chia-ting. Later he switched sides again and served the Prince of Kuei in Kwangtung and Kiangsi. He was killed at the battle of Hsin-feng in April 1649. There is an English biography of him in Hummel, *Eminent Chinese*, p. 452.

103. *Ming-chi nan-lueh*, pp. 252–254.

104. Wang, of course, had authored the note rejecting Liu Liang-tso's original offer of amnesty. Hsia had intervened to save the magistrate in the early days of the resistance movement.

105. Taking his cue from Han T'an, Hu Shan-yuan (Hu Shan-yuan, *Chiang-yin i-min*, p. 6) maintains that Hsia and Wang were beheaded at this time. Standard accounts like the local and national gazetteers list their names among biographies of other loyal officials killed when the city fell.

modation in order to preserve their stake in the postwar settlement of Kiang-nan. This predicament was triply significant: it made loyalism a genuine commitment because of the sacrifices entailed; it kept the gentry vacillating between engagement in the struggle and cautious withdrawal from it; and it permitted a relatively disinterested outsider like Yen Ying-yuan to be more royalist than the king. Of course, Yen was not without a certain gentry cachet of his own. Unlike Ch'en Ming-yü, he did hold a Ming examination degree. Both men, too, could take pride in holding Ming office, lowly as it was. When Wu Chih-k'uei had urged the city to surrender, Yen had sar-castically called down from the wall, "A general should have died sooner," because he—a mere warden—still held out.[106] It was therefore possible for Yen, who had already appropriated the suicidal commitment of Sui-yang wang, to begin to play a self-consciously historical role; and once he had become wrapped in the mantle of a loyalist hero, every action was thereafter prescribed by an established mythology of resistance. Like a *chanson de geste*, the epic mode in Chinese history (which compensates for its absence in Chinese literature) demands a ritual of events: betrayal, struggle against stupendous odds, inevitable defeat, and heroic death or suicide. History and myth thus melded for Yen Ying-yuan because his perception of himself was colored by the same kinds of siege chronicles which he knew Chiang-yin would leave behind. He was, in other words, both conscious of an historical audience and the spectator of his own drama. He even could have predicted his future enshrinement by the Ch'ien-lung emperor as a loyalist paragon[107] because Yen and his contemporaries believed that exemplary history was recorded and judged with constant and permanent criteria.

But this sort of enshrinement was ultimately parahistorical; it denied the Chiang-yin defenders their specificity. Like seventeenth-century localism, loyalism could not resist appropriation by the imperial government—even when the latter was ethnically alien. For, the "shrines to loyalty and righteousness" extolled abstract devotion to a dynasty—*any* dynasty. Since loyalism so defined could have happened at any time, in any Confucian place, it (to use an earlier image) divorced the *chi* from the *she*, the person from his land (*pang*), and dutiful obligation from sentimental attachment. Loyalism in the high Ch'ing was thus a generalized value alone, a mode of behavior and not a goal-oriented belief; motives were transformed into ends.

Though parahistory sometimes seems like parody,[108] we would do the Chiang-yin resisters an injustice to cast it in such a light. For once the dice

106. Han T'an, *Chiang-yin ch'eng*, p. 184.

107. The emperor honored Yen Ying-yuan ("loyal paragon"), Ch'en Ming-yü, and Feng Hou-tun in 1776, when he approved the erection of a shrine of the three dukes (*san kung tz'u*) at the eastern gate of Chiang-yin. *CYHC*, p. 216

108. For instance, when the city fell, four anonymous lower degree-holders decided to drown themselves together. Sitting beside the well they had chosen, they made a suicide pact which was sealed by a last toast of rice wine. But one toast led to another, each congratulating the others on their common sense of righteousness and duty. When Ch'ing troops came upon the

were cast, once Yen Ying-yuan had rejected the Ch'ing commander's final offer, there came a moment of unmistakable grandeur and pathos. At this time of mortal crisis, the gentry transcended its predicament. What a cynic might retrospectively view as residual ideals of loyalism struggling to survive in a world where real interest always prevailed had become the entire normative world of action for those who stood by Yen. The transcending was much like that of a man who had learned to accept death, and so knew that the contradiction between interest and ideal was no longer vital. At that point, honor had become a matter of dignity for all who realized that this was the final arena, and who shared with Yen the conviction that others would remember their deaths in times to come. A similar sentiment is expressed by the Greek poet Cavafy in his lament for the dying defenders of Thermopylae:

> And they merit greater honor
> When they foresee (and many do foresee)
> That Ephialtes will finally appear,
> And in the end the Medes will go through.[109]

MASSACRE

That year the autumn moon festival fell on October 4. A kind of truce, a momentary interlude, hushed the fire on both sides of the lines. As Yen Ying-yuan arranged for the distribution of holiday cakes, the defenders strolled peacefully along the city walls, viewing the full moon over the long river to the north. The scholar Hsu Yung even composed a special ode for the occasion, and as the lutes carried its melody across the moats, voices took up the song together. It is said that Han soldiers in the Ch'ing camp wept when they heard the lyrics.

> The moon begins to rise, as we protect the city of Chiang-yin.
> The moon glows on this great land; Chiang-yin belongs to the great Ming.
> The moon gradually ascends; heroic the courage of the people of Chiang-yin.
> Holding on to the rivers and mountains of the great Ming, our lives are as swansdown.
> The moon is at its zenith; brave and virile the people of Chiang-yin.
> The Manchus—three kings and eighteen generals—disappear without shadow or trace.
> The moon is slipping down; Chiang-yin city an hibiscus bloom.
> How elegant and beautiful the hibiscus, how variegated the rivers and mountains of the great Ming.
> The moon sinks in the west; the Tartars bitter, bitter cold.

---

scene, they found the four men, by then quite drunk, still maudlinly praising each other. The four were ignominiously beheaded on the spot. Ch'a Chi-tso, *Kuo shou lu*, p. 165.

109. *The Complete Poems of Cavafy*, trans. Rae Dalven (New York: Harcourt, Brace and World, 1961), p. 9.

Chiang-yin will not fall. Our eyes will see the rivers and mountains of the great
Ming grow as old as the heavens.[110]

During the next twelve days Liu Liang-tso's men prepared carefully for the
final onslaught.[111] Two dozen siege cannons which had been ferried down
from Nanking were zeroed in on the densely populated northeastern corner
of the city. The barrage opened on October 8—so intensely that even those
outside the walls could hear the screams of the wounded within. The next
morning another two hundred smaller pieces were directed against that
same portion of the wall, which then began to crumble. A noon squall suddenly swept across the river. The driving rain eroded the shot-pierced battlements, while Ch'ing officers ordered their men to advance under the cover of
the storm. Before the defenders were hardly aware of the enemy, Liu's infantry had scaled the wall behind Hsiang-fu temple and began to clear that
quadrant of the city. By dusk they felt confident enough to filter through the
connecting streets into the rest of the city.

Hearing that the Ch'ing were within the walls, Yen Ying-yuan knew that
the end had come. He called for brush and paper to address a final message to
his comrades. "For eighty days we kept our hair," he wrote, "devoted to
loyalty, commemorating the worthies of [Ming] T'ai-tsu's seventeen reigning
generations. One hundred thousand people share this feeling by dying for
righteousness, holding on to three hundred leagues of rivers and mountains
for the great Ming."[112] Then he gathered the remnants of his elite force and
mustered as many horses as could be found to sally forth one last time from
the west gate. Within moments Yen was struck by three arrows. Too weak to
deliver his own *coup de grace*, he staggered into a shallow pond. There enemy
soldiers found him barely breathing. He was quickly carried to Liu Liang-
tso's command post in the hall of the Buddhas at Hsiang-fu temple. Yen's
last words were, "We only die once. Quickly, kill me."[113]

That same afternoon the rest of Chiang-yin's leaders—finally united—
either committed suicide or were killed. Ch'en Ming-yü immolated his entire
entourage in the yamen; Feng Hou-tun hanged himself from the rafters
of a temple; Hsu Yung locked his family in their house before setting it on
fire.[114] The death toll continued to mount the next day, for Peking's orders

110. This version is given in Hu Shan-yuan, *Chiang-yin i-min*, p. 4. Jerry Dennerline has
compared variants of this *yueh-fu*, concluding that all of the texts were related and therefore
followed a given version fairly closely. Jerry Dennerline, "A Preliminary Analysis," pp.
24–25.

111. Liu abandoned his plan of directly attacking the city's flank. Instead, he took the advice of a monk, learned in military tactics, to concentrate on one corner of the walls. The
monk had told him that "The city of Chiang-yin is shaped like an hibiscus. If you attack by
striking at the petals, then the more you strike, the more compact remains the center or stem.
The stem is its northeast corner. Strike only at Hua-chia embankment. Then once the flower's
stem disintegrates, the petals will fall by themselves." Han T'an, *Chiang-yin ch'eng*, p. 192.

112. Ibid., p. 193. This is also given in *CYHC*, p. 437.

113. Han T'an, *Chiang-yin ch'eng*, p. 193. Yen's entire family committed suicide.

114. Ch'ien Su-yüan, *Nan chung chi* [Annals of southern loyalists], in *Chia-shen chi-shih,*

to Liu Liang-tso were to "fill the city with corpses before you sheathe your swords."[115] General Liu did proclaim that only adult males were to be killed, but his soldiers indiscriminately incinerated women and children in their houses. The spreading fires drove others to water, so that the Huang-t'ien River and the city's deep wells were clogged with corpses. Not until two days after the breaching of the wall did the fires burn out and the slaughter finally end. A few survivors, hiding on rafters or in temples, dazedly straggled into the open. Of an initial population near 100,000, only 53 were reportedly left alive within Chiang-yin's shattered walls.[116]

HISTORY AND MYTH

Modern Chinese historians claim that the dead were not sacrificed in vain. The siege was said to have taken an equally terrible toll of the conquerors. The Ch'ing supposedly used 240,000 troops to subdue the city, and lost 74,000 of their men before the fighting ended. By tying down so many of the enemy just after the Nanking regime fell, Chiang-yin's defenders gave other Ming loyalists in the south time to regroup under the Prince of Lu.[117] This, at least, was the belief of the people of Chiang-yin in the early nineteenth century. "To this day," a scholar then noted, "the city folk pass down the story of three [Manchu] princes and eight generals dying when the city fell."[118]

But that same nineteenth-century scholar, the statecraftsman Wei Yuan (1794–1856), was more skeptical of such lore than modern national historians have been. Wei scrupulously checked the biographies of all important Han and Manchu officials active then, only to discover that none had actually died at Chiang-yin. Certainly no Manchu princes had been present; and, as in some other infamous massacres of the period, the slaughter was actually conducted by Chinese troops, not Manchu bannermen. Furthermore, the sum total of soldiers on the Ch'ing side was nowhere near 240,000. At the very most—Wei Yuan conclusively showed—there were only 10,000 troops

wan-Ming shih-liao ts'ung-shu [A record of 1644: a compendium of historical materials of the late Ming] (Shanghai: Chung-hua shu-chü, 1959), p. 114.

115. Hsieh Kuo-chen, Nan-ming shih-lueh, p. 85.

116. Ibid. The compilers of Chiang-yin's local gazetteer also give this figure: "At the end of the Ming and the beginning of the Ch'ing, when the Ch'ing army moved south, Chiang-yin city held out alone for eighty-three days, and when the city fell the dead numbered over one-hundred thousand." CYHC, frontispiece and p. 858. Wei Yuan, however, took the figure of 74,000 as a likely number of victims. Wei Yuan, Sheng-wu chi [Record of imperial military exploits] (Taipei: Cheng-hua shu-chü, 1960), 13:6.

117. See, for example, Hsieh Kuo-chen, Nan-ming shih-lueh, p. 86. Despite his extraordinary bibliographical control over the sources of the late Ming and early Ch'ing, Hsieh accepted the figure of 60,000 Manchu deaths, and argued that a total of 172,000 civilians were killed throughout the entire district of Chiang-yin. Ibid., p. 85. These figures are routinely accepted by popularizers like Hsieh Ch'eng-jen, who also stresses the military importance of Chiang-yin's sacrifice. Hsieh Ch'eng-jen, I-ch'ien-liu-pai-ssu-shih-wu-nien, p. 61.

118. Wei Yuan, Sheng-wu chi, 13:6.

actually committed to the siege.[119] Since the massacre at Chiang-yin more likely inspired other areas to submit rather than defy the Ch'ing, what availed the ninety or hundred thousand civilians who died there?

Mythical battles are sometimes more significant than the historical reality of defeat or victory.[120] Chiang-yin's siege was no myth, but its defenders certainly were mythopoeic. Yen Ying-yuan, Ch'en Ming-yü, and the others all believed that they were engaged in the engraving of a moment destined to be remembered. Yet the myth that eventually prevailed was not the one they had envisioned. Theirs was a personal effort, an aggregate instance of individual loyalism, rather than a manifestation of the localist sentiment which later national historians perceived. In its modern embellishment this myth stressed the harmonious effort of thousands of Chiang-yin Chinese who collectively sacrificed themselves in the defense of the homeland. Of course, in spite of the actual struggle between Ch'en and the gentry, or Yen and the peace party, there did at the time exist a sense of communal identity (devotion to *pang* or land) which strengthened over the course of the Ch'ing. The Ch'ien-lung emperor in 1776 intended to honor only the Chiang-yin leaders as exemplary individuals, but the inscription on their shrine did delicately mention that "great numbers of the gentry and people had followed them into death."[121] And by 1825, when the Tao-kuang emperor approved a supplementary shrine for the 138 "righteous gentry and people" who had died defending their locale, the emphasis was already shifting to communal loyalism.[122] During the last years of the Ch'ing this collective sacrifice was stressed all the more, and altars venerated those people who had left such "an eternally lasting impression on later generations."[123] By the time of the republic, in fact, the citizens themselves had engraved on the south wall of the city the characters *chung i chih pang* (land of loyalty and righteousness)— words which were partially removed with dynamite by the Japanese in 1937, and then restored in Chiang Kai-shek's own hand when the city was retaken in 1945.[124]

As "land" replaced "loyal paragon," the loss of so many people acquired a new significance. Willingness to die for the "land of Su-Hang" symbolized a

119. Ibid., 13:6–7. The available Ch'ing forces in that part of China were then roughly divided between the headquarters garrison at Nanking and the attack on Hangchow. Wei Yuan implies that this left very few soldiers for Kiangnan: a little over 1,000 cavalry at Soochow and only 2,000 or so at Wu-sung. However, Jerry Dennerline has shown that Dodo's problem was not lack of troops. For 238,000 had surrendered to him at Yangchow and Nanking. It was to his advantage to disperse these troops, so he garrisoned them in small units across all of Kiangnan. Jerry Dennerline, "Resistance and Tragedy" (unpublished paper, Yale University, 1973).

120. Michael C. Rogers, "The Myth of the Battle of the Fei River (A.D. 383)," *T'oung Pao* 54:50–72. Frederic Wakeman, Jr., *Strangers at the Gate: Social Disorder in South China, 1839–1861* (Berkeley and Los Angeles: University of California Press, 1966), pp. 19–21.

121. *CYHC*, p. 216.

122. *CYHC*, p. 221.

123. *CYHC*, frontispiece.

124. *CYHC*.

commitment to native soil which was, after all, one of the basic sentiments of modern nationalism. But localism, if it was too parochial, could also conflict with national interests. We have seen how, during the seventeenth century, localism was taken to be a check on imperial despotism, rather than a principle of political organization. By 1900, though, the same body of statecraft theory which wished to invest prefecturalism with "the spirit of feudalism" was being used to justify a new kind of political autonomy in the form of local self-government and provincial assemblies. Provincialism, too, became a deeper attachment, whether in Cantonese anti-foreignism or Hunanese reformism, so that for a time strong local identity helped form an individual's national identity. Yet localism soon was set against nationalism, whether in the guise of regional warlords or venal local landlords. As the twentieth century ground on, the classical ideal of gentry rule even came to represent political disinvolvement and a petty scrambling to protect local economic interests.

How did the *pang* of Chiang-yin fare during this transformation? Just as the Ch'ing rulers had transformed Chiang-yin's leaders into abstract paragons, so did twentieth-century mythmakers turn the siege from a mere defense of locale into an exemplary act of collective devotion and sacrifice. Then numbers really were significant, because the dead were not seen as individuals, or even as residents of a particular *pang*, but rather as a people, a *min-tsu* or race. First as anti-Manchu men of the Han, then later as Chinese peasants opposed to foreign invaders and wealthy landlords, the defenders of Chiang-yin came to symbolize populism, not localism.

In the famous question which began this essay, Calderón likened glories to dreams, and had Segismundo ask where, in the end, truth finally lay. My response to that question has been to show that men who act for posterity can never be certain that their animating values will survive the historical future. Not only that; sometimes the acts themselves matter less than their images—however distorted—which are re-formed in the eyes of subsequent perceivers. This does not mean that historical myth is merely fiction, since events must have credibly occurred for the story to be effective. But it should warn any historical actor that "our virtues," as Shakespeare wrote in *Coriolanus*, "lie in th'interpretation of the time (IV. vii. 49–50)." Audiences are fickle, ideals labile, and glories fleeting. Conviction, after all, is the least—and noblest—of human certainties.

Fiscal Reform and Local Control:
THE GENTRY–BUREAUCRATIC ALLIANCE
SURVIVES THE CONQUEST

Jerry Dennerline

THE CONTEXT AND MEANING OF FISCAL REFORM

The bureaucracy of late imperial China was an institution of doubtful efficiency but incredible durability.[1] It survived economic growth, urbanization, rebellion, invasion, and alien rule. The key to its success was the alliance between local officials and gentry families, an arrangement fraught with social and political tensions which varied from place to place and from generation to generation. The present study examines this alliance under stress in two separate cases of fiscal reform in the seventeenth century. The first was in Ch'ang-lo district, Foochow prefecture, in the last decade of Ming rule. The second was in Sung-chiang prefecture, eastern Kiangsu, during the 1660s. The reforms dealt with service obligation law (*i-fa*), the regulations which assigned responsibility to landowners for registration and collection of taxes. The reformers were associated with the political and intellectual movement which began at the Tung-lin Academy around the turn of the century and continued into the early Ch'ing period. Our purpose is to relate the reformers' strategies to the ideals of the movement and also to demonstrate how the reforms strengthened the gentry–bureaucratic alliance. In order to understand the reforms, we must discuss them in the context of fiscal administration in general. In order to understand the reformers, we must view them in the context of the movement as a whole. First let us turn to the fiscal context.

The most important development in fiscal administration between the fourteenth and nineteenth centuries was the Single Whip method of taxation

1. This paper is the result of research conducted in Taiwan and Japan in connection with my dissertation program at Yale University. It would not have been possible without the support of the Foreign Area Fellowship Program of the American Council of Leaned Societies and the cooperation of the National Central Library, the National Palace Museum Library, and the Institute of History and Philology of the Academia—all in Taipei— and the Institute of Humanistic Studies of Kyoto University.

—a simplified means of assessment and collection designed to increase revenues through greater bureaucratic efficiency and fiscal control. The method grew out of a wide variety of simplifications worked out by reformers at the local level over a period of more than a hundred years. Grand Secretary Chang Chü-cheng (1525–1582) finally ordered it implemented universally in 1581, and from that time on it was supposed to be the legal method of taxation for all of China. In fact, however, bribery and evasion blocked its implementation, and before long it was clear that the promised revenues were not coming in. Reformers then set about trying to stop the evaders. At this point the key to making the Single Whip work was accurate registration, and it was *i-fa* that covered administration of the registers. The *i-fa* reforms were thus the last phase of a sequence of administrative developments usually described under the broader category of Single Whip.

The *i-fa* regulations originally had prescribed the obligations of the rural populace for corvee labor and various categories of local administration. Among the latter was the *li-chia* system, in which landowners in rotation shared responsibility for serving as the local headmen who distributed quotas among the landowners and delivered the tax goods to the yamen. Under the Single Whip all the service obligations were supposed to be converted to silver payments and combined with the land tax. Landowners would then pay the combined tax directly to the yamen. But many landowners managed to avoid registration, and the yamen had to squeeze the tax quotas out of the *li-chia* headmen. The registers of the *li-chia* system assigned responsibility for meeting tax quotas to the headmen. If the bureaucrats would eliminate the *li-chia* system, they would have to revise the registers in such a way as to shift responsibility for payment to the owners. In some places, such as northern Chekiang, reformers succeeded in doing away with the *li-chia* system in the late sixteenth century; in others, bureaucrats continued to rely on headmen until well into the Ch'ing period.

In Ch'ang-lo the reform magistrate, Hsia Yun-i (d. 1645), began phasing out the headmen just before the Manchu invasion. His plan, which we shall examine in detail, included eliminating the *li-chia* exemptions of the gentry. This meant that the gentry shared responsibility for local tax quotas for the first time. The reform thus restricted gentry privilege, but it also drove the gentry to cooperate with the yamen. It was a model of how the gentry–bureaucratic alliance could work. In Sung-chiang, however, *i-fa* reform was delayed until after the Manchu conquest. The prefectures of eastern Kiangsu were the most heavily taxed in the empire, and land-tax evasion had been common there throughout the Ming period. If Ming magistrates had been unable to get the land registered, the invasion could only intensify the problem, for then a whole new class of bureaucrats would confront the gentry with tax claims. The tension reached critical proportions with the Kiangnan tax clearance case of 1661. In the spring of that year, under pressure from the new K'ang-hsi regents, the Kiangsu governor charged thousands of gentry and local functionaries with tax evasion and began to strip them of status and wealth. The gentry–bureaucratic alliance was on the brink of disaster. But by the following spring the crisis had eased, and the Sung-chiang gentry were ready to cooperate in new reform efforts. The result was a new system of registration patterned after the same model that Hsia Yun-i had used in Ch'ang-lo.

The gentry reformers in Sung-chiang were direct descendants of the political–intellectual movement of which Hsia Yun-i had been a leader. In the early 1600s the Tung-lin Academy in Wu-hsi, Kiangsu, had become a center of reaction against "radical intuitionism" and profligacy among the governing elite. The political influence of this movement grew until a group known as the Tung-lin faction was the largest political force within the bureaucracy. The eunuch faction decimated its influence in Peking with the famous purges of 1625, but the movement only grew larger as a result. When the new Ch'ung-chen emperor threw out the eunuch faction in 1628, the movement again dominated the bureaucracy. By this time it had clearly outgrown the traditional political category of "faction." During the 1630s a huge coalition of societies with a combined membership of nearly three thousand bureaucratic aspirants and intellectuals spread the movement's influence beyond the bureaucracy into the world of local politics. This alliance was usually referred to as the Fu-she (Restoration society), after the group which first began to organize the coalition in eastern Kiangsu. Hsia Yun-i was part of that group as well as the organizer of the Chi-she, an affiliated society in Sung-chiang. The intellectual themes which characterized the movement were classical idealism and practical statecraft. The *i-fa* reforms reflected these themes and demonstrated one of the movement's central concerns—the desire to make the gentry–bureaucratic alliance work.

The gentry involved in this movement at the end of the Ming had a special political relationship with the bureaucracy. They had relatives, friends, and other political allies in high places, and many of them served personally in high-level posts. Because of their political influence, which some families had been accumulating for generations, the traditional category of "gentry" is not sufficient to identify them politically or socially. Although the term "gentry" conventionally means a social stratum made up of civil service degree-holders, a concept which equates social status with political power is flawed. There were some politically influential gentry whose involvement in government was enough to make them separate their economic from their political interests for the sake of bureaucratic efficiency. While these men favored the state's economic interests over those of the gentry class, they also fought for gentry influence in opposition to the arbitrary power of the state in local affairs. At the same time there were gentry whose influence was limited to the privileges attached to their status; this gave them certain economic advantages, which all gentry had, but did not give them political connections outside the district through which they could influence local affairs. The interests of these two groups were diverse enough to justify our drawing a social distinction between the gentry with bureaucratic influence and the gentry without. For the purpose of understanding the *i-fa* reforms, this distinction is more useful than the distinction between gentry and nongentry.

The Fu-she movement, which produced the *i-fa* reformers in both cases, clearly sprang from the influential gentry group. The Manchu invasion restricted the movement's influence considerably, but the reformers continued to work for the gentry–bureaucratic alliance. It is important to realize that while the Sung-chiang reform forced the gentry to divide their economic and political interests, the influential gentry themselves had recognized and tried to exploit such a division before the conquest. Imperial pressure alone does not sufficiently explain this coalition. In historical context the *i-fa* reforms demonstrate the complexity of the forces which made the influential gentry and the bureaucracy cooperate in matters of local control.

INSTITUTIONAL CONFLICT: THE BUREAUCRACY AND THE LOCAL ELITE IN FISCAL ADMINISTRATION

The dominant themes in the fiscal history of the Ming are simplification and centralization. Over the course of 270 years, the tax schedules were reduced from a veritable maze of items and dates to a few regularly scheduled silver payments, and the handling of the taxes passed from rural conscripts to the district yamen.[2] The land tax unquestionably remained the major source of revenue for the imperial state, in spite of the growth of capital enterprises and the continuation of economic diversification. In fact, administrators clung to the agrarian tax base until the middle of the nineteenth century.[3] Commerce was taxed, to be sure, but in contrast to its role in the fiscal life of

2. The basic outline of the local tax system may be found in *Ming-shih* [Dynastic history of the Ming], Kuo-fang yen-chiu yuan ed. (Taipei, 1962), chüan 77–79. The best secondary accounts are still Liang Fang-chung, "I-t'iao pien fa" [The Single Whip method], *Chung-kuo chin-tai ching-chi shih yen-chiu chi-k'an* [Journal of modern Chinese economic historical research] 40:1, also trans. by Wang Yü-ch'uan, in *The Single Whip Method of Taxation in China* (Cambridge: East Asian Research Center, Harvard University, 1956); and Liang Fang-chung, *Ming-tai liang-chang chih-tu* [The Ming tax chief system] (Shanghai, 1957). Also see Wei Ch'ing-yuan, *Ming-tai huang-ts'e chih-tu* [The Ming Yellow Register system] (Peking, 1961); and Heinz Friese, *Das Dienstleistungs-system der Ming-Zeit* (Hamburg, 1959). Other sources are cited below when relevant.

3. In 1735 the Ch'ing imperial revenue totaled 34,695,000 taels from land taxes and *ting* quotas, and 9,628,000 taels from all other sources; in 1865 the figures were 22,000,000 taels and 37,000,000 taels, respectively; and in 1895 the figures were 23,737,000 taels and 52,102,-000 taels. See Hsiao Kung-ch'üan, *Rural China: Imperial Control in the Nineteenth Century* (Seattle: University of Washington Press, 1960), p. 141, table 9. By way of comparison, the land tax assessment in the Hung-wu period (1368–1399) was 29,430,000 piculs of rice. Up to the end of the Ming, this figure was altered only by occasional surtaxes. See Ku Yen-wu, *Jih-chih lu chi-shih* [Record of daily knowledge], SPPY ed., 10:7. The conversion rate at the end of the Wan-li period (1573–1620) was one tael per picul. See *T'ai-ts'ang chou-chih* [T'ai-ts'ang *chou* gazetteer] (1642), 8:49.

the Northern Sung it remained only a minor contributor to state coffers. The surtaxes with which administrators attempted to finance the Ming armies during the last decades of the dynasty emphasized the inflexibility of this policy. In the face of bankruptcy, reformers consistently sought to shore up the fiscal base rather than expand it.[4] The common denominator in nearly all of these fiscal problems was tax evasion. Chu Yuan-chang, the Ming founder (reigned 1368 to 1398), had tried to punish the big landowners of Kiangnan for supporting his rival, Chang Shih-ch'eng, by classifying their property as official land (*kuan-t'ien*) and taxing it ten to fifteen times as heavily as private land (*min-t'ien*). Soochow prefecture alone was assessed for one-tenth of the state's land tax, most of it being applied to official land at a rate of 30 to 70 percent of the crops' value.[5] It is doubtful that the wealthy families of Kiangnan ever complied. As early as 1380 these taxes were lowered by one-fifth, and in 1400 the rates were limited to about 5 percent of crop value. But the Yung-lo emperor (reigned 1403 to 1425) again singled out the Kiangnan area for tax punishment, and by the time his successor tried to deal with the problem, widespread tax evasion was evident.[6] For the next two hundred years reformers sought to make the tax burden more equitable; they simplified and centralized. But the root of the problem remained tax evasion, and each reform was specifically designed to fight it.

This situation produced considerable tension between local administrators and landowners. A magistrate needed to meet his tax quotas in order to protect his career, but he also needed the cooperation of the local gentry. Many magistrates simply passed on the blame for deficits to sub-bureaucratic corruption, "bad elements," and the weather, but some elected to reform. It was these reform magistrates who made fiscal history, and their struggles demonstrate how the gentry–bureaucratic alliance worked.

The Ch'ang-lo and Sung-chiang reforms dealt with service obligations (*i*), a set of institutions with a history of their own. According to classical ideals, every household should provide not just a contribution for administrative expenses and public welfare, but a certain amount of administrative service as well. Service obligations, then, were more than a form of conscription or taxation; they grew out of a classical system of participatory administration. Eventually they came to include conscription for corvee labor and militia service, and even taxes to pay the salaries of local functionaries. Wang An-shih's (1021–1086) "new policies" generated the most famous debate concerning service obligations, as his reform replaced local service obligations

4. In his article, "Ni Yuan-lu: 'Realism' in a Neo-Confucian Scholar-Statesman," in Wm. Theodore de Bary, ed., *Self and Society in Ming Thought* (New York: Columbia University Press, 1970), pp. 415–451, Ray Huang suggests that opposition reformers might have turned to other sources of revenue in the last years of the Ming, but that they were restricted by imperial will, factional opposition, and institutional barriers. I believe that reformers were more interested in reestablishing control of the agrarian fiscal base.

5. Ku Yen-wu, *Jih-chih lu*, 10:7, 13.

6. *Ming-shih*, 78:824.

with a tax to be used for hiring public servants. Conscript service (*ch'ai-i*) became hired service (*ku-i* or *mu-i*), and local administration at the sub-bureaucratic level was turned over to professionals. The conservatives led by Ssu-ma Kuang (1019 to 1086), who opposed the reforms, argued that taxation placed a heavier burden on the people than conscription because it shifted obligations from the wealthier landowners to the rural populace in general. Because payments were in cash, the farmer had to convert his produce to meet his quotas; and because the value of cash was beyond his control, he invariably lost on the conversion.[7] But the conservatives produced no workable alternative and the debate continued until the Ming period.

The Ming founder revived the ideal of participatory administration by reintroducing conscription for local service. His chief innovation was the *li-chia* system, which was designed to allow local landowners to share the responsibility for distributing the other service obligations in their communities. Service obligations in general fell into several categories, since there was a fundamental distinction between services involving regular administration, called *ssu-ch'ai* (four conscriptions), and those which were extraordinary, called *tsa-fan* (miscellaneous). Into the miscellaneous category fell the standard corvee responsibilities: manpower for dike repairs, dredging, bridge building, and the like. The four conscriptions, on the other hand, provided regular public servants. Three of the four conscriptions—*chün-yao* (conscripted sub-bureaucratic functionaries), *min-chuang* (popular militia), and *i-ch'uan* (courier service)—were based on quotas distributed among the rural populace. The fourth—*li-chia*—was based on rotation. All landowning households were subject to conscription and all were registered in *li-chia* units. Each household provided its own unit's headman once every ten years, and this headman distributed the conscription quotas within the unit.[8]

Li-chia units were arbitrarily organized into a decimal system, with 110 households forming a single *li*. The ten wealthiest households were responsible for providing the *li-chang*, or *li* headman. The remaining hundred households were divided into ten separate units called *chia*, and the ten households in each *chia* shared responsibility for providing the *chia-shou*, or *chia* headman, for their own unit. It is important to note that only landowners were subject to conscription and headman service, and that *li-chia* units contained a fixed number of households, not varying numbers of households in fixed communities or with fixed amounts of land. The *li-chang* was responsible for distributing obligations among the 110 households in his unit regardless of who they were, where they lived, or how much they were worth. He was not the headman of

7. James T. C. Liu, *Reform in Sung China* (Cambridge: Harvard University Press, 1959), pp. 98–116.

8. See Liang Fang-chung, "I-t'iao pien fa," pp. 1–20; *Ming-shih*, 77:817–818, 78:823, 827–828. The most thorough description of the *chün-yao* obligations is in Friese, *Das Dienstleistungs-system*. On the evolution of *min-chuang*, see Saeki Tomi, "Minshin jidai no minsō ni tsuite" [The popular militia of the Ming-Ch'ing period], *Tōyōshi kenkyū* [Studies in Far Eastern history] 15 (1957).

a village or any other social unit; he was the headman of an artificial administrative unit.[9] This fact bore heavily on the evolution of *li-chia* as an institution.

According to the Ming founder's ideal, land taxes were to be administered separately from service obligations. The land and its owners were listed in both land and household registers so as to provide a cross-reference. Household registers (*huang-ts'e*) listed the names of land-owning households and appended information about their property. These registers also divided the households into *li-chia* units and listed the names of family members, categorizing able-bodied males between the ages of 16 and 60 as *ting*. A given household's conscription quota depended on its wealth and the number of *ting* registered. Land registers (*yü-lin t'u-ts'e*), on the other hand, listed every plot of land in the district, appending the name of the owner, the location, the quality, and the produce of the land. The land-tax quota, which was determined by this listing, was assessed on the appended households. In other words, the two sets of registers determined conscription and land-tax quotas separately.[10] In fact, however, the household registers came to determine all tax quotas because of the special role of the *li-chia* system in the administration of tax collection.

Originally the Ming founder had tried to introduce a new kind of tax collector, called *liang-chang* (tax chief), who was not dependent on *li-chia* conscription. The *liang-chang*, whose jurisdiction covered a district subdivision loosely defined as an area paying 10,000 piculs of grain in taxes, was selected from among the wealthiest families of that area.[11] Chu Yuan-chang reportedly intended the *liang-chang* to form an entirely new group of bureaucrats, owing their status to excellence in public service rather than success in the examination system. Having never achieved official civil service rank, they were allowed an indefinite tenure of office. If one performed well as *liang-chang*, he might receive imperial honors and eventually be granted regular bureaucratic status. The measure of his excellence was his efficiency in meeting the tax levies for his area. He was also charged with supervising the delivery of tax goods to prefectural and district storehouses. Under his management, *li-chia* conscripts labored to calculate the amounts due from each landowner, measured the payments, converted the required portions to cash, and physically transported it all to the proper depots. The entire administration of tax collection was thus left to the local people; the *liang-chang* supervised and answered to the bureaucrats, while the *li-chang* coordinated the landowners in their units.

If participatory government encouraged honesty and efficiency, punitive taxation certainly did not. From the beginning the large landowners of

9. Liang Fang-chung, "I-t'iao pien fa," pp. 1–20.

10. See *Ming-shih*, 77:817–819.

11. The following discussion of the *liang-chang* follows Liang Fang-chung, *Ming-tai liang-chang chih-tu*; also see *Ming-shih*, 78:825.1; Ku Yen-wu, *Jih-chih lu*, 8:11b.

Kiangnan had been unwilling to pay the Ming founder's heavy taxes, and devised means to avoid registering their ownership of land. In collaboration with corrupt yamen functionaries, a rich or powerful landowner could register his land under a category of exemption or reduced assessment. Much private land was falsely registered as belonging to temples, military households, households from other districts, or households that no longer existed. Productive land was listed as fallow or of poor quality. A whole new system of split property rights developed to facilitate this kind of evasion. Owners could sell the rights of cultivation without transferring tax liability to the buyer, and the buyer would pay a premium for the exemption. This practice rendered the land registers useless for proving tax liability.[12]

In the face of widespread evasion by manipulation of the land registers, tax officials were forced to meet their quotas by extralegal means. The demand for meeting quotas fell most heavily on the *liang-chang*, who had to answer to tax officials regardless of the accuracy of the land registers. If he could not meet the quotas, he faced public humiliation and possible corporal punishment. As a result the position of *liang-chang* was not very attractive to wealthy landowners, who could find other ways to advance their prestige. By the 1430s the Ming tax system, which had depended upon the ideal of cooperation between wealthy landowners and the state, was in complete disarray. The post of *liang-chang* was eliminated altogether in the 1450s, and although it was nominally restored in the next decade, its functions and in many cases its title had in fact passed on to the *li-chang*.[13] The subsequent history of fiscal reform was marked by a sequence of frustrating attempts to rid the *li-chang* of the responsibilities of tax collection.

As tax evasion became an established fact, the move toward centralization and simplification began. Three trends were already discernible in the 1430s. First, taxes previously payable in grain were being converted to nonperishable items. Significantly, the initial steps in this direction were in response to tax deficits; the conversions made later payments possible.[14] Eventually most of the land taxes would be commuted to silver, making nonpayment less defensible and squeeze less difficult. Second, distinctions in categories of land began to disappear, ostensibly eliminating a major source of false registration.[15] Finally, the sub-bureaucratic posts originally filled by conscription were becoming salaried positions. In other words, *ku-i* was replacing *ch'ai-i* as the norm in local administration.[16] As land taxes and

12. On split property rights, see Niida Noburo, *Tochi shoyūsei* [The system of property rights], in *Chūgoku hōseishi kenkyū* [Studies in Chinese legal history] (Tokyo, 1960–1964), pp. 164–182.

13. *Ta-Ming hui-tien* [Collected statutes of the Ming dynasty] (1587), 29:1, 19:4a–b.

14. Ibid., 29:3b–4.

15. See *Ming-shih*, 77:818f.; Ku Yen-wu, *Jih-chih lu*, chüan 10.

16. Liang Fang-chung, "I-t'iao pien fa," pp. 1–20. Also see Yamane Yukio, "Mindai no richō no shokuin ni kansuru ichi kōsatsu" [An inquiry into Ming *li-chang* personnel], *Tōhōgaku* [Oriental studies] 3:79–87. On the reassignment of responsibility for transporting tax

service obligations merged into lump-sum silver payments, the magistrate himself came under increasing pressure to meet district quotas, and by the sixteenth century responsibility had shifted completely from the participatory administration system to the district yamen.[17]

These trends culminated in the Single Whip reform of 1581. The Single Whip ultimately simplified the tax structure by commuting nearly all categories to silver payable in two semi-annual installments. It finally central-ized responsibility for meeting district quotas by officially assigning the old, headman functions of collecting (shou) and delivering (chieh) to the yamen and converting the old obligation of headman itself into an annual silver payment to cover the costs. The new system was appropriately called kuan-shou kuan-chieh (official collection and delivery). In order to implement the reform, Chang Chü-cheng ordered a new land survey of the entire empire. A new set of registers—the Fu-i ch'üan-shu (Complete book of land taxes and service obligations), based on the new survey and distributing quotas on the basis of land values—replaced the old land and household registers. In the new register, household and property were listed together, enabling bureau-crats to fix tax liability on the basis of a single record. Theoretically, the state now had the means to collect taxes directly from the landowners and to prosecute the evaders. The survey put millions of new mou on the tax rolls, and the imperial treasury showed an immediate gain. But Chang Chü-cheng's dramatic reform succeeded primarily in registering old imperial land grants in the north.[18] Evasion in the south had depended on the ability of the landowners to manipulate the land registers, and the reforms so far did not prevent them from doing this. Unable to overcome the corruption in land registration, magistrates continued to use the li-chia system. The Fu-i ch'üan-shu quotas were distributed among the geographical units described by the registers, and the registered households shared the responsibility of paying. It was then that reformers began to focus their attention on i-fa.

Since the failure of the land registers to provide revenue in the early dec-ades of the Ming, magistrates had depended on the li-chia system to squeeze their quotas out of the registered households. The legal function of the li-chia headman for tax collection was prompting (ts'ui), or serving notice of payments due. But as long as some landowners could avoid paying, the func-tion of ts'ui was in fact the function of taxpayer. The headman was held re-sponsible for the entire quota of the unit in which he was registered. Wealthy landowners, of course, managed to falsify the household registers just as they had falsified the land registers. In order to avoid being a taxpayer, one need

goods first to hired laborers and then to the local garrisons, see Wu Ch'i-hua, Ming-tai hai-yun chi yun-ho ti yen-chiu [A study of sea and canal transport in the Ming dynasty] (Taipei, 1961), pp. 91–104; and Shimizu Taiji, "Mindai no sōun" [Ming grain transport], Shigaku zasshi [Historical study miscellany] 39:3.

17. Ta-Ming hui-tien, 29:5–15b.

18. See Ming-shih, 77:819, 78:827; Chu Tung-jun, Chang Chü-cheng ta chuan [Biography of Chang Chü-cheng], K'ai-ming shu-chü ed. (Taiwan reprint, 1962), 12:305.

only exempt one's household from the *li-chia* obligation. The best way to do that was to attach one's land to a gentry household. According to the Ming code, gentry exemptions were limited, but in fact gentry households of even the lowest rank enjoyed complete exemption from service obligations.[19] Most significantly, they did not serve as *li-chia* headmen. By the seventeenth century large amounts of land were exempted from taxation through commendation (*t'ou-hsien* or *t'ou-k'ao*) and trusteeship (*chi-t'ien*).[20] Commendation meant giving one's land to another in exchange for privilege and protection.[21] Trusteeship meant registering one's land under another household.[22] The latter was often referred to as fraudulent trusteeship (*kuei-chi*), since the trustee household need not, in fact, have had anything to do with the land. If a landowner had sufficient control over the household registers, or sufficient influence among the yamen clerks, he could simply falsify the registers and exempt himself from the *li-chia* obligation. Regardless of who owned the land, a single gentry household could keep thousands of *mou* off the tax rolls. This form of gentry privilege thus accounted for most of the evasion as long as the *li-chia* system was the established means of tax collection.

This particular method of manipulating the registers emphasizes the distinction between the economic and political power of the local elite. Fraudulent trusteeships were not in the interest of the gentry; they were in the interest of people who would usurp gentry privilege for economic gain. A gentry family with broad political influence was not necessarily a big landowner. In fact, the longer the family's tradition of gentry status, the more likely it was to depend on other sources of income, be they bribes, public emoluments, or commercial speculations in which their connections gave them an advantage. Hilary Beattie has shown that by the late seventeenth century the most prominent families could be extremely concerned about the dissolution of their landholdings.[23] With no system of primogeniture to guarantee that an estate remain intact, the most prominent civil servant in the late Ming might retain as little as a hundred *mou* of the ten thousand *mou* estate of a fifth-generation ancestor. The rest of the estate, whether sold to speculators or still belonging to distant relatives, might well be registered

19. *Ta-Ming hui-tien,* 20:19; see Friese, *Das Dienstleistungs-system,* pp. 33–35, 37; Ku Yen-wu, "Sheng-yuan lun" [A discourse on *sheng-yuan*], in *T'ing-lin wen-chi* [Collected prose of (Ku) T'ing-lin] (Peking: Chung-hua shu-chü, 1959), 1:22–26; *T'ai-ts'ang chou-chih,* 8:34; *Ch'ang-lo hsien-chih* [Ch'ang-lo district gazetteer] (1639), 4:46. The Ch'ang-lo gazetteer was edited by Hsia Yun-i.

20. On types of evasion by manipulation of household registers, see Liang Fang-chung, "I-t'iao pien fa," 11–12.

21. On commendation abuses, see Shimizu Taiji, 'Tōken kō" [An examination of *t'ou-hsien*], in *Mindai tochi seidoshi kenkyū* [Studies in the history of the Ming land system] (Tokyo, 1968), pp. 385–405. Also see *T'ai-ts'ang chou-chih,* 5:8b.

22. On the use of trusteeship for evasion, see Shimizu Taiji, "Tōken to kiki no igi" [The meaning of *t'ou-hsien* and *kuei-chi*], and "Mindai ni okeru dento no kiki" [Fraudulent trusteeship of arable land in the Ming], in *Mindai tochi,* pp. 421–459.

23. H. J. Beattie, "Landowning and Great Families in China in the Seventeenth Century: The 'Heng-ch'an so yen' of Chang Ying" (unpublished paper).

under the gentry household in the form of trusteeships. One can imagine many variations on this theme, and it is clear that in such cases the gentry neither benefited from the evasion nor controlled the evaders. The *i-fa* reforms were directed against the misuse of gentry privilege, not against gentry political power. Fiscal reform in general, depending as it did on the cooperation of local bureaucrats and gentry families, must be seen to reflect the interests of the politically influential.

The course of reform up to the Single Whip was toward greater yamen control. The ideal of reformers for over a century had been *kuan-shou kuan-chieh*, and now the *i-fa* reforms sought to end the gentry privilege that stood in the way of its implementation.[24] The reformers were pursuing bureaucratic efficiency, but it was crucial that they not sacrifice gentry influence in the process. They did not fail to recognize the dangers of centralized authority to the gentry–bureaucratic alliance, and the reforms reflected their concern. Rather than push for more bureaucratic control, they managed a compromise between the power of landed wealth and the state. This paradoxical turnabout in the course of reform is explained in part by the distinction between political and economic, or public and private, interests of the influential gentry. But it also reflects a paradox in the classical ideology of the reforms.

INTELLECTUAL CONTRADICTION: CLASSICAL IDEALISM AND PRACTICAL STATECRAFT IN THE IDEOLOGY OF REFORM

The paradox arose from the fundamentalist character of the Tung-lin movement.[25] Born of idealistic dissent at Wu-hsi in 1604, the movement gained political momentum during the second decade of the seventeenth century by capitalizing on the concern of some influential gentry about the

24. See Liang Fang-chung, "I-t'iao pien fa," p. 58; Ch'i Piao-chia, "Ch'en min-chien shih-ssu ta hai shu" [Fourteen great nemeses of the people], *Ch'i Chung-hui kung i-chi* [Posthumous collection of the writings of Ch'i Chung-hui], 1:11b, in *Ch'ien-k'un cheng-ch'i chi* [A collection of writings of loyal ministers] (Taipei: Huan-ch'iu shu-chü, 1966), 30:16444.

25. The best sources in English to date are Heinrich Busch, "The Tung-lin Shu-yuan and Its Political and Philosophical Significance," *Monumenta Serica* 14:1–149; Charles Hucker, "The Tung-lin Movement of the Late Ming Period," in John Fairbank, ed., *Chinese Thought and Institutions* (Chicago: University of Chicago Press, 1957), pp. 132–163; and Ulrich Mam-mitzsch, "Wei Chung-hsien (1568–1628): A Reappraisal of the Eunuch and Factional Strife at the Late Ming Court" (Ann Arbor: University Microfilms, 1968). There is essentially nothing in English on the societies movement. For the basic outlines, see Hsieh Kuo-chen, *Ming-Ch'ing chih chi tang-she yun-tung k'ao* [Examination of the factional movement from Ming to Ch'ing] (Shanghai, 1934; Taipei reprint, 1966); Ono Kazuko, "Minmatsu no kesha ni kansuru ichi kōsatsu" [An inquiry into associations at the end of the Ming], *Shirin* [History grove] 45 (1962), 2:37–67 and 3:67–92; and Jung Chao-tsu, "Shu Fu-she" [Explaining Fu-she], *Pei-ta kuo-hsueh chou-k'an* [Peking University national studies weekly] 1 (1925), 7: 145–150 and 8:173–178. Also see Frederic Wakeman, "The Price of Autonomy: Intellectuals in Ming and Ch'ing Politics, "*Daedalus* (Spring 1972), pp. 35–71.

decline of traditional moral values within the bureaucratic world. This momentum brought it into direct conflict with the most influential members of the imperial household and its eunuch entourage, resulting in the temporary demise of the Tung-lin faction toward the end of the T'ien-ch'i reign (1620–1627). As the Fu-she leader Chang P'u (1602–1641) expanded the movement in the years that followed, the fundamentalist attitudes of the original Tung-lin Academy members continued to dominate. In the 1630s the geographical locus of the movement shifted from Wu-hsi and Peking to several regional political and intellectual centers. Most important were T'ai-ts'ang, then part of Soochow prefecture and home of the Fu-she, and the prefectural city of Sung-chiang, home of the Chi-she. Two of the Chi-she's founders, Ch'en Tzu-lung (1608–1647) and Hsia Yun-i, had met Chang P'u and several other promising young degree candidates in Peking during the height of Tung-lin influence there and vowed to form an alliance to further their ideals. Under their leadership the movement's attitudes toward reform became identified with two intellectual themes: classical idealism and practical statecraft.

The revival of classical idealism, in which the movement played a major role, went hand in hand with the widespread rejection of the most challenging implications of Wang Yang-ming's (1472–1529) intuitionism among Confucianists in the seventeenth century. In fact, there had been two basic types of intuitionism flourishing in the sixteenth century, one radical and the other conservative.[26] The radical branch, called leftist by some modern scholars, placed a high value on reasoning without the aid of classical models. The conservatives, on the other hand, interpreted Wang Yang-ming's doctrines in traditional terms, erasing the distinctions between Wang's concept of knowledge and that of the Sung classicists. As long as intuitionism so thoroughly dominated the intellectual climate, the more radical implications of Wang's thought were largely ignored. But the radical interpretation was capable of fostering attitudes that went beyond the world of reason, and by the end of the century a few extremists began to display their hostility to Confucian values in general on the basis of intuitive understanding. When conservatives began to identify these attitudes with intuitionism in general, the climate changed and classical studies began to come into vogue. The Tung-lin creed explicitly rejected radical intuitionism as a perversion of traditional values.[27]

26. The best discussion in English to date of the varieties of intuitionism and their implications is Wm. Theodore de Bary, "Individualism and Humanitarianism in Late Ming Thought," in de Bary, Self and Society, pp. 145–249. Also see Jung Chao-tsu, Ming-tai ssu-hsiang shih [History of Ming thought] (Shanghai, 1940; Taipei reprint, 1962); Shimada Kenji, Chūgoku ni okeru kindai shii no zasetsu [The frustration of modern thought in China] (Tokyo, 1949); and Hou Wai-lu, Chung-kuo ssu-hsiang t'ung-shih [Comprehensive history of Chinese thought] (Peking, 1960).

27. See Busch, "The Tung-lin Shu-yuan," pp. 114–115; Hucker, "The Tung-lin Movement," p. 146.

The Fu-she charter extended the fundamentalist trend by reviving the concept of "restoring the old" (*fu ku*) in literary style and in education.[28] Thinkers such as Ku Yen-wu (1613–1682), Huang Tsung-hsi (1609–1695), and the orthodox philosopher Lu Shih-i (1611–1671), all of whom took part in the Fu-she movement, continued to look to classical ideals in the early Ch'ing period. The bases for a society built on classical ideals were a subsistence economy, public ownership of land, and participatory local administration. The only true wealth was in the land and its produce, and the wealthiest class should be the governing class. The wealthy were most likely to provide good government, since what was good for them and what was good for the community were the same.

Most social theorists of the time advocated partial restoration of the enfeoffment and well-field systems,[29] trying to make classical ideals relevant to current institutions. In an essay on local administration in his *Ming-i tai fang lu* (A plan for the prince), Huang Tsung-hsi applied his ideals to *i-fa*:

> The yamen functionaries of old were one thing and the yamen functionaries of today are quite another. Of old, the use of government clerks and runners was a good way to keep registers and fix tax schedules. In cases where people would avoid the responsibility, rural householders were chosen to serve. Since Wang An-shih replaced conscription with hiring, those who would evade the responsibility have become functionaries themselves. Therefore, if one would eliminate the harm done by irresponsible functionaries, one should restore conscription; and if one would eliminate the harm done by the functionaries who keep registers and make tax schedules, one should use gentry (*shih-jen*) . . .
>
> In good government one should also consider the role of power. Power may do evil; even though it is formally restricted, there may be no stopping it. But the power that is incapable of doing evil is that power which stops of itself before it needs to be restricted. Conscription of public servants is a sure way to make power incapable of doing evil. Those who dispute this say that after Wang An-shih revised the system, in every generation up to the end of the Sung there were those who wanted to restore conscription but they were unable; was it not that people were upset by conscription? My reply is that the only harm done by conscription was in the case of yamen workers, and this is why Wang An-shih hired professionals to relieve them. But now, when there is no alternative to conscription for such as storehouse and transport workers, should that

---

28. Lu Shih-i, "Fu-she chi-lueh" [Fu-she summary], in *Chung-kuo chin-tai nei-luan wai-huo li-shih ku-shih ts'ung-shu* [Collectanea of historical anecdotes of internal disorder and external catastrophe in China in the modern period] (Taipei, 1966), 1:181. See also Jung Chao-tsu, "Shu Fu-she," and Hsieh Kuo-chen, *Ming-ch'ing chih chi*, 7:152–162.

29. For example, Ku Yen-wu, "Chün-hsien lun" [On the prefectural system], *Ku T'ing-lin wen-chi*, 1:12–17; Lu Shih-i, *Ssu-pien lu chi-yao* [Essentials from a record of thoughts and analyses] (Shanghai: Ts'ung-shu chi-ch'eng ch'u-pien, 1936), chüan 18–19.

which did no harm not be restored? When Sung people wanted to restore conscription, they thought that taxing for salaries was harmful. To this I say that the harm done by taxing for salaries is small, but the harm done by the functionaries is great.[30]

For Huang the classical ideal of participatory administration was still very much a live issue. Yamen functionaries were notorious for their corruption; to make them responsible for keeping the registers was to invite disaster. It was better to increase the responsibility of the local populace, including the gentry, than to apply legal restrictions to yamen activities. To misplace power and then try to control it was simply bad government.

Huang Tsung-hsi was defending a theory, but the administrative reformer had to face the long-confirmed unwillingness of wealthy families to act in the public interest at all. Here was the contradiction. According to classical ideals, the power which the Single Whip would give bureaucrats was badly misplaced, yet no administrator would dream of giving more power to prominent wealthy landowners. Typical of the reform movement's dilemma was Fan Ching-wen's (1587–1644) frequently quoted memorial of 1630. Service obligations had burdened the poor, he wrote, because the wealthy could always avoid conscription.

> Policy makers sympathized and passed the Single Whip reform, converting conscription for services to a standard tax assessment. This method should have provided some relief; but look at the people! Who is it that is not spending all his time racing to keep up with his public obligations; and who is it that is not selling his whole family, emptying his life to make up for public deficits? Implementation of the Single Whip has proceeded apace, but the reform of the wealthy families has not yet begun.[31]

In fact, implementation of the Single Whip had stopped short of giving control to the yamen. When Fan Ching-wen wrote of "the reform of the wealthy families," he meant just that. They would have to be made to co-operate if the Single Whip was to work. The idealistic reformer was caught between the power of the wealthy and the power of the state.

This type of contradiction helped to shape the movement's political philosophy. Along with its emphasis on classical idealism, the movement developed its own method for dealing with administrative problems—statecraft (*ching-shih chi-min*). One of the primary goals of the Fu-she movement was to prepare administrators to find classically consistent solutions to administrative problems, and its greatest contribution toward this end was

30. Huang Tsung-hsi, "Hsu-li" [Yamen functionaries], *Ming-i tai fang lu* [A plan for the prince] (Taipei: Kuang-wen shu-chü, 1965), p. 102.
31. Fan Ching-wen, "Ko ta-hu hsing chao-mu shu" [A memorial on replacing the great households with hired clerks], *Fan Wen-chung chi* [Collected works of Fan Ching-wen], 2:8b, in *Ch'ien-k'un cheng-ch'i chi* [A collection of writings of loyal ministers], 26:14004. See also *Ming-shih*, 78: 828.

the publication of a massive collection of memorials and essays on state problems, the *Ching-shih wen-pien* (Selected essays on statecraft). It appeared in 1638 when Ch'en Tzu-lung, Hsu Fu-yuan (1599–1665), and Sung Cheng-pi selected over a thousand such essays and memorials from among those they and their Chi-she friends had studied over the past ten years.

In his introduction to the collection, the Fu-she leader Chang P'u praised the work as the most significant aid to classical problem-analysis yet to appear.[32] Its editors explained why it was essential for bureaucrats to study statecraft. Hsu Fu-yuan lamented that reformers had helped to erode the Ming founder's institutions by sacrificing integration and consistency for stopgap measures in the interest of administrative efficiency. Such measures were "created by methodology and born of precedent, simple at first but complex in the end. People have made miniscule amendments one at a time, thinking them convenient, until the alterations have become so numerous that both form and content of the ancestral institutions have been perverted. The institutions of our sage founder were once likened to the strands of a rope and to a weaving of threads, this one the warp and that one the woof; obviously they can no longer be."[33] Under the circumstances, he argued, it was necessary to analyze the evolution of the institutions in order to keep them from eroding further. Then "the means by which to mend and save them should be obtainable." The problem was not only that reformers had lost sight of the classical ideal, but that they were lost when pressed for historical analysis. As Sung Cheng-pi put it: "The literati of our era—'clouds in the wind and dew in the moonlight.' They are not lacking in eloquence, but not one in ten writes about statecraft."[34] Ch'en Tzu-lung argued further that historians had tended to obscure the problems by recording words rather than deeds, and that the purpose of history was to show how statesmen dealt with the specific problems of their time. The *Ching-shih wen-pien*, he explained, would also enable historians to "broaden their corpus of facts," providing an analytical tool for administrators and scholars alike.[35]

Through historical analysis of administrative institutions and problems, classical ideals became relevant to fiscal reform. If the institutions of the Ming founder had eroded because reformers had sought efficient solutions to tax problems, statecraft reformers would seek solutions that were classically consistent. The key remained "the reform of the wealthy," because neither the state nor the evaders could be allowed to dominate. Devotion to this principle could lead to some paradoxical stances, and there is no more dramatic example than the Ch'ien Shih-sheng affair of 1636.

Ch'ien Shih-sheng (1575–1652) was the most successful member of a prominent family from Chia-shan, a district in Chia-hsing prefecture just outside

32. "Chang hsu" [Chang P'u preface], in *HMCSWP*, pp. 2–4.
33. "Hsu hsu" [Hsu Fu-yuan preface], in *HMCSWP*, p. 4.
34. "Fan-li" [Precedents], in *HMCSWP*, p. 6b.
35. "Ch'en hsu" [Ch'en Tzu-lung preface], in *HMCSWP*, p. 7b.

Sung-chiang.[36] He placed first in the palace examination in 1613 and entered the Hanlin Academy, becoming in effect a candidate for grand secretary, or privy councillor. Although he avoided factional politics himself, his brother was purged as a Tung-lin sympathizer in the 1620s and his nephew was one of the original Fu-she clique, along with Hsia Yun-i.[37] The Ch'ien clan dominated the Fu-she movement in Chia-hsing, and Hsia Yun-i himself married his only son into Shih-sheng's branch.[38] Ch'ien finally became a grand secretary in 1633, giving the Fu-she a much needed sympathizer in the inner council of imperial advisors. Such an advance could not be taken lightly, but Ch'ien resigned at the peak of his career in protest to a proposal that the state confiscate the land of the wealthy families of Kiangnan.

The issue arose when the Ch'ung-chen emperor, who was extremely active in state affairs and even-handed in his approach to factional intrigue, turned to a new source for policy advice in 1635. Skirting around the civil bureaucracy and the imperial household, he singled out the memorials of one Ch'en Ch'i-hsin, a lowly military *chü-jen*, for special attention.[39] These memorials attacked the civil service itself as representative of an ineffectual intellectual elite, and advocated abolition of the examination system.[40] At the height of the commotion surrounding these radical proposals, another military *chü-jen* by the name of Li Chin memorialized that in order to meet financial exigencies the state should demote all the gentry of Kiangnan to commoner status and reclassify their land as state property (*kuan-t'ien*). Because of the emperor's campaign to encourage proposals from outside the bureaucracy, the chief grand secretary, Wen T'i-jen, decided to let the memorial pass on to the emperor himself. Ch'ien Shih-sheng was enraged. Refusing to submit to Wen T'i-jen's politically circumspect advice that he should say nothing, because the emperor would never accept such a proposal anyway, Ch'ien wrote out his rebuttal in the heat of emotion and delivered it directly to the emperor. His argument went like this:

> According to the text, Mr. Li would have the names of all the gentry and the powerful families (*hao yu*) reported to the authorities, and then implement a plan to strip them of their wealth and status. This is the sort of recklessness in government that characterizes the darkest of ages. If it were in the pages of history one could hardly bear to cast eyes upon it, and now one should dare to spread it out for your own sagely perusal! The brashness of mean men that goes so far can only be termed mali-

36. For a biography of Ch'ien Shih-sheng and a brief account of the affair, see *Ming-shih*, 251:2846. On the Ch'ien family, see P'an Kuang-tan, *Ming-Ch'ing liang tai Chia-hsing ti wang-tsu* [Clans of Chia-hsing in the Ming and Ch'ing dynasties] (Shanghai, 1947), pp. 24–25.

37. Wu Shan-chia, *Fu-she hsing-shih chuan-lueh* [Biographical summaries of the Fu-she name list], 5:13–32.

38. Kuo Mo-jo, *Li-shih jen-wu* [Historical personalities] (Shanghai, 1950), p. 131.

39. See Ku Ying-t'ai, *Ming-shih chi-shih pen-mo* [Topical accounts from Ming history] (Taipei: Taiwan Commercial Press, 1956), 72:114 ff.

40. Lu Shih-i, "Fu-she chi-lueh," 3:227–234.

ciously slanderous and insensitively self-aggrandizing. It would alarm the soothsayers, and it would have no place in your sagely era.

When he writes that among the gentry and the powerful families the biggest are worth millions, the middling are worth hundreds of thousands, and those worth tens of thousands are beyond enumeration, your minister does not know to what he is referring. To take issue in the case of Kiang-nan, the number of *mou* owned by wealthy families, gentry and commoner alike, will suffice as a rebuttal. In broad terms, those in the hundreds account for six or seven tenths, those in the thousands account for three to four tenths, and those in the tens of thousands are one or two in a thousand. If this is the case for Kiangnan, one can imagine the other provinces. But to speak of hundreds of thousands and millions—even the wealth of a formidable state should not be so great. This is vacuous nonsense! More-over, what he finds disgusting about the wealthy is that they consolidate control over the little people and cheat their fellow villagers. But for there to be wealthy familes in the provinces is also beneficial to the little people.

Here follows a long discourse on how the wealthy protect the poor. They lend them money and provisions in times of need, spring to their defense when bandits appear, manage public works, and so on. Without the wealthy, he argued, the little people would be poorer still.

The *Rites of Chou* lists twelve policies for avoiding economic calamity, and first among them is conservation of wealth. But now there are military shortages, and the blame comes to rest on the wealthy; there is talk of confiscating their estates and their profits, of destroying their heritage. Such a thing was beyond even Ch'in Shih-huang and Han Wu-ti. It is absurd.

At this time all across the country, from the north and west and even down to the edge of the Yangtze delta, the emergence of local insurgents from their lairs is leaving no place at peace. Only those few prefectures of Kiangnan are still undisturbed by the malcontents. And in the areas afflicted with insurgency, only one or two gentry and a few commoners join with officials to protect their stranded cities. Just sound out such a policy and fear will rise in every quarter. This is the way to cause the rootless and reckless elements to take over and bring hardship to the wealthy. This is the way to transform all the gentry and other powerful men, the wealthy traders and big-time merchants, from one end of the country to the other, into poor folk. If it is not rooted out, all the people of the country will become rootless insurgents. If it is not stopped, the mak-ings of a great insurrection will surely come of it.[41]

41. The complete text of Ch'ien's memorial is recorded in *Chia-hsing Ch'i-chen t'iao-k'uan* [Items concerning Chia-hsing in the T'ien-ch'i and Ch'ung-chen reign periods], 4a:34–35. The explanation of the circumstances under which he presented it is based on his personal

Propriety demanded that Ch'ien be dismissed for the impertinence of his remarks, making him a martyr for private wealth and losing the Fu-she its voice with the emperor. The men who had the emperor's ear were attacking the politically influential gentry, equating gentry influence with landed wealth. Ch'ien paradoxically denied this equation while still defending the wealthy. He was surely aware that the wealthy families of Kiangnan evaded the responsibilities he claimed they shouldered. But he also realized how disastrous it would be to alienate them. There was simply no alternative but to accept the power of the wealthy until they could be made responsible. In that sense Ch'ien was being completely consistent with the ideals of the movement, and in fact defending its intentions to reform the wealthy families. Meanwhile the movement was devising its own solution for dealing with tax evasion, and Hsia Yun-i was about to apply it in his *i-fa* reform in Ch'ang-lo.

DENYING THE CONTRADICTION: A MAGISTRATE APPLIES HIS IDEALS TO FISCAL ADMINISTRATION

Hsia Yun-i had passed the provincial examination in Chekiang in 1618. During the next two decades he devoted himself to his studies and to the scholarly and literary activities of the Chi-she. Finally in 1637 he passed the palace examination and assumed the position of magistrate of Ch'ang-lo. Five years of service there earned him recognition as one of the outstanding administrators of the realm. His career, like those of many of his closest friends and relatives, ended abruptly when the Manchus invaded. He committed suicide after a brief, unsuccessful attempt at resistance in 1645.[42] Although he was remembered chiefly for his Chi-she activities and his martyrdom, he must have regarded his tenure as magistrate as the high point of his life. By the late 1630s the Fu-she coalition was strong enough to place favored bureaucrats in many positions. Hsia's influence might have won him a position of prestige in Peking, but he accepted a lesser post in which he could actually execute reforms on the statecraft model at the level closest to the people. In Ch'ang-lo he had the basis for a solid working relationship with gentry families. One young bureaucrat from Foochow prefecture had contributed to the *Ching-shih wen-pien* project, and Ch'ang-lo itself claimed ten Fu-she associates.[43] Such connections were essential if a magistrate intended to implement reforms, and Hsia set about reforming immediately.

The precedent for Hsia's reform was the development of a system called

---

note, which is appended to the text. The *Ming-shih* and *Ming-shih chi-shih pen-mo* accounts reflect the desire of early Ch'ing historians to place the blame for Ch'ien's dismissal on Wen T'i-jen and the anti-Tung-lin faction.

42. See *Ming-shih*, 277:3113, and Kuo Mo-jo, *Li-shih jen-wu*. On Hsia's role in the Chi-she, see Hsieh Kuo-chen, *Ming-Ch'ing chih chi*, pp. 187–204.

43. Compare Wu Shan-chia, *Fu-she hsing-shih chuan-lueh*, 7:1–7, and "Fan-li," in *HMCSWP*, p. 14.

chün-t'ien chün-i (equal fields and equal service) in Chia-hsing and Hu-chou prefectures in northern Chekiang in the sixteenth century. The system had been proposed as a means for overcoming inequities in Soochow and Sung-chiang prefectures as well. The editors of the *Ching-shih wen-pien* had included one such proposal, a memorial by Huang T'ing-hu. According to Huang, *chün-t'ien* meant distributing the entire obligations tax quota (*i*) of a given district evenly over all the taxable land of the district, allowing only limited cash exemptions for an approved list of gentry households. *Chün-i* meant giving each of the geographical subdivisions of the district the responsibility of administering the tax. This would "eliminate the complications that arise from the yamen's handling of administrative details."[44] In other words, the landowners themselves, including the gentry, would control their own registers, but they would also be held responsible for tax deficits. Hsia selected these principles from the *chün-t'ien chün-i* model and made the compromises he deemed necessary to implement them in his own magistracy.

The ability to compromise without losing sight of his principles characterized Hsia's success in this reform. He needed the cooperation of the local gentry in restricting gentry privilege. He also needed to relieve the *li-chang* of duties of tax collection without losing revenue.[45] The tax structure which he confronted upon his arrival in Ch'ang-lo was based on a Foochow prefectural reform of 1572. At that time the *li-chang*'s function of *ts'ui* had already been legally eliminated. New land registers had replaced the old household records, and the district's tax quotas were distributed among 110 geographical subdivisions of the district, called *t'u*. But this was as far as the reform had proceeded. Although each *t'u* was further divided into ten units which retained the name *chia*, these *chia* were in fact nothing but the basic units of the old *li-chia* structure. They were units of households, not of land, and the distribution of land among them was quite uneven. The member households of the *chia* continued to serve as headmen and share the responsibilities of tax administration in rotation. Furthermore, the *i* tax, or obligations quota, was still assessed in terms of *ting*, or able-bodied males. The *ting* quota for Ch'ang-lo was quite large, amounting to 10,060 taels in all. This quota was distributed over a total of 23,293.5 *ting* units at the time of the reform.[46] In other words, each *ting* was assessed at .405 taels. By way of comparison, the land tax

44. *HMCSWP*, 503:1–8.

45. Other magistrates faced the same problems, and their solutions were often just stopgap measures. In Chia-ting, Soochow, for example, 170,000 *mou* of land previously hidden by fraudulent trusteeships had been added to the household registers toward the end of the Wan-li period, but by the 1630s, it was hidden once more and magistrates had taken to making up the difference by raising the levies and adding new *ting* to the registers. See *Chia-ting hsien-chih* [Chia-ting district gazetteer] (1880), 4:41b.

46. *Ch'ang-lo hsien-chih*, 4:11b–13. (See note 18.) The *li-chia* obligation had been converted to silver as "*kang-yin*," a common feature of the Single Whip in Fukien. The *ssu-ch'ai* obligations were assessed separately, but were collected in a lump sum of silver on the basis of *ting*.

quotas were 8,560 taels silver and 2,234 piculs of rice. Clearly, half the district's tax quotas had not yet been attached to the land at all.

Hsia's reformed system continued to use the existing *t'u* units, and converted the *chia* into geographical subdivisions. These new divisions were called *chün-chia* (standard or equal *chia*). Technically a *chün-chia* was a unit of arable land making up one-tenth of a *t'u* and assessed for a standard amount of *i* tax. In fact, allowing for small differences in the quality of the land, each *chün-chia* contained about two hundred *mou*.[47] The completely reformed system was to include 1,100 *chün-chia* in all. If the *ting* quotas were distributed evenly among them, each *chün-chia* would be worth 8.5 taels in *i* tax and about 200 *mou* of land tax each year.[48] In this way it would realize the Single Whip's intention of attaching all levies to the land.

Implementing the new system of registration was, of course, the biggest problem. Hsia's intention was that it be implemented gradually. Retaining the existing *t'u* quotas and allowing the old *chia* and the new *chün-chia* to function simultaneously, he guaranteed that revenues would increase as implementation progressed. The tax quota was fixed for any given *t'u*, then distributed among the *chia* on the basis of the old registers. Each time one or

47. *Ch'ang-lo hsien-chih*, 4:36–39.
48. Ibid., 4:1–13b. The figures may be summarized as follows:

Total cultivated land		224102.7 *mou*
Land Tax Quota		
kuan-t'ien mi	3220.336 piculs	
min-t'ien mi	9598.628 piculs	
Total	12818.964 piculs	
Converted to silver	10584.584 piculs	
Payable in silver		8560.481 taels
Payable in kind		
to prefectural granary	144.424 piculs	
to district granaries	2089.956 piculs	
Total	2234.380 piculs	
Total *ssu-ch'ai* quota in silver		10060.329 taels

If all categories were evenly distributed on the land, the quotas would be:

Land tax in silver.... 8560.481 taels/224102.7 *mou* = .038 taels per *mou*;
Land tax in kind .... 2234.380 piculs/224102.7 *mou* = .010 piculs per *mou*;
Obligations quota ...10060.329 taels/224102.7 *mou* = .045 taels per *mou*.

This would mean a total of less than .1 tael per *mou*. In Chia-hsing prefecture one *mou* of rice land yielded from two to three piculs of rice, and rice brought about one tael per picul. See Ts'ing Yuan, "Aspects of the Economic History of the Kiangnan Region during the Late Ming Period, ca. 1520–1620" (Ann Arbor: University Microfilms, 1969), 17–18. If the yield in Ch'ang-lo was similar and if the tax conversion rate of .81 taels per picul reflected the value of rice crops, then the total tax should have been about 4 to 5½ percent of the gross value of a rice crop and considerably less of a cash crop.

a group of households agreed to register as much as one-tenth of the land of that *t'u* (about 200 *mou*) as a *chün-chia*, the *t'u* was reorganized. The *chün-chia* registers included only those households which owned land in the new *chün-chia*, while the land which was not registered in *chün-chia* continued to be attached to households in the old *chia* units. Each reorganization attached 8.5 taels (the *ting* quota for a *chün-chia*) of *i* tax to the land. Since this land was properly registered, tax revenues were guaranteed. In the remaining old *chia* units, the yamen continued to squeeze however much it could from the headmen. The *chün-chia*, on the other hand, did not have headmen. Tax liability was fixed for each household individually by the new registers, and responsibility for registration and distribution of the quotas within the *chün-chia* was shared by the member households. Hsia called this method of shared responsibility *chün-pan* (equal management).[49]

The *chün-pan* method naturally appealed to those landowners who would not or could not hide behind gentry privilege. It freed them from the arbitrary squeeze of the *li-chia*. Hsia also implemented other reforms in payment procedures which further protected properly registered households from extortion.[50] All this encouraged the cooperation of those who suffered under the old *li-chia* system and those who would not seek to evade their taxes under an equitable system. But the real evaders, of course, would not submit to *chün-chia* registration as long as they could continue to hide behind gentry exemptions. Dealing with the wealthy required a different approach.

Hsia's campaign against the evaders demonstrates clearly how the gentry-bureaucratic alliance could work toward reform. It also shows where the reformers felt the interest of the gentry should lie. The key to Hsia's attack was his enlistment of gentry support against the usurpers of gentry privilege. Legal exemptions under the Ming code were quite small; the universal exemption which gentry enjoyed under the existing system was extralegal. Hsia decreed a new schedule which increased legal exemptions dramatically for those members of the gentry most likely to have an interest in the bureaucracy. In terms of the amount of land that would be exempted, the exemption for government students (*sheng-yuan* and *chien-sheng*) increased only from 30 to 50 *mou,* while for *chü-jen* holding office it increased from 30 to 300 *mou.* For *chin-shih* in lesser bureaucratic posts, it increased from as little as 45 *mou* to 400. The maximum exemption was fifty taels, for *chin-shih* with civil service rank five or above, and this was about the equivalent of 625 *mou* of tax quotas at the time of the reform. The increases for higher ranking bureaucrats were not great, but for lesser provincial officials they were as much as 520 *mou.*[51] Hsia's schedule of exemptions thus clearly distinguished between the *sheng-*

49. *Ch'ang-lo hsien-chih,* 4:48.
50. Ibid., 4:36.
51. Ibid., 4:49. The old exemptions had been calculated in piculs and *ting;* the new ones were fixed in silver. But to describe them in the terms most meaningful to a landowner facing

yuan, many of whom were notorious for abusing gentry privilege,[52] and the lower-ranking bureaucratic gentry, all of whom were involved in administration themselves. It encouraged the cooperation of the active bureaucratic gentry by allowing them ample exemptions, while it greatly restricted the amount of land that gentry privilege could keep off the tax rolls. In short, the reformer was not attacking the gentry's privilege per se; he was splitting its political and economic interests.

Hsia was also careful not to blame the gentry directly for evasion. His approach to the subject of "trusteeships" was diplomatic:

> The earth in Ch'ang-lo is barren and the people are poor. For the number of households, the government students (*sheng-yuan*) are few. Much of the land around them is held in fraudulent trusteeships, and this provides some support for their studies. . . . [But] when there are fraudulent trusteeships there cannot help but be usurpations, and when there are usurpations there cannot help but be extended tax delinquencies. This is why prompting (*ts'ui*) becomes more and more urgent, and the evasions of the students become more and more impossible to follow.

---

chün-chia registration, we have converted the cash values of the exemptions to the amount of land that would be exempted at the current tax rate in the following list:

Conversion factors
1 picul (pls) = .8 taels (tls)
1 *ting* = .4 taels
Total tax quota = .08 taels per *mou*. (See above, note 48.)

Status	Old schedule in pls; ting	Cash value in tls	Land equivalent in mou	New schedule in tls (increase)	Land equivalent in mou (increase)
sheng-yuan, or chien-sheng	2; 2	2.4	30	4 (+1.6)	50 (+20)
kung-sheng	2; 2	2.4	30	8 (+5.6)	100 (+70)
kung-sheng bureaucrat	2; 2	2.4	30	16 (+13.6)	200 (+170)
chü-jen bureaucrat	2; 2	2.4	30	24 (+21.6)	300 (+270)
chin-shih, low rank	3; 3	3.6	45	32 (+38.4)	400 (+355)
chin-shih, 6A provincial	6; 6	7.2	90	32 (+24.8)	400 (+310)
chin-shih, 6A metropolitan	12; 12	14.4	180	32 (+17.6)	400 (+220)
chin-shih, 5B provincial	7; 7	8.4	105	50 (+41.6)	625 (+520)
chin-shih, 5B metropolitan	14; 14	16.8	210	50 (+33.2)	625 (+290)
chin-shih, 1A metropolitan	30; 30	36.0	450	50 (+14.0)	625 (+175)

52. For example, Ku Yen-wu, "Sheng-yuan lun."

Rather than attack the *sheng-yuan* openly, Hsia excused them as victims of the usurpers. He even allowed an extra exemption of four taels for trusteeships held outside one's own *t'u*. Such an exemption would still keep only fifty *mou* off the rolls, leaving the gentry household liable for the rest.[53]

In sum, Hsia's reform coaxed and coerced the locally powerful into a new form of registration while it guaranteed increasing revenues during the transition. Smaller landowners submitted eagerly to escape the pressure of the rotation system and share the responsibility for a small, fixed amount of land. Hsia first tried his responsibility-sharing plan in select *t'u* where payment had been slowest, and he found that they began paying promptly.[54] As for medium landowners, one could register an estate of two hundred *mou* as a *chün-chia* in itself, becoming responsible for payment of that unit's quota without incurring liability for another man's land. In one case an exempt estate became two *chün-chia*. In another some "military surplus" land became a *chün-chia*. In a third an estate formerly assessed as a single *chia* by special arrangement now became two *chün-chia*.[55] Bit by bit the registration progressed.

It is instructive to note Hsia's choice of words. His unit of registration was based on the land, but he called it *chün-chia*. *Chia* were groups of people, and the people of the *chia*—even if it was only a single landowner—were in charge of their registers and their quotas. He revised the registration system in order to "affix the service obligations" on the land.[56] These obligations (*ts'ui, shou,* and *chieh*) were the functions of the old *liang-chang* and *li-chang*. As they reverted to the *chün-chia*, the process by which the taxpayers met their quotas was called *tzu-ts'ui tzu-chieh* (self-prompting and self-delivery), clearly indicating that responsibility for distribution of quotas and conversion of goods to silver belonged to the *chia* rather than the yamen.[57] His term was in contrast to the more common *kuan-shou kuan-chieh* of Single Whip vocabulary. Conversion had first been assigned to the silversmiths and then to the clerks in the treasury, "but there was no overcoming the corruption in either case. There was nothing to do but make it a local obligation (*li-i*)."[58] In his own eyes, his reform must have brought fiscal institutions a step back toward the original ideal of participatory administration.

All this reflected the same attitude that Huang Tsung-hsi expressed in his essay on yamen functionaries. Some administrative responsibility simply had to remain with the landowners. Before the *i-fa* reforms, responsibility was not fixed sufficiently to enable the yamen to press its tax claims. If responsibility had been fixed on the state, then the yamen would have had the final word in tax disputes. But without strict legal controls, the notoriously corrupt func-

---

53. *Ch'ang-lo hsien-chih*, 4:46a-b.
54. Ibid., 4:48.
55. Ibid., 4:44–46.
56. Ibid., 4:40.
57. Ibid., 4:49.
58. Ibid., 4:36.

tionaries would have had free rein to speculate in claims of tax liability and even ownership. Strict legal controls would mean greater centralization of power and less gentry influence. The *chün-chia* system fixed responsibility on the owners. In any dispute over tax liability or ownership, the burden of proof rested on them. On the other hand, splitting the land up into standard-sized units for registration meant that functionaries could not win false claims unless the owners were remiss. The reform balanced the power of wealth against the power of the state, making further centralization unnecessary. Hsia Yun-i had found a classically consistent solution which was in the interest of both bureaucratic efficiency and gentry influence.

RESOLVING THE CONFLICT: THE LOCAL ELITE FINDS
A VALVE TO RELIEVE IMPERIAL PRESSURE

Before the Fu-she movement could implement similar reforms in Soochow and Sung-chiang, the heartland of gentry power and tax evasion, the Manchus invaded, sweeping away the movement's complex political structure. Many leaders, like Hsia Yun-i, Ch'en Tzu-lung, and Hsu Fu-yuan, died in active resistance or committed suicide. Some, like Sung Cheng-pi, did join the Ch'ing civil service, but the movement's influence in the highest bureaucratic levels was severely curtailed. The political networks of the late Ming were well enough developed to allow local gentry groups to govern appointments to local and provincial posts.[59] The same networks placed friends and relatives in censorial and imperial advisory posts in Peking. Local and provincial officials helped the networks' candidates reach the *chin-shih* examinations, and friendly central officials judged the local officials' administrative performances.[60] In the event of conflict between local officials and gentry, the latter could appeal to political allies who were capable of bringing considerable pressure upon the official in question.[61] In 1645 all this came to

59. I shall describe the extent of family and factional influence on appointments during the late Ming in a future study. Here are a few relevant examples. Collaboration between Fu-she leaders in T'ai-ts'ang and the magistrate, Liu Shih-tou, who was a Fu-she associate, brought charges of subversion against the group in the 1630s. See Lu Shih-i, "Fu-she chi-lueh," chüan 4. A later T'ai-ts'ang magistrate, Ch'ien Su-yueh, was also a Fu-she associate. He and Chang Ts'ai published a new edition of the local gazetteer including many of their own essays on local administrative problems. See *T'ai-ts'ang chou-chih*. Ch'ien Mei, the new magistrate of Chia-ting in 1644, was the seventeen-year-old son of Ch'ien Chan, a charter member of the original Fu-she group. Ch'ien Chan had married a daughter to Hsia Yun-i's son, and Hsia Yun-i had married a daughter to a son of Hou Ch'i-tseng. The Hous were the most prominent Fu-she family in Chia-ting. (See below, note 95.) Hou T'ung-tseng, Ch'i-tseng's elder brother, had also received an appointment in the Ch'iens' native prefecture of Chia-hsing with the help of two old friends in the Board of Civil Appointments, one of whom was also a native of Chia-hsing. See Hou Yuan-ching, "Nien-p'u" [Chronological biography], 1:16–18b, 3:1, in *Hou Chung-chieh kung ch'üan chi* [Complete works of Hou T'ung-tseng] (1933).

60. Lu Shih-i, "Fu-she chi-lueh," chüan 1 and 2, describes the extent of Fu-she influence in metropolitan appointments and examinations.

61. When Hou T'ung-tseng pressed charges of negligence against an influential Fu-she bureaucrat from Chia-hsing in a murder case involving the man's servant, for example, a

an end. The Manchus beheaded the networks by eliminating their influence
at the highest levels of government and disemboweled them by placing
bannermen in key provincial posts and appointing outsiders of lowly status as
prefects and magistrates. In Kiangnan during the last century of Ming rule,
for example, magistracies had been virtually reserved for *chin-shih* (or highest-
degree-holders) alone. But in the Shun-chih period (1645 to 1661) only one-
quarter of the magistrates of Sung-chiang and Soochow prefectures were
chin-shih, and not even half had passed the provincial examinations. Moreover, nearly three-quarters were from Manchuria or the extreme northern
provinces.[62] Under these conditions tension between gentry and local bureaucrats was sure to mount. One of the most obvious areas of conflict was fiscal
administration, and the most famous incident was the tax-clearance case
(*tsou-hsiao an*) of 1661.

Chinese historians have singled out the tax-clearance case as a paradigm of
Manchu–Chinese conflict.[63] But in the context of fiscal history, it falls into a
pattern established long before the invasion. Pressured to meet their tax
quotas, administrators resorted to force. The local gentry resisted, and the
two sides eventually compromised in the interest of the gentry–bureaucratic
alliance. From our point of view, the Manchus had only aggravated an
existing conflict with their appointments policies. In 1636 the influential
gentry had prevented confiscatory policies before force was applied, predict-
ing loss of support for the Ming state. In 1661 lacking the necessary political
influence to reach the ear of the regents, the gentry failed to prevent such
policies. But once force was applied, their earlier predictions were borne out
and the regents had to back down. The pattern is clear in the development of
fiscal administration leading up to the confrontation.

When the Manchus took over the state apparatus in 1644, they continued
to use the existing *Fu-i ch'üan-shu* registers. They espoused the Single Whip

---

host of influential gentry back in Soochow sent letters urging him to drop the case. See Hou
Yuan-ching, "Nien-p'u," 3:3b. The Fu-she also succeeded in blackballing Soochow prefectural judge Chou Chih-k'uei from bureaucratic service altogether for his refusal to cooperate in the Liu Shih-tou case. (see note 59.)

62. In the century before the conquest, the district of Chia-ting, for example, had only two
magistrates who had not passed the palace examinations. See *Chia-ting hsien-chih*, chüan 10.
Between 1645 and 1661, twenty-six of one hundred magistrates in Soochow and Sung-chiang
prefectures were *chin-shih*; fifty-four had not even passed the provincial exams. Eighteen
magistrates came from outside China proper or were bannermen, and fifty-four came from
the northern provinces of Chihli, Honan, Shansi, Shensi, and Hupei. See *Chiang-nan t'ung-
chih* [Kiangnan provincial gazetteer] (1737), chüan 107–109. Only four of fifty-three prefects in Kiangsu during the Shun-chih period were *chin-shih*, while sixteen had no degree at
all. Only one of six Kiangsu governors was a degree-holder, and the governor-generalship
went exclusively to bannermen after Hung Ch'eng-ch'ou's incumbency from 1645 to 1647.

63. See Meng Sen, "Tsou-hsiao an" [The tax clearance case], *Hsin-shih ts'ung-k'an* [Col-
lected writings of Meng Sen], Ser. I, pp. 1–15; also in *Ming-Ch'ing shih lun chu chi-k'an* [A
journal of writings and discourses on Ming-Ch'ing history] (Taipei, 1965), pp. 434–452. Also
see Hsiao Kung-ch'üan, *Rural China*, p. 127, n. 193; and Ch'ü T'ung-tsu, *Local Government in
China under the Ch'ing* (Cambridge: Harvard University Press, 1962), p. 185.

method of taxation but legalized the old *li-chia* system of collection which was still in use across most of the empire. Once the new regime was established, fiscal administrators began compiling a new edition of the *Fu-i ch'üan-shu* which still would depend on existing local methods of registration and assessment. Wang Hung-tso, the revenue official who headed this project, became president of the Board of Revenue in 1658 to preside over implementation.[64] In the meantime pressure on local officials to meet their tax quotas increased. The first schedule of punishments under the Ch'ing was light. In 1657 it was revised, denying promotions for magistrates who showed a 10 percent tax deficit in their districts.[65] Still the pressure on the magistrate was less than it had been before the conquest, and provincial officials frequently appealed successfully for remissions. Then in 1659, with the publication of the new *Fu-i ch'üan-shu*, the pressure increased dramatically. Each magistrate was required to file a statement of account (*tsou-hsiao ts'e*), listing the names of all gentry and local yamen functionaries whose taxes were in arrears.[66] This set the stage for the crisis of 1661.

The K'ang-hsi regents, under the leadership of Oboi, precipitated the conflict when, scarcely three weeks after the Shun-chih emperor's death, they ordered the boards of revenue and civil appointments to draw up a new set of regulations governing tax deficits.[67] The new regulations, which appeared on March 30, were severe. Any official, from magistrate to governor, who showed a tax deficit was ineligible for promotion. Punishments for prolonged deficits ranged from demotion and transfer to expulsion from the civil service.[68] The regents were determined to wipe out tax evasion by forcing provincial officials to perform. Those officials, lacking political connections among the local gentry, were obliged to attack with only the imperfect registers of the Board of Revenue to help them. In Kiangsu, Governor Chu Kuo-chih indicted 13,517 of the local gentry and 254 yamen functionaries for tax evasion. When his memorial reached the regents on June 28, they ordered the arrest and prosecution of those indicted.[69] The state had directly attacked the prominent families of Kiangnan for the first time since the early Ming.

The reaction in Kiangsu was swift. Popular accounts of the case which have survived of course emphasize the innocence of the accused. We have seen how hopelessly confused the registers were. Once the Ch'ing officials

64. *Ch'ing-shih* [Dynastic history of the Ch'ing], Kuo-fang yen-chiu-yuan ed. (Taipei, 1961), 122:1463–1464; also see *Ta-Ch'ing hui-tien* [Compendium of Ch'ing institutional law] (1690), 24:20.

65. *Ta-Ch'ing hui-tien*, 25:8b, 10b.

66. Ibid., 24:20.

67. *CSL*:SC, 1:16b; quoted in Meng Sen, "Tsou-hsiao an," pp. 434–435; see also *Yen-t'ang chien-wen tsa-chi* [Miscellaneous collection of observations by Yen-t'ang], T'ung shih ed. (Shanghai, 1911), pp. 34, 35b.

68. *CSL*:SC, 2:1b; *Ta-Ch'ing hui-tien*, 25:13.

69. *CSL*:SC, 3:2b.

alienated the gentry and yamen functionaries, there could be no hope of meeting tax quotas. Even before the actual indictments a group of gentry had begun to turn the screws in the other direction, bringing charges of fraud against one magistrate and getting him dismissed. Chu Kuo-chih had the accusers executed, fearing they would implicate him next. With that they became martyrs and the conflict intensified. The regents could hardly have wished for this kind of confrontation. By midwinter the governor had abandoned his post and was summarily demoted, and by the following summer the regents had officially pardoned all those accused of tax evasion, whether already detained or still awaiting arrest.[70]

The fiscal crackdown reflected the hard-line approach of the regents toward affairs of state in general. Oboi's faction had advanced the hard line with respect to Manchu involvement in Chinese bureaucratic affairs.[71] When Oboi became regent he applied it to fiscal policy as well. Prior to the Shun-chih emperor's death, Wang Hung-tso and civil appointments minister Sun T'ing-ch'üan had been the chief advocates of leniency toward officials with tax deficits.[72] By May of 1661, their adversaries prevailed in the boards of revenue and civil appointments,[73] and both Wang and Sun took leaves of absence when the tax clearance case broke.[74] But the hard line faltered rapidly. On September 1, Wang Hung-tso was recalled because the Board of Revenue was "in a state of confusion,"[75] and by the end of the year the regents had abandoned plans to revive the notorious late Ming surtaxes and granted emergency tax remissions to no fewer than twenty-nine districts for "bad crops."[76] The softer line reached Kiangsu in the spring, when Han Shih-ch'i replaced Chu Kuo-chih as governor with a mandate not to perform but to reform.[77] Han arrived with instructions to act on a proposal offered by an obscure official in the Board of Revenue.[78] According to the proposal it was irregularities in registration rather than willful gentry evasion that caused tax deficits. Landowners were at the mercy of whoever controlled the registers. These manipulators, gentry and nongentry, had increased the number of fraudulent trusteeships "until fully half the land reg-

---

70. *Yen-t'ang*, p. 38b.

71. Robert Oxnam, "Policies and Factionalism in the Oboi Regency, 1661–1669" (Ph.D. thesis, Yale University, 1969).

72. *Ch'ing-shih*, 251:3809; 264:3895.

73. *CSL*:SC, 2:17, 2:26b. On Chu Chih-pi, the hard-liner in Revenue, and his debate with Wang Hung-tso, see *Ch'ing-shih*, 251:3809, 264:3898.

74. *CSL*:SC, 3:3b, 3:14. Sun had also run afoul of Oboi on his choice of a posthumous name for the Shun-chih emperor at the very outset of the regency. See *Ch'ing-shih*, 264:3895.

75. *CSL*:SC, 4:2.

76. *CSL*:SC, 5:19b, 21.

77. See *Man-chou ming ch'en chuan* [Biographies of eminent Manchu officials], 19:34. Han received honorary titles ranging as high as president of the Board of Works, partly on the basis of his reputation as the governor who managed to meet the province's tax quotas.

78. The memorial is summarized in *Lou hsien-chih* [Lou district gazetteer] (1788), 7:6–7; and *Sung-chiang fu-chih* [Sung-chiang prefectural gazetteer] (1817), 27:24–26b; also see *CSL*: SC, 3:15b; *Chiang-nan t'ung-chih*, 76:10.

istered as gentry land is a mirage." The way to eliminate tax deficits, the argument went, was to implement a system of registration called *chün-t'ien chün-i*. The old statecraft solution to the conflict was thus revived.

First to implement the reform was Lou district, Sung-chiang. The local magistrate, Li Fu-hsing, was a *chü-jen* of 1646 from Wu-ting, Shantung. Less of an outsider than most Ch'ing appointees, Li began consulting the local gentry about the tax problem immediately upon his arrival in 1664. A group of local "students" eventually devised the plan which Li implemented.[79] The reformers also depended on the cooperation of a local yamen clerk by the name of Ma T'ien-ch'i, whose faithfulness to the reform is extolled in the local gazetteers. This little group was not without its detractors. Opponents of the clique managed to have Li dismissed in 1667 on charges of maladministration of waterworks, and "those who would subvert the law" then launched an attack on Ma T'ien-ch'i. But there was enough local support for Ma and the reform to weather this crisis, and the implementation of *chün-t'ien chün-i* continued.[80]

Like its antecedents, the Lou reform organized the district's land into geographical units of equal size.[81] Lou district's land units, called *chün-t'u*, included around 280 *mou* each, corresponding roughly to Ch'ang-lo's *chün-chia*.[82] Within the *chün-t'u* the rotating headman duties were eliminated. Li, like Hsia Yun-i, would have to pay special attention to registration in order to guarantee that the transition from *li-chia* to *chün-t'u* be made without loss of revenue. Under the new Ch'ing system the magistrate had to forward an annual statement of accounts (*tsou-hsiao ts'e*). The reformers would have to account for all the land in the district while they changed the registers, and they would gain nothing by transferring mistakes from the old registers to the new. They solved the problem by keeping both sets of registers active, making sure that any given field appeared in only one place but that every field was listed either in an old *t'u* or a new *chün-t'u*. First they surveyed the land and registered each field by number. Then they took the old *t'u* household registers and reorganized them, attaching households to the fields which the

79. *Chiang-nan t'ung-chih*, 7:5b; *Sung-chiang fu-chih*, 27:28b. Ch'ü T'ung-tsu, *Local Government*, 327, n. 81, cites "Sung chün chün-i ch'eng shu" [The complete documentation of the equitable service obligation system in Sung-chiang] as the source of information for his example of magistrate-gentry cooperation involving Li Fu-hsing and "a *chü-jen* adviser." This source was not available to me when I made the present study. There is a copy in the Harvard-Yenching Rare Book Collection. It contains a number of articles dating from 1667 to 1684 and a few brief comments dating as late as 1726. Most have to do with the method of registration, and the most important of these are reprinted or excerpted in the gazetteers. *Lou hsien-chih*, 11:6, lists *Li kung chün-i ch'üan-shu*, an anonymous collection of documents concerning *chün-i*. *Sung-chiang fu-chih*, 27:24, cites *Chün-i ch'eng-shu* as the source for K'o Sung's memorial.

80. *Lou hsien-chih*, 19:11b, 25:14b.

81. The following outline is based on Li Fu-hsing, "Chün pien t'iao-i" [Itemized case for equitable registration], in *Sung-chiang fu-chih*, 27:29b–31b; see also *Lou hsien-chih*, 7:9–10.

82. 841,432 *mou*/3000 *chün-t'u* = 280.5 *mou/chün-t'u*. Compare Ch'ang-lo: 203.6 *mou/chün-chia*.

registers claimed they owned. The landowners were asked to verify their ownership. Once they did this, the fields were removed from the old registers and listed in new ones, so that all the verified landholdings of a single household were combined in the new listings. When the total acreage of verified land reached 280 *mou*, allowing for differences in quality of the land, the properly registered land became a new *chün-t'u*. Meanwhile the land which was not verified continued to be listed under households in the old *t'u* registers. In this way there was no land which was not registered under households, and Li could claim that "there is no untaxed land."

Exemptions were still the crucial problem. On this point Li's reform was less generous than Hsia's. It eliminated exemptions from service obligations entirely. In fact such a move was less dramatic than it might seem, since service obligations in Sung-chiang were minimal. In Ch'ang-lo the *i* tax in silver averaged out to .045 taels per *mou*, amounting to half the total assessment. In Lou district it was an insignificant .0012 taels per *mou*, while the land tax was nearly six times that of Ch'ang-lo.[83] Hsia's limited exemptions had been a compromise encouraging gentry cooperation; such a move would have been meaningless in Sung-chiang. But in both cases eliminating the privilege of avoiding headman duties was the key to taxing gentry land.

An anonymous essay praising Li's registration reform as one of the most significant works of statecraft in the history of the prefecture recalls the debates of the 1630s. "Land-holding people are good people," it proposed. "When equitable registration was implemented, they accepted it gladly. Regardless of how much land they had, it was all declared openly and the irregularities by which service obligations had been avoided ceased." The reform rendered useless the corrupt practices of "local villains" and yamen

---

83. *Lou hsien-chih* does not include tax figures for the early period. The total amount of *shu-t'ien*, or prime tax land, was 841,432 *mou* when Lou *hsien* was carved out of Hua-t'ing district in 1656. The total number of *ting* was 44,406. Compare *Lou hsien-chih*, 6:2, 6:12. The *ting* quota for Lou district in the Yung-cheng period (1723–1735) was .0012 taels per *mou*. See *Chiang-nan t'ung-chih*, 69:31. The 1737 figures include Lou and Chin-shan district quotas. Chin-shan was carved out of Lou district in 1724. See *Chiang-nan t'ung-chih*, 69:30–33. If we assume that the tax quotas did not increase greatly between 1661 and 1737, we may estimate the tax for Lou district as follows:

Land tax in silver........115,377.73 taels
Land tax in kind ....111,913.73 piculs
Obligations quota .... 1,009.89 taels

Distributed evenly throughout the district, they would amount to:

Land tax in silver........ 0.137 taels/*mou*
Land tax in kind .... 0.133 piculs/*mou*
Obligations quota .... 0.0012 taels/*mou*

As for the exemptions in terms of *ting*:

Obligations quota .... 1,009.89 taels/44,406 *ting* = 0.023 taels/*ting*.

Compare Ch'ang-lo: .405 taels/*ting*.

functionaries, it asserted, by eliminating the variables on which their tactics had depended.[84] Such a glowing assessment suggests that the wealthy families had now been reformed. The major theme of the body of literature surrounding the reform implies that the gentry had won the registration battle, not lost it. One is tempted to conclude that Chu Kuo-chih's purge had forced the gentry to cooperate and that now they were apologizing for their defeat. But we have seen that Chu himself was the last victim of the purge, and we have also seen that the reform had its parallels before the conquest. In his *Ching-shih wen-pien* essay urging adoption of the Chekiang reforms in Kiangsu, Huang T'ing-hu had asked rhetorically, "If it is said that the gentry stand in the way [in Sung-chiang], does this mean that there are no influential gentry in Chekiang?"[85] The Sung-chiang gentry who finally devised the means to implement *chün-t'ien chün-i* were Huang's heirs in statecraft.

Most prominent among Li Fu-hsing's local gentry advisors was Wu Ch'in-chang, a *chü-jen* of 1639 who lived in retirement in Sung-chiang after the conquest.[86] Wu's family had been active in government service since before 1550.[87] His father, Wu Chia-ying, had also been a *chü-jen* and was one of the *Ching-shih wen-pien*'s many local consultants.[88] Others in the reform group also had ties with the Chi-she. Two were from the lineage of Hsu Fu-yuan; one may even have been his son.[89] Two more were cousins of the Chi-she's historian, Tu Teng-ch'un, who was himself the son of another Chi-she founder.[90] These families had long histories of bureaucratic service—the Hsu's had produced a chief grand secretary a hundred years before. Clearly Li's advisors were more than just intellectual heirs of the Ming reform gentry; they were literally its sons. The forces which drove them to cooperate with Li Fu-hsing were the same forces that had driven their fathers and uncles and grandfathers to cooperate with Ming bureaucrats. Chu Kuo-chih's purge had only demonstrated that neither gentry nor bureaucrat could survive without this cooperation.

84. "Chün pien yao-lueh shu" [An outline of equitable registration], in *Sung-chiang fu-chih*, 27:31b–33b.

85. *HMCSWP*, 503:1–8.

86. *Lou hsien-chih*, 23:2b, 25:16.

87. Ibid., 23:2b. In 1550, Wu's grandfather passed the provincial examination in Peking, indicating that the family already had enough influence to be in the capital.

88. "Fan-li," in *HMCSWP*, p. 16. For Wu Chia-ying, see *Lou hsien-chih*, 24:9.

89. *Lou hsien-chih*, 24:25. Hsu Fu-yuan's biographer relates that after Hsu's death in 1646, a son who had accompanied him to Fukien to participate in the resistance movement returned to Sung-chiang and wrote of his father's experiences. The son's name was Yung-chen, the "*chen*" of which was the same as that in Yun-chen, suggesting that the two were brothers or cousins.

90. Ibid., 24:1b and 25:5b. Chi-ch'un, Heng-ch'un, and Teng-ch'un all share the character "*ch'un*." Wu Shan-chia, *Fu-she hsing-shih chuan-lueh*, 3:10b, also lists Teng-ch'un's brother, Chia-ch'un. Their father, Tu Lin-cheng, a *chin-shih* of 1631, was the grandson of a famous scholar, son of a *chin-shih*, and co-founder of the Chi-she. Chia-ch'un was a *kung-sheng* of 1643; Teng-ch'un was a *kung-sheng* of 1651 and author of "She shih shih-mo" [The societies affair from the beginning to the end]. See Hsieh Kuo-chen, *Ming-Ch'ing chih chi*, p. 187.

THE ALLIANCE REAFFIRMED: SPECULATIONS ON THE BUREAUCRATI-
ZATION OF THE GENTRY

It remains for us to bring together the evidence we have uncovered in the
i-fa reforms and speculate on the pressures which forced the politically influential gentry of the time to cooperate with the bureaucracy. We shall
divide the pressures into four categories—economic, intellectual, social, and
political—and we shall assume that the movement which produced the *i-fa*
reformers saw itself as expressing the interests of the influential gentry as a
whole.

Economic pressure on the gentry of Kiangnan during the late Ming came
from two sources. The first, which was not unique to the period, was the
absence of primogeniture. All land-owning families faced the problem of
economic insufficiency that came with dividing up the land among several
sons who had to seek other forms of income if they were to live as well as the
previous generation. The second was the changing substance and methodology of agriculture. During the Ming period the economy of eastern Kiangsu
became dependent on cotton and textile production. This trend encouraged
speculation in land, managerial landlordism, and the concentration of
landed and commercial wealth in the hands of entrepreneurs.[91] Some scholars
have argued that the more progressive gentry were developing bourgeois
attitudes through economic ventures and that the Single Whip reflected their
interest in freeing the land from feudal obligations.[92] But although the influential gentry clearly felt the pressures of economic growth and the Single
Whip did represent a response to these pressures, there is simply insufficient
evidence concerning the reformers' own sources of income to attribute such
interests to them.[93] Moreover, economic pressure need not have produced a
more progressive gentry. We should keep in mind that while the Single Whip
facilitated the exchange of land and freed it from obligations, the *i-fa* reforms

91. See Fu I-ling, *Ming-tai Chiang-nan shih-min ching-chi shih-t'an* [An investigation of bourgeois economy in Kiangnan in the Ming] (Shanghai: Jen-min ch'u-pan-she, 1957).

92. Wang Fang-chung, "Ming-tai i-t'aio pien ti ch'an-sheng chi ch'i tso-yung" [The
origin and the function of the Ming Single Whip], in Chung-kuo jen-min ta-hsueh Chung-kuo
li-shih yen-chiu shih, ed., *Ming-Ch'ing she-hui ching-chi hsing-t'ai ti yen-chiu* [Studies in the social
and economic characteristics of Ming and Ch'ing] (Shanghai, 1957).

93. The most prominent adherents of the movement did maintain both country estates and
city residences, but we have found no mention of their involvement in or hostility to industry,
trade, or finance. The Fu-she families of Chia-ting, for example, had had country and city
residences for some time. The Hou family had been the chief advocates of both the permanent commutation of grain tribute to silver and private landowners' responsibility for waterworks. See *Chia-ting hsien-chih*, passim. In neighboring T'ai-ts'ang, the Fu-she advocated local
responsibility for military stores, arguing that this would help to encourage the cultivation of
staple crops in place of cotton. See Chang Ts'ai, "Chün-ch'u shuo" [A discussion of military
stores], *Chih-wei t'ang wen-ts'ung* [Extant prose of Chang Ts'ai], 11:18. On balance, the Fu-she
seemed to favor cotton interests and still oppose the commercialization of agriculture. One
should also keep in mind that bureaucratic use of silver was not necessarily beneficial to commercial interests. See Fu I-ling, *Ming-Ch'ing shih-tai shang-jen chi shang-yeh tzu-pen* [Merchants
and commercial capital in the Ming-Ch'ing period] (Peking, 1956), p. 36.

restored a degree of administrative responsibility to landowners and prevented any further encroachment of entrepreneurial wealth on gentry political influence. One reformer's view of the commercialization of his native
Hui-chou is exemplary:

> The city of Hui-chou sits amid a myriad mountains, rather like a rat in a
> cave. The earth is barren, the fields narrow, and not one in ten is able to
> make a living off the land. If one has nothing to feed one's family, how
> can one stand about and watch them die? One is forced to go out and seek
> provisions in distant places. . . . Although the people may handle the
> wealth when they engage in commerce, the wealth is not really their own;
> they borrow it from rich families in distant places and pay interest of 20
> or 30 percent. But when people hold the wealth in their hands it appears
> that it is their own, and it is taken to be the wealth of the people. How the
> people are cheated! This wealth which they handle is not wealth at all!
> It's like a field which a stranger cultivates to feed himself; one morning it
> is taken away. It's like a field floating on the sea. If a field does not belong
> to one but is rented from another, when one loses it one has nothing to
> offer the owner and one loses his life as well.[94]

Even if the author himself depended on commercial wealth, his attitude was
less bourgeois than physiocratic.

The intellectual roots of *i-fa* reform in classical ideals also confirm the conservative outlook of the influential gentry. Statecraft neither diverged from
classical theories with respect to a subsistence economy nor abandoned
traditional ideals with respect to agrarian values. The extreme intuitionism
to which the societies' movement was partly a reaction was clearly more
congenial to commercial interests than was classicism. Li Chih (1527–1602),
the famous iconoclast, symbolized the extreme to which intuitionism could
go, denouncing the tyranny of classical ideals and denying the wisdom of
Confucius himself. For this he paid with his life, and his writings were banned
for all time. Ku Yen-wu spoke for the movement when he wrote, "From
antiquity to the present, of all the petty men who were impudent enough to
reject the sages, Li Chih was the worst." This conscious rejection of intuitionism's challenge was consistent with the interests of the influential gentry.
Statecraft was their alternative to iconoclasm.

The social pressures on the influential gentry were more than just the
traditional ones from competitive status-seekers and the merchant community. The influential group had a special interest in the imperial bureaucracy which was more important than gentry status per se. The group
included members of families which had been serving the government for
over five generations, like Ch'ien Shih-sheng and Hsu Fu-yuan. It also included

---

94. Chin Sheng, *Chin T'ai-shih chi* [Collected works of Chin Sheng], 4:16–17b, in *Ch'ien-
k'un cheng-ch'i chi* [A collection of writings of loyal ministers], 32:17879; see also Fu I-ling,
Ming-Ch'ing shih-tai shang-jen, p. 26.

those with virtually no history of service in the family, like Hsia Yun-i. The social ties among these civil servants guaranteed their influence as a group, and were surely stronger than the bonds of arbitrary social strata determined by degree alone.[95] Established influential families could marry their daughters to bright young men of obscure origin and their sons to influential families outside the district. They could form study societies for civil service candidates excluding the sons of wealthy neighbors. Such activities could not help but incur the enmity of those among their gentry peers who lacked influence beyond their own communities. This enmity added pressures on the influential from within the gentry status group. Since it was their influence which set them apart from the gentry as a whole, this naturally increased their interest in the efficient use of bureaucratic power.

Finally, for the influential gentry social pressures were closely related to political pressures. Gentry political power depended on bureaucratic influence. Prominent gentry families which had built up their influence carefully over several generations could rely on a vast network of connections with other such families to influence local appointments and administrative policies. Politically, the Fu-she movement was just such a network. But there were also other powerful groups which had little or no bureaucratic influence. Among these were those landowners, gentry and nongentry alike, who were excluded from the political networks of the bureaucrats. Such a group might ally with yamen functionaries, local garrison commanders, imperial relatives, or commercial interests to oppose the influential locally. The gentry who did have bureaucratic influence were thus driven politically as well as socially to use the power of the state. Their political interest was divided between gentry and bureaucratic power.

All of these pressures contributed to the *i-fa* reforms. The reformers limited both the privileges of the gentry and the power of the yamen, splitting the economic and political interests of the gentry as a whole and strengthening the alliance between the influential gentry and the state. The influential gentry of the late Ming found political power to be more important than economic power. They could ill afford to risk losing their influence by evad-

95. Preliminary findings based on my own research indicate that prominent gentry families in Chia-ting, with marriage ties reaching into Sung-chiang and Chia-hsing prefectures, were the leaders of the local Fu-she clique, but that only 17 of 38 members had won gentry status or came from gentry families themselves. The Hou family seems to have pursued a policy of continuing marriage ties with one well-established local gentry family on the one hand, while seeking out new alliances outside the district on the other. Of the six male offspring in the generation that came of age in the 1630s, one married a Kung (the traditional alliance); one married a Sun of Chia-ting and Shanghai—a family his grandfather had patronized; one married Hsia Yun-i's daughter; one married a cousin of the Hsia family, a Sheng from Chia-hsing; one married a daughter of Yao Hsi-meng of Ch'ang-chou district; and one married a Ning, whose family I have been unable to trace. Significantly, both Yao Hsi-meng and Hsia Yun-i were men of considerable influence who had risen from obscure circumstances with the help of influential patrons. See Jerry Dennerline, "The Mandarins and the Massacre of Chia-ting: An Analysis of the Local Heritage and the Resistance to the Manchu Invasion in 1645" (Ph.D. thesis, Yale University, 1973).

ing taxes, and they could better use their influence not to accumulate wealth but to control it. Their solution to the tax problem was classically consistent, and it affirmed the gentry–bureaucratic alliance. The Manchu invasion did not fundamentally alter the balance of local power. It eliminated the existing political networks of the influential gentry, but local political adversaries did not gain much in the long run. The influential survived Chu Kuo-chih's purge and helped to restore the alliance with the same kind of solutions their fathers had urged before the conquest.

The reformers succeeded in implementing *chün-t'ien chün-i* in Lou district between 1664 and 1667. The prefect then ordered its implementation throughout Sung-chiang, and in 1674 it became the law for all Kiangsu. By 1684 it was strictly illegal for a magistrate to use the *li-chia* system to collect taxes in Kiangnan.[96]

In the final analysis the *i-fa* reforms succeeded in making the Single Whip method of taxation work, but the "reform of the wealthy families" remained a mirage. Even if the big landowners did enter the tax rolls, they could easily pass on the burden to tenants in the form of higher rents. Not even the idealists believed that the wealthy would sacrifice their own economic interests for the public welfare. As Lu Shih-i put it:

> In ancient times the one who was enfeoffed in the seat of power would bestow a hundred *mou* of farmland upon a citizen. When the citizen was in the prime of life it was granted to him, and when he grew old it reverted to the seat of power. But if latter-day wealthy families were to bestow the land of their forefathers upon the tillers, they would base their tenure on standards of diligence and their rents on considerations of the crops' abundance. The advantages and disadvantages involved in distributing land are things which they learned in their youth; they need not engage in much calculation before their extortions would be beyond measure.[97]

But this perception did not prevent Lu or other idealists from practicing statecraft.[98] Their intention was to work in the interest of good government within an imperfect society. In a more perfect society, like the classical one which Lu Shih-i described, the interests of the wealthy should coincide with the public good. The *i-fa* reformers pursued their goal of a more perfect society by limiting the legal power of the state and the economic power of landowners. They helped perpetuate the gentry–bureaucratic alliance which would enable statecraft to continue the process of restoring classical ideals. But statecraft was a phenomenon of the seventeenth century, and the gentry of succeeding generations were not distinguished by their reform zeal. It has

96. *Chiang-nan t'ung-chih*, 76:13b.
97. Lu Shih-i, *Ssu-pien lu chi-yao*, 19:191.
98. Lu Shih-i was the architect of the plan by which the long-overdue dredging of the Lou River, a major artery in eastern Kiangsu, was finally carried out in 1672. Compare Lu Shih-i, "Lou-chiang t'iao-i" [Itemized case for the Lou River], in *Ti-hsiang chai ts'ung-shu* [Ti-hsiang chai collectanea], with *Chiang-nan t'ung-chih*, 63:23.

been argued that gentry power moved into the administrative towns by the mid-Ch'ing, and that administrators lost touch with their agrarian base.[99] This would have been consistent with increased bureaucratic efficiency and the declining power of landed wealth. Ironically, the i-fa reforms must have accelerated this trend. In effect, the reformers had only engaged in a holding action on behalf of gentry influence. Gentry historians of later times praised them for their ideals, and the imperial bureaucracy lumbered on toward the twentieth century.

99. See John Watt, "The Yamen as a Socio-political System," Conference on Urban Society in Traditional China (Wentworth-by-the-Sea, N.H., 1968).

Local Control
of Convicted Thieves
in Eighteenth-Century China

Fu-mei Chang Chen

Banishment and penal servitude, two of the so-called "five punishments" in Ch'ing China, involved forcibly removing a convicted man from his native place (*yuan-chi*).[1] A less harsh feature of Ch'ing law was its goal of rehabilitating offenders through their forced integration into the society of their native community. Presumably replete with family members, friends, and acquaintances, the criminal's native place was considered ideal for carrying out a policy of supervision and rehabilitation. Nonetheless, very little is known of the treatment of criminals in eighteenth-century China. Were exconvicts and undesirable elements treated like second-class citizens? How much freedom did they enjoy? Was it true that the government would not interfere with private individuals' lives as long as they had not transgressed the law? What techniques and procedures might officials use to control the populace? To answer these questions and to evaluate the effectiveness of local control will no doubt require years of thorough research. By investigating the methods by which thieves were punished and controlled in their native place, this paper takes a small step towards understanding such problems.

There are a number of factors favoring the selection of theft offenders over other types of criminals for this study. First, because theft was a common occurrence, almost every district magistrate had to deal with it. Second, theft tends to have a high rate of recidivism; presumably, effective control and supervision would pay off in combating that crime. Furthermore, unlike other crimes, theft had a wide range of prescribed punishments corresponding to the value of the goods stolen, ranging from sixty blows of the heavy bamboo

1. I wish to acknowledge the help given by Professors Randle Edwards and Frederic Wakeman.

121

to strangulation after the assizes.[2] Actual execution of thieves, however, was rare, and even the punishment of banishment was said to have been infrequently imposed.[3] Thus the government was confronted with the task of controlling a large number of convicted thieves, some of whom were to be reintegrated into the society either as soon as the sentence of beating and canguing was imposed, or immediately after they had served up to three years of penal servitude.

While using the control of thieves as an example for our study of local control of criminals in Ch'ing China, we should bear in mind the limitation of such a study. Since theft seemed to exhibit a high rate of recidivism, theft offenders were probably less amenable to rehabilitation than other criminal offenders. For that reason future research on other types of criminals may reveal a somewhat different mechanism of social control from that depicted in this paper. However, we must not go so far as to assert that convicted thieves were basically not rehabilitable. Even though they had once been stigmatized as bad elements in the society, as long as they truly repented and refrained from violating the law they were to be treated as ordinary citizens. Their right to be free from police harassment was clearly protected by law, and in a 1769 Hupei case this right was upheld by the courts.[4]

The main sources used in this study are the various rules and regulations adopted by the Ch'ing central and local governments prior to the end of the eighteenth century, case reports from the same period, and writings by sundry local officials. Since the records are better preserved and more easily accessible for the Ch'ien-lung reign (1736–1795), that period is covered more fully than others.

CONVICTED THIEVES AS POLICE OR POLICE AIDS

One general provision in the Ch'ing code of 1646 stated:

All robbery and theft offenders who have been tattooed with appropriate characters shall be returned to their place of origin to serve as police aids (*ching-chi*). If they are sentenced to penal servitude, they shall be so returned immediately after they have finished their sentence and shall serve as police aids. However, if they are sentenced to banishment, such duty shall be carried out in the place where they have been banished. Whoever is found guilty of destroying the characters on his tattoo so as to render them illegible shall be punished with sixty blows of the heavy bamboo, and the characters shall be tattooed anew.[5]

2. *Ch'ing code* III, 2069–2071; Staunton, pp. 284–285. For an unsuccessful theft offense, the punishment was fifty blows of the light bamboo.

3. *HTSL*, XIX, 15039, 15087; *TLCA*, ts'e 20, under *pu-wang*, pp. 24–26.

4. *PAHP*, II, 557–566. The *li* in question is found in *Ch'ing code*, IV, 2983; *HTSL*, XIX, 15349.

5. *Ch'ing code*, III, 2319; Staunton, p. 301. According to this provision petty thieves who had

However, this code provision for the systematic enrollment of convicted thieves into the police force actually reveals little about the exact scope of the work of a police aid or the length of his service. Was he ever allowed to remove the tattooed characters if he later repented and became a good citizen? When we trace the origin of this legislation, we learn that it was borrowed verbatim from the Ming code of 1397.[6] In addition, in the Ming ordinance (*Ming-ling*) there is a closely related provision which stated that tattooed thieves should serve as police aids for two years for the first offense and three years for the second offense. However, if they were able to catch either three or more robbers, or five or more thieves, during the period of their police duty, their tattooed characters would be officially removed and their service terminated.[7]

The available Ming records are very sketchy as to the actual enforcement of such regulations. In 1439 the Cheng-t'ung emperor (reigned 1436 to 1449) issued an order that degree-holders who committed bribery, sex offenses, robbery, or theft were to be sent to their place of origin to serve as police aids.[8] Then in 1500 the Hung-chih emperor ordered that musicians who had been found guilty of theft, pickpocketing, or unarmed robbery would receive the same treatment.[9] However, in the late 1500s a Ming code commentator named Lu Chien attributed the rapid rise in the crimes of theft and robbery to the government's failure to enforce the regulations on making police aids out of convicted thieves as well as to its authorizing the removal of the tattooed characters after stipulated conditions were met.[10] In short, the founder of the Ch'ing dynasty adopted the law in spite of the fact that the "tattooed-thief-as-police-aid" institution was no longer in existence. It is more likely that the government did so simply for expediency (as it borrowed most of the Ming code provisions) rather than with the intention of reviving the old system.

That being the case, one wonders if convicted thieves ever served in any capacity connected with Ch'ing police forces. There is one piece of evidence showing that they probably were not asked to be police aids in the seventeenth century. Chu P'ei, a *chin-shih* of 1646 who later rose to be a censor, once

been given the punishment of bambooing in their native place were also apparently required to serve as police aids.

6. *Ta-Ming hui-tien* [Collected statutes of the Ming dynasty], 1587 ed. (Taipei: Tung-nan shu-pao she, 1963), V, 2347. The police aid institution was probably first initiated in the mid-thirteenth century under the Yuan. See *Ta-Yuan sheng-cheng kuo-ch'ao tien-chang* [Collected statutes and cases of the Yuan], 1908 ed. (Taipei: Wen-hai Publishing Co., 1964), pp. 676–677; also pp. 656–657, 663, 667, 678, and 683.

7. *TLTI*, 31:64b–65. The Ming ordinance was adopted in 1367. See a discussion on this legislation in Naito Kenkichi, *Chūgoku hōseishi kōshō* [Studies on Chinese legal history] (Osaka, 1963), pp. 90–91.

8. *Ta-Ming hui-tien*, V, 2442.

9. Ibid., V, 2439; IV, 2253–2254.

10. *TLTI*, 31:65. It is to be noted that by the early seventeenth century the exact meaning of *ching-chi* (police aid) was already unclear. See Kao Chü, comp., *Ming-lü chi-chieh fu-li* [The annotated Ming code, with special provisions appended], 1610 ed. (1908), 18:80b–81.

called the government's attention to the said provision of the code, and requested that convicted thieves be so treated.[11] This suggests that during Chu's time this law existed only on the statute books. Indeed, my own search of case records and various statutory regulations indicates that the requirement was probably not enforced at all before 1740.

When referring to police, we must bear in mind that a modern police system did not come into being in Ch'ing China until the early twentieth century. Prior to that time, the closest equivalent to policemen was one group of government runners called *pu-i* or *pu-k'uai*, whose duties were to catch robbers and thieves and to serve as night watchmen. The number and wages of policemen varied from area to area. Since the government allocated no funds for investigation and arrest of robbers and thieves, the policemen's salaries were primarily donated by the district magistrate, although sometimes they were allowed to demand various fees from the victims of robbery and theft. Although their authority to arrest could inspire awe among the people, by and large the policemen's fate was pitiable. Under the pressure of meeting his own statutory deadline to catch robbers and thieves, the magistrate often imposed an even stricter deadline on policemen. Failure to make an arrest would invariably make the policemen liable to corporal punishment. In fact, policemen were social outcasts called *chien-min* (mean people), and were classed together with actors, prostitutes, and beggars.[12]

Before discussing the new 1740 legislation which again imposed police service on convicted thieves, let us examine a few regulations which were adopted during the two decades preceding that date. In 1725 the government decreed that a thief convicted of a first offense and given the punishments of bambooing and tattooing should be handed over to his *pao-chia* headman for supervision. If the offense was committed away from home, the offender was to be returned to his native place, and was then forbidden to leave his district without first obtaining permission from the government.[13] Although the local officials were required frequently to check up on those placed under their supervision, the police aid requirement was not mentioned at all. Instead, a person under surveillance was required to visit the yamen periodically. Should he leave the district without permission, he was apparently punishable by the law on "doing what ought not to be done" (forty blows of the light bamboo or eighty blows of the heavy bamboo, depending on the circumstances of the case).

Two years later this rule on surveillance was extended to cover more serious criminals in Peking who were sentenced to penal servitude. They (thieves included) were returned to the capital of their native province and,

11. Chu P'ei, "Ch'ing hsing-yü shen ch'u-chao shu" [On being careful at the inception of criminal interrogation], in *HCCSWP*, 93:26b.

12. Ch'ü T'ung-tsu, *Local Government in China under the Ch'ing* (Cambridge: Harvard University Press, 1962), pp. 57, 60, 62–63, 66, and 69–70.

13. *HTSL*, XIX, 15073; but at p. 15172 the date is given as 1727 rather than 1725.

upon the completion of their penal servitude, were sent to their native place and handed over to the presiding official for supervision. Attempts to escape were punished by banishment to a distant province.[14] However, the relatively wide coverage and the harsh punishment of this legislation on Peking criminals were reevaluated under the Ch'ien-lung emperor.[15] As a result, only thieves, robbers, and scoundrels (*kuang-kun*)[16] who had been sentenced to penal servitude in Peking were placed under surveillance on completion of their term of servitude. The punishment for unauthorized departure from the district was reduced to eighty blows of the heavy bamboo. The government pointed out that a change was needed because, "People are returned from Peking to their native place after being sentenced to penal servitude. Upon the completion of their sentence they must leave their home region to make a living. If they are strictly prohibited from leaving, it is tantamount to depriving them of a living."[17]

In other words, thieves expelled from the capital continued to be considered dangerous and had to remain in their native place for close watch, but the Ch'ien-lung revision did enable most other offenders who had likewise served penal servitude to leave freely. The fate of theft recidivists as well as of offenders who had been sentenced to penal servitude for theft committed outside of Peking remained unclear. In theory they too were required to serve as police aids in their native place. But, as pointed out earlier, there is no evidence of any actual enforcement of this stipulation of the Ch'ing code.

In 1740 the Ch'ing government carefully revised the penal code, adopting a *li* (special provision) modelled after the Ming ordinance cited above. This provision permitted the removal of tattooed characters if convicted thieves who served as police aids were able to capture other thieves or robbers.[18]

14. *CSL*:YC, 57:14b; *HTSL*, XX, 15489. (The date was entered as 1725 by mistake.) No mention was made of the punishment of the offenders' family members, relatives, or *pao-chia* heads. According to a regulation of the Board of Civil Appointments, also dated 1727, the officials in charge of controlling these two categories of offenders should submit an annual report to the Board of Justice on the number of people under surveillance, if they were law-abiding and residing in their home locale. Should one single person escape, the official would be given the administrative sanction of forfeiting one month's salary. *HTSL*, VIII, 6743. (Note: The words "in Peking" were probably inadvertently omitted at the beginning of this entry.)

15. *HTSL*, XX, 15490.

16. The regulations on scoundrels are generally found under the code section entitled *K'ung-he ch'ü-ts'ai* [Extortion], *Ch'ing code*, III, 2165–2196; Staunton, pp. 288–289.

17. *HTSL*, XX, 15490.

18. *HTSL*, XIX, 15169. In the same year, new legislation was introduced to govern the treatment of convicts who were to be dispatched to their native place. Beginning in 1673, offenders sentenced to banishment or penal servitude would receive their bambooing only after they arrived at their destination; this was designed to eliminate the unnecessary hardship of walking long distances while one's buttock was severely injured from the corporal punishment. See *HFC*, p. 46. No provision had been made concerning offenders sentenced to bambooing who were required to be taken to their native place. This often resulted in the misery of minor offenders. Therefore, the 1740 legislation also called for the delayed execution of the punishment of beating until the offenders had reached their home district. In addition,

According to this legislation, convicted thieves should serve in their native place for an undetermined period as patrolmen (*hsun-ching*). After they had demonstrated their repentance and ability to catch thieves, their tattooed characters would be officially removed, restoring the criminals to the status of good people who could be incorporated into the regular *pao-chia* system. The vagueness of this law no doubt enabled the officials to adjust it to the needs of their local conditions.[19]

In 1745 Yen Ssu-sheng, the governor of Hupei, memorialized to the Ch'ien-lung emperor, proposing the enactment of a new law to deal with theft recidivists.[20] He argued that the punishment of bambooing and tattooing was not harsh enough to deter thieves. After having received such a punishment for the second time, a thief should be forced to wear the cangue and a bell while serving as a patrolman for three years. This treatment would have been considerably harsher and more humiliating than that prescribed in the 1740 legislation. The ringing bell could serve to deter potential wrongdoers, but it could also defeat the purpose of capturing real offenders by surprise. If the exconvict did not commit a new theft during the three years

---

during the transit different treatment was to be accorded those offenders who had been sentenced to penal servitude and above and those offenders sentenced to bambooing and less. Those in the former group were placed under strict guard, and during each overnight stop they were put in a detention house, whereas those in the latter group were taken to inns, though accompanied by runners. *CSL:CL*, 119:14b–16; *HTSL*, XX, 15538; *Ch'ing code*, V, 3503.

19. This law was revised in 1838; the new version made the condition for release more specific. If while serving as a police aid a convicted thief did not repeat the offense for two or three years and if he could catch either two or more robbers, or five or more thieves, he was allowed to be freed and have the tattooed characters removed. The revised law also stressed that after the thief's status was restored to that of "good people," the local officials might not arrest him unless he again committed theft or other offenses. The newly revised *li* resembled the Ming ordinance mentioned above, except the latter seems to have been more reasonable. The Ming regulation encouraged positive contribution by a thief: if he could capture a certain number of thieves or robbers, he was eligible for immediate release. But even if he failed to fulfill this quota, a Ming thief could be relieved of police duty and have the tattoo removed after the lapse of three years. Not so in the case of the 1838 *li*: the release was conditioned on both the ability to catch other offenders and the fulfilment of the police duty for a definite period of time. It is foreseeable that even though many years had elapsed and the convicted thief never transgressed the law, he could still be denied the right to have his tattoo destroyed as long as he was unable to catch other thieves or robbers. Conversely, even if a Ch'ing thief could fulfill the quota of capturing other offenders, he had to wait for the passage of two or three years. See *Ch'ing code*, III, 2321–2322.

The only other code provision stipulating police duty as a control mechanism is the one on *Lao-kua tsei* [old melon thief], organized robbers whose main target was travelers. According to a 1741 special provision of the code, anyone acquainted with an "old melon thief" was required to report this fact to the government; failure to report incurred the punishment of 100 blows of the heavy bamboo. Moreover, the person failing to report was considered guilty by association with the highway robbers and was forced to serve as a policeman and to make a semimonthly appearance at the yamen as if he were a convicted thief. *HTSL*, XIX, 15028. However, when this *li* was revised in 1870, both the police duty and the regular visit at the yamen were deleted because, according to Hsüeh Yün-sheng, "these requirements had not been enforced for a long time." *TLTI*, 26:65b.

20. *CSL:CL*, 249:26b–27.

of active duty as a patrolman, the cangue and bell would be removed, but his name would remain in a special register for three more years, during which time he would be required to make periodic reports to his supervising local magistrate. After the passage of six years without repeating his offense, the exconvict would be given money by the government to enable him to start a new life.[21]

Yen's proposal did not arouse the enthusiasm of the emperor, who curtly commented: "The art of governance depends on the man rather than on the law. Why don't you try out your program first!"[22] What the emperor probably had in mind was the futility of enacting new national legislation to cope with theft recidivism in the absence of data supporting the feasibility of the proposed program. If the Hupei governor wished to force theft recidivists all over the empire to wear the cangue and bell, then he should first experiment with it in his own province. However, Yen's project was probably never carried out, since he resigned from public service to care for his mother a month after submitting his proposal.

In Szechwan province, at least, convicted thieves were indeed forced to serve as policemen in accordance with the 1740 li. In January 1775, Li Cheng-jung of Nan-ch'uan, Szechwan, committed a theft. He was sentenced to bambooing and tattooing, and was also forced to wear a pole (kan) and serve as a policeman. In April 1778 Li's father moved to Cheng-an, Kweichow, to settle as a tenant farmer, leaving Li behind. One year later Li managed to desert from his police duty and joined his father in Kweichow. Two weeks after he arrived, several villagers reported that their pigs had been stolen. Ch'en Kuei, the p'ai-t'ou (the head of ten households), asked them not to report the case while he was conducting an investigation. Soon Ch'en discovered that Li, an exconvict, had escaped from the neighboring province. Suspecting that Li was the pig thief, Ch'en asked various theft victims to meet at his house while he tried to coax Li to join him for a drink. Li gladly accepted the invitation and went to Ch'en's house, where he was attacked by the group. Li attempted to defend himself with a knife, but Ch'en snatched the weapon and stabbed Li a few times in the legs. That evening Li died from his wounds.

In the report submitted to the Board of Justice, the governor of Kweichow referred to the deceased as a criminal (tsui-jen). "Li Cheng-jung committed a theft in Szechwan. After his capture he was punished and tattooed. During the course of his [involuntary] service as a policeman, while still wearing a pole as part of the punishment for his theft offense, he seized a chance to

21. Governor Yen may have been inspired by the practice in Kiangsu and Kiangsi where a thief convicted for the second time was forced to wear the cangue and bell. The experience of Kiangsu will be discussed later.

22. CSL:CL, 249:27. Another version of the same account, given by the HTSL, did not include the remark made by the emperor. Instead it said that the governor's proposal was approved and presumably became a law. HTSL, XIX, 15088.

escape. Therefore, he was a guilty person (*yu-tsui chih jen*)."²³ It is to be noted that prior to his escape, Li had already served as a policeman for over four years. The case report does not indicate how long he was required to serve in that capacity, but it certainly does seem that so long as Li was not relieved from his police duty he was not free to leave the area.

TATTOOING AND THE CANGUE AS SUPPLEMENTARY PUNISHMENTS

Although convicted thieves probably were not enlisted as police aids during the first century of the Ch'ing period, there is ample evidence in case records showing that those offenders were indeed tattooed throughout the dynasty. The law regulating tattooing was very complicated. The code of 1646 stipulated that appropriate characters such as *ch'ieh-tao* (theft) and *tao-kuan-yin* (stealing government money) should be tattooed on the right forearm of an offender. If he repeated the same offense, he should be tattooed on the left forearm. The size of the character was also carefully regulated.²⁴

Certain groups were by law exempted from tattooing: women, the aged (seventy or above), the young (fifteen or below), and offenders guilty of stealing the property of a family member.²⁵ Furthermore, if thieves turned themselves in either to the government or to the property owner, they were exempted from all punishment, including the tattoo. Even if their confession was found to be inaccurate, they were still entitled to reduction in punishment and to exemption from tattooing. However, thieves might not resort to voluntary surrender more than once. If they subsequently committed the offense of theft, they would be tattooed and given the statutory punishment even though they had surrendered voluntarily.

In the 1646 code tattooing was required for thieves, but it was not imposed on robbers until 1725.²⁶ This disparity probably could be explained by the fact that because most robbers were scheduled to die, there seemed to be no need to have them tattooed.²⁷ This was not so in the case of thieves. On the

23. *PAHP*, VI, 3031–3038. This passage was recapitulated by the Board of Justice in its memorial to the emperor. Both the governor and the board members agreed that Ch'en Kuei was authorized to arrest Li as a suspect, but they considered him guilty of the unauthorized killing of a captured offender. Consequently, Ch'en Kuei was sentenced to strangulation after the assizes in accordance with a general provision of the code which stated that, if a police officer killed a criminal who was not capitally punishable, and who had surrendered or been overtaken, such police officer should be punished according to the law on "killing in an affray," which in turn prescribed the death penalty. *Ch'ing code*, V, 3351, and IV, 2497; Staunton, pp. 442, 311. This practice of forcing a thief to wear a pole is also intriguing. An 1814 imperial regulation required a special type of thief in Szechwan to wear iron poles (*t'ieh-kan*) in addition to the punishments of bambooing and canguing. It is interesting to note that from the 1820s the Szechwanese practice of wearing iron poles became a frequently-imposed punishment in many parts of the country. *HTSL*, XIX, 15083, 15090–15091; *HAHLF*, III, 1179–1186; *Ch'ing code*, III, 2092–2098.

24. *Ch'ing code*, III, 1933, 1945, 2027, and 2069; Staunton, pp. 278–279, 283–285.

25. *Ch'ing code*, I, 227, 383, 409, 415, and III, 2153; Boulais, p. 26, sec. 40, and p. 76, sec. 135; Staunton, pp. 22, 23; *HAHLF*, I, 415, and III, 1186; *HTSL*, XIX, 1517.

26. *HTSL*, XIX, 15169.

27. According to the code of 1646, if robbery was successful, all the participants were

one hand, thieves might be sent back to their native place, where their distinctive markings presumably could serve to humiliate them into repenting. The tattoo could also deter other potential criminals as well as enable local residents to guard against crime-prone elements. If, on the other hand, the thieves were banished or imprisoned, the tattooing would make it difficult for them to escape without being noticed.[28] The tattoo on the right or left forearm, however, was not considered conspicuous enough to achieve the deterrent effect, as people could easily conceal it with long sleeves. Thus, beginning in 1692, the tattoo was put on the thief's face.[29]

Exemption from tattooing was often crucial to the life and death of an offender, for the number of times he had been tattooed was taken as the basis for determining the appropriate punishment for a theft recidivist. Prior to 1735, a third-time theft offender would invariably receive strangulation after the assizes, but after that year the death penalty was meted out only if the value of the stolen property exceeded fifty silver taels.[30] Thus it is understandable that many judicial officials were extremely careful about administering the tattoo. Their attitude is best portrayed by Yao Wen-jan, who became the president of the Board of Justice in the late seventeenth century. He said: "For the third theft offense the punishment is strangulation [after the assizes]. The number of times an offender has been tattooed is used as the basis for calculating recidivism. Therefore, when you administer the tattoo to a person once, you have already deprived him of a third of his life!"[31]

Under the Yung-cheng reign, when there was a general tendency to tighten control over the officials and the populace, the penalties for theft were increased.[32] Many officials, presumably for humanitarian reasons, refrained from tattooing thieves, because the mandatory sentence for theft was now death after having been tattooed twice. The Yung-cheng emperor threatened to impose severe administrative sanctions upon officials who were lenient toward thieves. He also increased the punishment for destroying the tattoo from sixty to a hundred blows of the heavy bamboo plus three months of canguing. If the removal was performed by someone other than the offender,

---

sentenced to immediate decapitation regardless of whether they were principals or accessories. *Ch'ing code*, III, 1953.

28. In fact, both of these purposes were articulated in an 1813 ruling of the Board of Justice. See *Ch'ing code*, III, 2320. Also see *HTSL*, XIX, 15172.

29. *TLCA*, ts'e 10, 18:17. Repeated in 1725, see *HTSL*, XIX, 15073. The code did not specify exactly which part of the face was to be tattooed. An official source, however, pointed out that the exact position was above the cheek but below the hairline; in other words, it was the temples. The characters would show in black. *HTSL*, I, 562; *HFC*, p. 60.

30. *Ch'ing code*, III, 2071 and 2082; Staunton, p. 285; Boulais, p. 505, sec. 1124; *HTSL*, XIX, 15078.

31. Yao Wen-jan, *Tao-fa kuan-liu wu tz'u-tzu shu* [On tattooing by mistake a thief who had cut government-owned willow trees], in *HCCSWP*, 92:50b.

32. In 1724 the emperor noted that according to the code, if stolen property was valued at 120 silver taels or more, the thief was to be sentenced to strangulation after the assizes even for a first offense, and if between 100 and 120 taels, to banishment; but judicial officials seldom meted out those punishments in compliance with the code.

he should be punished with a hundred blows of the heavy bamboo plus two months of canguing. The destroyed characters were of course restored.[33]

In 1741 the policy of tattooing thieves on the face came under review. It was decided that if a thief was sentenced to bambooing it would be better to have the tattoo administered on his right forearm for a first offense and on the left face for the second offense. But if a thief was sentenced to penal servitude, the place for the tattoo was the left face for both the first and second offenses.[34] This pattern persisted until the end of the dynasty. The reason for the change of place of tattoo for petty thieves was not given, but I believe that it was probably designed to make first offenders less conspicuous and more easily reintegrated into the society. Although one of the avowed purposes of the tattoo was to humiliate the offender and thus arouse his sense of shame, it was felt that the stigma effected by tattooing often unduly closed all the avenues for repentance and reform.[35] This type of humane consideration would not be repeated if the petty theft offender should become a recidivist.

Judging from case records, unauthorized removal of tattooed characters was not uncommon. No doubt a convicted man would be eager to erase this reminder of his past offense when he desired to return to his normal life. And where he chose to continue his association with hoodlums, it was even more important to have the characters destroyed. Ch'iu Yang-wen, a mid-eighteenth-century district magistrate in Nan-ch'ung, Szechwan, reported that robbers and thieves ganged up in that province to form a society of "red-cash brothers" (*hung-ch'ien ti-hsiung*). But if a person had been tattooed, he was rejected by that gang and had to seek membership among the "black-cash brothers" (*hei-ch'ien*).[36] The mere fact that a man had been convicted and tattooed relegated him to a somewhat inferior position even among the population of robbers and thieves.

For recidivists the humilation of conspicuous tattooing was further compounded by public display in a cangue. As a form of punishment, the cangue, a large wooden board worn around the neck, was used more widely by the Ch'ing than by earlier dynasties. At first the cangue was primarily applied to bannermen for a specific number of days in lieu of penal servitude and banishment.[37] As time went on, more and more statutory regulations prescribed the cangue as a supplementary punishment for common people.[38]

---

33. *TLCA*, ts'e 20, under *pu-wang*, pp. 24–27; *CSL:YC*, 14:12b–13 and 16b.

34. *HTSL*, XIX, 15073.

35. Wang Yu-liang, "Chi Yu-ssu shih" [Some events of the Board of Justice], in *HCCSWP*, 75:28.

36. Ch'iu Yang-wen "Lun Shu kuo-lu chuang" [On Szechwan's *kuo-lu* bandits], in *HCCSWP*, 75:28.

37. Derk Bodde and Clarence Morris, *Law in Imperial China, Exemplified in 190 Ch'ing Cases (Translated from the Hsing-an hui-lan) with Historical, Social and Judicial Commentaries*, Harvard Studies in East Asian Law (Cambridge: Harvard University Press, 1967), p. 96.

38. A good example is the *li* enacted in 1724 governing the removal of tattooing mentioned

Like tattooing, the cangue served to stigmatize the offender. After being displayed in public with a placard indicating his offense, it was hoped that he would feel ashamed, and other crime-prone elements of the society would be warned against violating the law. Li Yü, a seventeenth-century writer, once declared that it was not difficult to stand the pain inflicted on one's body, but it was hard to endure the humiliation caused by canguing.[39]

Nevertheless, the cangue was still considered a relatively light punishment and so was often used by magistrates as a postconviction supplementary punishment along with bambooing. It was especially applied to theft recidivists.[40] In August 1760, Su Erh-te, the judicial commissioner of Kiangsu, memorialized to the emperor, requesting increased punishment for such criminals. He recommended one month of canguing for a recidivist guilty of stealing property valued at less than ten silver taels, one and a half months for ten to thirty taels, and two months for thirty to fifty taels. When the value exceeded fifty taels, the punishment would be penal servitude or above; in that case Su felt that canguing would not be needed. However, the Board of Justice counterproposed a standard by which the canguing would correspond directly to the seriousness of each theft offense: where the original punishment was sixty blows of the heavy bamboo, twenty days of canguing should be added. Each additional ten blows would incur five more days of canguing, thus culminating in forty days of canguing for one hundred blows of the heavy bamboo. The emperor approved the board's proposal, and the beating-canguing of theft recidivists remained in force until the twentieth century.[41]

---

above. Another example is the 1725 *li* which imposed one month of the cangue plus 100 blows of the heavy bamboo on adulterous women and their paramours, while the original punishment for adultery prescribed in the general provisions of the code was only 90 blows of the heavy bamboo. After 1740, however, women were allowed to redeem the punishment of canguing. *HTSL*, XX, 15414, and XVIII, 14441; *Ch'ing code*, IV, 3209, and I, 226; Boulais, p. 682, sec. 1590, and p. 26., sec. 39.

39. Li Yü, "Lun hsing-chü" [On the instruments of punishment], in *HCCSWP*, 94:16b. The size and weight of the cangue was carefully regulated by law: it measured 3 × 2.9 *ch'ih* (Chinese feet) and normally weighed 25 catties. However, in the course of time some abuses occurred; one cangue was found to have weighed as much as 130 catties. Moreover, it was designed in such a way so that the man locked in the cangue could not feed himself. Not until 1812 was a reform effected to reduce the size to 2.5 × 2.4, presumably to allow self-feeding. The weight was also limited to 25 and 35 catties respectively for the ordinary and the extra-heavy cangues. (1 *ch'ih* = 14.1 inches, and 1 catty = 1.3 English pound.) *Ch'ing code*, I, 166 and 220; Boulais, 5; *HTSL*, XVIII, 14429, 14431, and 14434. There are some mistakes contained in Bodde's account on the cangue; see Bodde and Morris, *Law in Imperial China*, p. 96.

40. For example, a late seventeenth-century district magistrate in Shantung named Huang Liu-hung wrote that soon after he arrived at his new post he apprehended theft recidivists and imposed the punishment of beating and the cangue on them, having them stand outside his yamen for public display. Huang Liu-hung, "I-tao chih-tao shuo" [On eliminating robbery by utilizing robbers], in *HCCSWP*, 75:22b.

41. *CSL*:CL, 616:11b–12b; *Ch'ing code*, III, 2088; Boulais, p. 505, sec. 1122; *HTSL*, XIX, 15074.

GUARANTOR'S LIABILITY

During the Ch'ing period the household was thought to constitute the basis of civil responsibility. The family was supposed to control the conduct of its individual members, while groups of households were aligned to form *pao* and *chia* units for mutual responsibility. Although the effectiveness of the *pao-chia* system during the mid-Ch'ing varied from locality to locality, the general consensus among scholars seems to be that overall it functioned reasonably well.[42] The task of supervising (*kuan-shu* or *yueh-shu*) bad elements in the society, such as those with a previous record of stealing, was assigned to the family and to the *pao-chia* apparatus because it was the cheapest and most effective way of local control.

At first, this supervisory duty was assigned to a relative of the thief. According to a 1672 regulation, the father or the elder brother of a theft recidivist was given fifty blows of the light bamboo even though he was not privy to the crime. The magistrate was also given some administrative sanction for his failure to prevent the thief from becoming a recidivist.[43] In 1732 the government further tightened up its control over the populace: the father or elder brother of a thief would be held vicariously liable even though the thief was only guilty of a first offense. The punishment for the relative was forty blows of the light bamboo.[44]

Beginning with new legislation in 1727, the postconviction supervisory duty over petty thieves (that is, those punishable by bambooing) was formally assigned to *pao-chia* heads. The latter acted as guarantors to assure that the supervised person would not repeat the same crime. However, this legislation did not stipulate the punishment to be imposed on the guarantor. Not until 1759 was a special provision adopted in the code to remedy the shortcoming. This provision prescribed the punishment of forty blows of the light bamboo for a guarantor if the thief under supervision committed a second theft offense punishable by bambooing or less, or eighty blows of the heavy bamboo if the theft offense was punishable by penal servitude or above. The basis of these punishments was the law on "doing what ought not to be done."[45] Moreover, this special provision also referred to the liability of a family member who had served as a guarantor. Therefore it seems clear that sometime between 1727 and 1759 the family member was again authorized to act as a guarantor.

42. Hsiao Kung-ch'üan discussed the *pao-chia* system in Ch'ing China at length. See his *Rural China: Imperial Control in the 19th Century* (Seattle: University of Washington Press, 1960), pp. 43–83. He also pointed out that some officials in the eighteenth and nineteenth centuries treated the *ti-pao* (local constable) as a *pao-chia* agent. Ibid., pp. 64–65. In this study we also found the existence of such confusion.

43. *HTSL*, XIX, 15086. It is also possible that the theft recidivist was instead sentenced to 60 blows of the heavy bamboo. Because the text only mentioned 20 *pan*, it could be either way. See Bodde and Morris, *Law in Imperial China*, p. 77.

44. *HTSL*, XIX, 15076.

45. *TLHP*, 1:72b–74 (1759); *Ta-Ch'ing lü-li an-yü* [Compilers' notes on the Ch'ing code] (1847), 54:59a–b.

Responsibility therefore alternated between the *pao-chia* and the family throughout the mid-Ch'ing period. Neither one seems to have been sufficient by itself, perhaps because it was often difficult to find guarantors in either case. A late seventeenth-century district magistrate in Shantung named Huang Liu-hung wrote that he often imposed beating and the cangue on theft recidivists. One day when he came out of his yamen, he noticed that under the blistering sun those offenders wearing the cangue looked like burned charcoals and appeared as weak as "floating silk." He took pity on them and sent for their relatives to come forth as guarantors to secure their release, but the relatives were reluctant to do so for fear of being implicated in the future. Soon those offenders all died.[46]

Sometimes neither father nor elder brother was available. Supervision could then be carried out by a younger brother, but this was contrary to Confucian ethics, posing intricate legal problems which are illustrated by a 1776 Kiangsu case. A man named S.C. was a troublemaker (*pu an-fen*) who was ordered by the district magistrate to be put under the control of his younger brother, Y.C. The younger brother intervened in a dispute between S.C. and a local landlord. When S.C. hit Y.C. in the ribs, the younger brother's reaction was as follows:

> Y.C. was struck by his elder brother S.C. Y.C. was incensed because S.C., who had been placed under his supervision, had the audacity to disobey him and commit a criminal act against him. Thereupon he wanted to drag S.C. to the government authority. In the struggle Y.C. hurt S.C. in the neck with his nails. He further took a rope to tie S.C.'s neck in order to pull him to the local constabulary.[47]

A neighbor who was drawn into the struggle mortally wounded S.C. in the chest. In his report to the Board of Justice on what had now become a capital crime, Sa-tsai, the governor of Kiangsu, proposed to sentence Y.C. to immediate decapitation and the neighbor to strangulation after the assizes. Sa-tsai argued that Y.C. should not have violated Confucian ethics by injuring his older brother and tying his neck. Moreover, if S.C. had not been tied, the neighbor probably could not have inflicted a fatal wound on him. The board rejected Sa-tsai's recommendation, stating that only the neighbor was to be held liable for the ensuing death; Y.C. should not receive the death penalty. By so refusing to subscribe to the governor's moral condemnation of Y.C.'s conduct towards his elder brother, the Board of Justice chose law over ethics and implicitly sanctioned the practice of allowing a junior to exercise supervision over his senior relative.[48]

46. Huang Liu-hung, "I-tao chih-tao shuo," in *HCCSWP*, 75:22b.
47. *PAHP*, V, 2263–2271.
48. Upon retrial the governor adopted the board's opinion: the neighbor's death sentence remained unchanged whereas the younger brother was held liable only for bodily injury, for which he was sentenced to three years of penal servitude and 100 blows of the heavy bamboo. However, the younger brother had died in prison before the sentence became final. Ibid.

In the absence of immediate family members, the supervisory duty tended to be imposed either upon the *ti-pao* (constable) or upon the *pao-chia* headman. In the case of the former, the constable would be held responsible for failing to prevent the crime of his charge, and accordingly punished.[49] The *pao-chia* form of supervision, however, posed special problems—some of which were outlined in a 1777 memorial submitted to the emperor by the acting judicial commissioner of Chekiang.[50] First, when the original guarantor died, the supervisory duty was occasionally not transferred to the new *pao-chia* headman.[51] Second, the supervised were sometimes allowed to leave the district freely.[52] Third, where the supervised repeated an offense, their guarantors were only punished "leniently" with bambooing. Finally, it was extremely difficult to secure guarantors. According to the Chekiang commissioner, a guarantor was required to submit a written document (*pao-chuang*) pledging that the person under his supervision would be law-abiding and that subsequent repetition of the theft offense by the supervised person would make the guarantor personally liable. Since being a guarantor meant subjecting oneself to possible criminal punishment, we can easily understand the general reluctance to assume such responsibility.

LOCAL VARIATIONS IN THE CONTROL OF THIEVES: KIANGSU

In 1740 Ch'en Hung-mou—who was considered by contemporaries to be an exemplary official—was appointed judicial commissioner of Kiangsu. During his tenure he submitted to the governor a comprehensive proposal

---

49. In 1751 a thief named Ch'eng from Anhwei was banished to Chin district, Chekiang, and placed under the supervsion of a *ti-pao*. Four years later, a man named Chao became the *ti-pao*. Since Ch'eng had no place to stay after the house he currently occupied was taken back by the landlord, and since he might get into trouble if permitted to roam, Chao made him stay in his house. Ch'eng lived by begging, but when it rained Chao had to provide him with food. One day Ch'eng picked up some old gambling cards on the road. Because he had learned carving before, he decided to get into the business of producing and selling gambling cards. His idea was approved by his guarantor Chao, for the latter was eager to make him self-supporting. Ch'eng successfully sold a few sets of cards but was soon caught by the authorities. For the offense of producing and selling cards for gambling, Ch'eng was sentenced to 100 blows of the heavy bamboo plus four years of hard labor to be carried out in the place where he was serving his banishment; whereas Chao, who had failed to stop Ch'eng's illegal act, received 90 blows of the heavy bamboo plus two and a half years of penal servitude. It is to be noted that in this case Chao did not simply fail to supervise properly: he actually knew and approved Ch'eng's crime. Ma Shih-lin, comp., *Ch'eng-an so-chien-chi* [Collection of seen cases] (Kwangtung: Tsai-ssu Studio, 1793), 34:11–13. For the statutes cited in this case, see *Ch'ing code*, IV, 3281, and I, 391; Staunton, p. 23.

50. *TLHP*, 24:34 (1777).

51. This memorial did not state whether or not a new guarantee was necessary when the *pao-chia* heads rotated each year.

52. This matter also proved of concern to the Board of Justice in a case which came up a few years after the 1777 memorial. In 1776 a man named Hung, from P'o-yang district, Kiangsi province, committed a theft in a neighboring district called Fu-liang. He was given the punishment of bambooing and tattooing, and sent back to his native place for supervision. Four years later his guarantor died, so he went to another area to seek employment. There

for crime prevention.[53] In this document he was quite sympathetic toward the plight of convicted thieves, since the relatively light punishments prescribed by the Ch'ing code for theft tended to lure people into committing that crime. In the case of multiple theft, if the largest sum stolen from any one property owner was valued at less than fifty silver taels, the punishment would not go beyond bambooing.[54] After a thief was caught, however, his face would be tattooed and even if he repented, his friends and neighbors would shun him. Often unable to find a job, he was frequently molested by government runners who would try to extort money from him. This was especially true when another theft occurred in the district. Ch'en felt that most first offenders still retained a sense of shame and were relatively susceptible to rehabilitation. He suggested that immediately after punishment and tattooing, the district magistrate should summon a thief's relatives or neighbors to take him home. They were to supply a written guarantee to a prospective employer that the latter would never be implicated if the exthief got into trouble again. If they found the exthief unruly, they should report the matter to the magistrate so that appropriate action might be taken against him.

Ch'en's concern for the well-being of convicted thieves reflected the traditional Confucian attitude of attempting to transform subjects through education and moral suasion. He saw the ultimate effect of the punishment of tattooing as making a man who had erred only once a social outcast, and consequently denying him a chance of true repentance. Although Ch'en did not go so far as to advocate the total abandonment of tattooing, he apparently did desire to eliminate it at least for the first offender. During his lengthy service as a local official—he served over twenty years as the governor of various provinces and also in other lesser local posts—he always stressed the importance of public education. His collected works *P'ei-yuan t'ang ou-ts'un-kao* (Writings from the P'ei-yuan studio), and his compendium of five treatises on moral and educational topics, entitled *Wu-chung i-kuei* (Five kinds of tradition), are replete with the examples of his strong commitment to this exalted goal. Ch'en's experience in Yunnan, where he successfully attended to the tutelage of a large number of Miao tribesmen, was apparently very heartening.[55] In the case of convicted thieves, it was only natural that Ch'en tried to mobilize the help of family members and neighbors to facilitate the convicts' reintegration into civil society.

To deal with theft recidivists, Kiangsu already had for some years enforced

---

he became involved in banditry and was captured by the authorities. The responsibility of the *p'ao-chia* heads in charge of Hung in his native place was deliberated by the Board of Justice, but they were exempted from punishment on the ground that after Hung had left the area they could not have discovered his wrongdoing. *PAHP*, II, 649–664.

53. Ch'en Hung-mou, *P'ei-yuan t'ang ou-ts'un kao* [Writings from the P'ei-yuan Studio], 10:6b–10.

54. *Ch'ing code*, III, 2069–2070; Staunton, pp. 284–285.

55. Arthur W. Hummel, ed., *Eminent Chinese of the Ch'ing Period (1644–1912)* (Washington, D.C.: U.S. Government Printing Office, 1943), pp. 86–87.

a regulation requiring them to wear the cangue and bell and to make semi-monthly appearances at the district yamen. The requirement of wearing the cangue and bell was waived if a relative or neighbor was willing to act as guarantor. As for those outcasts who could find no one as their guarantor, life was very miserable because they could do nothing but beg for food while wearing the cangue and bell. Thus Ch'en Hung-mou suggested three ways to help them:

1. Throughout Kiangsu urban residents usually hired people to guard the city walls or other barriers at night, while rural inhabitants employed patrolling night watchmen. The theft recidivists could be paid to perform this function. Instead of wearing the cangue and bell, their feet would be fettered to such an extent that they could walk slowly but never be able to run. If the area patrolled by them was free from thievery for three years, they should be set free.

2. The government's mint at Soochow, the provincial capital, had twelve hearths which needed many laborers. Since the mint had a tight security system, the theft recidivists did not have to wear the cangue and bell. They would be supervised by the head of each hearth and receive regular wages.

3. If the two channels mentioned above failed to absorb all the forlorn theft recidivists, each district magistrate should assign a few rooms near the yamen as a detention house (*chi-hou so*) to confine them for an undetermined period. The cost of their food was to be borne by the magistrate's voluntary contribution. During the daytime they would be forced to work on some handicraft, whereas at night they would be locked up under the guard of a few government runners.

Both the governor of Kiangsu and the governor-general of Liang-Kiang had some reservations about Ch'en Hung-mou's proposals on the control of theft recidivists. To have a unified system of theft control throughout the province was thought to be impractical, and it was more important to have each district devise means to meet its own needs. Therefore, district magistrates throughout Kiangsu were encouraged to try out their own programs. Meanwhile, Ch'en's proposals were circulated in all the districts and comments were invited.[56]

Many magistrates responded to the provincial circular by submitting reports on the implementation of their theft control programs. Some districts reported over ten theft recidivists who had to wear a cangue and bell because no one wanted to be their guarantor; other *hsien* reported no such outcasts. The consensus among the magistrates was that the best policy was to let thieves become beggars. Not a single magistrate liked the idea of entrusting thieves to act as night watchmen, guards, or police. Instead, they favored three other methods of control.

Fourteen of the responding magistrates preferred forcing thieves to wear a

56. Ch'en Hung-mou, *P'ei-yuan t'ang*, 10:19–22b.

small cangue, a long spear (*ch'ang-ch'iang*), or wooden handcuffs. During the daytime they could beg and at night they would be placed under strict guard in a detention house within the yamen. Depending on their ability, thieves could be ordered to make mattresses, weave, or carry dirt for the government's construction work in order to earn a living. If they were unruly, they would lose their freedom completely.

However, the magistrates of T'ung-shan and T'ao-yuan pointed out that it was extremely difficult to live by begging in districts without sizable marketplaces. In such areas thieves should be dispersed and assigned to small townships or villages where postal stations or other governmental agencies were located. During the daytime the thieves could go to nearby villages to beg for food, and in the evenings report back to their detention house. On the cangue or the spear that they were wearing, the name of the thief and the government unit in charge of him should be distinctively carved. Residents in that area would be warned against permitting those thieves to stay overnight at their houses.

Finally, one magistrate suggested hiring exthieves to work at the postal stations as porters. Currently, most of the porters were part-time beggars who were placed under the control of a government-appointed chief beggar. Thieves would also be assigned to the latter's jurisdiction.

After reviewing these sundry opinions, Ch'en Hung-mou continued to urge the magistrates to encourage thieves to reform. If thieves genuinely repented, furnished a written guarantee, and were able to persuade the local constable to provide another written guarantee for them, they should be set free. In case of future theft offense, both the exthief and the constable were to be punished. Although the local constable's guarantee would be hard to obtain, it was still not impossible for a thief to regain his pre-conviction status as a "good person." Ch'en further recommended exempting convicted thieves from the semi-monthly visit to the yamen if they were only first offenders and were able to find a guarantor. Government runners were warned not to arrest or interrogate convicted thieves unless they had been identified as suspects in a subsequent theft or were found to be in possession of stolen property.

Ch'en's view on how to treat exthieves contrasted sharply with those of his contemporaries. His proposed program for assisting theft recidivists was seriously questioned by his superiors and by his subordinate local officials as well.[57] Perhaps under the influence of the popular notion that exthieves were unworthy of trust and that they tended to collaborate with other undesirable

57. In 1741 the various magistrates' opinions along with some of Ch'en's recommendations were submitted to the governor and the governor-general, who presumably approved them. In the same year Ch'en was promoted to the post of financial commissioner of the same province and then to the post of governor of Kiangsi. Since neither his own writing nor other sources contain information on the theft-control program, we cannot evaluate its success or failure.

elements of the society, the governor-general, the governor, and magistrates throughout Kiangsu province declined to adopt Ch'en's proposal for hiring those former criminals as patrolmen or mint workers. Ch'en wanted to give the exthieves a chance to prove that they could cooperate with the authorities and eventually become respectable people again. However, most officials preferred the conventional and conservative approach of degrading theft recidivists by making them beggars. This approach was justified not only on the ground that such criminals well deserved harsh punishment because of the harm they had done to the society, but also because the officials in charge would be relieved from the extra burden of supervising the rehabilitation program.

LOCAL VARIATIONS IN THE CONTROL OF THIEVES: CHEKIANG

In 1756 Chu A-p'ei, from Lin-hai, Chekiang, was convicted of theft.[58] As a result of imperial amnesty, he was either pardoned or spared from penal servitude. According to a regulation adopted by the Chekiang provincial government, however, all exthieves were to be rounded up and placed in preventive detention at the end of each year. This was because thievery usually reached its peak when the farming season was over and people were desperate to get money for the festive Chinese Lunar New Year.[59] The Chekiang government regulation did not specify how many years such preventive dentention should continue, nor the length of each individual detention. Therefore, in spite of the fact that Chu never got into trouble again after his conviction, he was arrested by government runners and locked in an official bandit house (fei-fang) every New Year for thirteen consecutive winters. In the winter of 1769, Chu finally reached his own limit. When two runners again appeared with a warrant, Chu resisted arrest, wounding one of the runners with a knife. For this offense Chu A-p'ei was sentenced to three years of penal servitude and one hundred blows of the heavy bamboo.[60]

Hsu, the acting judicial commissioner, reported the case to the governor, Hsiung Hsueh-p'eng, requesting that the regulation in question be revised. Hsu pointed out that preventive detention was merely a local device to cope with the rising rate of theft. The imperial Ch'ing code required only that convicted thieves be supervised by the local constable (ti-pao).[61] If the offenders had repented and refrained from repeating the same crime, they should be left undisturbed. It would be difficult for them to make a living should the government continue to detain them at the end of each year.

58. *Chih-Che ch'eng-kuei* [Established regulations for governing Chekiang province] (ca. 1837), ts'e 7, pp. 15–17b.
59. Also see Ch'en Hung-mou, *P'ei-yuan t'ang*, 10:9a-b, 14:37.
60. *Ch'ing code*, IV, 2703, 2642–2643; Staunton, pp. 334, 325.
61. This probably refers to the 1727 legislation that formally assigned the *pao-chia* heads the duty to supervise thieves. See *HTSL*, XX, 15490, and XIX, 15169, with respect to "controlled exclusively by *pao-chia* heads."

Commissioner Hsu therefore recommended that three years should be the proper limit for the winter quarantine.

The governor was not quite convinced by Hsu's argument. Fearing that the three-year limit on preventive detention might be detrimental to the larger society, he urged Hsu to discuss the matter with Fu-le-hun, the financial commissioner. Hsu soon left his post, but his replacement as judicial commissioner, a man named Hao, continued to pursue the matter. In fact, shortly afterwards Hao and Fu-le-hun submitted a joint opinion favoring the past practice of requiring a theft recidivist to wear the cangue and bell for three years, after which time he would be allowed to go free if he had demonstrated good conduct.[62] The Chekiang practice of winter confinement, on the other hand, denied thieves the opportunity of self-rectification, so that the government inevitably forced them to become outlaws. Finally convinced, the governor consented to the proposal and put the revised law into effect in October 1770.[63]

CONCLUSION

During the Ch'ing period, petty thieves punishable by beating were tattooed, sent back to their native place, given blows of the heavy bamboo, and finally handed over to a guarantor for supervision. More serious theft offenders who had been sentenced to penal servitude were also tattooed and, after completing penal servitude, were likewise returned to their native place to be supervised. The practice of tattooing, the forcible return, and the imperial regulation of 1760 which required theft recidivists to wear the cangue in a public place for twenty to forty days prior to their beating, all reflected the Ch'ing attempt to combat crime by capitalizing on shame ("loss of face") and the fear of social ostracism.

Ch'ing society can be roughly divided into two major groups: "good people" (consisting of commoners and officials) and "mean people" (social outcasts). The latter category was primarily composed of people who engaged in such demeaned professions as prostitution, acting, or begging. Because of the tattooing imposed by the state, convicted thieves were similarly ostracized and, along with other hardened criminals, became identified as outcasts.

Except in serious cases, thieves were normally not sentenced to death; they were instead expected to live with respectable members of society. The

---

62. They were probably referring to the 1745 ruling. Kiangsu had a similar practice, see above.

63. Chekiang was probably not the only province that used such a winter quarantine. Kiangsi also seems to have had a program that called for temporary detention of thieves if a theft case was concluded and the offender should have been set free during the winter. One entry in *chüan* 2 of the *Hsi-Chiang cheng-yao* (see note 64) is called *Tsei-fan lung-tung fa-lo chan-hsing chi-chin* (Temporary confinement of thieves whose cases were concluded in the cold winter). Unfortunately, due to faulty binding its text has been left out.

avowed and foremost purpose of tattooing and canguing was to make convicted thieves conspicuous among the populace, arousing a feeling of humiliation and thus, hopefully, stimulating a sense of shame and a resolve to become respectable citizens. Implicit in such a penal policy was a promise to remove any permanent trace of the tattoo and restore the criminals to their preconviction status as "good people" if true repentance had been manifested. Nevertheless, frequently such a promise was either forgotten or purposefully disregarded, so that this corporal punishment amounted to a cruel retribution against wrongdoers.

Preoccupied with other administrative and judicial tasks, the magistrate was often too busy to worry about the sufferings of the small segment of his subjects who had been stigmatized through the legal process. And even if he did have the time to concern himself with such matters, the magistrate had to choose between two different legal philosophies. The first was closely associated with the statecraft tradition, exemplified during the eighteenth century by Ch'en Hung-mou. By resorting to guarantors and by encouraging self-respect, this school tried to rehabilitate convicts by reintegrating them into a regular social setting. Since the guarantors were chosen from among a convict's immediate relatives or his close neighbors, they were likely to be sympathetic to the convict while carrying out an effective surveillance. Furthermore, the physical discomfort imposed on criminals should be reduced to the minimum: as long as the prescribed sentence had been completed, a properly supervised convict need not be further humiliated by wearing a cangue or bell, or inconvenienced by a semimonthly appearance at the district yamen.

The second philosophy derived from the traditional legalist view. Once a man was convicted for theft, he deserved the humiliation of becoming an outcast. Even though statutory punishments of tattooing and canguing alone sufficed to ostracize convicted thieves, additional measures might be adopted to insure maximum discomfort: the imposition of a bell, cangue, iron stick, handcuffs, or winter detention, as in Chekiang. Such measures were not necessarily motivated by the desire for retaliation. Rather, the advocates of this school were mainly concerned about the security and welfare of the society as a whole, believing that an individual's transgression of the law was clear evidence of his evil nature. Consequently, it was too much of a risk to the community for convicted thieves to be permitted to roam freely, even though they had completed the sentence meted out by the state. This was especially true in the case of thievery where the rate of recidivism was known to be high. As we have seen, the Ch'ing code did prescribe that convicted thieves serve as police or police aids. Although we lack sufficient evidence to confirm that this requirement was enforced all over the empire, we can still suppose that the hesitation of many officials to entrust such an important duty to suspicious characters accounted for the nonenforcement of this particular policy.

The latter failure in turn suggests that the provincial governments enjoyed a considerable amount of freedom in their implementation of imperial law. Most of the provisions of the Ch'ing code were very detailed, even to the point of being meticulous. Yet at times we also find legislation drafted in such a way as to enable each province to take care of a wide range of local variations. One example is the *li* promulgated in 1740 by the Ch'ien-lung emperor which required that convicted thieves assume police duty. The emperor neither specified the period and condition of service nor limited it to the theft recidivist alone. Thus each province was clearly authorized to devise a program most suited to its needs.

Even in a case where the national regulation was unequivocal, we see the provincial authorities at times making modifications in the application of law. A case in point is the 1760 *li* which standardized the imposition of twenty to forty days of the cangue on a theft recidivist prior to the punishment of bambooing. In the following year the government of Kiangsi ruled that he should be given an additional three years' police duty while wearing the cangue and bell. It is possible that the provincial government was relying on the aforementioned 1740 *li* on police duty, yet the justification given by Kiangsi officials was that it would be too dangerous to let the convict free after merely forty days of canguing![64] At best, what the Kiangsi government did can be termed an extremely broad construction of the principles set forth in the penal code.

There were other examples showing that differences in local situations necessitated flexibility for control and even provided latitude for local officials to choose within a spectrum ranging from rehabilitation to inner banishment of convicted theft offenders. Chekiang officials asserted the need for preventive detention even though they clearly recognized that such measures were nowhere contemplated in the penal code. The allowable range of provincial variations was not precisely stipulated by the central government. If in doubt, local officials could always address their problems to Peking for guidance. On the whole, however, the impression is that flexibility in local control mechanisms was accepted by the majority of officials.

This is not to imply that the Ch'ing central government abdicated its power in the wake of growing regionalism. In the seventeenth and eighteenth centuries, Peking's control was still very strong, enabling it to check local deviations from the national norm. Therefore, it seems that the attempt to achieve optimum accommodation in varying geographical locations was the main consideration behind the central government's acquiescence in letting the provinces enjoy some degree of legislative autonomy.

Finally, I would like to offer a tentative appraisal of how successful the theft-control policy was during the course of the dynasty. Although statistics are lacking on the incidence of theft among the populace and on the convic-

64. Kiangsi an-ch'a-ssu ya-men [Kiangsi provincial judicial commissioner's office], *Hsi-Chiang cheng-yao* [The essentials of governing Kiangsi province] (ca. 1900), 5:6–7, 19–20.

tion rate, it seems safe to conclude that the government did arrest a substantial number of thieves and punish them in accordance with law. (At
least not much complaint was heard about the government's ability to do
so.) The success of prevention of theft recidivism was, however, quite another
matter. Since most officials seem to have preferred inner banishment of
convicted thieves to their rehabilitation and reintegration into the society,
the harsh treatment given exthieves left much to be desired. It goes without
saying that the legal philosophy of safeguarding the society's interests mili-
tated against thieves' returning to the civilly respectable world.

Opium Smoking
in Ch'ing China

Jonathan Spence

Opium addiction in Ch'ing China is a large subject.[1] At one level, it is a story of international trade, warfare, and diplomacy. At another level, it concerns the psychic needs or the demoralization of individual Chinese, and the local economic arrangements that were made to grow and to distribute the prepared opium. At yet another level, it concerns the most complex interactions between Western powers and individual Chinese: the triumph of trading interests over morality and the collapse of older agricultural ideals; the linkage of "evil" with "the foreigner"; the growth of special interest groups such as Canton merchants, Triads, Shansi bankers, and Parsee firms; shifts in Chinese taxation patterns; and the final shattering of images of the emperor as paternal protector.

To date most studies on opium in China have focused on the areas of international commerce and diplomacy.[2] This essay is an attempt to widen the area of debate by developing certain themes that show opium smoking as a phenomenon that radically affected all levels of Chinese society. Further-

1. My special thanks to Andrew Hsieh, for much help with bibliography and translation; to Fu-mei Chen and Randle Edwards for crucial legal references, and for correcting several mistakes in the draft paper; to John Fairbank for perceptive comments as discussant; and to Janis Cochran for typing so often from my longhand without objections. Thanks also to many people who discussed this paper with me, or supplied references: Leonard Adams, Charles Boxer, Edward Brecher, Rosser Brockman, Chang Te-ch'ang, Sherman Cochran, Herbert Kleber, Jao Tsung-i, Sue Naquin, Jonathan Ocko, Saeki Tomi, Jack Wills.

2. The most interesting studies include: Hosea Ballou Morse, *The International Relations of the Chinese Empire*, 3 vols. (Shanghai and London, 1910–1918); John King Fairbank, *Trade and Diplomacy on the China Coast, The Opening of the Treaty Ports, 1842–1854* (Cambridge: Harvard University Press, 1953); Chen Ching-jen, "Opium and Anglo-Chinese Relations," *Chinese Social and Political Science Review* 19:396–437; Yü En-te, *Chung-kuo chin-yen fa-ling pien-ch'ien shih* [A history of the prohibitions of opium in China] (Shanghai: Chung-hua shu-chü, 1934); Chang Hsin-pao, *Commissioner Lin and the Opium War* (Cambridge: Harvard University Press, 1964); Charles C. Stelle, "American Trade in Opium in China, 1821–1839," *Pacific Historical Review* 9:425–445 and 10:57–75; David Edward Owen, *British Opium Policy in China and India* (New Haven: Yale University Press, 1934); Michael Greenberg, *British Trade and the Opening of China, 1800–1842* (Cambridge, England: Cambridge University Press, 1951); and *YPCC*.

more, I have attempted to marshal the data in certain categories that will encourage two areas of comparative study: first, opium addiction as a problem of deviance and control in Ch'ing China, and second, opium addiction as an economic and social problem that can be compared with drug dependencies in other cultures. The categories I have tried to isolate are consumption, prohibition, distribution, and economic function.

There is one other category, that of motivation, which should have a section for itself, only the data is extraordinarily elusive. Opium was highly regarded in China, both as a medicinal drug (that checked diarrhea and served as a febrifuge),[3] and as an aphrodisiac.[4] Therefore, people might become addicted either because they took opium intensively during an illness —for instance, in the great cholera epidemic of 1821[5]—or because they had vigor, leisure, and money and wanted to make the best of it.[6]

Such general considerations aside, it is obvious that different occupational and economic groups had different motivations, but in many cases one can only guess what these might have been. For the eunuchs and members of the imperial clan, there was a boring life in sheltered circumstances, without the possibilities of release that political power had given them in other times—for instance, the late Ming for eunuchs, or early Ch'ing for the Manchu nobles.[7] Soldiers, whether banner or green standard, had similar elements of boredom, compounded by a routine life and the forbidding to them of release through trade or other gainful employ; furthermore, the officers were unlikely to use the opium-addicted soldier in crucial combat situations.[8] For Chinese literati,

3. Chang Lu, *Pen-ching feng-yuan* [Clear exposition of medical classics] in *Chang-shih i-shu* [The medical works of Chang Lu] (preface dated 1709), 3:11–12; Joseph Edkins, *Opium: Historical Note, or the Poppy in China*, Imperial Maritime Customs, China, vol. 2, special ser. no. 13 (Shanghai, 1898). As a febrifuge, especially for the poor in marshy areas or for boatmen, see *RoyCom*, I, 112, no. 1637.

4. Most early eighteenth-century sources mention its aphrodisiac quality. See Lan Tingyuan, *Lu-chou ch'u-chi* [Collected works from Lu-chou] (1731 ed.); and Huang Shu-ching, *T'ai-hai shih ch'a lu* [Notes on a mission to Taiwan] (Taipei: T'ai-wan wen-hsien ts'ung-k'an, 1957). Liang Kung-ch'en cites a mid-Ch'ing prostitute for more graphic details. See Liang Kung-ch'en, *Pei-tung-yuan pi-lu* [Notes from the northeast garden], in *Pi-chi hsiao-shuo ta-kuan* [A broad view of random essays and fiction] (Taipei: Hsin-hsing shu-chü, 1962), 3rd ser., 2:21b. There are strong parallels with one element of heroin motivation here: both opium and heroin initially prolong male erection and postpone ejaculation, though in later stages of addiction, desire decreases markedly. See *RoyCom*, I, 167, for the interesting testimony furnished by the Sydney Police Department on Australian prostitutes consorting with Chinese addicts.

5. The epidemic is discussed in K. Chimin Wong and Wu Lien-teh, *History of Chinese Medicine* (Tientsin: The Tientsin Press, 1932). For the extent of the epidemic, see *Ch'ing-shih* [Dynastic history of the Ch'ing], Kuo-fang yen-chiu-yuan ed. (Taipei, 1961), I, 671.

6. On opium smoking in circumstances of great prosperity, see the evidence for Szechwan collected by S. A. M. Adshead, "The Opium Trade in Szechwan, 1881–1911," *Journal of Southeast Asian History* 7:93–99.

7. The waning of eunuchs' power and their dissatisfaction is considered by Chang Te-ch'ang in "The Economic Role of the Imperial Household (*Nei-wu-fu*) in the Ch'ing Dynasty," *Journal of Asian Studies* 31:243–273. Manchu nobles had little power after Yung-cheng's reign.

8. The interpretation of becoming addicted so as to avoid dangerous combat assignments

mu-yu (private secretaries), and officials, opium provided a relief from career frustrations and stresses generated within the family;[9] it may also, for Chinese humiliated by their positions under barbarian conquerors, have been a surrogate for withdrawal, a form of eremetism in one's own home. If such a proposition has any validity, things must have been even more depressing after 1842, when the Manchu overlords were themselves humiliated. This may explain why a man like Yen Fu became an addict.[10] Merchants sometimes smoked because they believed opium sharpened their wits and helped them to drive shrewder business deals with their competitors.[11] They and other wealthy Chinese also took and offered opium to guests after dinner parties as a social gesture.[12] Students took opium during their key state examinations, thinking that it helped them to do better work.[13]

Sometimes the explanations for addiction are rather tortuous; thus, the *Gazetteer of Amoy* reported that many rich Chinese encouraged their sons to stay at home and smoke opium rather than indulging in debauchery or gambling.[14] This motive, with an additional social twist, was sufficiently accepted to provide the theme for the first feature film made by a Chinese production company, "Wronged Ghosts," shot by the Huei Hsi company in 1916. The synopsis of the film begins: "A wealthy miser has a son who is enthusiastic about public welfare and gives money generously to relieve the poor. His father fears that the family fortune will be wasted in the son's hands, and he persuades the son to start smoking opium, hoping that this will keep him idle and at home."[15]

For the rich, or those with some surplus cash, the rewards from opium must have been sharper perception, greater social ease, removal from present worries, and a pleasing distortion of time sequences; but unfortunately there is no literature in praise of opium that can match the euphoric compendia on tobacco written by eighteenth-century Chinese.[16]

---

which had not occurred to me, though it should have, was suggested by Dr. Herbert Kleber.

9. A theme beautifully illustrated in Mao Tun, *Midnight* (Peking: Foreign Language Press, 1957). Charles de Constant guessed in the late eighteenth century that women smoked for similar reasons. See Louis Dermigny, *Les Memoires de Charles de Constant sur le commerce à la Chine* (Paris: École Pratique des Hautes Études, 1964).

10. As mentioned by Benjamin I. Schwartz, *In Search of Wealth and Power* (Cambridge: Harvard University Press, 1964), p. 31.

11. *RoyCom*, I, 110, no. 1631, and 116, no. 1733.

12. *RoyCom*, I, 116, no. 1739, and 131, nos. 2026–2032.

13. *RoyCom*, I, 30, no. 389.

14. *Hsia-men chih* [Gazetteer of Amoy] (1839), 15:17.

15. Jay Leyda, *Dianying, Electric Shadows: An Account of Films and the Film Audience in China* (Cambrdige: M.I.T. Press, 1972), pp. 17–18.

16. Much data is in the collections by Wang Shih-han, comp., *Chin-ssu lu* [Notes on tobacco] in *Ts'ung-mu Wang-shih i-shu* [Collection of Mr. Wang's posthumous papers] (1886); Lu Yao, *Yen-p'u* [Notes on tobacco] in *Chao-tai ts'ung-shu, ting-chi* [Chao-tai collection, 4th ser.] (1833), chüan 46; and Ts'ai Chia-wan, *Yen-p'u* [Notes on tobacco] in *Pai-mei shan-fang chi shang-shu* [Writings from the house on Pai-mei mountain] (1836). These discuss tobacco smoking as being good for health and relaxation and as an aid in forgetting sadness; all three presumably would have been emphasized by opium smokers had a *Ya-p'ien p'u* [Notes on

Those who ate regularly and well did not show physical deterioration resulting from their addiction;[17] but for the poor, addiction was a serious health hazard (even though, ironically, it was often first taken for health reasons), since scarce cash resources were put to opium rather than food purchases. The rewards for the poor were a blurring of the pains of prolonged labor, and an increase in work capacity over short periods of time.[18] Thus there was heavy addiction among coolies and chair-bearers,[19] and among such groups as boatmen who had to work their boats upstream, and stonecutters working outside in cold weather.[20] The last Chinese to become addicted seem to have been the peasants, though as they grew more opium crops the incidence of heavy opium smoking rose, and by 1902 one could find entire rural communities that were in desperate straits because addiction had become almost total.[21]

By the late Ch'ing, it seems that no major occupational group was without its addicts. We can give individuality to some of these forgotten opium smokers by describing them in terms of their relationships: they were Ch'en Tu-hsiu's grandfather, Kuo Mo-jo's brother, Feng Yü-hsiang's parents, Hu Shih's stepbrother, Ch'ü Ch'iu-pai's father, Lu Hsun's father.[22] Others survive only in fiction—the lean servants in Pa Chin's *The Family* who told their stories to Chieh-hui while the little boy, rapt, watched the light of the opium lamps play over their faces.[23]

We cannot tell why they all smoked; but we can, at least, begin to sketch in the story of why the opium was available to them.

CONSUMPTION

The habit of opium smoking in China was an offshoot and development of tobacco smoking. Tobacco reached the Fukien coast sometime late in the Wan-li reign (1573–1619),[24] and was first transplanted in the Shih-ma area of

---

opium] ever been written. The joys of opium in a Chinese literati setting of the 1930s are wonderfully caught in Emily Hahn's essay, "The Big Smoke," *Times and Places* (New York: Crowell, 1970).

17. *RoyCom*, I, 48, no. 627 and *passim*, for Indian testimony.

18. Brief summary in *RoyCom*, VI, 51. Again, there was much detailed study of the effects of opium on Indian laborers.

19. *RoyCom*, I, 47, no. 611.

20. *Roycom*, I, 95, no. 1320.

21. Francis H. Nichols, *Through Hidden Shensi* (New York, 1902), ch. 5.

22. For examples, in order, see: D. W. Y. Kwok, *Scientism in Chinese Thought, 1900–1950* (New Haven: Yale University Press, 1965), pp. 50–60; David Roy, *Kuo Mo-jo, The Early Years* (Cambridge: Harvard University Press, 1971), p. 46 (Kuo's father also dealt in opium; ibid., p. 9); James Sheridan, *Chinese Warlord, The Career of Feng Yü-hsiang* (Stanford: Stanford University Press, 1970), p. 9; Chou Hsia-shou (Chou Tso-jen), *Lu Hsun ti ku-chia* [Lu Hsun's home] (Shanghai: Shang-hai ch'u-pan kung-she, 1953), sec. 26, p. 70; Donald Klein and Ann Clark, "Ch'ü Ch'iu-pai," *Biographical Dictionary of Chinese Communism, 1921–1965* (Cambridge: Harvard University Press, 1971), I, 239.

23. Pa Chin, *The Family* (Peking: Foreign Languages Press, 1958), pp. 91, 117–118.

24. *Fu-chou fi-clil* [Foochow prefectural gazetteer] (1754), 25:24; L. Carrington Goodrich,

Chang-chou.[25] Tobacco grew so luxuriantly in China that it rapidly became an important domestic cash crop, dashing the Portuguese hopes for developing an oriental outlet for their Brazilian tobacco.[26] By the K'ang-hsi reign tobacco smoking was a national Chinese habit; Shih-ma and other brand names were inscribed on the shop signs of hundreds of tobacco retail stores in downtown Peking,[27] and large fields of tobacco were growing just outside the city walls.[28]

The earliest Chinese reference that I have found to the fact that opium too could be smoked is a comment by Chang Ju-lin (who died in 1626) that appears in the *Gazetteer of Macao.* Appended to a note on snuff he has this remark: "There is also opium (*ya-p'ien-yen*); in a raw state it looks like mud, but it can be treated so that it's smokable. There's a prohibition against selling it."[29] The delight taken by Chang Ju-lin and his family in the widest range of sensual delights is well known,[30] and they would be worthy candidates for the mixed honor of being China's first opium smokers. There is evidence that Chinese in Jakarta were smoking opium as early as 1617, and Chinese in Batavia were dealing in opium and tobacco mixtures in 1671.[31] More detailed records on opium smoking appear in the 1690s, when Kaempfer was in Java and noticed shops that sold pipefuls of opium mixed with tobacco to passersby.[32] Opium smoking may have been introduced to Taiwan by the Dutch when they controlled the island early in the seventeenth century, but again the first careful description only comes much later—in a comment given by Lan Ting-yuan in 1724, after he had returned from the campaign against Chu I-kuei.[33]

Lan described opium smoking as being a harmful trap, set by the barbarians in Taiwan to ensnare Han Chinese: neophytes were given free meals and free opium at first, but once they were hooked they were made to pay.

"Early Prohibitions of Tobacco in China and Manchuria,"*Journal of the American Oriental Society* 58:638–657; Berthold Laufer, *Tobacco and Its Use in Asia,* Anthropology leaflet no. 18 (Chicago: Field Museum of Natural History, 1924).

25. "Wu-ch'an-chih" [Section on produce], 1:7b, in *Fu-chien t'ung-chih* [Fukien provincial gazetteer] (1870 ed.; reprint, Taipei), p. 632.

26. André Joao Antonil, *Cultura e opulencia do Brasil por suas drogas e minas,* ed. and trans. Andrée Mansuy (Paris: Institut des Hautes Études de l'Amérique Latine, 1968), p. 333.

27. See the illustrations in *Wan-shou sheng-tien* [Compilation of K'ang-hsi's sixtieth birthday celebrations] (1717), showing the tobacco shops along Peking streets.

28. John Bell, *A Journey from St. Petersburg to Pekin, 1719–1722* (Edinburgh: Edinburgh University Press, 1965), p. 167.

29. Wang Shih-han, *Chin-ssu lu,* p. 2.

30. Arthur W. Hummel, ed., *Eminent Chinese of the Ch'ing Period* (Washington, D.C.: U.S. Government Printing Office, 1943–1944), I, 53.

31. For 1617, see L. C. D. van Dijk, "Bijvoegsels tot de geschiedenis van het handle en het gebruik van opium in Nederlandsch Indië," in *Bijdragen tot de Taal-, land, en Volkenkunde van Nederlandsch Indië,* 211; for the resolution of 1671 to forbid further Chinese dealing, see *Algemeen Rijksarchief,* K. A. 586, fol. 256. Both of these references were supplied by Jack Wills.

32. Engelbert Kaempfer, *Amoenitatum Exoticarum politico-physico-medicarum* (Langoviae, 1712), cited in Edkins, *Opium,* p. 155.

33. Lan Ting-yuan, *Lu-chou ch'u-chi,* 2:16.

Addiction was common in Taiwan, and smoking had been widespread in Amoy for over ten years. Lan gave no details about smoking methods, save that the opium "is heated in a copper pot and smoked through a pipe like a short club." But Huang Shu-ching, who recorded his impressions after returning from a stint as Taiwan inspecting censor in 1723, wrote that the opium, after being mixed with plants and boiled in a copper pan, was added to tobacco and smoked through a bamboo tube filled with coir fibres.[34]

None of these sources sheds much light on the smokers, or gives exact details as to what was being smoked. Lan and Huang merely noted that those who smoked were either the criminal or the gullible, while Chang Ju-lin didn't say who was smoking. Nor is the first detailed prohibition of opium smoking, which appeared in 1729, much help on this point; it merely refers in general terms to the seduction with opium of minors from worthy families (*liang-chia tzu-ti*) as being particularly reprehensible.[35]

This 1729 prohibition struck at distributors but not at smokers, and does not seem to have been strongly enforced; so we may assume, though we cannot prove, a gradual spreading of opium and tobacco smoking throughout the eighteenth century. Charles de Constant discussed the widespread smoking of opium mixed with tobacco in the Canton of the 1780s,[36] and Abel in 1816 described the smoking of opium imbedded in tobacco, or of tobacco steeped in opium solution, as being common "in all parts of the Empire."[37]

The vagueness of this data has led to an understandable imprecision about who was smoking what and when, and has even led some students to reject the data altogether. Thus Ch'en Ch'i-yuan, reviewing some evidence from 1729, concluded that the officials could not have known what they were talking about, since opium is not smoked with tobacco.[38] The problem is solved if we realize that there are two different types of opium derivative under consideration. Until the late eighteenth century most Chinese were smoking madak, not pure opium. Madak is crude opium that has been dissolved in water, boiled and strained, boiled a second time till it reaches a syrupy consistency, then mixed with shredded leaves preparatory to smoking. It is smoked in a regular pipe, like tobacco, and yields about 0.2 percent of morphia by volume.[39] Huang Shu-ching had partly understood this process in 1723, when he wrote that the crude opium was mixed with *ma* and *ko* leaves and then cooked.[40] His testimony is not decisive, but it is backed independently by the Dutchman Valentyn who saw madak being smoked in Java in

34. Huang Shu-ching, *T'ai-hai shih-ch'a lu*, p. 43.
35. Cited in Yü En-te, *Chung-kuo chin-yen fa-ling*, p. 16.
36. Dermigny, *Charles de Constant*, p. 207.
37. Clarke Abel, *Narrative of a Journey in the Interior of China* (London, 1818), pp. 214–215.
38. Ch'en Ch'i-yuan, *Yung-hsien chai pi-chi* [Notes from the Yung-hsien study], in *Pi-chi hsiao-shuo ta-kuan* [A broad view of random essays and fiction] (Taipei: Kuang-wen shu-chü, 1960), 8:22.
39. *RoyCom*, VI, pt. 1, p. 117.
40. Huang Shu-ching, *T'ai-hai shih-ch'a lu*.

1726.[41] The smoking of madak, or of tobacco dipped in opium solution, can be seen as the connecting point between tobacco and opium proper. The moderate pleasure of madak—perhaps equivalent to taking a few inhalations of marijuana—were rejected by many smokers when they discovered the smoking of pure opium. When properly refined and aged, a unit of smokable extract (chandu) yields between 9 and 10 percent of morphia.[42]

The 1760s has been suggested as the time when the smoking of pure opium began in China, and the date is a plausible one, though there seems no way of definitely proving when *ya-p'ien yen* comes to refer to unadulterated opium.[43] It was in the 1770s that Charles de Constant observed that the Chinese had suddenly developed "une passion pour ce narcotique qui passe toute croyance,"[44] and perhaps this new passion—echoed by a quadruple rise in imports from around 1,000 chests in 1773 to 4,000 chests per annum in 1790[45]—was the result of encounters with the stronger drug. Nevertheless, the demand was not yet immense, since it was in 1782 that Warren Hastings dispatched the *Nonsuch* with 1,000 chests of Patna opium and found almost no buyers at Canton, being forced to sell to Sinqua at only $210 a chest.[46]

There is an extremely detailed passage on opium smoking in Chao Hsueh-min's continuation of the *Pen-ts'ao kang-mu*; the preface to this is dated 1765, so here we have a rare source of Ch'ien-lung reign opium practices from the Chinese viewpoint. Though the author gives the nod to previous writers by saying the opium is mixed with tobacco and smoked, it is obvious from his description that he is describing pure opium:

> When you're going to smoke you must get a group of people together, and take it in turns. Place a mat on the *k'ang* and have everyone recline on it; put the lighted lamp in the middle and smoke (*hsi*), from a hundred to several hundred puffs. The smoking pipe is a tube of bamboo, eight or nine *fen* in diameter, filled with coir fibre and hair. Bind each end firmly with silver bands, and at one end open a hole the size of your little finger. Mold some clay into the shape of a gourd, hollow it out, dry it in an oven, and push it into the little hole on the top of this gourd. You only take a little bit of the opium, and it is all used in one inhalation. It makes a gurgling sound.[47]

Apart from the fact that one person could not make a hundred inhalations, and that the text does not say how the opium is heated over the lamp before

41. *RoyCom*, VII, pt. 2, appendix B, p. 33.

42. *RoyCom*, VI, pt. 1, p. 117.

43. Chen Ching-jen, "Opium and Anglo-Chinese Relations," *Chinese Social and Political Science Review* 19:388.

44. Dermigny, *Charles de Constant*, p. 205, n. 1.

45. Morse, *International Relations*, I, 173–174.

46. Chang Hsin-pao, *Commissioner Lin*, p. 237, n. 6.

47. Chao Hsueh-min, *Pen-ts'ao kang-mu shih-i* [A continuation of the medical classic *Pen-ts'ao kang-mu*] (Hong Kong: Shang-wu yin-shu kuan, 1969), pp. 34–35. Also, pp. 25–34 have a great deal of data on tobacco.

inhalation, this is a full enough description to leave no doubt that pure opium is the substance being smoked, not some tobacco mixture or madak.

The dissemination of opium smoking, however widespread, did not rouse the Ch'ing emperors to action until it became noticeable at court in the early nineteenth century; thereafter, the interplay of memorials and edicts enables us to trace the spread of addiction through the bureaucracy in some detail. By 1813 there were a number of opium smokers among the palace guard officers (*shih-wei*), and Chia-ch'ing suspected that eunuchs were smoking as well.[48] He was posthumously proved right, in a sensational investigation conducted by the directors of the Imperial Household in December 1831. The directors found that a large number of senior eunuchs were opium addicts, and that some of them had been smoking for twenty or thirty years; also, they sometimes smoked with Manchu members of the imperial clan.[49] But the wide range of smokers had already been graphically described in a remarkable memorial written four months earlier by Lu Yin-p'u (grand secretary and concurrently president of the Board of Justice) together with six other board presidents and vice presidents. Tracing the origins of opium smoking to corrupt secretaries and merchants, the memorialists found that it had spread from them to the sons of great families and rich city merchants, and from them to the common people. "At the present time, there are opium smokers in all the provinces, with special concentration in the various yamens; we estimate that among governors-general and their subordinates, and at every level of both civil and military officialdom, those who do *not* smoke opium are few in-deed."[50]

In 1832 it was finally proven beyond doubt that opium addiction in certain parts of the army had become so serious that the troops were incapable of combat. After investigating the reasons why the troops of the Liang-Kuang governor-general, Li Hung-pin, had been roundly defeated by the Yao rebels in the area of Lien-chou (in northwest Kwangtung, near the Hunan and Kwangsi borders), the Manchu imperial commissioner, Hsi-en, concluded that: "Six thousand combat troops were sent [from Kwangtung], but they were not used to the mountains; and many of the troops from all the coastal garrisons were opium smokers, and it was difficult to get any vigorous response from them."[51]

The extent of these revelations alarmed Tao-kuang and many senior officials, and from this time onward the opium debates developed in intensity, reaching an initial climax in the legalization–prohibition arguments in 1836. The most graphic account of widespread opium smoking appears in Chu

48. *TCHT* p. 15, no. 442 (828:4b).

49. *YPCC*, pp. 454–456; *CSL*:TK, pp. 3562, 3579, 3587; *HAHL*, p. 909.

50. *YPCC*, p. 436. Chang Hsin-pao, *Commissioner Lin*, p. 34, shows that Pao Shih-chen had estimated 100,000 addicts spending about 10,000 taels a day in the Soochow of 1820.

51. *SCL*:TK, pp. 3893, 3895, 3897, 3899; biography of Li Hung-pin in *Ch'ing-shih lieh-chuan* [Biographies of the Ch'ing dynasty] (Taipei: Chung-hua shu-chü, 1962), 36:46b; *HAHL*, p. 863.

Tsun's memorial of that year. Chu Tsun attacked the arguments made by Hsu Nai-chi and his friends in Juan Yuan's Canton academy—they wanted legalization for the common people and prohibition for scholars, officials, and soldiers[52]—as being hopelessly impractical, since there was no way to control private smoking unless the ban was total. Chu Tsun analyzed the smoking population as follows: "The great majority of those who at present smoke opium are the relatives and dependents of the officers of government, whose example has extended the practice to the mercantile classes, and has gradually contaminated the inferior officers, the military, and the scholars. Those who do not smoke are the common people of the villages and hamlets."[53]

The spread of opium to the common people can be gauged through three different groups of sources: import figures, analyses of domestic production, and the guesses of informed observers.

Imports—of Bengal, Malwa, and Turkish opium—stayed within the 4,000 to 5,000 chest mark until 1820. During the 1820s they hovered around the 10,000 chest mark, with a sharp upward jump in 1828 to 18,000.[54] By 1832 they had passed the 20,000 chest mark, and reached 40,000 by 1839.[55] The steady climb continued, to 76,000 chests in 1865 and 81,000 by 1884.[56] There followed a slow drop until the 1900s, when imports stabilized around 50,000 chests.[57] This imported opium was smoked mainly by the rich, who found it better quality than the domestic—both in flavor and strength.[58]

Chinese domestic production of opium has been traced back to the T'ang dynasty, and the poppy seems to have flourished in western China, particularly Yunnan, Szechwan, and Kansu.[59] By the early Ch'ing we find that the gazetteers of Kweichow and Fukien also listed Ying-su poppy among their plants, though they did not elaborate on production methods or uses.[60] Hsu Nai-chi, in 1836, pointed to domestic production in Kwangtung, Fukien and eastern parts of Chekiang, as well as Yunnan.[61] Trying to back up his legalization arguments, Hsu pointed out that domestic Chinese opium was milder than foreign, and hence addiction could be more easily eliminated; he drew a parallel with the tobacco plant, showing how, after domestic prohibitions were relaxed, native gentle Chinese tobacco ousted its harsh, diz-

52. Chang Hsin-pao, *Commissioner Lin*, pp. 87–88; and *Chinese Repository* 5:139–144.

53. *Chinese Repository* 5:396.

54. Chang Hsin-pao, *Commissioner Lin*, p. 223, appendix B.

55. Morse, *International Relations*, I, 209–210.

56. Stanley F. Wright, *Hart and the Chinese Customs* (Belfast: Wm. Mullan, 1950), p. 544.

57. Morse, *International Relations*, III, 437.

58. IMC, *Native Opium, 1887; with an Appendix: Native Opium, 1863*, vol. 2, special ser. no. 9 (Shanghai: Inspector General of Customs, 1888), p. 6, and app. on 1863; and IMC *Opium: Crude and Prepared*, vol. 2, special ser. no. 10 (Shanghai: Inspector General of Customs, 1888), p. 38.

59. *Ku-chin t'u-shu chi-ch'eng* [Historical encyclopedia of the Ch'ing] (Shanghai: Chung-hua shu-chü, 1934), as cited in Edkins, *Opium*.

60. *Fu-chou fu-chih: Kuei-chou t'ung-chih* [Kweichow provincial gazetteer], 1741 ed.

61. *YPCC*, p. 474; for Kwangtung, *YPCC*, p. 440; for Chekiang, *YPCC*, p. 465.

zying Philippines competitors. Unfortunately, Hsu's argument had little weight, since wealthy opium smokers wanted strength, not mildness. As Chang Lu, certainly the most widely known doctor and medical writer of the K'ang-hsi reign, had written in 1705, the domestic opium can still cure some maladies but "its strength is less and it is not so efficacious" as the foreign.[62] Presumably, the same strength differential held true through the 1840s, when domestic poppy cultivation had spread to Kwangsi, Hunan, and Hupei as well.[63] Thomas Wade estimated Kwangtung domestic opium production at between 8,000–10,000 piculs in 1847, noting that it sold well locally and was often mixed with other types: "It resembles Patna in smell, is not equal to Bengal in strength. . . . When two years old it is preferred by some smokers to any foreign drug." On the other hand, Fukien opium, said Wade, "is weak in quality, coarse in flavor, and is not produced in qualities sufficient to compete with the foreign article."[64] The price of this inferior domestic product was, however, only $250 a picul, whereas Hsu Nai-chi had listed the imports at $800 per picul for Wu-t'u (Bengal opium), $600 for White Skin (Bombay), and $400 for Red Skin (Madras).[65]

Since Kwangtung was not the area where the great opium fields were to be found, we can guess that western Chinese production was already several times this 8,000-picul level, and internal prices were often lower than $250. In this case, Chinese production and consumption almost certainly exceeded the estimates made by the British consuls in 1847[66]—and were vastly greater than the estimates made by Hart's Imperial Maritime Customs survey of 1863.[67] It would seem probable that this domestic production, though initially spurred by a desire to cash in on the available market among the wealthy, came to cater mainly to Chinese workers—especially the coolie laborers, chair-bearers, and boatmen who seem to have become addicted on a massive scale by the 1870s.[68] Besides its cheap price—in Kansu, Indian opium could be ten times the cost of the local product[69]—Chinese domestic opium had the additional advantage that it could be smoked more times in residue than Indian.[70] Chinese workers were also willing to accept opium that had been repeatedly adulterated—not only with husks or pods from the poppies, but with pork fat, sesamum seed cake, willow shoots, and thistle juice, according to an observer in Manchuria.[71] Though richer Chinese had

62. Chang Lu, *Pen-ching feng-yuan*, 3:11.
63. *RoyCom*, I, app. 6, pp. 168–169.
64. *RoyCom*, I, app. 6, p. 169.
65. *YPCC*, p. 471. For the much higher earlier prices, compare Chang Hsin-pao, *Commissioner Lin*, pp. 21–22. In 1821 Bengal had been over $2,000.00, and in 1817 Patna had been $1,300.00.
66. Fairbank, *Trade and Diplomacy*, p. 242.
67. IMC, *Native Opium*, app. on 1863.
68. *RoyCom*, I, 39, no. 503; 47, no. 611, 112, no. 1637. Also IMC, *Native Opium*, p. 40.
69. *RoyCom*, I, 44, nos. 553–554.
70. IMC, *Opium: Crude and Prepared*, p. 5.
71. IMC, *Opium: Crude and Prepared*, p. 16.

long smoked blends of domestic and Indian, they seem to have swung to pure domestic opium out of desperation; thus the prolonged famine around the Chefoo area from 1875–1878 forced the wealthy city dwellers faced with shrinking rents to smoke domestic opium. They got used to it and never changed back, with the result that Indian sales slumped in the area.[72] This process was accelerated as Chinese producers grew wiser on the question of quality control, and their wealthy buyers grew more numerous.[73]

Smoking among the peasantry, we may again estimate, probably began on a massive scale during the 1870s, when domestic production was increasing so rapidly. That the growing of opium does indeed encourage the growers themselves to smoke has been proved for a later period of Chinese history. J. L. Buck found that peasants came to consume about a quarter of their own opium production themselves.[74] And though high yields depended on moderately favorable weather conditions, there were plenty of advantages in growing opium poppy as a cash crop. It would yield at least twice the cash of an average cereal crop on a given acreage;[75] it could be planted in the tenth month and harvested in the third when nothing else would grow; it could survive on very poor soil, as long as there was a reasonable amount of fertilizer; it could be interspersed with food crops such as beans or potatoes, or planted in alternate rows with tobacco.[76] Winter growing was especially profitable to tenants holding lands on metayer tenure—that is, paying the landlord a fixed percentage of the yield of the *summer* crop.[77] Furthermore, though techniques for gathering poppy juice were labor-intensive, they were very simple.

Increasingly, opium poppies began to be grown on good soil. By comparing Baron von Richthoven's 1872 surveys with W. D. Spence's in 1882, we can see how the poppy had come down from the hills to the valleys in southwest China.[78] Robert Hart tried to estimate addiction on the basis of a ratio between population and known production, and came up with a figure of just under 1 percent.[79] But most observers found this far too low—Chang Chih-tung insisted that smokers were 80 percent of the population in Shansi cities and 60 percent in the countryside,[80] (though Tseng Kuo-ch'üan thought rural smoking was even greater than urban).[81] Kansu observers also

72. IMC, *Native Opium*, p. 8.
73. IMC, *Native Opium*, p. 6.
74. John Lossing Buck, *Land Utilization in China* (Shanghai: Commercial Press, 1937), p. 234.
75. IMC, *Native Opium*, p. 41; *RoyCom*, II, 384.
76. *RoyCom*, II, 383. A photograph of opium and tobacco growing in alternate rows is in Buck, *Land Utilization*, facing p. 206.
77. W. D. Spence, acting consul at I-chang, claims to have investigated tenancy relations in 1882; see *RoyCom*, II, 383–384. His report is fascinating, but it is by no means clear how thoroughly his investigation was conducted.
78. *RoyCom*, II, 384.
79. *RoyCom*, I, 17, no. 212; *RoyCom*, II, 386.
80. *PGT* (1892), p. 125.
81. *PGT* (1878), p. 45.

came up with an 80 percent figure.[82] Accurate figures are unobtainable, but a sensible figure seems to be that of a 10 percent smoking population, which James Legge arrived at as he jolted on his mule-cart through the Shantung poppy fields en route to Confucius' tomb.[83] Legge's guess in turn can be modified by the separate estimate of the experienced Dr. William Lockhart, who also estimated a 10 percent opium-smoking population, but felt that only 3 to 5 percent were smoking "in excess."[84] This would give an 1890 figure of somewhere around 15 million opium addicts in China; if they smoked about one-third of an ounce a day or seven pounds a year—which local observers found common[85]—this means that around 105 million pounds were required each year. Hence the estimate that in the 1880s, 850,000 acres of land in Szechwan were producing 177,000 piculs (23.5 million pounds) per year at an average of 50 ounces per *mou* seems not unreasonable.[86] Feasibility cross-checks may be made to more accurate studies in the twentieth century: 29,750 *mou* of land under opium poppy in the Kunming district of Yunnan;[87] 23,000 piculs from the Fu-chou district of Szechwan alone;[88] around a million *mou* under poppy cultivation in Shansi;[89] and half a million *mou* and a million and a half smokers in Shensi.[90] A general estimate for turn-of-the-century interregional trade in domestic production yielded these figures: rice, 100 million taels; salt, 100 million taels; opium, 130 million taels.[91] Undeniably, opium was being smoked in China on a gigantic scale.

PROHIBITION

Much of the legal history of opium prohibition in Ch'ing China revolved around the search for a precedent. Tobacco prohibition might seem to have been a logical point from which to build—but even the tobacco prohibitions were vague in formulation and execution.

Abahai (Ch'ing T'ai-tsung) discussed the tobacco problem at some length in 1635, and noted some of its ambiguities as a problem. Certainly it was

82. *RoyCom*, I, 44–45, nos. 559–560, 2nd 129, nos. 1977–1979.

83. *RoyCom*, I, 15–17, nos. 193 and 212.

84. *RoyCom*, I, 113, no. 1643.

85. *RoyCom*, I, 18, nos. 221–222. Estimates of annual consumption vary widely; one observer in 1865 thought two pounds per year a better guess for medium smokers, with four pounds for heavy smokers. See "Opium-Raucher und Esser in China und Japan," *Wiener Medizinische Wochenschrift* 15:1568–1569.

86. *RoyCom*, II, 387. Alexander Hosie, *On the Trail of the Opium Poppy* (London, 1914), p. 265, estimated that 200,000 piculs were produced in Szechwan in 1904, of which 180,000 piculs were smoked locally.

87. *Agrarian China, Selected Source Materials from Chinese Authors* (Chicago: University of Chicago Press, 1938), p. 118. "Catties" in this source appears to be a misprint for ounces.

88. *Agrarian China*, p. 124.

89. Hosie, *On the Trail*, p. 237.

90. Hosie, *On the Trail*, pp. 242–243.

91. S. A. M. Adshead, *The Modernization of the Chinese Salt Administration, 1900–1920* (Cambridge: Harvard University Press, 1970), p. 13.

wrong, he said, for officers to forbid all smoking in their offices and then to smoke at will in their own homes; but that did not mean that a good example was absolutely essential, and that the lower orders necessarily aped the ways of their betters. In any case, Abahai continued, he was going to ban smoking for one reason, and one only: smokers were ignoring their retainers' wretched condition and using what money they had to buy tobacco, and he found this inexcusable.[92] The argument here was clearly one relating to military morale. In 1638 two Manchu generals collected and publicly burned all the tobacco that they found in the western section of Mukden. Strict penalties against sellers and smokers were both promulgated and implemented in 1641; but that same year the attempt at suppression was abandoned. Henceforth planting for one's own use was to be legal, and a fair price of three *ch'ien* per catty (*chin*) was fixed.[93] In partial explanation of this turnabout, Abahai stated that the prohibition had proved unenforceable, and also that tobacco smoking was a minor crime compared to neglect of archery. It was to this latter that the Manchus should apply themselves.[94]

The Koreans had known tobacco since the 1620s, calling it "smoke-tea" (*yen-ch'a*) or "smoke-wine" (*yen-chiu*); believing that it gave the power to foretell the future, and noting its habit-forming qualities, they also termed it "magical herb" (*yao-ts'ao*).[95] The Chinese also believed that it had strong powers and was useful in quelling disease. In his authoritative medical treatise *Ching-yueh ch'üan-shu* (Complete medical works), the Ming scholar Chang Chieh-pin observed that tobacco smoking had saved troops in Yunnan from malaria, and that this had increased its popularity.[96] The late Ming tobacco prohibitions in 1637 and 1640 seem to have been initially promulgated because it was believed tobacco was helping the Manchu military cause: "Those who hawk clandestinely tobacco, and sell it to foreigners, shall, no matter the quantity sold, be decapitated," and "the people beyond the [northern] border are subject to diseases caused by extreme cold, and cannot be cured without tobacco."[97] The Ming withdrew these prohibitions because the morale of their own troops was suffering without tobacco.[98] K'ang-hsi had smoked as a child, but issued a prohibition in 1676 against smoking in the palace areas; his motive here was fear of fire, not moral uplift.[99] The prohibition was clearly not very effective, and was rephrased in

92. Walter Fuchs, "Koreanische Quellen zur Frühgeschichte des Tabaks in der Mandjurei zwischen 1630 und 1640," *Monumenta Serica* 5:89.

93. Fuchs, "Frühgeschichte," p. 96, and edict of 1639 in Goodrich, "Early Prohibitions," p. 652.

94. Fuchs, "Frühgeschichte," p. 99.

95. Fuchs, "Frühgeschichte," p. 93.

96. Chang Chieh-pin, *Ching-yueh ch'üan-shu* [Complete medical works] [n.d., 17th century ed.), 48–25.

97. Goodrich, "Early Prohibitions," pp. 650–651.

98. Ibid., p. 651.

99. *T'ing-hsun ko-yen* [K'ang-hsi's conversations], translated in Goodrich, "Early Prohibitions," p. 654.

1684. K'ang-hsi now stated that since his grandmother feared the possibility of fires in the palace, people should not smoke carelessly.[100]

These were not useful precedents, and when Yung-cheng was apprised of the opium smoking problem and tried to stop it, his legal advisers had to look elsewhere in the Ch'ing code. The first opium prohibitions in Chinese history, formulated between 1729 and 1731, reflected this uncertainty.[101] Opium dealers were to be sentenced, in accordance with the law for those handling forbidden goods, to a month in the cangue and military banishment; those who opened opium dens and seduced the worthy were to be sentenced, in accordance with the law for teachers of heterodox religions, to strangulation after the assizes; soldiers and runners abusing the new laws and engaging in extortion were to be punished proportionately in accordance with the laws on bribery in connection with unlawful objects (*wang-fa*). Further prohibitions in 1730 were directed specifically against those using Taiwan as a base for opium dealing—they were to be punished and sent back to their native places.[102] Perhaps because of a general feeling that it was the distributors who were the problem, the penalties for smokers and planters were not so serious—they were to receive one hundred blows in accordance with laws for violating an imperial decree.

Some isolated attempts were made to tighten and coordinate the laws against smoking as a whole. Grand Secretary Fang Pao submitted proposals for banning tobacco planting in 1736, and Chang Jo-chen, financial commissioner of Shansi, tried the same tactic in 1751. According at least to later Ch'ing legal opinion, legislation against both dry tobacco smoking and water-pipe smoking was a *sine qua non* for successful opium prohibition, and the failure of the ministries to back up either Fang or Chang made the spread of opium inevitable.[103]

A further confusing element came from the fact that throughout this period opium in small amounts was coming into China on a fixed tariff as a medicinal drug; the tax was two *ch'ien* per ten *chin* in 1589, and the assessment was raised to three *ch'ien* in 1686.[104] In the late K'ang-hsi reign, as we have seen, it was also being smoked in some quantities, mixed with tobacco. The only detailed account of a prosecution case that I have been able to find for this period[105]—involving an opium seller named Ch'en Yuan in Ch'ang-

---

100. Yü Min-chung, *Kuo-ch'ao kung-shih* [History of the Ch'ing palace] (Taipei: Hsueh-sheng shu-chü, 1965), p. 26.

101. Yü En-te, *Chung-kuo chin-yen fa-ling*, p. 16; *TCHT*, 828:1.

102. Yü En-te, *Chung-kuo chin-yen fa-ling*, p. 16; *TCHT*, 828:1.

103. *TLTI*, 22:63b–64; Fang Pao, *Fang Wang-chi hsien-sheng ch'üan-chi* [Fang Pao's collected works], 1746 ed. (Shanghai, 1935), p. 457.

104. Yü En-te, *Chung-kuo chin-yen fa-ling*, p. 15; F. Hirth, "The Hoppo Book of 1753," *Journal of the North China Branch of the Royal Asiatic Society*, new ser. 17:221–235.

105. The case is in *Yung-cheng chu-p'i yü-chih* [Vermilion endorsements of the Yung-cheng emperor] (Shanghai, 1887), 14:22b, and has been translated by Fu Lo-shu, *A Documentary Chronicle of Sino-Western Relations, 1644–1820*, A.A.S. Monographs and Papers no. 22 (Tucson: University of Arizona Press, 1966), I:162–164. I am grateful to Professor Saeki Tomi for using

chou fu, Fukien, in August 1729—shows the complexities of enforcing the law. There was no easy way to have opium (*ya-p'ien*) freely available as a medicinal drug while forbidding the sale of *ya-p'ien-yen* or "opium ready for smoking," since the one was directly linked to the other, separated only by a process of further refining. Ch'en Yuan, who had sold some opium to a prefectural stoolpigeon, was sentenced by the prefect under the terms of the new law to the cangue and military banishment. This sentence was overthrown by the governor, who defended Ch'en's right to sell opium as a medicinal drug, and Yung-cheng agreed that the governor was right in so doing. Both governor and emperor agreed further, however, that the overzealous prefect should not be punished, lest the ignorant common people think that the "prohibitions against opium for smoking have been relaxed."

If these laws were hard to interpret and enforce in China, they were nevertheless taken seriously by foreign traders at this time, as is shown by an alarmist order issued to commanders of East India Company ships in June 1733 by members of the council:

> On board the *Windham* June 16th
>
> It having been a usual thing heretofore, for shipps bound from Fort St. George, to carry ophium with them for sale to China, & not knowing but that there might be some of that commodity now on board your ship design'd for the same markett, we think it our Duty (lest you should be a Stranger to itt) to acquaint you with the late severe laws enacted by the Emperour of China for yᵉ prohibition of Ophium, the penalty, should any be seiz'd on board your Ship, being no less than yᵉ confiscation of Ship & Cargoes to the Emperour, as well as death to the person who should dare offer to buy it of you; upon these considerations therefore, & the more effectually to prevent any such like misfortune attending of us, you are hereby required to take the best measures you possibly can, by a strict enquiry & search in your ship, to be well informed whether there be any such thing on board or not, & in case there be, that you then take effectual care to have it removed out of your Ship before you leave Malacca, since upon no consideration whatsoever, you are neither to carry, nor suffer any of it to be carry'd in your Ship to China, as you will answer the contrary to the Honᵇˡᵉ Company at your peril.[106]

After 1729 there seems to have been no further development in anti-opium legislation until the Chia-ch'ing reign (1796–1820), so that the Ch'ien-lung reign saw the domestic spread of smoking and the increased boldness of foreign traders. Even the well-known early Chia-ch'ing prohibitions, though they included sections on domestic growing, were mainly directed at foreign

his index of the *chu-p'i yü-chih* to check that there were no other Yung-cheng references to opium cases.

106. H. B. Morse, *The Chronicles of the East India Company Trading to China, 1635–1834* (Oxford: Oxford University Press, 1926), I:215.

merchants bringing opium from India.[107] It was not until 1813 (Chia-ch'ing 18) that the Chinese seriously tackled the problem of tightening their internal laws to cope with the mounting foreign trade and smuggling of opium.

The Board of Justice in 1813 noted that though precedents (e.g., 1729) existed for punishing dealers and owners of opium dens, the law against purchasers and smokers had never been specifically clarified in the Ch'ing code and they had been punished with a hundred blows in accordance with the laws for violating an imperial decree. It was now time to tighten up the law and to distinguish between officials and common people.[108] The new penalties for opium smokers were to be as follows: guards, officers, and officials would receive punishment of a hundred blows, plus dismissal and two months in the cangue; soldiers and commoners would receive a hundred blows, plus one month in the cangue. Dealers and den owners should be punished as before, but more care should be taken to try to separate ringleaders from their subordinates. Chia-ch'ing agreed to these proposals, adding that he had also heard rumors that eunuchs in his own palaces were smoking; should they be discovered, they would be sent as slaves to Heilungkiang after two months in the cangue.

This attempt to handle opium smoking under the laws for "violating an imperial decree" with extra penalties attached, must have proved quite inadequate, an apparent exception being Juan Yuan's arrest of sixteen Macao dealers in 1821.[109] A further flurry of legislation came in 1830 following the memorial by censor Shao Cheng-hu on the extent of domestic opium planting and sales.[110] Henceforth, domestic growers and refiners were to be handled in accordance with the old laws on dealers. Local headmen who took bribes were to be punished on the same scale as the principal offenders. New provisions were that those growing opium poppy were to have the plants torn up and their land confiscated by the government. However, Tao-kuang was very skeptical about this provision, since he castigated Juan Yuan for daring to suggest that local opium could be successfully rooted up.[111] Also the senior provincial officials were to order their subordinates to carry out meticulous cross-checks at the village level, and to procure annual affidavits that local areas were clear. Regulations incorporating new refinements were added in 1831: manufacturers of opium pipes and other smoking equipment were to be sent to military banishment, in accordance with the laws against those making gambling utensils, and boatmen or landlords who leased space for smoking would be banished or beaten like those who leased rooms to gamblers; parents whose children dealt in opium

107. Yü En-te, *Chung-kuo chin-yen fa-ling*, p. 22. Fu Lo-shu, *Documentary Chronicle*, I:381–383, has a translation of the 1811 prohibition edict and the Liang-kuang governor-general's reply.
108. *TCHT*, p. 15, no. 442 (828:4b).
109. Chang Hsin-pao, *Commissioner Lin*, p. 20.
110. *TCHT*, p. 15, no. 443 (828:5).
111. *YPCC*, p. 439, interlinear endorsement.

or smoked it would get forty blows, in accordance with the laws against "parents who cannot stop their children from stealing."[112] In the same year of 1831 a new dimension was added to existing penalties: in the future all accused smokers would receive the standard penalties as long as they named the dealers and those dealers were arrested, in line with the laws covering gamblers who named those who supplied their equipment; failure to name and catch the dealers would lead the smoker to be treated as if he himself were a dealer.[113]

Officials in the Board of Justice struggled to make these laws work, and cases have survived which show how they argued over the special problems raised by opium addiction. In the case of the P'an brothers in Kwangtung in 1827, for example, where the younger brother was an opium dealer who involved his elder brother and other outsiders in his deals, the board corresponded at length with the Kwantung governor on the correctness of ascribing blame to the elder brother in accordance with normal legal practice.[114] The argument centered on the problem of whether opium dealing constituted "direct injury to the person," and was continued by the Board of Justice and the governor of Anhwei in 1831; the conclusion was that opium sellers were like sellers of gambling equipment in that they did not deliberately seek to do harm, but only wanted profit.[115] In another ruling, however, it was specifically stated that an opium seller should not be treated leniently, even if "his parents were very old and he were the only male descendant."[116]

The increasing complexity and severity of these laws—new categories were added and finer distinctions drawn in 1839, 1850, and 1870[117]—did not make them any more effective as a means of control. Nor did the smokers respond to an additional law that promised them pardon if they gave themselves up.[118] Contemporary Ch'ing officials were fully aware of the difficulties behind enforcement. Ho Ch'ang-ling pointed out that the opium smokers were simply not dissuaded by punitive legislation: they grew their opium locally and smoked it themselves not because they were evil, but just because they were weak, like drinkers or lechers. Also smoking could be done in secret: the severer the penalties the more secret the smoking, so it got harder and harder to catch the smokers—their main danger was from blackmail or other harassment.[119]

The levels that this blackmail and harassment had reached long before the Opium War is clearly shown in a case reported in late 1831 by Ch'ü Yung, a

112. *TCHT*, p. 15, no. 443 (828:6); *HAHL*, pp. 905–906.
113. *TCHT*, p. 15, no. 443 (828:6b); *HAHL*, pp. 904, 906–908.
114. *HAHL*, pp. 482–483.
115. *HAHL*, p. 484.
116. *HAHL*, p. 906.
117. *TCHT*, p. 15, no. 443 (828:6b); *TLTI*, 22:60b–61b; Morse, *International Relations*, I:548.
118. *TLTI*, 4:42b.
119. *TLTI*, 22:62b–63.

circuit censor with special responsibility for northern Peking who had proved expert at rounding up preparers of raw opium.[120] A certain Wen Cho-chiao had purchased a post in the banqueting court, and brought a supply of opium with him when he moved from Kwangtung to Peking. Wen's cook, aware that his master was smoking, told two ward runners, and they in turn told a local constable. This group, together with some other servants, climbed over the wall of Wen's residence one night and caught him smoking with two friends. They locked up the three smokers, impounded two and a half boxes of opium and three pipes, and the constable Wang San blackmailed Wen for 1,000 taels. Wen handed over twenty-five taels in cash (of which fifteen were immediately passed on to the cook) and gave a promissory note for the rest. Later on a friend told Wen to refuse to pay: but the constable and his friends came back with reinforcements and forced Wen to disgorge 600 taels. The opium was distributed among the various accomplices. Nobody reported the case to the authorities.

Such a case suggests the prevalence of both dishonesty and fear, and gives real force to the arguments of such men as Chu Tsun. Chu was passionately against any legislation that might leave opium available—e.g., to commoners—while making it prohibited for officials. In his words (made more eloquent by the *Chinese Repository* translation of January 1837):

> And if the officers, the scholars, and the military smoke the drug in the quiet of their own families, by what means is this to be discovered or prevented? Should an officer be unable to restrain himself, shall then his clerks, his followers, his domestic servants, have it in their power to make his failing their plaything, and by the knowledge of his secret to hold his situation at their disposal? We dread falsehood and bribery, and yet we would thus widen the door to admit them. We are anxious to prevent the amassing of wealth by unlawful means, and yet by this policy we would ourselves increase opportunities for doing so. A father, in such a case, would no longer be able to reprove his son, an elder brother to restrain his junior, nor a master to rule his own household. Will not this policy, then, be every way calculated to stir up strife? Or if happily the thing should not run to this extreme, the consequences will yet be equally bad: secret enticement and mutual connivance will ensue, until the very commonness of the practice shall render it no longer a subject of surprise.[121]

What Chu Tsun wanted—and in this desire he was at one with Hsu Nai-chi and Lin Tse-hsu—was consistency in the law, for only thus would there be a control system that was enforceable. But what began to emerge after 1842, and became the norm after 1860, was a legal patchwork: the sporadic punishment of opium offenders in the midst of legalized foreign opium im-

120. *YPCC*, p. 458.
121. *Chinese Repository* 5:396.

ports and accelerating domestic production.[122] Examples taken from the *Peking Gazette* during the 1870s and 1880s show the range of opium offenses punished, and often the *nature* of the offense hints graphically enough at the types of abuse that were commonplace.

An imperial clan member is punished for both living in and operating an opium den in northern Peking;[123] a musketry instructor in the Foochow Arsenal kills his servant for breaking his opium pipe;[124] a Kiangsu magistrate is banished for *selling* opium;[125] a eunuch is beheaded for opium smoking in the palace *and* operating an opium den (*yen-kuan*) inside the Imperial Equipage Department;[126] the correctors of a batch of *chü-jen* examination papers are addicts;[127] a boy is condemned to death by slicing for providing his mother with opium—he had apparently thought that she wanted to smoke but she used it to commit suicide, thus making him guilty of "wilfully causing a mother's death";[128] a sedan chair carrier operates his own den and has connections with a military officer;[129] two others are accused of smuggling opium on their own patrol vessel;[130] a *chü-jen* has the nerve to prosecute some rowdies for breaking up an opium den which he *himself* owned and operated;[131] and most poignant historically, perhaps, among random cases of officials dismissed for being addicts[132] we find the name of the Wuhu taotai, son of the once prestigious treaty negotiator Ch'i-shan.[133]

The ambiguity and inconsistency of the law in such cases made the spread of addiction and distribution patterns quite uncontrollable.

DISTRIBUTION

The more widely opium was smoked, the more complex the distribution network must have been, but it is not easy to locate the network's various components. The following analysis, therefore, which concentrates on *Chinese* distributors, is both episodic and sporadic.

As early as 1674 a Chinese merchant named "Bonsiqua" was buying substantial quantities of opium from the Dutch in Batavia; he had trouble disposing of it, and it was eventually sold at public auction.[134] Only three

122. See the survey for the 1840s in Fairbank, *Trade and Diplomacy*, pp. 240–242.
123. *PGT* (1874), p. 141.
124. *PGT* (1882), p. 132.
125. *PGT* (September 12, 1878).
126. *HAHLF*, p. 4971.
127. *PGT* (1881), p. 32.
128. *PGT* (1872), p. 115.
129. *HAHLF*, p. 4971.
130. *PGT* (1879), p. 98.
131. *PGT* (1872), p. 130.
132. *PGT* (1877), p. 175.
133. *PGT* (1881), p. 135.
134. Algemeen Rijksarchief, K. A. 589, fol. 55, Council Resolution of May 8, 1674. This reference is also courtesy of Jack Wills.

years later the Dutch signed a new treaty with the Mataram prince of Java, and one of the objects of this treaty was to check the bulk trade that Chinese merchants had built up in cloth and opium.[135] I do not know whether Bonsiqua or these merchants might have had contacts with Taiwan customers or not, but a Batavia/Taiwan/Amoy route is certainly feasible. Also, early opium sales areas were often identical with tobacco areas, and already-established tobacco transport and marketing patterns may have been utilized for distribution of madak. Ch'en Yuan, the man convicted and then pardoned in the 1729 case already discussed, had obtained his opium from a merchant he was unable (or unwilling) to name in Kwangtung; he traded orange cakes he had brought from Fukien for the opium, and himself carried the opium back to Ch'ang-chou fu. He sold it as a medicine in his store.[136]

Chang Hsin-pao has described how, in the early nineteenth century, the brokerage houses (*yao-k'ou*) of Chinese partners in the Canton area would pay for the opium at the Canton factories and then send out their "smug boats" to pick up the opium from the foreign receiving ships anchored off shore.[137] The *yao-k'ou* sold to brokers who followed certain set routes—westward to Chao-ch'ing, and thence to Kwangsi and Kweichow; northward to Lo-ch'ang and Nan-hsiung for shipping to Hunan and Kiangsi; and eastward via Ch'ao-chou to Fukien.[138] This latter was the route taken by Ch'en Yuan.

This analysis can be extended through the testimony of Feng Tsan-ch'in, a Kwangsi-born censor in Hu-kuang[139] who was deeply interested in distribution methods in the Canton area and made a detailed report on them in 1831.[140] The large brokerage houses (*ta yao-k'ou*), said Feng, were collaborating with local criminal interests who took advantage of two interlocking fears: the foreign merchants' fear of landing on Chinese soil, and the Chinese merchants' fear of putting out to sea. The criminals set up so-called money-changing shops which they used to monopolize the opium trade; it was in these shops that Chinese merchants met with the Westerners and signed a contract for the deal. The shops were located either in the thirteen factories or in Lien-hsing Street, and from these bases the criminals sent out their boats, "fast crabs" with three masts, fifty or sixty oars, iron nets to protect them from cannonballs, and a capacity of several hundred piculs. They were so swift that the local slang for them was "glued-on wings" (*ch'a-i*); but many patrol boats would not catch them even if they could, since they were all in league together, and the trade took place openly by daylight. In such places

135. *RoyCom*, VII, app. B, p. 35; memorandum by F. C. Danvers on the Dutch trade in opium during the 17th century.
136. Fu Lo-shu, *Documentary Chronicle*, I:163.
137. Chang Hsin-pao, *Commissioner Lin*, p. 32.
138. Chang Hsin-pao, *Commissioner Lin*, p. 33, and map on p. 25.
139. Fang Chao-ying and Tu Lien-che, eds., *Tseng-chiao Ch'ing-ch'ao chin-shih t'i-ming pei-lu* [Index to the Ch'ing dynasty *chin-shih* holders], Harvard-Yenching Institute Sinological Index Series, Supplement no. 19, reprint (Taipei: Ch'eng-wen, 1966), p. 151, 2/76 in class of 1820.
140. *YPCC*, pp. 433–434.

as Amoy, Tientsin, Hainan, and southwest Kwangtung there was no need for the "fast crab" boats, though even here merchants had to work through the *yao-k'ou* brokers, and the same brokers had bases in other cities of Kwangtung and thus controlled distribution beyond the provincial borders. Once the opium had moved inland, it was handled by other criminals and yamen clerks through local brokerage houses (*hsiao yao-k'ou*) and sold in small amounts at the local markets.

Other memorialists in 1831 filled out this picture a bit more. In Shantung the opium was ferried to deserted parts of the shore, far from harbors or garrisons, by shallow-draft lighters (*po-ch'uan*), and sold for distribution right there at the water's edge.[141] In Kweichow it was entering along the established trade routes from Kwangtung, and being sold by local merchants who were private operators, there being as yet no opium dens (*yen-kuan*) in the area.[142] The Kwangsi governor similarly denied any knowledge of local production, claiming that opium was only found in certain prefectures bordering the West River where merchants brought it in from Kwangtung.[143] The governor-general of Szechwan admitted that there were many smokers and some domestic production in his area, and noted that "when there are so many smokers there must be many distributors." His proposal was to check at customs points and defiles on the established trade routes, and to concentrate on certain key interprovincial junctions: K'uei-chou-fu for the Kwangtung and Chekiang traffic, Ning-yuan-fu for the Yunnan traffic, Kuang-yuan-fu for Hupei, and so on.[144]

In Peking itself distribution had become fairly complex, as can be seen from three examples of police raids conducted during the late summer of 1831.[145] Wang Erh ran his opium business from his own house near the Hsuan-wu gate, where he also kept dice and a set of account books; these latter he managed to burn before the raid. Chiao Ssu operated out of the hostel for merchants from Fu-shun in Szechwan (Fu-shun *k'o-tien*), and also had dice, dominoes, and other equipment for gambling. Hsiao Shen sold his opium in the Kwangtung Provincial Hostel (Yueh-tung *hui-kuan*). All three distributors had an ample supply of bags (*tai*, perhaps used for take-away orders), copper pots, and other equipment for heating and smoking opium. All three seem to have performed the same role of buying the crude opium and selling it in smokable form (*mai-t'u mai-yen*); they claimed that their source was either sea-going vessels at Tientsin or the sales section for Cantonese goods (*Kuang-huo tan-shang*), but none of the three would identify their sources of supply by name.

We have already noted above that by 1831 the Ch'ing were trying to force

141. *YPCC*, p. 444.
142. *YPCC*, p. 447.
143. *YPCC*, p. 449.
144. *YPCC*, pp. 451–452.
145. *YPCC*, p. 453.

smokers to reveal the names of their distributors without success; in this case
we see how small-scale distributors similarly defended their wholesalers from
exposure. The lengths to which a smoker might go in order to throw officials
and police off his tracks can be seen from the testimony made by the eunuch
Chang Chin-fu to investigating officials of the Imperial Household:

> At first the opium that we used was bought in small quantities directly
> from the Moslem Chu Ta. Then I learnt that when the sea vessels came
> into Tientsin the opium prices got cheaper, so I asked K'o-k'o-ssu-pu-k'u
> for a loan of 100 string of local cash and I also sold my mule cart for cash.
> I took [my servant] Ch'in Pao-ch'üan with me to Tientsin, and got Ch'in
> Pao-ch'üan's old friend Yang Hui-yuan to act as an agent and buy 160
> ounces of opium from Chang Erh for 240 strings of cash. I gave Yang a
> commission of three strings and 800 wen.[146]

In this particular case, careful investigative work by the censors and a
rather full confession led to the discovery of a certain sequence: smoker to B
to C to distributor. But the distributor himself was only a small time dealer,
and as we saw in the previous case of the three Peking distributors the trail
often went no further than these minor intermediaries. The rounding up of
distributors depended to a large extent on local agencies—the police magistrates, their assistants, and the constables. When the constables themselves
were involved in blackmailing smokers and in selling opium, as they were in
the 1831 blackmail case, even the most admirable laws would not work.

Any final analysis of opium distribution would have to include a full section on police activities and procedures. Here we may draw some cases from
the *Peking Gazette* to show the dimensions of the problem, both in Peking and
the provinces. Local opium distribution might be dominated by groups of
deserters from the army who would use "foreign pistols" to fight off police.[147]
An opium shop might be owned by a member of the imperial clan.[148] Even
those constables on the rolls were not paid their full wages,[149] and local
citizens were growing so jumpy that they would fire their guns off at random
through the night.[150] Smuggling of goods over city walls involved so many
people that "the police are afraid to interfere";[151] on one occasion members
of an entire police patrol were robbed of their sheepskin coats as they went
about their duties in winter.[152] It seems likely that when the police did get
up the evidence or the courage for a raid, they only struck at the small dealers.

In the latter part of the nineteenth century the distribution of opium took
place in a three-tiered system, in what looks like a logical extension of the two-

146. *YPCC*, p. 455.
147. *PGT* (1872), pp. 79 and 89.
148. *PGT* (1874), p. 141.
149. *PGT* (1875), p. 49.
150. *PGT* (1890), p. 189.
151. *PGT* (1882), p. 46. In this instance wine was the smuggled article.
152. *PGT* (1887), p. 12.

tiered brokerage house system described by Feng Tsan-ch'in. These were first, the big wholesale dealers; second, the large-scale retailers; third, the local sellers.

The big wholesalers bought in bulk both from the British and from domestic growers. R. E. Bredon in 1887, thought that this group was dominated by men from Swatow and Ningpo.[153] They were men of great wealth, and we can contrast the vast resources at their disposal with the scanty funds generally made available for "self-strengthening" or other enterprises. Thus in 1881 Li Hung-chang memorialized that a syndicate headed by the Cantonese merchant Ho Hsien-ch'ih wanted to corner the entire Indian opium stocks through a company Ho would head in Hong Kong; they offered the Ch'ing government at least three million taels in additional annual taxation, in return for sole distribution rights in Chinese ports. Ho was going to capitalize the company initially at $Mex 20,000,000. As Li Hung-chang commented:

> I've heard that Ho Hsien-ch'ih and the others are very rich, and have long been doing business in the Kwangtung and Hong Kong area. They understand both Chinese and foreign business methods. Other rich merchants have heard of this and want to put up capital and get stock; they all know that a company with a monopoly of the opium trade is bound to make a profit, and not to fail, so it's not hard to raise capital.[154]

Li himself sent taotai Ma to Calcutta, to negotiate directly with Lord Ripon.[155] His plan was to combine some kind of Chinese monopoly with a graded decrease in imports, spread over twenty or thirty years, until the trade stopped entirely.[156] Even if the scale of such deals was exceptional, there were regular opium fairs in major cities where half a million taels or more would change hands.[157] These wholesalers affected opium trade on a provincial scale; the Chekiang governor noted in 1887 that though there was plenty of opium growing in his province, it did not cross the provincial boundaries because there were "no large merchants to undertake its export."[158] Sung Ts'ai, the comprador for Sassoon's in Chinkiang, sold one and a half million taels of opium in 1875 alone.[159] One would assume that these

153. IMC, *Opium: Crude and Prepared*, p. 18. For Swatow men, see also Edward Le Fevour, *Western Enterprise in Late Ch'ing China: A Selective Survey of Jardine, Matheson and Company's Operations, 1842–1895* (Cambridge: Harvard East Asian Research Center, 1968), pp. 23–24.

154. Li Hung-chang, *Li Wen-chung kung ch'üan-chi* [The complete works of Li Hung-chang] (Shanghai, 1905), 41:32. For Samuel's role in the deal, see Morse, *International Relations*, II, 385.

155. Robert Hart, "Letters to James Duncan Campbell," unpublished ms. at Harvard University, pp. 413 and 697.

156. Hart, "Letters," pp. 701 and 706.

157. *RoyCom*, II, 384.

158. *PGT* (1887), pp. 182–183.

159. Yen-p'ing Hao, *The Comprador in Nineteenth-Century China* (Cambridge: Harvard University Press, 1970), p. 103.

men were above police harassment, and that even officials handled them carefully.

The large-scale retailers, who may be seen as descendants of the earlier small brokerage houses, were those who kept the retail shops (*t'u-tien*) and joined in the local opium dealers' guilds (*t'u-pang*).[160] They also refined the raw opium by boiling off the impurities so that it was ready for smoking, a process that involved simple equipment but a fairly sophisticated knowledge of relative yields and prices—as we can see from a table on Tientsin preparation prepared for Robert Hart—since 100 catties Malwa would yield 70 catties boiled, with a price shift from 506 to 567 taels, whereas 100 catties of local opium would yield 50 to 60 catties boiled, involving a shift from 285 taels to anywhere between 304 and 364 taels.[161] This refining process could not be done in secret (as Ch'ing officials had noted well before the Opium War) since the smell was so strong and also the treacly *yen* was much harder to transport than the raw *t'u*;[162] so these retailers clearly operated with official connivance.

These large-scale retailers may have sold some stocks to wealthy purchasers for use in their homes, but probably their main customers were the two main groups of local sellers: the owners of opium divans and the itinerant merchants. These men sold opium in lots of a few cash, for smoking on the spot. The amount of divans in any city was very high by the late Ch'ing: one observer counted 170 in Tientsin;[163] one guessed at over a thousand in Hangchow;[164] in Lanchow, Kansu, there were "five stalls in one street, within fifty yards from the shops";[165] in Chungking there were 1,230 opium shops of various kinds.[166] Ratios of population to number of divans suggest either that one divan catered to very few people, or else that the divans in large towns catered to large numbers of out-of-town visitors. Thus Chefoo had an estimated 132 dens for a population of 32,500, while Wenchow served a population of 80,000 with 1,130.[167] Sometimes a city was subject to reforming zeal; thus Ting Jih-ch'ang's anti-opium proclamations in 1869 led to the closing of 3,700 opium shops and dens in Soochow according to Young J. Allen; but, as Kuo Sung-t'ao noted, such urban prohibitions had absolutely no effect on the countryside where business continued as usual.[168]

160. IMC, *Opium: Crude and Prepared*, p. 18.
161. Ibid., p. 7.
162. *YPCC*, p. 467.
163. IMC, *Native Opium*, p. 6.
164. *RoyCom*, I, 47, no. 618.
165. *RoyCom*, I, 45, no. 562.
166. *RoyCom*, II, 386.
167. Emile Bard, *Chinese Life in Town and Country*, adapted by H. Twitchell from the French (New York, 1907), pp. 159–160. It is possible that these divans catered to peasants visiting town in connection with their periodical marketing journeys; if so, this would be another item to add to the analysis of market structures made by G. William Skinner, "Marketing and Social Structure in Rural China," in 3 pts., *Journal of Asian Studies* 24:3–43, 195–228, 363–399.
168. *Chiao-hui hsin-pao* [Mission news] 2:65 (December 11, 1869); Kuo Sung-t'ao, *Yang-*

Along all major transportation routes there were stalls or booths where opium could be bought; a detailed study of the tea export routes showed opium constantly available, like tobacco.[169] The coolies would often stop for about an hour after each three hours' work for a smoke of opium and a rest.[170] Here, also, they could buy some opium to carry if they knew there would be no chance to smoke along the next stage of their journey; either little balls of opium, bits of which could be broken off and chewed;[171] or some smokable extract that could be carried in a little cup at the belt and licked off the finger;[172] or even, perhaps, one of the concentrated tablets which Westerners had thoughtfully provided as an aid to withdrawal from addiction. Dr. William Gould was surprised, in Swatow, at how quickly his 50,000 morphia tablets sold,[173] and duty-free morphia—known as "Jesus Opium" because it was often sold by Chinese Christians—became a major import in the late Ch'ing.[174]

Itinerant vendors also did a major business at annual fairs and festivals, setting up their booths near the temples in advance of the festivities, and then doing a brisk business with the holiday crowds who came in from the countryside.[175] This would have been a good way to widen the market, as those in high spirits with loose cash in their pockets (for probably the only time in the year) might well contract a habit that would last a lifetime.

ECONOMIC FUNCTION

For at least the last fifty years of the nineteenth century, opium played an important role in the Chinese economy, and it did so in three major areas: it served as a substitute for money, it helped local officials meet taxation quotas, and it helped finance the self-strengthening program.

Both British and American merchants saw, after the Opium War, how useful opium would be as a medium of exchange in the *interior* of China; and though they themselves were still restricted to the treaty ports, they sent their compradors inland with large stocks of opium that could be exchanged for upcountry tea or Soochow silk.[176] Ahee, for example, was entrusted with $440,065 of specie and opium by Jardine's in 1855.[177] Similarly, in the Taiping-induced financial crisis at Shanghai in the early 1850s, it was the

chih shu-wu wen-chi [Collected prose works of Kuo Sung-t'ao] (Taipei: Wen-hai ch'u-pan she, 1964), 12:21b.

169. Fairbank, *Trade and Diplomacy*, p. 297.

170. *RoyCom*, I, 47, no. 611.

171. *RoyCom*, I, 45, no. 567.

172. *RoyCom*, I, 114, no. 1670, and 115, no. 1693.

173. *RoyCom*, I, 59, no. 836.

174. Hilary Beattie, "Protestant Missions and Opium in China," *Harvard University Papers on China* 22A (1969): 104–113.

175. *PGT* (1888), p. 88.

176. Yen-p'ing Hao, *The Comprador*, pp. 77, 79, 82.

177. Ibid., p. 81.

Western companies with large opium stocks that were able to exploit the tea market most successfully.[178]

Non-comprador Chinese were equally quick to see the advantages of opium as a substitute for cash. One reason was its light weight. In a number of homicide cases in the later Ch'ing, we find that travelers were often murdered because their boatmen or bearers had guessed from the heaviness of their baggage that they were carrying silver bullion.[179] Though opium of course was worth less by unit of weight than silver, it was far lighter than a copper cash equivalent, and its bulk and weight distribution might confuse the bearer. For this, or other, reasons it was early used by small shopkeepers in Hong Kong to remit funds to the mainland,[180] and it was commonly used as currency in western China; even students traveling to Peking for the examinations would take opium with them to pay their expenses along the way.[181] Others used it as a temporary investment to increase their earnings. Thus, at the lowliest economic level, coolies who had pulled barges up the Yangtze would load up with opium in Szechwan, and then carry this opium on foot through the mountains and sell it to dealers in Hupei (or sometimes carry it on a commission basis).[182] At a more sophisticated financial level, the expectant prefect Wu Shu-heng in Szechwan in 1881, asked by the financial commissioner to take 30,000 taels to Hupei, invested the money in opium, in hopes of reselling it at a profit when he reached his destination. As he could find a local market for only 37 of his 168 piculs of opium, he asked the Hupei governor to sell the rest for him at Hankow.[183]

Opium revenue was a boon to harried magistrates trying to fill their tax quotas. Especially after the great rebellions of the mid-nineteenth century, the magistrate's position was extremely precarious. Where agricultural production had slumped while quotas remained unchanged, the magistrate would run the risk of serious local unrest—and hence of losing his job—if he tried to squeeze more from the conventional agricultural sector. Tso Tsung-t'ang reported three magistrates and one deputy magistrate accepting fees from local poppy growers in return for exempting their fields from uprooting in 1874,[184] and a local censor found matters even worse in Shansi, where only two prefects in the whole province did anything to check growing. Everywhere else, people and officials were linked by the desire to make money from opium.[185] Some of the officials who "levied opium taxes without authori-

---

178. Fairbank, *Trade and Diplomacy*, pp. 405–406.
179. A graphic case is in *PGT* (1888), p. 160; another in Fairbank, *Trade and Diplomacy*, pp. 405–406.
180. Fairbank, *Trade and Diplomacy*, p. 238.
181. IMC, *Native Opium*, p. 16.
182. *RoyCom*, II, 385.
183. *PGT* (1881), p. 52.
184. *PGT* (1874), p. 46.
185. *PGT* (1874), p. 87.

zation"[186] had been formally approached by the local people. For instance, on taking up his new office, one magistrate was visited by the local farmers and gentry and given a lump sum (of unspecified size); a few months later he was given 1,163 taels in cash and opium worth 3,000 taels. The agreement seems to have been that he would receive a percentage of the yield.[187] On another occasion, it was the local military officer who was bribed not to report 2,500 *mou* of opium fields.[188]

The general trouble, as the Shansi governor Pao Yuan-shen analyzed it, was that opium had now become "routine"; local officials both needed the revenue and were unwilling to irritate the people they governed by attacking "one of the prevailing customs of the day."[189] (Kuo Sung-t'ao, incidentally, mocked Pao for the inefficiency of his suppression moves, which made Pao the butt of jokes in Peking. According to Kuo, people would simply pull up a few poppies along the roadside when they heard that one of Pao's inspectors was coming; apart from that, they took no notice of the prohibitions.)[190] In Kiangnan, Governor-general Shen Pao-chen echoed Pao's sentiments: opium, once regarded as a deadly poison, was now treated as if it were tea or rice,[191] though Shen continued to dismiss officials in his own jurisdiction who were opium smokers.[192] That taxes for opium growing were quite public in some areas can be seen from the example of Ning-hsia. In 1878 the local inhabitants kept their best land for opium, saying that otherwise they could not pay their taxes; and the prefect refused to send grain relief to Shensi because half his land was now under opium and he had no grain surplus.[193]

Taxes on local growth, tacit acceptance of local growth, or bribery to permit local growth, all took place in the context of the traditional tax system and the traditional bureaucracy. Quite the opposite was the case with likin, where one had a new tax, levied in a new way, to be applied to new purposes. Proposals for taxing opium had predated the Opium War. They were revived in 1853, when a censor suggested a rate of forty taels for each imported chest.[194] In 1856 a collection of twelve taels per chest was started by the taotai in Shanghai, and in 1857 the same rate was levied in Ningpo. The 1858 tariff agreements between Britain and China settled on an import duty of thirty taels per picul; opium had to be sold by the importer at the port and could be transported inland only by Chinese as Chinese property.[195] Inland taxation on opium in transit was a difficult question both

186. *PGT* (1875), p. 36.
187. *PGT* (1875), p. 147.
188. *PGT* (1878), p. 225.
189. *PGT* (1876), p. 105.
190. Kuo Sung-t'ao, *Yang-chih shu-wu wen-chi*. 12:18b.
191. *PGT* (1877), pp. 184–186.
192. *PGT* (1878), p. 13.
193. *PGT* (1878), p. 176.
194. Morse, *International Relations*, I, 549.
195. Ibid., I, 551–555.

for the Chinese and the British, and it remained a separate problem in the inclusive import-duty debates—where the British 7.5 percent and the Chinese 12.5 percent had ended up with a 10-percent compromise that was never implemented.[196] In the original Chefoo convention, opium was granted treatment "different from that affecting other imports," since each provincial government was to be free to assess its own likin rates and collect them from the Chinese distributors. Debate continued on this question through the 1870s and 1880s. Tso Tsung-t'ang wanted a uniform rate of 120 taels per picul; Li Hung-chang swung between 60 and 90 taels; Thomas Wade suggested raising import rates to 45 taels, and thought 40 taels would then be a generous likin assessment. The final ratified 1885 agreement was for retention of 30 taels as import duty and a payment of 80 taels likin, which would exempt the opium from all further inland taxation.[197] On an annual import rate of 50,000 chests, this would yield 5,500,000 taels to the Chinese government.

In 1881, writing to the secretary of the Anti-Opium Society, Li Hung-chang stated: "Opium is a subject in the discussion of which England and China can never meet on common ground; China views the whole question from a moral standpoint, England from a fiscal."[198] But in fact it was the very complexity of the fiscal role that opium revenue played in late Ch'ing China's economy that made suppression so difficult. We can note a progression in the practical experience of several great officials: Chang Chih-tung in 1884 was most eloquently pleading to banish all opium from Shansi; in 1890 he was reorganizing the taxes on Hupei opium, in 1899 he was raising them, and in 1904 still discussing the use of funds from Hupei-processed opium for the purchase of foreign weapons.[199] Tso Tsung-t'ang had been savagely efficient in attacking smokers in Kansu and Shensi in the early Kuang-hsu reign; by 1881 he was talking of raising taxes on local opium to discourage smoking.[200] Tseng Kuo-ch'üan had been a powerful opium suppressor in Shansi; in Kiangnan by 1887 he was discussing uses of opium revenue in the handling of Shanghai affairs.[201]

Li Hung-chang's memorials yield the richest amount of evidence. There, between 1862 and 1889, we find opium taxes used to make up deficits in the merchants' taxes—Tientsin opium for Chihli defense, Tientsin opium taxes to pay for Peking police, Tsingtao opium to pay for new patrol boats, coal for the cruiser *Chen-hai* to be bought with opium funds, opium to pay off interest on foreign loans to the new armies, and so on.[202]

Most of this revenue was doubtless import tax revenue collected at port

196. Ibid., II, 375.
197. Ibid., II, 379.
198. Ibid., II, 376.
199. Chang Chung-li and Stanley Spector, eds., *Guide to the Memorials of Seven Leading Officials of Nineteenth-Century China* (Seattle: University of Washington Press, 1955), pp. 364, 379, 391, 396.
200. Ibid., pp. 173–174.
201. Ibid., p. 231.
202. Ibid., pp. 245, 277, 311, 328, 329, 335.

of entry, but in some cases likin is specified, and one censor insisted that almost all local likin revenues came from domestic opium.[203] A survey of the *Peking Gazette* yields several examples of likin on both locally-produced and foreign opium in transit, which show how tightly bound some self-strengthening and modernizing enterprises were to opium revenues. In 1877 the Kwangtung governor-general reported that sixteen gunboats were being built at the Canton Arsenal; the cost to date of 96,860 taels plus the 4,148 taels a month in wages and sundries was all drawn from opium-likin revenue.[204] The same work was continuing in 1880, on a base revenue from opium likin of 110,000 taels p.a. (the total collected was 230,000, of which 120,000 was sent to court as a "subsidy").[205] In 1887 the governor of Taiwan, Liu Ming-ch'uan, was given Takow and Tamsui opium likin revenues to meet his naval and military expenses.[206] In the same year the Szechwan Arsenal drew 67,771 taels from opium likin that were used to make machinery, guns, cartridges, and percussion caps.[207]

Opium became such a major component in overall likin receipts that shifts in distribution patterns or changes in legal enforcement procedures could have wide-ranging fiscal repercussions. The case of Honan in 1870 illustrates this. In that year the governor reported that nearly all wholesale dealers were now based in Yü-chou, which had had no likin office since the Taiping days; the lesser dealers in Shen-chou, Ho-nai-hsien, and Ch'ing-hua-chen, who had "compounded" for their likin payments, were going broke for lack of business, whereas Yü-chou had "several scores of new firms." Opium was a key part of likin, and most of it originally came from the produce of Shensi and Kansu. Tso Tsung-t'ang's prohibitions of opium in northwest China had upset the conventional opium trade patterns; it was now *Szechwan* opium that was flowing into Honan, and new branch stations were needed to catch the new revenue. Teng-chou was a key town at which to tap the Hu-kuang and Honan shipments.[208] After approval had been granted, the governor set up his new stations as well as smaller substations to "inspect the opium duty certificates" and stop "the adoption of circuitous routes" by tax-evading merchants.[209]

Such reports as this must have been studied by the Board of Revenue, for in 1887 they tried to standardize domestic opium likin on a fixed payment plan—as foreign opium had been standardized at 80 taels in the 1885 agreements—deciding on a rate of 45 taels per picul. Just as harsh tax collection in times of dearth led peasants to riot, so did increased opium taxes lead to discontent. News of the higher likin rate caused a mob led by a military graduate

203. *PGT* (1874), p. 87.
204. *PGT* (1877), pp. 116–117.
205. *PGT* (1880), p. 58.
206. *PGT* (1887), p. 197.
207. *PGT* (1887), p. 142.
208. *PGT* (1879), pp. 200–201.
209. *PGT* (1881), pp. 52–53.

to sack the magistrate's yamen at Yuan-ch'ü in Shansi.[210] Two years later, at Hsiangshan near Ningpo, two local growers and an opium seller joined forces to whip up a crowd on market day and sack the magistrate's yamen and destroy the three new likin barriers that had driven up local opium prices.[211] (The rioters may have had a point, in that such likin-opium stations seem to have been prone to rather extraordinary graft—furthermore, at least one corrupt likin station was run by an expectant magistrate, which suggests that this may have developed as a new and lucrative post that could be used to relieve bureaucratic unemployment.)[212]

The revenue potentials of native opium grew more and more tantalizing to the Ch'ing. In 1891, through a system of official dues which were to replace likin, the central government started to collect opium revenue itself.[213] In 1896, when the twenty million taels of annual Imperial Maritime Customs revenue was already 80 percent pledged to cover foreign loans, they approached Robert Hart. The Board of Revenue asked Hart on May 16 if he would take over all collections on inland native opium.[214] In mid-June they renewed the offer. As Hart, who had hoped for such an offer since 1894,[215] wrote to Campbell:

> I have again been asked to take *Native Opium* in hand and consented; but it will be no easy job for it extends our work over all China, will be disliked by officials and people and will take years to getting into anything like efficient condition. As I said before—if I had only twenty years more work in me, or, better if I was twenty years younger, I might now look forward to doing something big and being really useful: so far all I have done has been to keep the customs on its legs and go on widening its base at every chance and so securing stability—now I might build, but "hélas!" that's for other men to do.[216]

Hart started work on an opium taxation memo, but the president of the Board of Revenue "funked it," according to Hart, on June 24.[217] Hart expressed his disappointment in a letter dated July 4, 1897, after the board had drafted their own plans:

> The *Hu-pu* stole my "thunder" and instead of giving me the *Native Opium* have directed the provincials themselves to deal with it: ordering them at once to collect Tls. 20,000,000 annually on chests 330,000—I had promised that result in *thirty* years time! Of course my plan is spoiled, and their experiment will fail.[218]

210. *PGT* (1888), p. 88.
211. *PGT* (1889), p. 117, and (1890), p. 232.
212. *PGT* (1877), p. 88.
213. Beattie, "Protestant Missions," p. 121.
214. Hart, "Letters," pp. 1957–1958.
215. Hart, "Letters," p. 1830.
216. Hart, "Letters," p. 1968.
217. Hart, "Letters," p. 1971.
218. Hart, "Letters," p. 2089.

No satisfactory system had been developed by 1906, when the mutual accords with Britain on a 10 percent per annum suppression rate were made.

We can see from the foregoing discussion that in seeking to eradicate opium addiction the Ch'ing state had to deal with a formidable array of vested interests. The damage that opium growing caused to Chinese agriculture and to peasant and urban morale has long been known to us; but we should also entertain the hypothesis that these vested interests—criminals, poor peasants, coolies, merchants, and officials—may have been so resistant to suppression just because opium had provided fluid capital and fresh revenue sources in a stagnating domestic economy. Only when moral outrage transcended these special interests could a successful suppression campaign commence. This moral outrage was coordinated by tough senior officials like Hsi-liang[219] who were not afraid to use military force against Chinese growers; and it was encouraged by the British, who had clearly lost their dominating position in the Chinese opium market, and with new types of investments in China and new sources of revenue for India were willing to be reciprocally gracious.[220]

The considerable success of the opium suppression campaigns between 1906 and 1915 points up the force of emergent Chinese nationalism and the recovery of a sense of social purpose,[221] just as the fall back into massive addiction between 1915 and 1945 points to the premature frustration of that nationalism and sense of purpose.[222] The success of the Communist suppression campaign reaffirms the cycle.[223] As a sequence, these events seem to indicate that in ending opium addiction psychological factors are more important than physiological ones.

219. An excellent account of his suppression campaign in Yunnan is in Roger V. Des Forges, "Hsi-liang, A Portrait of a Late Ch'ing Patriot" (Ph.D. thesis, Yale University, 1971), pp. 252–281.

220. With some reservations, as noted in Mary C. Wright, ed., *China in Revolution, The First Phase, 1900–1913* (New Haven: Yale University Press, 1968), pp. 14–15.

221. There is intriguing data in Edward Friedman, "Revolution or Just Another Bloody Cycle? Swatow and the 1911 Revolution," *Journal of Asian Studies* 29:289–307, esp. pp. 301–302.

222. These are among the themes in a recently registered Yale Ph.D. thesis by Leonard P. Adams, III, "The Tarnished Crusade: Opium Suppression in China, 1880–1930."

223. The Communists had also learned a great deal about local option and minority group sentiments, as can be seen from their February 1950 anti-opium provisions: *Chung-yang jen-min cheng-fu fa-ling hui-pien* [Collection of laws and decrees of the People's Republic of China] (Peking: Fa-lü ch'u-pan she, 1952), I, 173–174.

Some Preliminary Statistical Patterns of Mass Actions in Nineteenth-Century China

C. K. Yang

NATURE OF THE STUDY

This is a quantitative sketch of mass unrests and social movements during the late Ch'ing period (1796–1911).[1] It attempts to use computer-processed historical data as a heuristic tool to discern the magnitudes and configurations of mass action incidents occurring in this critical period of dynastic decline and social transition. The paper offers only a sample view of the rather extensive data which is still being processed. The portion presented here is based on availability from the processing operations, not on logical selection or conceptual considerations. As a presentation of sample items, therefore, this paper is not systematically conceived; it contains inconsistencies, gaps, ambiguities, omissions by data limitation, and other characteristics of an ongoing process of analysis.

DATA AND TREATMENT

The primary data is extracted from 2,247 *chüan* of the *Ta-Ch'ing huang-ti shih-lu* (Veritable records of the Ch'ing emperors), covering the turbulent period from the first year of the Chia-ch'ing reign (1796) to the last year of the Hsuan-t'ung reign (1911). Four kinds of information most closely related to social change were culled from the volumes: (1) mass action incidents, each involving five or more participants and creating public issues ranging

1. This study, which received support from the Air Force Office of Scientific Research and the Center for International Studies of the University of Pittsburgh, constitutes a part of the project on Comparative Study of Social Movements. This project's co-investigators are C. K. Yang, studying the Chinese case, and Burkart Holzner studying the German case. The conceptualization and instruments used in these two cases represent the joint efforts of the two investigators. The task of data extraction from the *Shih-lu* was undertaken by the staff of the Modern Chinese History Institute of the Academia Sinica in 1966–1968. Dr. Chok-king Liang did the computer processing. Mr. Chong-chor Lau checked and corrected the statistics.

from famine riots to battles of rebellion; (2) imperial honors awarded to exemplary persons in support of such critical traditional values as loyalty, filial piety, and chastity; (3) government relief for famines and disasters, an indicator of economic dislocation; (4) cases of punishment of officials, denoting political ineffectiveness and disorganization.

The first category of data provides factual information on the development of social unrest and on social movements, which compelled increasingly drastic changes in Chinese society through successive waves of mass action. The second category represents an effort to shore up basic traditional values as one form of system response to threats against society's stability. The third and fourth categories provide indicators of economic and political forces which helped to generate social unrest and movements for change.

This paper offers a sample view mainly of the first category in the form of initial item counts without sophisticated computation or cross-tabulation. A limited amount of data on the second category has been included, but figures for categories three and four are not yet available.

METHODOLOGICAL CONSIDERATIONS

More specifically stated, the study tries to identify on a national scale the institutional locuses of the complex social process leading to the Republican Revolution of 1911 and the Communist Revolution of 1949 which eventually brought about the transformation of traditional Chinese society. The eventual collapse of this social order was not the result of short-term occurrences of several years or even several decades, but the fermentation of over a century. Neither was the transformation generated from a single locality, but from the interplay of regional forces encompassing the entire nation. Case data of historical accounts have their limitations in dealing with long-term development over such extensive territory. Although case accounts may be able to examine the details of prominent events which are relatively limited in number, they may not be able to cope with the innumerable smaller occurrences which could have causal significance for those prominent events. The present attempt at quantitative analysis hopes to reveal new features in the long-term national development of social forces which led to revolutionary change.

Another ground for the present attempt is to exploit the quantitative approach which may yield information beyond what case accounts could achieve. We may note that certain cases occurred in cities, but if we produce a quantitative pattern showing that a significant proportion of the same type of events, big and small, occurred in cities instead of in the countryside, this may indicate the urban sector to be the locus of forces generating unrest. Case studies of uprisings show that sectarian and secret societies played a strategic role, but our understanding of sectarian and secret societies as a motivating force in popular uprisings will be enhanced if we can learn the proportion of incidents of social unrest in which such societies take a part, as compared to the total number of incidents of social unrest. A quantitative pattern of individual facts can offer unsuspected views of a problem, at times in opposition to accustomed opinions.

However, quantitative analysis of historical data, now vastly facilitated by computer processing, faces the extreme difficulty of available sources of data which yield systematic and long-term (e.g., over a century) information on a national scale, while still being manageable in terms of time, manpower, and other related costs. After long deliberation and consultation with Chinese historians, the *Shih-lu* was selected as the main source of data, using such supplementary sources as local gazetteers for references.

The selection is based partly on its extensive day-to-day coverage of events and partly on practical considerations which necessitate the use of a single source. Although the *Shih-lu*, a record of the emperors' utterances and edicts and of officials' memorials on matters of government, includes all events of national significance, it also reflects certain biases. Information had to filter through various levels of the bureaucracy before it reached the court and became a part of the records, so that many categories of information were altered to protect the interests of the officials involved. The political nature of incidents was minimized, as were events incriminating to officials, such as incidents of looting and plundering by government troops or cases of bureaucratic corruption.

To evaluate the completeness and accuracy of information in the *Shih-lu*, data pertinent to categories one and three have been extracted from the local gazetteers of forty *hsien* (about 3 percent of all *hsien* in the late Ch'ing) covering the same period as the *Shih-lu*, and this will be compared with the *Shih-lu* data at some future time. These *hsien* are distributed over six provinces: Kwangtung, Hunan, Szechwan, Chekiang, Shantung, and Honan. The first four provinces have a heavy concentration of social unrest, while the last two represent areas with a high frequency of natural disasters (floods and droughts), which supplied the classic generating forces of socio-political disturbances pressing for change. Although the gazetteer information is not available for this paper, a preliminary impression of this corroborative data suggests that the *Shih-lu* has sufficient coverage of events for the present purpose of attempting a broad analytic sketch of mass action patterns in nineteenth-century China.

A final methodological point concerns the unit of data. The basic statistical unit is the "mass action incident" which represents an action by groups of any size (from five persons to an army) involving public issues. Interlinked incidents constitute an event. A chain of events on a sustained pattern with defined goals forms a social movement. Thus, a single "rice riot" is an incident, while a series of such riots in the same region which snowballed into a local uprising (such as attacking the county magistracy) will constitute an event. A battle for a strategic point is an incident, while a series of battles in a prolonged struggle over a major location or territory will make an event. Uprisings and prolonged battles provide the components for certain types of social movement, such as the Taiping Rebellion or the Republican Revolution. This paper deals mainly with statistics of incidents, although events and movements are discussed on occasion.

FREQUENCY OF MASS ACTION INCIDENTS

Table 1 presents the frequency of mass action incidents from 1796 to 1911 in ten-year intervals,[2] except for the last interval, which consists of sixteen years. In subsequent tables the grand total of incidents may be slightly higher or lower than the 6,643 given in this table, due to differences resulting from

TABLE 1:

FREQUENCY OF MASS ACTION INCIDENTS

	1796–1805	1806–15	1816–25	1826–35	1836–45	1846–55	1856–65	1866–75	1876–85	1886–95	1896–1911	Total
Number of Incidents	107	131	117	206	258	959	2483	1020	391	315	566	6643

multiple entries of certain items of information or to faulty card-punching. But the variation is generally within twenty cases, and is insignficant for a total of over six thousand.

The frequency pattern fully supports our common understanding of modern Chinese history. The large number of incidents in the three decades from 1846 to 1875 corresponds to the extensive turmoil of the Taiping and Nien rebellions. The Taiping Rebellion consisted of 1,152 incidents of individual actions, and the Nien Rebellion of 490 incidents, as recorded in the *Shih-lu*. In addition, there were scores of nonaffiliated incidents (e.g., Hakka-Punti feuds) which the *Shih-lu* did not differentiate from the Taiping or the Nien rebellions, while many other separately recorded outbreaks (e.g., Miao uprisings and sectarian movements) were actually linked to the Taiping or Nien forces.

The high number of incidents in the sixteen-year interval of 1896–1911 mirrors a general outbreak of mass action incidents in the country, seemingly continuing the Taiping and Nien efforts after a short lull of two decades, and heralding the Republican Revolution of 1911. Neither the Boxer Rebellion nor the Republican Revolution contributed significantly to this high total, for only ninety incidents were recorded in the *Shih-lu* for the Republican Revolution, and we excluded all but sixteen incidents of the Boxer Rebellion

2. The ten-year interval could be reduced to five years for greater efficiency, but this is not practical for the present and may be done later.

because our concern is only with actions inside the Chinese social system. Battles with foreign powers (mainly government action) were included only when they involved spontaneous popular resistance to foreign invaders.

A large portion of the six thousand-odd incidents took the form of single local actions, but many of them were a chain of unit actions constituting an event, and a series of related events might be linked into a social movement having some enduring stability. This treatment of the data is not included in this paper.

At this stage of analysis it may not be fruitful to indulge in elaborate speculation on the statistical pattern of this frequency series, because the necessary interpretative data concerning such phenomena as agricultural failures or political misrule cannot be incorporated in the form of correlations or time sequences. One could, however, observe that in general the empire never really recovered from the impact of the Taiping and Nien catastrophe, for the number of mass actions climbed back to a high level after a respite of only two decades during which incidents of unrest continued in substantial number. This suggests the possible persistence of outstanding problems which these two rebellions failed to resolve. It would be interesting to see the development of the frequency trend after 1911, if comparable data were available for the republican period.

MAGNITUDES OF MASS ACTION BY DURATION, AREA, AND PARTICIPANTS

Tables 2, 3, and 4 convey an impression of the magnitude of the mass action incidents as measured by duration of time, the extent of area affected, and the number of participants. In all three tables, let us keep in mind that

TABLE 2:

DURATION OF EACH INCIDENT

Duration	1796–1805		1806–15		1816–25		1826–35		1836–45		1846–55	
	No.	%	No.	%	No.	%	No.	%	No.	%	No.	%
13 months and more	27	25.2	7	5.3	4	3.4	3	1.5	6	2.3	24	2.5
1 month to 12 months	27	25.2	46	35.1	36	30.8	40	19.4	83	32.2	321	33.5
1 month and less	31	30.0	61	46.6	43	36.7	80	38.8	116	45.0	475	49.5
Unknown	22	20.6	17	13.0	34	29.1	83	40.3	53	20.5	139	14.5
TOTAL	107	100.0	131	100.0	117	100.0	206	100.0	258	100.0	959	100.0

Duration	1856–65		1866–75		1876–85		1886–95		1896–1911		TOTAL	
	No.	%	No.	%	No.	%	No.	%	No.	%	No.	%
13 months and more	77	3.1	44	4.3	12	3.1	8	2.6	39	5.9	251	3.8
1 month to 12 months	567	22.8	319	31.3	72	18.4	52	16.5	126	19.2	1689	25.4
1 month and less	1562	62.9	437	42.8	286	73.1	219	69.5	425	64.8	3735	56.2
Unknown	277	11.2	220	21.6	21	5.4	36	11.4	66	10.1	968	14.6
TOTAL	2483	100.0	1020	100.0	391	100.0	315	100.0	656	100.0	6643	100.0

the unit is the individual mass action incident, not an event or a movement, for the nature of the unit affects the interpretation of the data. Time limitation precludes the use of any sophisticated statistical analysis, such as precise trend measurements. Simple percentages are provided in these three tables to facilitate cursory analysis.

For the entire period, more than half of all the incidents were short-term actions lasting from a few hours or a day to less than a month, while about one-fourth lasted from over a month to a year. Incidents lasting over twelve months were few (Table 2). Most of the mass actions were short- or middle-term incidents which terminated without subsequent development. But the continual outbreak of brief incidents indicates persistence of the causes which generated them, leading to the development of long-term regional or national movements as organized efforts to eliminate the sources of social unrest.

While we need further computations to interpret the fluctuations of the long- and middle-term incidents, even visual inspection discloses the steady growth of short-term incidents of less than a month. The growth became pronounced after the three mid-century decades of massive upheaval (1846–1875) marked by the Taiping and Nien rebellions. The violent suppression of these two great uprisings seems to have generated a rash of spontaneous momentary actions all across the troubled land. Although the imperial army may have been able to suppress a large-scale insurrection, it was much less effective when confronted with innumerable small disturbances spreading throughout the country.

The next measurement of the magnitude of mass actions is by the percentage of area in a province affected by each incident (Table 3). For the entire period, 96.7 percent of all incidents were local affairs restricted within an area of 10 percent or less of a province. For the most part, incidents were confined within a single *hsien*, with those affecting 11 to 49 percent and those

TABLE 3:

PERCENTAGE OF AREA IN A PROVINCE AFFECTED BY A MASS ACTION INCIDENT

Percentage of Area	1796–1805		1806–15		1816–25		1826–35		1836–45		1846–55	
	No.	%	No.	%	No.	%	No.	%	No.	%	No.	%
Greater than 50%	0	0	0	0	0	0	0	0	1	0.4	2	0.2
11–49%	4	3.7	6	4.6	5	4.3	22	10.7	19	7.4	20	2.1
10% and less	103	96.3	125	95.4	112	95.7	184	89.3	238	92.2	937	97.7
TOTAL	107	100.0	131	100.0	117	100.0	206	100.0	258	100.0	959	100.0

Percentage of Area	1856–65		1866–75		1876–85		1886–95		1896–1911		TOTAL	
	No.	%	No.	%	No.	%	No.	%	No.	%	No.	%
Greater than 50%	10	0.4	2	0.2	2	0.5	0	0	0	0	17	0.2
11–49%	51	2.1	46	4.5	5	1.3	10	3.2	17	2.6	205	3.1
10% and less	2422	97.5	972	95.3	384	98.2	305	96.8	639	97.4	6421	96.7
TOTAL	2483	100.0	1020	100.0	391	100.0	315	100.0	656	100.0	6643	100.0

affecting 50 percent of a province accounting for 3.1 and 0.2 percent of all cases respectively. If we look for trends, it can be seen that although small local incidents had always been predominant, tending to increase slightly after the fourth decade of the century, incidents of medium range exhibited a tendency to decrease following the same decade. Large-scale incidents affecting over half of a province, however, occurred in small numbers only in the four decades of 1836–1885, which saw the two great upheavals—the Taiping and the Nien rebellions. No category has been provided for incidents affecting over a whole province, because the unit of count is the individual incident, not a complex event or a continuous long-term movement. A single incident often spilled over a provincial boundary, but it affected only a portion of a province or its equivalent, and the provincial boundary is insignificant for the purpose of estimating the extent of area affected by an incident. It is necessary to keep in mind the fact that even such extensive movements as the Taiping and the Nien were constituted by large numbers of smaller incidents.

As a partial effort to extend our view of mass actions beyond the individual incident level, Appendix 1 presents the duration and the provinces affected by 45 major sample cases of social unrest, ranging from events of uprisings to prolonged social movements. Among these cases, 20 lasted one year or less, and 7 lasted one to five years. The longest ones include the Nien Rebellion

TABLE 4:

NUMBER OF PARTICIPANTS OF MASS ACTION INCIDENTS

Number of	1796–1805		1806–15		1816–25		1826–35		1836–45		1846–55	
Participants	No.	%	No.	%	No.	%	No.	%	No.	%	No.	%
1,000,000+	0	0	0	0	0	0	0	0	0	0	0	0
500,000+	0	0	0	0	0	0	0	0	0	0	0	0
100,000+	0	0	0	0	0	0	1	0.5	0	0	2	0.2
10,000+	3	2.8	7	5.3	3	2.6	5	2.4	5	2.0	59	6.2
1,000+	8	7.5	14	10.7	6	5.1	18	8.7	21	8.1	104	10.8
100+	6	5.6	15	11.4	23	19.7	26	12.6	21	8.1	42	4.4
99–	1	0.9	34	26.0	35	29.9	57	27.7	40	15.5	80	8.4
Unknown	89	83.2	61	46.6	50	42.7	99	48.1	171	66.3	671	70.0
TOTAL	107	100.0	131	100.0	117	100.0	206	100.0	258	100.0	959	100.0

Number of	1856–65		1866–75		1876–85		1886–95		1896–1911		TOTAL	
Participants	No.	%	No.	%	No.	%	No.	%	No.	%	No.	%
1,000,000+	0	0	0	0	0	0	0	0	1	0.2	1	0.0
500,000+	1	0.0*	0	0	0	0	0	0	0	0	1	0.0
100,000+	34	1.4	2	0.2	0	0	2	0.6	0	0	41	0.6
10,000+	146	5.9	62	6.1	1	0.2	5	1.6	14	2.1	310	4.7
1,000+	90	3.6	48	4.7	18	4.6	16	5.1	25	3.8	368	5.5
100+	34	1.4	47	4.6	12	3.1	14	4.5	18	2.8	258	3.9
99–	59	2.4	39	3.8	91	23.3	60	19.0	81	12.3	577	8.7
Unknown	2118	85.3	821	80.6	269	68.8	218	69.2	517	78.8	5087	76.6
TOTAL	2483	100.0	1020	100.0	391	100.0	315	100.0	656	100.0	6643	100.0

* 0 registered for miniscule percentages.

and the Miao uprising in Kweichow (eighteen years in both cases), the Yunnan Moslem uprising (seventeen years), the Republican Revolution (sixteen years), and the Taiping Rebellion (thirteen years). An initial impression of this data reinforces the patterns of time and space magnitude established by statistics based on the individual incident as the unit, with the magnitudes of the larger mass actions tending to fluctuate without any persistent secular trend lasting longer or affecting larger areas.

The magnitude of mass action incidents measured by the number of participants is presented in Table 4. The large number of unknown cases is caused by the extremely cryptic nature of the *Shih-lu* text. For the whole period, the largest category consists of incidents involving less than 99 persons. These were mostly small riots, local acts of banditry, scattered uprisings, and limited sectarian disturbances. The few large incidents involving upward of 100,000 persons were full-scale battles between government troops and rebels. No time trend is apparent to cursory inspection because of the high degree of irregularity from decade to decade.

One observation can be made, however. The number of participants in mass action incidents seems related to that pattern of social organization which has the function of mobilizing people for collective action on common issues. Participants in local incidents may be restricted to relatively small numbers because of the small-group nature of local community organizations (kinship organizations, villages, urban neighborhoods, local gangs) which could mobilize only those within its restricted network of social relations. On the other hand, the large formal organizations of the national political system (the imperial government and extensive rebel organizations like the Taiping forces) could mobilize impressive numbers of participants for large-scale actions. This will be supported by data to be presented below on the organizational nature of the incidents. Other implications of the data may gain some clarification when we examine the materials on the contents of the incidents in subsequent sections of this paper.

ECOLOGICAL PATTERNS OF MASS ACTIONS

We may begin interpreting the foregoing general figures by examining their geographical pattern in Table 5, which presents the distribution of mass action incidents by provinces. The provinces are ranked by the total number of incidents for the entire period. To bring out the pattern in this rather irregular distribution, we can rearrange the data by regional configurations, as in Table 6.

The regional pattern emphasizes the fact that the largest numerical concentration of incidents occurred in north China. This region is characterized by two factors relevant to the generating of social unrest: it contains the center of national political power, Peking, and it has been chronically plagued by recurrent famines following such disasters as floods, droughts,

TABLE 5:

NUMBER OF INCIDENTS BY PROVINCE, 1796–1911

Province	1796–1805	1806–1815	1816–1825	1826–1835	1836–1845	1846–1855	1856–1865	1866–1875	1876–1885	1886–1895	1896–1911	TOTAL
Chihli	1	21	17	26	26	86	126	68	89	90	111	661
Anhwei	2	3	4	11	8	73	298	14	8	7	16	444
Kiangsu	4	5	9	10	14	68	216	35	7	14	35	417
Kansu	6	0	3	5	8	25	140	178	8	9	20	402
Honan	4	11	8	7	8	68	190	26	16	9	28	375
Kiangsi	2	4	4	13	9	57	205	30	8	9	23	364
Kwangtung	14	8	4	23	24	100	88	28	16	19	40	364
Kweichow	2	2	2	5	2	26	169	104	11	7	20	350
Hupeh	13	7	6	4	26	96	115	31	18	11	23	350
Shantung	1	14	15	8	14	47	141	40	10	14	27	331
Yunnan	9	5	7	3	7	12	96	101	27	22	29	318
Chekiang	1	3	4	9	20	22	164	21	26	11	34	315
Kwangsi	2	2	3	3	5	76	79	37	22	16	53	298
Szechwan	13	14	4	10	16	17	75	26	29	18	55	277
Shensi	8	7	1	4	1	5	110	81	3	1	18	239
Hunan	2	2	3	5	13	67	61	21	12	15	26	227
Sinkiang	2	3	3	30	11	19	55	46	20	3	7	199
Fukien	9	9	6	12	7	37	72	11	7	12	8	190
Fengtien	2	0	2	4	7	23	32	39	13	5	18	145
Shansi	4	2	4	4	5	15	14	10	9	0	15	82
Kirin	0	1	0	1	2	2	8	30	7	6	10	67
Taiwan	2	4	4	4	10	5	17	5	6	8	0	65
Inner Mongolia	0	0	2	1	2	3	6	10	1	4	7	36
Outer Mongolia	0	0	1	0	3	1	0	15	6	0	7	33
Heilungkiang	0	1	0	0	1	0	3	6	4	4	11	30
Tibet	1	1	0	1	1	3	3	4	8	0	4	26
Tsinghai	2	1	1	2	7	5	0	1	0	0	2	11
Unknown	1	1	0	1	0	1	0	2	0	1	8	15
TOTAL	107	131	117	206	258	959	2483	1020	391	315	656	6643

and pests. We may also speculate that the proximity to Peking might have led to a higher frequency of reporting of incidents in north China than in more distant sectors of the empire. The concentration of turbulence in a region of central political power collaborates with the information that the majority of all mass action incidents were directed against the government or related to political problems, and that a dominant portion of the incidents took place in political centers. The politically centered nature of this century's incidents of mass unrest has many implications. One of these is the gradual deterioration of the traditional socio-political system and its eventual collapse under the pressure of increasingly drastic movements which tried to end the government's persistent failure to correct administrative weaknesses

TABLE 6:

DISTRIBUTION OF MASS ACTION INCIDENTS BY REGION, 1796–1911

Region	Province	Number of Incidents (1796–1911)	TOTAL
North China: Plain	Chihli	661	
	Honan	375	
	Shantung	331	1,367
North China: Plateau	Shensi	239	
	Shansi	82	321
Central China	Anhwei	444	
	Kiangsi	364	
	Hupeh	350	
	Hunan	227	1,385
Southwest	Kweichow	350	
	Yunnan	318	
	Szechwan	277	945
South China	Kwangtung	364	
	Kwangsi	298	
	Fukien	190	852
East China Coast	Kiangsu	417	
	Chekiang	315	732
Northwest	Kansu	402	
	Sinkiang	199	601
Manchuria	Fengtien	145	
	Heilungkiang	30	
	Kirin	67	242
Mongolia	Outer Mongolia	33	
	Inner Mongolia	36	69
Tibet and Tsinghai	Tibet	26	
	Tsinghai	21	47
Taiwan		65	65
TOTAL			6,626

within and to successfully resist foreign invasions without. The term "political" is used here to mean the exercise of political power and the functioning and malfunctioning of the government bureaucracy.

The other characteristic of the north China region, the high frequency of famines, will gain added weight if we consider Shansi and Shensi, the two drought-cursed provinces, as a part of the north China region. Famines are undoubtedly linked to the development of social unrest, although the direct and indirect linking process remains a research problem. (The *Shih-lu* data on famine will be analyzed in this light on a further occasion, but not in this paper.)

The total of 1,385 incidents of social unrest for the central China region compares closely with the 1,367 incidents for the north China plain. Central China, like south China (852 incidents) and the east China coast (732 incidents), was a region long plagued by misgovernment, banditry, and ex-

TABLE 7:

THE RANKING OF MASS ACTION INCIDENTS BY PROVINCE*

Province	1796–1805	1806–1815	1816–1825	1826–1835	1836–1845	1846–1855	1856–1865	1866–1875	1876–1885	1886–1895	1896–1911	Total scale points	Final rank	Number of incidents
Chihli	21.5*	1	1	2	1.5	3	9	5	1	1	1	47	1	661
Kwangtung	1	6	11	3	3	1	13	14	8.5	3	4	67.5	2	364
Szechwan	2.5	2.5	11	7.5	5	17	15	15.5	2	4	2	84	3	277
Kiangsu	9	9.5	3	7.5	6.5	6.5	2	10	20	7.5	5	86.5	4	417
Hupeh	2.5	7.5	6.5	17	1.5	2	10	11	7	10.5	11.5	87	5	350
Shantung	21.5*	2.5	2	10	65	10	7	7	13	7.5	9	96	6	331
Honan	9	4	4	11	13	6.5	4	15.5	8.5	13	8	96.5	7	375
Yunnan	4.5	9.5	5	20.5	16.5	19	12	3	3	2	7	102	8	318
Kiangsi	15	11.5	11	4	11	9	3	12.5	13	13	11.5	118	9	364
Chekiang	21.5*	14	11	9	4	15	6	17.5	4	6	6	118.5	10	315
Kwangsi	15	17.5	16.5	20.5	19.5	4	14	9	5	5	3	129	11	298
Anhwei	15	14	11	6	13	5	1	20	16.5	16.5	17	135	12	444
Fukien	4.5	5	6.5	5	16.5	11	16	21	20	9	21	135.5	13	190
Hunan	15	17.5	16.5	13	8	8	17	17.5	11	6	10	139.5	14	227
Kansu	7	25.5	16.5	1	13	13	8	1	16.5	13	13.5	140	15	402
Sinkiang	15	14	20	13	9	16	18	6	6	22	23	146.5	16	199
Kweichow	15	17.5	23	17	23	12	5	2	12	16.5	13.5	149.5	17	350
Shensi	6	7.5	23	17	26	21	11	4	25	23	15.5	179	18	239
Fengtien	15	25.5	20	17	16.5	14	19	8	10	19	15.5	179.5	19	145
Shansi	9	17.5	11	17	19.5	18	21	22.5	14	25.5	18	193	20	82
Taiwan	15	11.5	11	17	10	21	20	25	22.5	15	27	195	21	65
Kirin	25.5	21.5	26	24	23	25	22	12.5	20	18	20	237.5	22	67
Tsinghai	15	21.5	23	22	16.5	21	26.5	22.5	27	25.5	26	251	23	21
Inner Mongolia	25.5	25.5	20	24	23	23.5	23	26	20.5	20.5	23	256.5	24	36
Tibet	21.5*	21.5	26	24	26	23.5	24.5	26	16.5	25.5	25	260	25	26
Outer Mongolia	25.5	25.5	23	26.5	21	26	26.5	19	22.5	25.5	23	264	26	33
Heilungkiang	25.5	21.5	26	26.5	26	27	24.5	24	24	20.5	19	264.5	27	30

*Ranking here is arranged according to the number of incidents in an area, with the highest score, 1, going to the area with the largest number of incidents. The range of the scale is based on the total number of areas, i.e., the number of provinces: from 1 to 27. Where two or more provinces had the same number of incidents, and therefore the same score, the individual score is computed by averaging the total score among such provinces.

TABLE 8:

The Ranking of Mass Action Incidents by Region*

Region	1796–1805	1806–1815	1816–1825	1826–1835	1836–1845	1846–1855	1856–1865	1866–1875	1876–1885	1886–1895	1896–1911	Total scale points	Final rank	Number of incidents
North China: Plain	7	1	1	1	2	3	2	3	1	1	1	23	1	1367
Central China	3	4	2	4	1	1	1	4	3	4	4	31	2	1385
Southwest	2	2	4	6	5	5	4	1	2	2.5	2	35.5	3.5	945
South China	1	3	4	2	3	2	5	6	4	2.5	3	35.5	3.5	852
East China Coast	5	6	4	5	4	4	3	8	5	5	5	54	5	732
Northwest	6	8	6	3	6	6	6	2	6	7	8	64	6	601
North China: Plateau	4	5	7	7	10	8	7	5	8	10	7	78	7	321
Manchuria	9.5*	9.5	10	8	7.5	7	8	10.5	7	6	6	85.5	8	242
Taiwan	9.5*	7	8	9	7.5	10	9	10.5	11	8	11	100.5	9	65
Tibet and Tsinghai	8	9.5	11	10	9	9	11	9	9	11	10	108	10	47
Mongolia	11	11	9	11	11	11	10	9	10	9	9	111	11	69

*For scoring, see note for Table 7.

tensive activities of secret societies. The Southwest (945 incidents) and the Northwest (601 incidents) were both troubled by prolonged ethnic violence, aboriginal and Moslem uprisings. Even the "sacred land" of Manchuria was affected by mass unrest after the fourth decade of the last century.

A question beckons: did the center of unrest move from one area to another during the past century? To throw some light on this intriguing problem, we have ranked the provinces and then the regions according to incident frequencies, and have computed rank scores to show the centers of highest incident concentration for different periods during the past century. The ranking pattern of provinces is shown in Table 7, and that for regions in Table 8. The results from these two tables show that north China has consistently been the leading geographical focus of unrest for the past century, with the high point of concentration in Chihli (Hopei) province where Peking is located. The three decades of 1846–1875 formed the only prolonged period when north China yielded to central China as the region with the highest incident frequency, due to the extensive development of the Taiping Rebellion in the central provinces. The leading implication of these two tables is that for a century the Ch'ing dynastic power, which was located in the north China region, was consistently the focus of social and political unrest.

Further elaboration of the ecological patterns of mass action is presented in Tables 9 and 10. Both tables contain some multiple entries, i.e., an incident may be listed in more than one category due to multiple characteristics. For example, certain subdivision capitals may also be put into the large town category, and many incidents in the seacoast category may also be put into the rural category. This is to show as many characteristics of the incidents as is methodologically permissible, and the distortion to the total number of incidents does not seem unduly large.

Table 9 shows two distributive patterns: the dominance of administrative centers as sites for mass action incidents for the entire period of the study, and the tendency for the incidents to concentrate in administrative centers in periods of large-scale disturbances.

In the total number of incidents for the entire period of the study, subdivision capitals (*fu, chou, hsien, t'ing*) led all types of sites of mass action incidents, and next to this category were incidents which took place in villages, rural areas, and the open sea (piracy). The leading role of subdivision capitals as the site of social strife emphasizes the political nature of the mass actions, as these were the points at which local government came in close touch with the life of the common people. The dominance of the political element in the majority of the incidents becomes even more apparent if we combine the individual items of national, provincial, and subdivisional capitals into a single category of administrative centers, with a total of 3,501 incidents. This total accounts for 52.7 percent of 6,643 incidents which represent the total number for the entire period without distortion by multiple

TABLE 9:

NUMBER OF INCIDENTS BY TYPE OF COMMUNITY

Type of Community	1796–1805 No.	%	1806–15 No.	%	1816–25 No.	%	1826–35 No.	%	1836–45 No.	%	1846–55 No.	%
Subdivision capitals	70	62.5	57	39.8	21	15.3	26	11.9	42	15.3	471	40.7
Villages, rural area, on sea	18	16.1	54	37.8	68	49.6	140	63.9	128	46.7	425	36.8
Large towns	2	1.8	7	4.9	9	6.6	18	8.2	13	4.7	97	8.4
Small towns	10	8.9	5	3.5	11	8.0	16	7.3	21	7.7	59	5.1
National capital	3	2.7	0	0	5	3.7	2	.9	2	.7	11	1.0
Border administrative areas	0	0	1	.7	6	4.4	12	5.5	33	12.1	32	2.8
Urban centers, unclassified	0	0	8	5.6	0	0	0	0	1	.4	3	.3
Provincial capitals	3	2.7	1	.7	1	.7	1	.5	5	1.8	24	2.0
Unknown	6	5.3	10	7.0	16	11.7	4	1.8	29	10.6	34	2.9
TOTAL	112	100.0	143	100.0	137	100.0	219	100.0	274	100.0	1156	100.0

Type of Community	1856–65 No.	%	1866–75 No.	%	1876–85 No.	%	1886–95 No.	%	1896–1911 No.	%	TOTAL No.	%
Subdivision capitals	1676	57.3	242	17.3	152	37.2	106	29.5	306	40.0	3165	40.1
Villages, rural area, on sea	715	24.5	667	47.7	130	31.8	113	31.4	211	27.9	2669	33.8
Large towns	273	9.3	173	12.4	20	4.9	13	3.6	51	6.8	676	8.6
Small towns	182	6.2	145	10.4	11	2.7	10	2.8	17	2.2	487	6.2
National capital	12	.4	8	.6	57	13.9	66	18.3	64	8.5	230	2.9
Border administrative areas	30	1.0	15	1.0	14	3.4	19	5.3	46	6.1	208	2.6
Urban centers, unclassified	10	.3	133	9.5	5	1.2	6	1.7	6	.8	172	2.2
Provincial capitals	13	.5	3	.2	6	1.5	4	1.0	45	6.0	106	1.4
Unknown	13	.5	11	.9	14	3.4	23	6.4	13	1.7	173	2.2
TOTAL	2924	100.0	1397	100.0	409	100.0	360	100.0	755	100.0	7886	100.0

entries. The large number of incidents occurring in Peking and in the provincial capitals poses many questions about the effectiveness of the nineteenth-century political order.

The incidents tend to concentrate in the countryside in periods of relative peace and stability, and to converge in the administrative centers when the country was plunged into major crises. Thus the proportion of incidents in administrative centers was high in the first two decades of our study, when the country was troubled by large-scale sectarian uprisings. In the subsequent three decades of 1816–1835, when there were only scattered disturbances, the incidents tend to disperse into the countryside. But the incidents increasingly converged in the administrative cities as social unrest built rapidly toward the great crises of the Taiping and Nien rebellions. It appears that when uprisings acquired large forces, their actions moved from the countryside to the cities where they fought for control of the political and economic centers which commanded regional resources. When the two rebellions were suppressed, subsequent incidents dispersed rapidly into the countryside in the decade of 1866–1875. But the urbo-centric tendency was resumed in the subsequent three periods when there was an increase in the number of large-scale sectarian rebellions and ethnic uprisings in response to the crises caused by the imposition of major reforms, the impact of foreign invasions, and finally the collapse of the ruling dynasty.

Despite these variations the data clearly shows the predominance of towns and cities as sites of mass actions in comparison to rural areas. There were 4,836 incidents which took place in national, provincial, and subdivision capitals, large towns, small towns, and unclassified urban centers (incidents recorded as happening in an urban place without specifying the type of location), accounting for 72.8 percent of the undiluted total of 6,643 incidents. The high urbo-centric figure assumes added significance when we consider the fact that urban inhabitants did not exceed 5 to 10 percent of the population in nineteenth-century China. Intriguing questions arise from the concentration of 72.8 percent of all incidents in places inhabited by 5 to 10 percent of the population. What made the urban environment such a favorite spawning ground of social unrest may be analyzed partly by the rural–urban classification of mass action types.

Table 10 categorizes the geographical environments of the incidents. The vast majority of the mass actions took place in farming areas, as would be

TABLE 10:

GEOGRAPHIC ENVIRONMENT OF INCIDENTS

Environment	1796–1805		1806–15		1816–25		1826–35		1836–45		1846–55	
	No.	%	No.	%	No.	%	No.	%	No.	%	No.	%
Farming	62	55.3	95	68.8	89	75.4	138	67.0	171	65.0	815	82.2
Mountains	16	14.3	12	8.7	7	5.9	20	9.7	27	10.3	67	6.8
Steppes	11	9.8	4	2.9	11	9.3	36	17.4	34	12.9	44	4.4
Coast	20	17.9	14	10.2	11	9.3	7	3.4	23	8.8	55	5.5
Lakes	0	0	0	0	0	0	2	1.0	4	1.5	5	.5
Mines	1	.9	1	.7	0	0	1	.5	1	.4	2	.2
Others	2	1.8	0	0	0	0	1	.5	0	0	0	0
Unknown	0	0	12	8.7	0	0	1	.5	3	1.1	4	.4
TOTAL	112	100.0	138	100.0	118	100.0	206	100.0	263	100.0	992	100.0

Environment	1856–65		1866–75		1876–85		1886–95		1896–1911		TOTAL	
	No.	%	No.	%	No.	%	No.	%	No.	%	No.	%
Farming	2135	85.4	739	71.6	306	77.9	272	85.5	557	83.8	5379	79.8
Mountains	229	9.1	201	19.5	54	13.7	27	8.5	65	9.8	725	10.8
Steppes	64	2.6	75	7.3	29	7.4	6	1.9	37	5.6	351	5.2
Coast	53	2.1	10	1.0	2	.5	11	3.5	4	.6	210	3.1
Lakes	5	.2	0	0	0	0	0	0	0	0	16	.2
Mines	2	.1	3	.3	0	0	1	.3	1	.1	13	.2
Others	0	0	0	0	0	0	0	0	1	.1	4	.1
Unknown	13	.5	3	.3	2	.5	1	.3	0	0	39	.6
TOTAL	2501	100.0	1031	100.0	393	100.0	318	100.0	665	100.0	6737	100.0

expected for an agricultural society. The large number of incidents in the mountain category indicates the possibility of both poverty and aboriginal ethnic discontentment as motivating forces of social strife. Most of the 351 incidents occurring on the steppes involved Moslem minority group violence. The 13 incidents in the mining areas may be an understatement due to incompleteness of the *Shih-lu* record, because mining communities have long been known to be common locations for mass violence due to harsh working conditions, merciless exploitation, and the nature of the labor force.

FORMS OF MASS ACTION

Table 11 presents the distribution of forms of mass action incidents in ten-year intervals in order to further clarify the nature of the past century's incidents of social unrest. This is a complicated set of data still in the process of cleaning and clarification, and any serious presentation is actually premature. At present we can offer only a general view of the nature of the mass actions which contributed to the turbulence of nineteenth-century China. The classification system is experimental and does not adhere to a system of well-defined criteria; inconsistencies and overlapping remain to be eliminated. Nevertheless, the imperfect table is presented because of the critical importance of the data.

For the entire period, by far the largest single item of mass action consists of armed suppression of anti-government groups, followed by suppression of banditry and piracy. To convey a clearer view of the nature of the incidents, the individual items of action have been regrouped into eight types in Table 12.

The first grouping consists largely of battles of suppression against organized rebel forces, such as in the Taiping and Nien cases, or of smaller but organized rebellions. Brief troop or police actions against organized local bands, which committed such illegal activities as gambling or forcing the release of arrested criminals, constitute a smaller item in this category.

The second category, anti-government actions, is in a sense a continuation of the first, for such actions were also objects of government suppression. The largest item here is the familiar activities of secret and sectarian societies, which have a firmly established role in the traditional political order. The heading of anti-government conspiracy is a translation from the term *mou-i*, plotting a rebellion, used in the *Shih-lu*, and it includes such cases as bandits in collusion with local militia for illegal action, and Moslem or mountain aboriginal groups gathering for suspicious collective action.

Collective resistance against unjust taxation or high agricultural rents was a familiar form of popular reaction against political and economic injustice. Some of the anti-taxation violence resulted in the killing of the local magistrate and the burning of the yamen buildings. The vast majority of the smuggling cases involved salt. The reliance on the salt monopoly as a major

TABLE 11:

FORMS OF MASS ACTION, 1796–1911

Forms of Action	1796–1805	1806–1815	1816–1825	1826–1835	1836–1845	1846–1855	1856–1865	1866–1875	1876–1885	1886–1895	1896–1911	TOTAL
1. Battles between government forces and organized groups	42	1	2	4	20	502	1792	554	35	25	94	3071
2. Skirmishes between government forces and local groups	1	4	0	13	11	11	9	4	14	10	17	94
3. Activities of secret and sectarian societies	8	37	31	28	24	25	19	29	27	36	29	293
4. Anti-government conspiracy	5	8	3	0	8	4	27	9	10	20	47	141
5. Resistance against taxation and rent	0	1	0	0	6	17	6	4	4	2	10	50
6. Smuggling	0	0	0	0	13	0	1	3	1	2	3	23
7. Banditry and piracy	42	51	46	97	85	266	302	183	204	156	240	1672
8. Local gangsterism	3	8	9	14	23	28	50	19	31	24	37	246
9. Riots	3	5	14	24	14	26	10	20	4	7	39	166
10. Strikes and boycotts	0	1	1	2	2	3	0	0	4	1	7	18
11. Demonstrations and noisy crowds	0	0	4	7	8	3	1	0	4	4	21	52
12. Agitation and propaganda	2	7	3	11	6	2	4	0	2	2	21	60
13. Panic and rumor	1	1	0	0	2	0	0	0	1	0	2	7
14. Mass flight from hunger, wars, and other miseries	0	0	1	2	15	5	0	8	5	1	4	41
15. Troop mutiny	0	0	0	1	1	2	37	24	9	3	13	90
16. Betrayal by troops and officials	0	0	0	0	0	1	2	1	0	0	0	4
17. Conflict between troops	0	0	0	0	1	3	8	5	1	0	2	20
18. Troop plundering	0	0	0	0	0	10	24	26	13	2	10	85
19. Feuds and property destruction	0	5	2	3	6	16	30	3	12	8	21	106
20. Christian proselytism	0	2	0	0	2	7	2	0	0	0	1	14
21. Anti-missionary actions	0	0	0	0	0	1	6	11	7	11	31	67
22. Resistance against foreign intruders	0	0	1	0	1	8	4	6	6	0	5	25
23. Collective donation to government military expenses	0	0	0	0	8	15	136	101	6	1	1	268
24. Local self-defense	0	0	0	0	2	4	13	10	0	0	1	30
TOTAL	107	131	117	206	258	959	2483	1020	391	315	656	6643

TABLE 12:

Grouping of Incidents by Form of Action

Grouping and form of action		Incidents 1796–1911	
		No.	%
I. Suppression of anti-government groups			
1. Battles between government forces and organized groups		3071	46.2
2. Skirmishes between government forces and local groups		94	1.4
	Subtotal	3165	47.6
II. Anti-government actions			
3. Activities of secret and sectarian societies		293	4.4
4. Anti-government conspiracy		141	2.1
5. Resistance against taxation and rent		50	.8
6. Smuggling		23	.4
	Subtotal	507	7.7
III. Action by predatory groups			
7. Banditry and piracy		1672	25.2
8. Local gangsterism		246	3.7
	Subtotal	1918	28.9
IV. Crowd actions			
9. Riots		166	2.5
10. Strikes and boycotts		18	.3
11. Demonstrations and noisy crowds		52	.8
12. Agitation and propaganda		60	.9
13. Panic and rumor		7	.1
14. Mass flight from hunger, war, and other miseries		41	.6
	Subtotal	344	5.2
V. Deterioration of government forces			
15. Troop mutiny		90	1.4
16. Betrayal by troops and officials		4	0
17. Conflict between troops		20	.3
18. Troop plundering		85	1.3
	Subtotal	199	3.0
VI. Intergroup conflicts			
19. Feuds and property destruction		106	1.6
	Subtotal	106	1.6
VII. Conflicts with foreigners			
20. Christian proselytism		14	.2
21. Anti-missionary actions		67	1.0
22. Resistance against foreign intruders		25	.4
	Subtotal	106	1.6
VIII. Popular support for government			
23. Collective donation to government military expenses		268	4.0
24. Local self-defense		30	.4
	Subtotal	298	4.4
TOTAL		6643	100.0

source of revenue led to the traditionalization of salt smuggling. The 23 cases cited represented only those which led to armed conflict with government forces, as the actual number of salt smuggling cases was very large.

The third category of predatory group actions refers to the traditional subject of banditry, piracy, and local gangs, with piracy in the minority. The preponderant number of banditry cases attests to the extensiveness of this chronic expression of the weakness of the traditional political order. Many of the so-called banditry cases were actually full-scale rebellions which took government forces many years to suppress, and many of the local bands would even "kill the officials and occupy the city [for brief periods]" (*hsiang-kuan chü-ch'eng*), which was a common expression of popular protest against misrule. Cases of plundering by "hungry bands" occurred even in the national capital of Peking. Gangsterism involved not only urban groups like laborers and such destitute elements as beggars, but also police and runners in the local yamen.

The fourth category, crowd actions, embodies a mixture of economically and politically motivated incidents. As a form of mass action, riots are characterized by their uninstitutionalized and rather unpremeditated nature, but they cover a wide range of disturbances. Several examples will illustrate this variety: the rioting crowd which broke into the community granary and kidnapped the official in charge, the Taiwan aboriginal crowd rioting over the purchase of rice from Chinese residents, the riot over the unjust adjudication of a court case by the local garrison officer and gentry, the riot of prisoners who killed their jail keeper. Strikes also were of many kinds: a town's businesses would strike against unjust police action; workers on a water control project would strike against an official taking a cut from their pay; students would strike against unfair government examinations. Cases of administrative injustice, excessive taxation, and in the latter part of the last century, the many cases of popular objection to the construction of railways and to Christian missionary proselytism, were also typical subjects for mass agitation, while disturbances were often caused by fleeing columns of victims from famines, wars, and other miseries, or by roaming bands of urban or rural paupers. A large proportion of these forms of crowd action have an anti-government political tone, and since any form of mass agitation and propaganda was likely to be regarded as subversive to public security and political order, they quickly became objects of suppression.

The fifth category of incidents clearly indicates the internal deterioration of government forces. This category subsumes the familiar cases of troop mutiny from shortage or default of wages (disintegration of government finance), the infiltration of rebel elements (secret societies, discontented ethnic groups) into the armed forces and civilian administration, armed conflicts between government forces over salt monopoly areas or other lucrative sources of revenue, and banditry of disgruntled or disaffected troops who plundered and burned as they rampaged over the countryside.

The sixth category of intergroup conflict consists of armed feuds and incidents of property destruction. Many of these actions were between clans and villages in the South, between minority groups or between ethnic groups and Chinese in border areas.

Conflict with foreigners is too familiar a category in modern history to need explanation. The final category, popular support for the government, comprises two leading types of group action: collective donation to government military expense, and local defense. The sizable number (298 incidents, or 4.4 percent of the total number of incidents for the entire period) denotes the continuity of popular support for the traditional political order. Collective donation to government expense was usually made by local communities which contributed money to the government in return for the increase of quotas of examination candidates for that territory. Thus it resembles the government's selling of official titles as a revenue-raising measure. Local self-defense was a part of the widespread local militia actions against banditry and rebellions when the government forces could no longer maintain law and order.

The foregoing comments are based on the total number of incidents of various categories for the entire period of our study. In the absence of statistical formulation, a few general observations can be made about the process of development of some categories of mass action. A cursory glance at Table 11 gives the impression that the significant growth in the number of most categories of mass action took place after the fifth decade of the nineteenth century. This is particularly true for the most preponderant single item, battles between government forces and organized groups, which account for 46.2 percent of the total number of incidents for the whole period. The high figures for the three decades following 1846 clearly reflect the large-scale and extensive operations against the Taiping and the Niens. Banditry and predatory gangs (piracy in far smaller numbers) were a persistent curse in the traditional countryside in all decades of our period, but the mid-century intervals show a drastic upswing in their numbers, which never were significantly reduced after that and which suggest the inability of the traditional socio-political system to re-establish its stability before the Taiping Rebellion. The persistence of activities by secret and sectarian societies in all intervals throughout the period indicates that covert actions were endemic to the authoritarian political order, whose ever-present fear of rebellion led to the proscription of any popular organized efforts to redress social or political injustice. The pronounced increase of incidents denoting deterioration of government forces in the three decades following 1846 again mirrors clearly the effects of the great open rebellions of that period, the internal weakness of the Ch'ing political system, and its subsequent inability to restore its effectiveness. Yet during those same three decades of 1846–1875, collective support for the government was quite prominent. The implication seems clear: the establishment dug deep into its coffers to prop up the tottering traditional order and protect its vested interests during three decades of widespread popular insurgence.

The data in Tables 11 and 12 stress the dominant political nature of the mass action incidents, and further details of this political factor in mass actions are presented in Table 13. Actions in items 1 to 8 are politically involved in some fashion, with a total of 5,253 incidents or 79.1 percent of the total for the entire period, and only 1,390 incidents or 20.9 percent of the total are not related in the *Shih-lu* to some political conflict or process. Incidents in items 1 to 5 may be regarded as anti-government actions in varying degrees, totaling 4,531 incidents or 86.2 percent of all the politically involved incidents for the period.

Some examples may serve to clarify the nature of the individual items in Table 13. The first and largest item, replacement of government, includes incidents aimed at toppling the Ch'ing dynastic government and replacing it with another traditional mode of government, typically the *fan-Ch'ing fu-Ming* (overthrow the Ch'ing and restore the Ming) type of activities current among secret and sectarian societies. The second item, change of officials, refers to mass actions attacking individual officials (typically the *hsien* magistrate) or demanding the recall of officials charged with misrule.

Actions categorized as attempts to overthrow the political system were those committed not only to overthrowing the Ch'ing dynasty, but also to building a nontraditional political order. They consist mainly of actions in the Taiping Rebellion and the Republican Revolution, with the extensiveness of the Taiping upheaval contributing to the large number of incidents in this category.[3] Gradual political reform actions also aimed at changing the traditional order, not by overthrowing the government but by piecemeal reforms, and this includes incidents in the Hundred Days Reform and the constitutional monarchy movement.

The item of action against the law includes large-scale banditry and piracy as well as local attacks on officials and government offices. Power struggle incidents are self-explanatory. The category of incidents politically related but lacking details includes many of the aboriginal uprisings and some of the secret and sectarian societies which had political designs but had not committed overt anti-government acts. Actions categorized as support of government were effected through collective financial donations and local self-

3. It is necessary at this point to recall again the use of the individual action incident as the unit of statistics. If complex events or movements were used as units, the number in this category could be small, for there were very few movements which had the ideology of building a nontraditional political system; most were of the renovative type, as contrasted to the unrenovative type which purports to reconstruct the government after the traditional model.

POLITICAL FACTOR IN MASS ACTION INCIDENTS

Type of Political Action	1796–1805	1806–1815	1816–1825	1826–1835	1836–1845	1846–1855	1856–1865	1866–1875	1876–1885	1886–1895	1896–1911	TOTAL
1. Replacement of government	38	16	11	9	23	210	954	570	62	30	79	2002
2. Change of officials	0	0	1	0	3	0	4	1	1	0	0	10
3. Overthrow of political system	15	0	0	0	0	302	887	3	0	1	58	1266
4. Gradual political reform	0	0	0	1	0	0	0	3	0	0	15	19
5. Action against the law	29	39	22	79	30	168	281	101	134	127	224	1234
6. Power struggle inside government	0	0	0	0	0	1	2	0	0	0	1	4
7. Politically related, lacking details	16	27	28	39	60	73	38	27	23	25	67	423
8. Support of government	0	0	0	2	5	18	151	109	7	1	2	295
9. No mention of political implication	9	49	55	76	137	187	166	206	164	131	210	1390
TOTAL	107	131	117	206	258	959	2483	1020	391	315	656	6643

ECONOMIC FACTOR IN MASS ACTION INCIDENTS

Type of economic factor	1796–1805	1806–1815	1816–1825	1826–1835	1836–1845	1846–1855	1856–1865	1866–1875	1876–1885	1886–1895	1896–1911	TOTAL
1. Economic dissatisfaction	3	44	23	46	66	190	189	156	162	134	168	1181
2. Serious economic deprivation	3	4	4	11	22	12	2	14	9	8	15	104
3. Related to organization of economic and financial matters	13	5	25	55	57	74	197	147	21	23	76	693
4. Campaigning for prosperous territories	0	1	1	3	9	3	0	0	0	0	2	19
5. Economically-related but unspecified	58	30	26	28	25	476	1941	560	150	103	197	3594
6. Economic factor unknown	30	47	38	63	79	204	154	143	49	47	198	1052
TOTAL	107	131	117	206	258	959	2483	1020	391	315	656	6643

defense, as previously explained. The final item refers to incidents for which the *Shih-lu* mentioned no direct political involvement, such as the numerous small disturbances created by local robberies and gangsterism or by Christian missionary activities.

Table 14 presents the economic nature of these mass actions. The largest definitely identifiable category of incidents related to the economic factor were those motivated by dissatisfaction with economic conditions, consisting mainly of the numerous local actions of scattered robbery and piracy, as well as troop mutiny caused by shortage or default of pay. Such incidents totaled 1,181 or 17.8 percent of the total for the entire period. Incidents of serious economic deprivation were mass actions involving famine victims, and include riots and plundering by them. The number of such reported incidents was relatively small, 104 cases or 1.6 percent of the total. Incidents related to organization of economic and financial matters refer to such actions as corruption and extortion by officials and local leaders, smuggling (mainly salt), and resistance against taxation and rent. There were 693 such incidents, accounting for 10.4 percent of the total. The cases of campaigning for prosperous territories refer to rebel military actions. The largest item in the table is economically related but unspecified incidents, numbering 3,594 or 54.1 percent of all the cases. These were unit actions of large-scale rebellions (Taiping, Nien), and acts of banditry with varying degrees of political and economic motivations. The economic causes of such rebellions and banditries were generally assumed, but they were complex and only cryptically specified in the *Shih-lu* source. Nevertheless, proponents of the deprivation theory of revolutions may draw considerable support and comfort from this set of data.

COMPOSITION OF PARTICIPANTS IN MASS ACTIONS

The composition of the participants in the mass action incidents is an important subject, as it may suggest the social sources of the unrest. Although the very brief passages in the *Shih-lu* contain little detailed description of the participants in the incidents, they generally mention the type of groups involved in an action. In many cases, incident leaders were mentioned by name, which facilitates the use of supplementary sources to trace further information. Those incidents in which the participating group can be identified are tabulated in Table 15. The largest single item was incidents committed by armed bands composed largely of bandits and pirates. If we group this type of incidents with those involving gangs (urban) and militia, police and office runners (*ya-i*), we have a total of 1,962 incidents of armed groups (29.5 percent of all incidents) which often preyed at will upon the unarmed and unorganized civilians. These predatory forces operated beyond the influence of traditional informal agents of social control such as kinship and neighborhood groups, thus leaving matters to the formal legal control system which proved to be ineffective.

TYPES OF PARTICIPANT GROUPS IN MASS ACTION INCIDENTS

Type of group	1796–1805	1806–1815	1816–1825	1826–1835	1836–1845	1846–1855	1856–1865	1866–1875	1876–1885	1886–1895	1896–1911	TOTAL
Minority	18	15	16	40	38	76	386	402	55	39	55	1140
Secret societies	37	19	8	13	19	193	103	55	36	41	87	611
Religious	1	30	22	34	16	43	357	173	34	22	30	762
Kinship	2	1	2	5	2	6	2	1	0	4	4	29
Localistic associations	0	1	2	3	3	7	11	4	3	2	6	42
Community	0	1	5	1	4	16	143	54	11	7	13	255
Neighborhood	0	2	1	3	2	5	6	2	0	0	2	23
Peasant	2	6	9	10	31	86	412	38	6	9	19	628
Worker	0	2	3	3	7	6	3	2	6	2	6	34
Guilds	0	0	4	7	13	13	6	4	0	1	8	56
Educational and literary	0	1	1	2	2	5	5	0	0	0	8	24
Gentry	0	0	2	3	8	7	5	7	6	2	30	70
Civic	0	0	1	3	3	6	7	1	0	0	1	22
Charity	0	0	0	0	0	1	0	1	0	0	1	3
Militia and police	5	3	2	2	7	27	129	41	42	9	64	331
Gangs	2	8	10	13	32	16	19	11	35	17	12	175
Armed bands	40	38	24	61	58	236	294	158	142	151	254	1456
Unclassified	0	4	5	3	13	210	595	66	21	9	56	982
TOTAL	107	131	117	206	258	959	2483	1020	391	315	656	6643

The next largest item was minority ethnic groups, mainly Moslems and aboriginals, which accounts for 1,140 incidents (17.2 percent of all incidents) and clearly reflects the large number of mass actions occurring in the border provinces.

The traditionally anti-government and often interchangeable groups, secret societies, and religious organizations (Chinese as well as non-Chinese, like Moslem and Christian), perpetrated a total of 1,373 incidents or 20.7 percent of the total.

We may discern a communal category of groups consisting of localistic associations (*t'ung-hsiang hui*), community groups (famine refugees from the home community), and neighborhood organizations. Actions committed by these groups total 320 incidents or 4.8 percent of all the incidents. Peasant organizations (intervillage self-defense and crop-protection associations), worker organizations (such as the Grand Canal sailors), and guilds in towns constitute another configuration of groups based on economic interests, which were responsible for 718 incidents or 10.8 percent of the total. The last constellation of groups consists of educational and literary societies, gentry organizations (alumni groups of examination candidates), civic groups (such as self-strengthening societies) and charity organizations. Their numbers were small—only 119 incidents or 1.8 percent of all incidents—but the dominant role of the gentry in all of these groups lends an importance to such incidents beyond their numerical size.[4]

SOCIAL POSITION OF INCIDENTS' LEADERS

Tables 16 and 17 give some hints about the social position of the incidents' leaders, as established by concrete information or clear inference from the *Shih-lu*. The statistical unit is the individual leader, and there could be more than one leader per incident. The number of unknown cases is very large.

The implications of this data may be explored through some illustrations. One's attention is immediately drawn to the 1,096 wealthy leaders, the largest of the three groups, which account for 58.7 percent of the 1,868 known cases. Constituting a significant part of this category of wealthy leaders were organizers of collective donations to government military expenses (268 cases) and local self-defense (30 cases), as such actions were generally sponsored by well-to-do citizens motivated obviously by self-preservation.

But there were other types of actions led by the wealthy elements. For example, they played a prominent role in community actions against the government in taxation disputes and in certain types of political resistance, injustice, or misrule. Local military leaders often led mob attacks on the civilian officials in defiance of the superiority of civil authority. There were

---

4. This category, of course, is somewhat skewed, because mass action incidents also include measures taken in defense of the traditional order.

TABLE 16:

Class Status of Incident Leaders

Status	1796–1805	1806–1815	1816–1825	1826–1835	1836–1845	1846–1855	1856–1865	1866–1875	1876–1885	1886–1895	1896–1911	TOTAL
Unknown	120	119	103	182	148	885	2236	936	342	305	534	5910
Wealthy	6	11	17	26	28	54	531	264	51	18	90	1096
Middle	3	3	16	2	27	33	10	4	5	5	47	155
Poor	1	33	21	33	85	64	189	64	30	20	77	617
TOTAL	130	166	157	243	288	1036	2966	1268	428	348	748	7778

TABLE 17:

Social Positions and Occupations of Incident Leaders

Position and occupation	1796–1805	1806–1815	1816–1825	1826–1835	1836–1845	1846–1855	1856–1865	1866–1875	1876–1885	1886–1895	1896–1911	TOTAL
Gentry	2	1	5	4	12	47	380	215	22	6	35	729
Officials	19	3	8	17	13	12	137	43	21	12	66	351
Nobility	2	2	4	7	3	6	0	10	3	1	9	47
Officials' servants, government runners	0	2	3	15	7	21	136	44	27	13	65	333
Soldiers	0	1	1	0	7	20	55	37	16	6	40	183
Priests	0	5	9	1	4	15	5	6	4	5	6	60
Landlords	1	0	6	2	5	42	362	212	12	4	9	655
Peasants in general	3	23	27	16	39	50	99	139	3	12	29	440
Farm tenants	0	0	2	0	2	5	0	1	1	1	1	13
Merchants	0	2	1	2	18	10	1	0	1	2	15	52
Craftsmen, miners, sailors	0	1	3	3	19	7	2	1	1	4	5	46
Nomads	0	0	0	5	34	34	4	2	0	0	4	83
Unemployed	0	25	21	14	25	24	11	8	5	51	40	224
"Mean people"	0	0	0	0	1	1	1	2	1	0	0	6
Others	7	10	13	24	1	7	10	9	2	1	3	87
Total Known	34	75	103	110	190	301	1203	729	119	118	327	3309
Total Unknown	79	91	54	133	98	736	1761	539	309	230	439	4469
TOTAL	113	166	157	243	288	1037	2964	1268	428	348	766	7778

also cases of banner officers leading bannermen in riots for pay. The category of middle-class leaders (155 cases or 8.3 percent of the known total) includes those in such illegal activities as banditry, gambling, and opium traffic. They include many sectarian leaders spreading subversive rumors, or local figures who disrupted the government examinations in order to protest against injustices such as excessive taxation. Leaders from the poor class (617 cases or 30.0 percent of the known total) were gangsters in local robberies, prominent elements in wandering bands of paupers engaged in plundering or extortion, or government office runners involved in extortion and expropriation actions. We can conclude that the well-to-do had the resources and prestige to lead a large proportion of the collective actions, while the poverty-stricken led only such common local incidents as robberies. This is again instructive for those committed to the economic deprivation interpretation of revolutions. The general comment may be ventured here that upper-class elements were prominent in the century of social unrest which eroded the foundation of the traditional socio-political order.

Further information on the social composition of incident leaders is given in Table 17. It is notable that, by individual items, the gentry (729 cases or 22.0 percent) and landlords (655 cases or 19.8 percent) rank first and second respectively. But the significance of the data may become clearer if we reclassify the figures into political categories. Gentry, landlords, officials, and nobility are distinctly elements of the ruling class; these four items total 1,782 cases or 53.8 percent of the known total. If we add soldiers, officials' servants, and government runners, the two traditionally predatory groups against the common people, as supporting force to the block of ruling class, then the total comes up to 2,298 cases or 69.4 percent of all leaders whose social position can be identified. If we further add established merchants[5] to this block because of the political influence their wealth commanded, the total is increased to 2,350 cases or 70.9 percent of the total. These figures indicate that it was the ruling stratum and its supporting forces which led most of the incidents of social unrest during the nineteenth century.

Table 18 reveals further information on the types of mass action committed by different categories of leaders. The gentry, who were the governing elite, concentrated their activities on actions in support of the traditional political order: donation to government military expenses and involvement in battle between government forces and organized groups. But, to a much lesser proportion, they provided leadership as well for anti-government actions: secret and sectarian societies, anti-government conspiracy, resistance against taxation and agricultural rent, riots, mob demonstrations, agitation and propaganda. The gentry also engaged with appreciable frequency in the leading forms of lawless enterprise: smuggling, banditry and piracy, local gangsterism, and troop plundering. Landlords, in close alliance with the

5. When the *Shih-lu* mentioned merchant, it meant generally an established businessman: the term hawker or peddler would be used for those engaged in petty commercial activities.

TABLE 18:

LEADERS' POSITIONS AND OCCUPATIONS IN VARIOUS FORMS OF ACTION

Form of action	Leaders' positions and occupations															TOTAL
	Gentry	Officials	Nobility	Officials' servants, government runners	Soldiers	Priests	Landlords	Peasants in general	Farm tenants	Merchants	Craftsmen, miners, sailors	Nomads	Unemployed	"Mean people"	Others	
1. Battles between government forces and organized groups	131	64	10	59	7	4	122	217	0	0	9	15	2	2	17	659
2. Skirmishes between government forces and local groups	11	5	2	4	4	3	4	8	2	5	2	4	5	0	1	56
3. Activities of secret and sectarian societies	4	4	1	4	3	17	4	17	2	2	3	0	9	0	4	74
4. Anti-government conspiracy	13	38	1	36	11	2	1	3	0	3	3	0	1	0	4	116
5. Resistance against taxation and rent	5	2	0	2	0	0	3	25	6	0	0	0	3	0	0	46
6. Smuggling	1	0	0	1	0	0	0	0	0	8	0	0	4	0	1	16
7. Banditry and piracy	16	84	14	65	17	9	13	55	2	0	6	51	150	2	33	517
8. Local gangsterism	14	34	6	44	5	4	10	18	1	5	7	5	35	0	11	199
9. Riots	7	11	5	10	1	4	8	28	2	7	6	0	9	0	8	106
10. Strikes and boycotts	2	0	0	0	0	0	0	0	0	3	2	2	0	0	0	11
11. Demonstrations and noisy crowds	14	10	0	9	1	0	2	3	0	1	1	1	0	0	0	48
12. Agitation and propaganda	14	1	4	0	0	3	3	10	0	4	2	0	2	0	4	42
13. Panic and rumor	0	1	0	1	0	0	0	4	0	1	0	0	0	1	1	6
14. Mass flight from hunger, wars, and other miseries	0	0	1	0	0	0	0	2	0	0	0	4	0	0	0	31
15. Troop mutiny	0	30	0	30	63	0	0	24	0	0	0	0	0	1	1	124
16. Betrayal by troops and officials	0	0	0	2	2	0	0	0	0	0	0	0	0	0	0	5
17. Conflict between troops	0	11	0	10	10	0	0	0	0	0	0	0	0	0	0	31
18. Troop plundering	1	33	0	35	49	0	1	0	0	0	0	2	1	0	1	121
19. Feuds and property destruction	6	7	2	9	7	4	5	22	0	0	4	0	2	0	1	74
20. Christian proselytism	1	0	0	1	0	9	1	0	0	0	0	0	0	0	0	13
21. Anti-missionary actions	7	3	0	3	4	1	5	0	0	0	0	0	0	0	0	22
22. Resistance against foreign intruders	5	1	1	0	0	1	2	3	0	4	1	0	0	0	0	20
23. Collective donation to government military expenses	449	7	0	0	0	0	446	0	0	4	0	1	0	0	1	914
24. Local self-defense	28	0	0	7	0	0	25	1	0	2	0	0	0	0	0	58
TOTAL	729	351	47	333	183	60	655	440	13	52	46	83	224	6	87	3309

gentry, followed a parallel pattern: dominance of supportive actions for the traditional political order, a lighter role in anti-government struggles, and a small share in criminal activities.

Government officials were a close ally to the gentry and landlords, but their forms of mass action departed somewhat from the gentry-landlord pattern. While their pro-government actions show a high frequency, as expected, it is surprising to find the highest frequency of their leadership to be located in the criminal category: banditry and piracy, local gangsterism, smuggling, troop plundering. Also surprising is the high frequency of their actions in categories ostensibly subversive of the old socio-political order: anti-government conspiracy, resistance against taxation and rent, riots, demonstrations, troop mutiny.

Officials' servants and government runners patterned their mass actions closely on those of their bureaucratic masters: the leading items were criminal in nature—banditry and piracy, local gangsterism, smuggling, troop plundering. Next to these were anti-government conspiracy, troop mutiny, riots, demonstrations and noisy crowds, betrayal by troops and officials, all having the connotations of political disaffection characteristic of socio-political disorganization in a period of dynastic decline.

Soldiers as a group formed a close partner to the ruling establishment, and their mass actions were dominated by disaffecting activities: troop mutinies and resistance against taxation and rent. Like their masters, soldiers show a high frequency of criminal activities: troop plundering, banditry and piracy, and local gangsterism.

Nobility and merchants were two numerically lesser components among incident leaders in the ruling group. As in the case of officials, noblemen provided leadership in government battles against organized rebel forces, but their leading activities were organized crime: banditry and piracy, and local gangsterism, although they were also involved in such other seditious activities as secret and sectarian societies, conspiracy, riots, agitation and propaganda. The noblemen as a group were no longer in full support of the socio-political order which gave them their privileged position.

In the item of smuggling, merchants had the highest frequency, as expected, but they were also considerably involved in lawless enterprises (banditry and piracy, local gangsterism) and in actions such as resistance against taxation and rent, secret and sectarian societies, strikes, boycotts, riots, demonstrations and noisy crowds, agitation and propaganda, all of which also contributed to the erosion of the socio-political order.

The numerically significant groups of peasants and the unemployed also generated social unrest. The dominant form of peasant actions was organized battles with the government forces, and next in frequency were banditry and piracy and local gangsterism. Also prominent among their mass actions were riots, resistance against taxation and rent, secret and sectarian societies, demonstrations and noisy crowds, agitation and propaganda, and conspiracy.

TABLE 19:

ETHNIC COMPOSITION OF INCIDENT LEADERS

Ethnic composition	1796–1805	1806–1815	1816–1825	1826–1835	1836–1845	1846–1855	1856–1865	1866–1875	1876–1885	1886–1895	1896–1911	TOTAL
Chinese	104	149	132	181	232	933	2532	658	354	302	651	6228
Moslems	0	3	6	29	17	31	290	396	21	5	14	812
Miao and other aboriginals	10	0	3	3	6	17	77	105	6	6	9	242
Tibetans	0	0	1	1	14	32	10	6	9	1	21	95
Manchus	0	0	1	2	3	6	4	9	5	2	11	43
Mongols	0	0	3	0	3	0	7	7	1	3	10	34
Others	15	11	8	18	13	13	40	15	22	29	23	207
Unknown	1	3	3	9	0	4	7	70	11	0	9	117
TOTAL	130	166	157	243	288	1036	2967	1266	429	348	748	7778

Peasants were prominent members in both the refugee columns fleeing from famines and wars and in the destructive feuds between clans and villages. But even though the peasants fought the government in both organized combat and other forms of mass action and contributed their share of lawlessness in chaotic times, they were a much more law-abiding group than the officials and their servants and runners.

The forms of mass action engaged in by the jobless elements were rather simple: they robbed when they could not gainfully produce, and the overwhelming majority of the incidents caused by them fell in the categories of banditry and piracy and local gangsterism. The remainder of their activities was scattered in small numbers among categories of social and political dissent. The nomads also showed a heavy concentration of activity in banditry and piracy. Priests as a group were distinguished by their high frequency of participation in secret and sectarian societies, due apparently to their relation to sectarianism.

The large number of incidents involving ethnic groups is reflected in the ethnic origins of the incident leaders in Table 19. The data are self-explanatory as a source for interpreting the role of interethnic relations in mass action incidents. The large number of Moslems among non-Chinese leaders is related to the large number of incidents involving that ethnic group.

VALUE ORIENTATIONS OF MASS ACTIONS

If the ruling class and their supporting elements figured preponderantly in mass actions during the nineteenth century, they followed traditional patterns for the most part. It was traditional values which guided the majority of the forms of mass action, whether they were supportive actions for the government, suppression of banditry and piracy, secret and sectarian conspiracy, rebellions of armed organizations, or resistance against Christian prosyletism. Out of the total of 6,643 incidents for the entire period, only 1,328 or 20.0 percent were clearly anti-traditional in their acceptance of certain foreign values. These were actions constituting the Taiping Rebellion (1,328 incidents), the Republican Revolution of 1911 (90 incidents), and Christian missionary activities which became political issues (15 incidents, not including anti-Christian mob actions). A small number (27 incidents or 0.4 percent) took on an eclectic orientation, trying to harmonize traditional with Western values. They include six incidents of the Hundred Days Reform, eight incidents in the constitutional monarchy movement, and agitation by self-strengthening societies (associations of intellectuals for strengthening China by self-reliance). After the anti-traditional Taiping flare-up, the traditional orientation maintained its continuity among the mass action incidents until the last decade of the nineteenth century.

The maintenance of traditional values by the ruling class in the face of mounting socio-political tension is expressed in another form of action, namely the awarding of imperial honors for exemplary observance of critical traditional values. The *Shih-lu* contains a complete record of imperial honor awards for loyalty, filial piety, and chastity, traditional values undergirding the political and kinship structures so essential to the Chinese socio-political order. Table 20 traces the pattern of a social system's response to threats

TABLE 20:

SOCIAL DISTURBANCE IN RELATION TO GOVERNMENT HONORS

	1796–1849	1850–1876	1896–1911
Average (weighted) Social Disturbance Incidents per year	65.91 (100)	507.42 (866)	114.04 (173)
Average Frequency of Government Honors per year	5,960.31 (100)	56,764.17 (905)	14,076.57 (235)
Average Number of Honors per Incident of Disturbance	90.43	111.86	123.43

against it from unrest and rebellion through reinforcement of traditional values, which were conceived as useful for tension reduction and system stability.[6] In other words, when the system was threatened by crises, one of its responses was to reinforce the faith in fundamental values in order to restore the effectiveness of traditional guidelines of social action. In this table the period is divided into three subperiods: 1796–1849, initial unrest; 1850–1875, nationwide uprising; and 1876–1911, attempted restoration. Each figure in the upper line represents the average annual number of incidents weighted by the size of the population, and figures in the second line in parentheses are indices with the first subperiod as the base. The data show clearly that as the frequency of mass actions increased, the political system responded by frantically increasing the number of honor awards to reassure the population of the soundness of traditional values. It is notable that the number of honor awards per incident of social unrest steadily increased as tension mounted against the traditional political order, an indication of the reaffirmation of faith in tradition as a response to the growing crises.

GOVERNMENT MEASURES AND FORMS OF SETTLEMENT OF MASS ACTION
INCIDENTS

Table 21, on the measures taken by the government concerning mass action incidents, and Table 22, on the ways in which the incidents came to an end (forms of settlement), may be considered as concluding information for this paper.

6. Table 20 is taken from Chok-king Liang, "The Pattern of Value Maintenance in Social Disturbance," unpublished paper, University of Pittsburgh, 1971, p. 40.

TABLE 21:

GOVERNMENT MEASURES ON MASS ACTION INCIDENTS

Measures	1796–1805		1806–15		1816–25		1826–35		1836–45		1846–55	
	No.	%	No.	%	No.	%	No.	%	No.	%	No.	%
Troops sent, number unknown	45	42.1	13	9.9	16	13.7	40	19.4	41	15.9	570	59.4
Over 10,000 troops sent	4	3.7	2	1.5	1	.9	21	10.2	0	0	40	4.2
1,000 to 9,999 troops sent	14	13.1	15	11.5	6	5.1	3	1.5	11	4.3	23	2.4
Less than 999 troops sent	11	10.3	35	26.7	25	21.4	96	46.6	23	8.9	10	1.0
Corrective measures of administrative nature	20	18.7	41	31.3	51	43.6	37	17.9	151	58.5	237	24.7
Unknown	13	12.1	25	19.1	18	15.3	9	4.4	32	12.4	79	8.3
TOTAL	107	100.0	131	100.0	117	100.0	206	100.0	258	100.0	959	100.0

Measures	1856–65		1866–75		1876–85		1886–95		1896–1911		TOTAL	
	No.	%	No.	%	No.	%	No.	%	No.	%	No.	%
Troops sent, number unknown	1545	62.2	632	62.0	112	28.6	103	32.7	241	36.7	3358	50.6
Over 10,000 troops sent	81	3.3	64	6.3	5	1.3	1	.3	4	.6	223	3.4
1,000 to 9,999 troops sent	296	11.9	26	2.5	15	3.8	25	7.9	32	4.9	466	7.0
Less than 999 troops sent	68	2.7	10	1.0	70	17.9	42	13.3	50	7.6	440	6.6
Corrective measures of administrative nature	346	13.9	206	20.2	163	41.7	123	39.1	247	37.7	1622	24.4
Unknown	147	6.0	82	8.0	26	6.7	21	6.7	82	12.5	534	8.0
TOTAL	2483	100.0	1020	100.0	391	100.0	315	100.0	656	100.0	6643	100.0

The first four items in Table 21 may be taken together to represent forcible repression. They give a collective subtotal of 4,487 incidents or 67.5 percent of all cases for the entire period. Among those cases for which there are estimates of government forces employed, incidents engaging small and medium numbers of government troops dominated, reflecting the prominence of small-scale local actions. Corrective administrative measures consisted mainly of punishment and change of officials involved in the incidents, and of such actions as strengthening the security measures (increase of garrison troops, organizing militia). The 1,622 measures constitute 24.4 percent of the total for the whole period. The data indicate clearly the predominance of forcible suppression as a means of dealing with social unrest despite the variation in this pattern for some intervals.

The use of force won temporary success in nearly half of all cases. In Table 22 government military victory is by far the largest single item, accounting for 3,796 incidents or 44.8 percent of the period's total. If we add the items of capture of leaders and surrender by rebels to the item of government military

TABLE 22:

SETTLEMENT OF MASS ACTION INCIDENTS

Type of Settlement	1796–1805 No.	%	1806–15 No.	%	1816–25 No.	%	1826–35 No.	%	1836–45 No.	%	1846–55 No.	%
1. Government military victory	76	45.2	67	33.9	33	21.2	146	45.7	59	18.0	441	38.2
2. Capture of leader	60	35.7	54	27.3	58	37.2	97	30.4	127	38.7	208	18.0
3. Surrender by rebels	1	.6	14	7.1	8	5.1	4	1.3	1	.3	0	0
4. Punishment of officials	2	1.2	3	1.5	2	1.3	14	4.4	16	4.9	78	6.8
5. Punishment of both officials and persons involved	3	1.8	12	6.0	1	.6	5	1.6	12	3.7	3	.3
6. Absorption of rebels into government troops	7	4.2	2	1.0	1	.6	0	0	3	.9	7	.6
7. No administrative action	0	0	0	0	2	1.3	2	.6	1	.3	1	.1
8. Negotiated settlement	0	0	0	0	1	.6	0	0	1	.3	0	0
9. Acceptance of rebels' demands	0	0	0	0	0	0	0	0	0	0	0	0
10. Government military defeat	0	0	1	.5	4	2.6	4	1.3	3	.9	166	14.4
11. Reward and others	4	2.4	2	1.0	0	0	3	.9	15	4.6	37	3.2
12. Consequences unknown	15	8.9	43	21.7	46	29.5	44	13.8	90	27.4	212	18.4
TOTAL	168	100.0	198	100.0	156	100.0	319	100.0	328	100.0	1153	100.0

Type of Settlement	1856–65 No.	%	1866–75 No.	%	1876–85 No.	%	1886–95 No.	%	1896–1911 No.	%	TOTAL No.	%
1. Government military victory	1647	55.0	674	47.1	190	37.3	179	46.0	284	34.6	3796	44.8
2. Capture of leader	398	13.3	357	25.0	130	25.5	70	18.0	182	22.2	1741	20.6
3. Surrender by rebels	58	2.0	51	3.6	5	1.0	6	1.5	4	.5	152	1.8
4. Punishment of officials	95	3.2	7	.5	17	3.3	14	3.6	56	6.8	304	3.6
5. Punishment of both officials and persons involved	23	.8	14	1.0	8	1.6	1	.3	9	1.1	91	1.1
6. Absorption of rebels into government troops	10	.3	2	.1	0	0	0	0	5	.6	37	.4
7. No administrative action	1	0	3	.2	0	0	3	.8	10	1.2	23	.3
8. Negotiated settlement	3	.1	3	.2	0	0	0	0	2	.2	10	.1
9. Acceptance of rebels' demands	1	0	1	0	0	0	0	0	1	.1	3	0
10. Government military defeat	225	7.5	49	3.4	5	1.0	4	1.0	16	2.0	477	5.7
11. Reward and others	161	5.4	119	8.3	15	3.0	16	4.1	45	5.5	417	4.9
12. Consequences unknown	370	12.4	152	10.6	139	27.3	96	24.7	207	25.2	1414	16.7
TOTAL	2992	100.0	1432	100.0	509	100.0	389	100.0	821	100.0	8465	100.0

victory, at the risk of duplication due to technical multiple-entry difficulties, we have an impressive figure of 5,689 incidents, or 67.2 percent of the period's total, representing government successes in suppressing unrests. Items 4 to 9 in Table 22 may be grouped together to represent the government's compromise with the situation, with a subtotal of 468 incidents or 5.5 percent of all the cases. Here the government yielded partly to the pressure of the situation, and the majority of the compromise measures took the form of punishment of officials (often just to ease popular resentment). Rebels' victories amounted to 477 or only 5.7 percent of all cases. The category of reward and others includes mostly cases of collective donation to government military expense and local self-defense (militia).

The above data certainly raise many important questions for the study of social unrest as a process of social change. In all major phases of analysis the data clearly converge on the political institution as the primary sector which failed to maintain the traditional social order and thus bred social unrest. The predominance of suppressive measures and the prominence of government military success had only questionable effectiveness in restabilizing the traditional socio-political order. Suppression and victories in one decade did not forestall the further rise of mass action incidents in the next decade, nor did they save the imperial power structure from its eventual downfall in 1911. Although this recalls the cliché that suppression may remove the symptom but not the cause of social tension, we must also point out that the statistical data in this paper have not been analyzed systematically in terms of the causes of social unrest. Hidden from view are many disruptive forces, such as secret and sectarian societies, which would rekindle social disturbances soon after their overt suppression. Some attention has been drawn to these underground organizations, but not much specific information is available regarding the number of such groups and their membership size in different periods. However, the above data on the relative frequency of incidents related to the secret and sectarian societies at least provide information on the role of such groups in proportion to other social and political groups.

The ineffectiveness of suppression as a means to quell unrest is also emphasized by the internal deterioration of the ruling class of late Ch'ing China. It is important to note from the previous statistical information that the ruling class and its supporting elements supplied the bulk of leadership for incidents of social unrest. In this sense, government suppressive actions may well be viewed as an internal strife or civil war among the rulers and their henchmen. The declarations of autonomy by the provinces, for example, may be viewed as a major final act in bringing down the curtain on the Ch'ing rule. The betrayals, mutinies, and power struggles, the countless mass actions led by local strongmen, wealthy landlords and corrupt gentry, who all aspired to prominence in the traditional socio-political order, fill a large portion of our data cards. The deterioration of the ruling elements often reached a point where the distinction seemed to vanish between bandits and predatory officials or their marauding soldiers. Nevertheless, great scholars arose to defend the traditional order in lengthy polemics, and the public did not foresake its traditional values, as shown in the above data. One can only wonder why the imperial order did not fall sooner than 1911. A century of internal chaos in the ruling stratum failed to resolve problems underlying social unrest, thus giving rise to systematically organized popular uprisings—the Republican Revolution and the Communist movement.

APPENDIX TABLE:

DURATIONS AND AFFECTED AREAS OF 45 MAJOR SAMPLE CASES OF SOCIAL SIGNIFICANCE*

Case	Period	Affected Provinces
1. White Lotus Sect uprising	Chia-ch'ing 1–8 (1796–1803)	Szechwan, Hupeh, Shensi
2. The rampage of Pirate Tsai Chien	Chia-ch'ing 5–9 (1800–1809)	Fukien, Chekiang, Kwangtung, Taiwan
3. Celestial Principles Sect uprising	Chia-ch'ing 18–19 (1813–1814)	Chihli, Honan, Shangtung
4. San-tsai lumber workers' uprising	Chia-ch'ing 18–20 (1813–1815)	Shensi
5. Yi aboriginal uprising	Chia-ch'ing 22—Tao-kuang 1 (1817–1821)	Yunnan
6. Moslem uprising	Chia-ch'ing 25—Tao-kuang 8 (1820–1828)	Sinkiang
7. Ethnic uprising	Tao-kuang 2 (1822)	Tsinghai
8. Aboriginal uprising	Tao-kuang 2 (1822)	Szechwan
9. Peasant uprising (Blue Lotus Sect)	Tao-kuang 6 (1826)	Taiwan
10. Li aboriginal uprising	Tao-kuang 11 (1831)	Kwangtung
11. Yao aboriginal uprising	Tao-kuang 12 (1832)	Hunan, Kwangtung, Kwangsi
12. Heaven-Earth Society uprising	Tao-kuang 12–13 (1832–1833)	Taiwan
13. Prebirth Sect uprising	Tao-kuang 15 (1835)	Shansi
14. Yao aboriginal uprising	Tao-kuang 16 (1836)	Hunan
15. Yi aboriginal uprising	Tao-kuang 17 (1837)	Szechwan
16. Opium War	Tao-kuang 19–22 (1839–1842)	Area of popular resistance undetermined
17. The peasant uprising of Chung Jen-Chieh	Tao-kuang 21–22 (1841-1842)	Hupeh
18. Moslem uprising	Tao-kuang 25 (1845)	Kansu
19. Moslem uprising	Tao-kuang 26 (1846)	Yunnan
20. Moslem uprising	Tao-kuang 27 (1847)	Sinkiang
21. Yao uprising	Tao-kuang 27 (1847)	Hunan
22. Taiping Rebellion	Hsien-feng 1—T'ung-chih 2 (1851–1863)	Kwangsi, Hunan, Hupeh, Kiangsi, Anhwei, Kiangsu, Chekiang, Honan, Shantung, Chihli, Shansi, Shensi, Kansu, Fukien, Kwangtung, Kweichow, Yunnan, Szechwan
23. Nien Rebellion	Hsien-feng 1—T'ung-chih 7 (1851–1868)	Anhwei, Honan, Shantung, Chihli, Kiangsu, Hupeh, Shansi, Shensi, Kansu
24. Heaven-Earth Society uprising	Hsien-feng 3—T'ung-chih 4 (1853–1865)	Kwangtung, Hunan, Kiangsi, Fukien

Case	Period	Affected Provinces
25. Small-Knife Society uprising	Hsien-feng 3–5 (1853–1855)	Shanghai (Kiangsu)
26. British-French Alliance invasion	Hsien-feng 6–10 (1856–1860)	Area of popular resistance undetermined
27. Miao uprising	Hsien-feng 5—T'ung-chih 11 (1855–1872)	Kweichow
28. Moslem uprising	Hsien-feng 6—T'ung-chih 11 (1856–1872)	Yunnan
29. Rampaging banditry	Hsien-feng 9—T'ung-chih 3 (1859–1864)	Yunnan, Szechwan, Shensi
30. Heaven-Earth Society uprising	T'ung-chih 1—3 (1862–1864)	Taiwan
31. Moslem uprising	T'ung-chih 2—12 (1863–1873)	Kansu, Shensi
32. Moslem uprising	T'ung-chih 3—Kuang-hsu 4 (1864–1878)	Sinkiang
33. Troop mutiny	T'ung-chih 4 (1865)	Kiangsi, Kwangtung, Hupeh
34. Troop mutiny	T'ung-chih 5 (1866)	Kansu
35. Li aboriginal uprising	Kuang-hsu 13 (1887)	Kwangsi
36. Aboriginal uprising	Kuang-hsu 14 (1888)	Taiwan
37. Aboriginal uprising	Kuang-hsu 14–15 (1888–1889)	Taiwan
38. Chin-tan (golden pill) Sect uprising	Kuang-hsu 17 (1891)	Chihli, Inner Mongolia
39. Moslem uprising	Kuang-hsu 21 (1895)	Kansu
40. Hundred-Days Reform	Kuang-hsu 24 (1898)	Area to be determined
41. Boxer uprising	Kuang-hsu 25–26 (1899–1900)	Chihli, Shansi
42. Constitutional Monarchy movement	Kuang-hsu 26—Hsuan-t'ung 3 (1900–1911)	Area to be determined
43. Republican Revolution movement	Kuang-hsu 21—Hsuan-t'ung 3 (1895–1911)	Nationwide
44. Troop mutiny	Kuang-hsu 30 (1904)	Kwangsi
45. Ethnic uprising	Kuang-hsu 34 (1908)	Tibet

*Sources:

1. Kuo T'ing-i. *A Day-by-Day Record of the History of Modern China*. Taiwan: The Commercial Press, 1963.

2. Hsiao I-shan. *The General History of the Ch'ing Dynasty*. Taiwan: The Commercial Press, 1963.

Gentry Hegemony:

SOOCHOW IN THE
T'UNG-CHIH RESTORATION

James Polachek

> Feng Kuei-fen was on intimate terms with the great houses of
> Soochow. With some, he was even related by marriage. But the
> agonized cries of the toiling masses never reached his ears. . . .
> For his troubles on their behalf, Feng was rewarded by the worthies
> of Soochow with a personal shrine, in tribute to his reputation as
> a scholar. Would it not have been more just if, in his stead, they
> had deified an ordinary farmer from the fields?
>
> Chang Ping-lin, *Chien-lun*

I would like to begin with an anecdote. The tale concerns Feng Kuei-fen
(1809–1874), a Confucian theoretician from Kiangsu whose views on statecraft (*ching-shih*) exercised enormous influence upon late Ch'ing social
thought. The story begins in 1854. In that year a clerk at the Soochow mint
was arrested for having pawned a stamp belonging to his office as a security
on a loan. The investigating magistrate, hearing that the author of the loan
(a Mr. Hsu) was very wealthy, decided to impose a ten thousand tael fine,
intending to use the funds to help defray the cost of a security force that had
recently been created to defend Soochow against a possible Taiping attack.
Outraged, the penalized financier took his case to the Militia Supply Bureau,
offering to make a large contribution to the defense effort if the fine were
annulled. But the chief of the bureau, Feng Kuei-fen, had a better idea. If
Hsu would transfer a fourth part of the proposed penalty to some of his
relatives who lived in the suburban market town of Kuang-fu *chen*, agreeing to
allow the money to be donated as the endowment for a badly needed public
mortuary, Feng would be pleased to intercede with the magistrate.[1]

The details took time to arrange, but early the next year Feng himself
moved out to Kuang-fu to supervise work upon the new mortuary and an

1. *WHC*, 30:11; *HCTC*, 3:32a-b.

attached "arboricultural foundation" in the hills overlooking Lake T'ai. On
the advice of the mortuary's manager, a young man named Hsu Tun-jen,
Feng invested in a small piece of adjacent land that had formerly belonged to
the Hsu family. While clearing the trees which obstructed the view from his
new ten-rafter dwelling, Feng discovered traces indicating that the site had
once belonged to the famed late-Yuan poet Hsu Ta-tso (1336–1374).[2] Upon
the very plot where his dwelling now stood, the great Kao Ch'i (1333–1395)
had once gazed across the lake below, wondering what fate lay in store for
his native Soochow should the Ming rebels succeed in fighting their way
down the Yangtze.

In the autumn of 1866, a cousin of Hsu Tun-jen asked Feng to handle the
remittance of taxes and collection of rents owed upon five *mou* of Hsu's rice
fields in the vicinity of Kuang-fu *chen*. Though Feng had been known in
earlier years to be opposed to this kind of arrangement, he did not hesitate to
comply. Gratitude to the Hsu's as well as sympathy for the difficulties faced
by a fellow landlord stood behind his willingness to help. Because the moun-
tainous western flank of Soochow prefecture bordering Lake T'ai had fared
much worse during the war against the Taipings than the flatlands to the
south and east of the prefectural seat,[3] many tenants had fled from the area.
The ones who now worked the land in their stead were a restless lot, willing
to wield a plow only so long as rents were minimal.[4] Taxes, though much
lower than before the war, were also much harder to evade, particularly
during 1865 when they were needed to pay for Li Hung-chang's campaigns
against the Nien rebels.

The two men soon reached a mutually beneficial agreement. Since his
return to Soochow after its recapture from the Taipings in 1853, Feng had
been living in Mu-tu *chen*, closer than Kuang-fu to the prefectural city, and
the rents on his Kuang-fu holdings, as well as the taxes charged upon them,
had been handled through a rent agency (*tsu-chan*) administered by his son,
Fang-chih.[5] If Mr. Hsu would agree to cover the cost of paying off the

2. *Ch'ing-shih lieh-chuan* [Biographical series of the dynastic history of the Ch'ing] (Shanghai, 1928), 73:44; Feng Kuei-fen et al., comp., *Su-chou fu-chih* [Gazetteer of Soochow] (Soochow, 1885), 45:23a-b, 51–52b; Chang Yu-yü, *Mu-tu hsiao-chih* [A modest gazetteer of Mu-tu]
(Soochow, 1921), 6:11; *HCTC*, 3:34a-b, 6:37b.

3. For Hsu Tun-jen's appearance in the Feng *tsu-chan* records, see Muramatsu Yūji, *Kindai
Kōnan no sosan: Chūgoku jinushi seido no kenkyū* [Landlord bursaries of the lower Yangtze delta
region in recent times: studies of the Chinese landlord system] (Tokyo: Kindai Chūgoku
kenkyū iinkai, 1970), pp. 580, 584. For the devastation of the western portion of Soochow
prefecture, see Wang Ping-hsieh, *Wu-tzu-ch'i shih wen-chi* [Collected prose from Wu-tzu-ch'i
hall] (Soochow, 1885), 6:4.

4. Li Wen-chih and Chang Yu-yi, comp., *Chung-kuo chin-tai nung-yeh shih tzu-liao* [Modern
Chinese agrarian history materials] (Peking, 1957), I, 289, cited from *I-wen-lu* [Record of
profitable hearsay], no. 101 (May 11, 1881).

5. For Feng Fang-chih's role as manager of the family estate, see Muramatsu Yūji, "Shinmatsu Shoshū fukin ichi-sosan ni okeru jinushi shoyūchi no chōzei kosaku kankei" [On the
relationship between tax collection and tenancy in a rent bursary in the vicinity of late-Ch'ing
Soochow], *Keizaigaku kenkyū* [Research in economic studies] 6:279. For Feng Kuei-fen's res-

Kuang-fu submagistrate (a friend of Feng's) and other incidental expenses that might arise should the tenants make difficulties, Feng would be happy to recommend the problem of collecting Hsu's rents to Fang-chih.[6]

And so the arrangement was made. Apparently it proved satisfactory to all parties concerned, for in 1869 Feng became the trustee of over one hundred additional *mou* of Hsu family property, likewise situated in the depressed western reaches of Soochow prefecture.[7] And later, when Feng's new residence at Mu-tu *chen* became the scene of feverish activity as work got under way on the compilation of a new prefectural gazetteer, Feng awarded the responsibility for the section on parks and mansions with characteristic aplomb to his devoted pupil, the senior licentiate Hsu Tun-jen.[8]

THE RIDDLE OF THE SOOCHOW RESTORATION

What justifies resurrecting this mini-scandal from its well-earned obscurity is the suggestion it contains for a re-evaluation of the character of the T'ung-chih Restoration. The presence of questionable motivations on the dynastic side of the struggle against the Taipings has not, of course, gone unremarked. The gaping sores revealed in the Chinese body politic during the conflict with France in 1884–1885, and with Japan a decade later, are rarely seen suddenly accompanying the accession of the Kuang-hsu emperor. Yet somehow the conceit adopted for purposes of self-vindication by the activists of the restoration era continues even now to influence the historiography of that period.

Our image of the restoration is, in short, still very much more colored by the paternal presence of Hu Lin-i (1812–1861) and Tseng Kuo-fan (1811–1872) than by the Machiavellian maneuvering of Li Hung-chang (1823–1901) and Feng Kuei-fen.[9] Even in the portrait of the age bequeathed to us by Professor Mary C. Wright, the Hunanese motif overshadows all else, by

---

idence in Mu-tu *chen*, see Ts'ao Yun-yuan, *Fu-an lei-kao* [Classified drafts of Fu-an] (Ch'ing-chou, Shantung, 1904), 3:7; and Chang Yu-yü's appendix to *Mu-tu hsiao-chih*, 1:37b.

6. For Feng's contact with the subdistrict magistrate at Kuang-fu, see *HCTC*, 5:62b. For the operation of the Feng bursary, see Muramatsu, "Shinmatsu shoshū," pp. 133–383 passim.

7. Muramatsu, *Kindai Kōnan*, pp. 580, 584.

8. *Su-chou fu-chih, tsung-mu*, p. 16b.

9. The dissimilarity of Tseng and Li, both as thinkers and doers, has been noted by Professor Spector in his monograph on Li's career as a military reformer. See Stanley Spector, *Li Hung-chang and the Huai Army* (Seattle: University of Washington Press, 1964), p. 153. K. C. Liu has likewise observed that "certain concrete situations which Li faced . . . —concerning armies and concerning the tax-collecting machinery—compelled him to accept administrative methods that were at variance with those employed by Tseng." See Kwang-Ching Liu, "The Confucian as Patriot and Pragmatist," *Harvard Journal of Asiatic Studies* 30:19. Liu further concedes that "the expedients to which Li resorted, not always consistent with Confucian principles, were, as we shall see, to condition his proposals for innovation and reform." Ibid. Strangely, neither commentator has chosen to make much of this dissimilarity. However, this may be because a precise definition of Li's heterodoxy hinges upon the definition of his counterpart's orthodoxy—in itself a formidable problem, once the simplistic equation of Confucianism with the cult of grand character is left behind.

implication if not by design. Healthy peasant troopers, fresh from the hills of the inner Yangtze provinces and bound by classically particularistic loyalties to their impeccably Confucian commanders, are still thought to comprise the core of the restoration armies. Hardy backwoods gentrymen, charged with concern for their imperiled native communities and untainted by the petty careerism common to the normal run of bureaucrat, still are envisioned as everywhere taking command of the struggle to put new life into the corruption-wracked state. The unwieldy civil service hierarchy, realizing its own limitations, is seen as yielding gracefully, allowing itself after only a few shudders of apprehension to be converted overnight from an instrument of repression and control into a pliant tool in the hands of the eager Yangtze gentry. For a brief moment China is surprised to find herself on the verge of realizing the old statecraft dream of literati self-rule. After years of subjugation under an alien dynasty, China's long-frustrated indigenous ruling elite is at last granted the powers necessary to serve the throne as it should be served, and the voluntarist paradise promised for centuries by Neo-Confucian seers seems not far distant. Unfortunately the miracle did not outlast the men who had brought it into existence. Consistent with the Chinese notion of restoration, the revival of dynastic fortunes achieved in the 1860s was gained "with excessive dependence on the particular qualities of particular officials."[10] As Tseng Kuo-fan himself commented on the reforms he had implemented, there was no expectation of good government outlasting good governors.[11] And so the triumphs of the restoration ebbed swiftly into the despair of the 1870s.

It is a difficult vision to challenge. As the depressing succession of blunders produced during the decade preceding 1860 show so well, the Manchu dynasty could not have been rescued from its mid-century peril by even the most adroit application of normal bureaucratic administrative techniques. Chinese bureaucracy in its normal condition was too much preoccupied with the division and balance of power, and too little concerned with the morale of the men who served it, to function as an effective ordering device once things got very far out of hand. Salvation for a regime simultaneously threatened by internal disorders and foreign incursions was unfeasible without new, decentralized methods of civil and military government. Insofar as Hu Lin-i and Tseng Kuo-fan pioneered the development of these methods in Hupei and Hunan and eventually won Peking's acceptance of them, these two men do indeed deserve the prominence that Professor Wright and others have afforded them in the history of the T'ung-chih Restoration.

But it was neither Hu nor Tseng who applied the new model of government

10. Mary C. Wright, *The Last Stand of Chinese Conservatism: The T'ung-Chih Restoration, 1862–1874* (New York: Atheneum, 1966), p. 94.

11. Tseng Kuo-fan, *Tseng Wen-cheng kung shu-cha* [The complete works of Tseng Kuo-fan], 28:46, as cited in Hsia Nai, "T'ai-p'ing t'ien-kuo ch'ien-hou Ch'ang-chiang ko-sheng chih t'ien-fu wen-t'i" [The land-tax problem in the Yangtze provinces before and after the Heavenly Kingdom], *Ch'ing-hua hsueh-pao* [Tsinghua University journal] 10.2:470.

to the task of restoring order in the key provinces of Kiangsu, Honan, and
Shantung. That vital assignment was performed by Tseng's student, Li
Hung-chang—a man whose political style and sense of priorities separated
him from his Hunanese mentors by as comparable a distance as the 2500 *li*
that intervened between Changsha and Shanghai. To the common folk of
Kiangsu, the disparity between the master and the pupil was striking.
Tseng's habit of making pilgrimages by night, in ordinary dress, to out-of-
the-way places of local interest soon won him the approving nickname
"Tseng-the-sober-robed," as well as complimentary comparison with the
great T'ang Pin (1627–1687). No such appreciation, however, was expressed
in the clumsily punning limerick by which Li Hung-chang (from Ho-fei,
Anhwei) and another key figure in the Kiangsu restoration, Weng T'ung-ho
(1830–1904; from Ch'ang-shou, Kiangsu), were enshrined in popular
memory.

> Though the Prime Minister is from Ho-fei[12]
> The empire starves.
> Though the Minister of Finance is from Ch'ang-shou[13]
> All under heaven go hungry.[14]

Obviously marketplace humor is no sure evidence of Li's insincerity nor of
the corruption of the political apparatus upon which his power was built.
Yet the disaffection reflected in that popular limerick is perceptible even
within the ranks of the literati of the Shanghai hinterland. Chang Ping-lin's
caustic indictment of Li's trusted advisor, Feng Kuei-fen, which introduces
this article, was not the first of its kind. Substantially identical charges against
Feng, and by implication his patron, Li Hung-chang, made their first appearance quite early in the Kuang-hsu period. In a widely-read jeremiad, "An
Inquiry into Rents," penned around 1876 by a neighbor of Feng's named
T'ao Hsu (1821–1891), Li Hung-chang's recently departed ally is excoriated
for a host of crimes, only the least of which is breach of confidence.[15]

This essay was prompted by the publication in 1876 of a posthumous
anthology of Feng Kuei-fen's extant writings, which included a lengthy piece
detailing, in rather self-congratulatory terms, Feng's recollections of his role
in the great tax reform of 1863, as well as several earlier tracts on fiscal reform
dating from the 1850s. T'ao Hsu's reaction was sarcastic:

> Reading over the essays on tax equalization (*chün-fu*) . . . I could not
> but be moved. How truly glorious is the philanthropic spirit which seeks
> to abolish the system of privilege enjoyed by the grandee households (*ta-*

12. Literally, "combined fertility."
13. Literally, "constant ripeness."
14. Chang Yu-yü, *Mu-tu hsiao-chih*, 6:21.
15. See T'ao Hsu, *Tsu-ho* [Inquiry into rents] (Soochow, 1884). This interesting text was
first discovered by Suzuki Tomō in 1959, and appears as an appendix to Suzuki Tomō et al.,
Kindai Chūgoku nōson shakai shi kenkyū [Studies in the history of pre-Communist Chinese rural
society] (Tokyo, 1967).

hu) and to render the assessment rates equal for all. Why is it, then, that
the age speaks not at all of the benefits of equalization, but murmurs
instead only of Master [Feng Kuei-fen's] accomplishments in negotiat-
ing the reduction of our taxes?

There can be no disputing the credit earned by Mr. Feng in drafting
[for Li Hung-chang] the memorial which moved the court to lessen our
taxes by one-third. . . . But in this very same memorial, Mr. Feng speaks
incessantly of the plight of the tenant farmers who comprise 90 percent of
the local population. Why is it, then, that the benefits of this one-third
discount have not been conveyed to the tenant farmer? . . .

In the "Memoirs on Tax Reduction," Mr. Feng . . . speaks of rent
reduction in tandem with tax reform. Is it permissible to speak of both
projects together, yet not implement them simultaneously?

In the same piece, Mr. Feng rebukes a certain official for his ignorance
of Ku Yen-wu's discussion, in the *Jih-chih lu* (Diary of daily learning), of
the procedure for "apportioning [deficits produced by resurveying]
among the [rate payers] of the entire county in question." Yet in this very
work, Mr. Feng speaks cheerfully of rents as high as twelve bushels of rice
per *mou*. It does not seem, to judge from this, that Mr. Feng himself ad-
hered to the prescriptions of Mr. Ku, who proposed a rent ceiling of eight
bushels.

I raise these points for the consideration of those who peruse Mr. Feng's
anthology believing its author worthy only of praise, and innocent of
misdeed, or who seek to excuse Mr. Feng on the grounds that he had at
least intended that rents too should be trimmed.[16]

But a divergence between theory and practice was only one of the faults
of the restoration leadership. In the sections of the "Inquiry" that follow, T'ao
Hsu pictures the Soochow gentry resorting to methods which are so draconian
as to call into question the very integrity of the restoration's champions in
that part of China. Since the reestablishment of loyalist hegemony in the
Shanghai hinterland in 1863, T'ao informs us, the gentry of Soochow have
shown themselves to be obsessively concerned with imposing their will upon
the local rural population. In former times it was often the pleasure of landlords to make special concessions to indigent sharecroppers who were stricken
by sickness, death in the family, or natural calamity. But the landed pro-
prietors of post-bellum Soochow were of a new and remorselessly tight-fisted
variety. The unfortunate lessee who could not meet his rent obligations in
full, or whose holdings failed to produce the required 10 percent profit for
their owner, would be shunted off to the yamen to be caged like an animal
until a more fortunate kinsman might pay his fine, or until his desperate
wife could auction her children to raise the requisite sum. Blame for this
harsh treatment did not, of course, rest entirely with Mr. Li and Mr. Feng.

16. T'ao Hsu, *Tsu-ho*, pp. 5a-b.

In 1876 (as opposed to 1911), the sins of these worthy gentlemen were still mainly those of omission, not of commission. But the implication is clear. By abdicating responsibility to see the reforms he initiated carried to their end, by loaning a philanthropic facade to the abortive fiscal reorganization of 1863, Feng and his fellow gentrymen had, in effect, applied their seal of approval to the brutal new order in southern Kiangsu.[17]

But T'ao had still another bone to pick with Li and Feng. Perhaps aware that the landlords' tendency to lapse from the ways of charity long antedated restoration, the irate inquirer into rents added to his accusation of hypocritical greed that of deliberate apathy with respect to the welfare of the rural economy. Worried only about making the countryside safe for *rentier* interests, the leaders of the restoration robbed the patient farmer both of the means and the will to maintain his industry. With production slipping, shopkeepers and workmen in the market towns felt the pinch of worsening recession. Yet the influential talked only of minting more coin, raising the opium tariff, and finding funds to build railways and steamships.[18] By directing the attention of China's rulers to the treaty ports, Feng Kuei-fen had been responsible for much of the topsy-turvy economic thinking of the age, consigning the agrarian sector to decay while the government dreamed of mines and railways.

A surfeit of passion and a dearth of convincing data may make T'ao's argument a bit incoherent. Yet from what we know of the behavior of Soochow's landlord class during the late Ch'ing, and from what glimpses contemporary Chinese and foreign sources afford into the economic condition of the Shanghai hinterland during the same period, it seems likely that at least his final two indictments, greed and apathy, are justified.[19] But what of the charge of hypocrisy? At what point, and in regard to what problems, will we find Feng Kuei-fen representing himself in a fashion specifically contradicted by his behavior in the restoration period? Tao's critique is unhesitating in singling out the issue of Mr. Feng's fiscal reform thinking in the prewar years. It is to this that our attention must accordingly turn.

MUDDLING THROUGH: 1825—1841

Feng Kuei-fen drew upon a tradition of fiscal reform which had its origins in the early Ming. In what was ultimately to prove a vain attempt to de-urbanize the ownership of landed property in the lower Yangtze region, the first of the Ming monarchs decided to impose an extravagantly high complex of corvee and tax obligations on the estates confiscated in 1368, which

17. Ibid., pp. 12–13.
18. Ibid., pp. 14–15.
19. For a summary of the most recently unearthed evidence concerning Kiangsu's economic decline during the latter part of the nineteenth century, see Wang Yeh-chien, "The Impact of the Taiping Rebellion on Population in Southern Kiangsu," *Harvard University Papers on China* 19 (1964):120–158.

would allow the lands to be profitable in the future only to a resident land-lord or farmer.[20]

Whether the scheme ever worked as desired is hard to say, but it rapidly became an anachronism with the removal of the capital from Nanking to Peking in 1403. Thanks to this relocation, much of the raw labor power made available to the state under the original corvee system became useless, and the schedule of obligations pointlessly oppressive. In 1430 an official named K'uang Chung began the arduous task of reforming the Ming founder's system to make it more consistent with the real needs of government and the actual capabilities of the social order. Between that year and 1442, K'uang and another official named Chou Ch'en (1381–1453) managed to curtail many of the more flagrant abuses created by the legacy of 1368. The corvee was simplified and partially commuted, and tax quotas were adjusted.[21] But though this sort of remedial tampering was repeated many times during the centuries which followed, the root cause of the disruptiveness of the sys-tem, an extremely high level of fiscal pressure unique to the lower Yangtze area, was never removed. By Ch'ing times Board of Revenue inertia on the matter of reducing the Su-Sung-T'ai quotas was very nearly an unquestioned assumption in reformist circles.[22] Though concerned officials continued as late as the nineteenth century to speak of tax reduction (*chien-fu*) as a major long-term priority, their concrete plans for institutional change came gradual-ly to deal almost exclusively with techniques for redistributing the assigned level of obligations (*chün-fu*) and reducing the corruption that made the existing burden more socially disruptive than was necessary.

The last flurry of such patching and mending in the Su-Sung-T'ai environs during the Ch'ing occurred in the period 1825–1841. As was normally the case in such matters, the immediate incentive for reform was the depletion of government treasuries (largely the result of the White Lotus disturbances) and widening deficits in the collection of public moneys.[23] But the Tao-kuang reforms were at the same time rather special in the extent to which they reflected concern from private and not merely bureaucratic quarters. The changes attempted in the 1820s and 1830s were designed not simply to restore the solvency of the state (*kuo-chi*), but to achieve this restoration in a way

20. Mori Masao, "Minsho kōnan no kanden ni tsuite" [On the *kuan-t'ien* system of the early Ming], *Tōyōshi kenkyū* [Research in oriental history] 19.3:1–22; and his "14-seiki kōhan Sesshi chihō no jinushisei ni kansuru oboegaki" [A note on the landlord system in the Che-hsi vicinity during the latter half of the 14th century], *Nagoya Daigaku Bungakubu kenkyū ronshū* [Research essays from the literature department of Nagoya University] 44:67–88.

21. Mori Masao, "15-seiki zenpan Soshū-fu ni okeru yōeki rōdōsei no kaikaku" [Corvee reforms in early fifteenth-century Soochow prefecture], *Nagoya Daigaku Bungakubu kenkyū ronshū* 41:105–124.

22. Ku Yen-wu, *Jih-chih lu* [Record of daily knowledge], *SPPY* ed., 10:7–17b; Lu Shih-i, "Su-Sung fu-liang k'ao" [On the excessive grain tax of Soochow and Sung-chiang], in *Fu-t'ing hsien-sheng i-shu* [The posthumous papers of Mr. Fu-t'ing] (Sung-chiang).

23. For an excellent study of the fiscal crisis of the early nineteenth century, see Suzuki Chūsei, "Shinmatsu no zaisei to kanryō no seikaku" [Late Ch'ing finance and bureaucracy], *Kindai Chūgoku kenkyū* [Research on modern China] 2:189–282.

that would buttress the economy (*min-sheng*) and help mend the badly tattered fabric of local society. Especially demanding of attention in this respect was the particular portion of the land tax known as tribute rice (*ts'ao-mi*).

Unlike the other major category of assessment levied upon the land (the land-and-capitation silver, *ti-ting yin*), the tribute rice obligation for which the Su-Sung-T'ai rate-payer was responsible in the nineteenth century still bore the signs of its feudal origins as a kind of regularized and geographically specific purveyance requisition. Though the district magistrate collected the tribute rice assessment largely in copper cash, the tax bills by which the rate-payers were assessed were calculated in piculs of clean, dry rice rather than ounces of silver. We need not look far to see why this was so. With the funds collected under the tribute rice rubric, the local authorities were expected not only to purchase the full amount of rice assigned their territories, but to amortize all of the expenses involved in shipping this rice from the Yangtze up the Grand Canal to the imperial granaries at T'ung-chou, near Peking. What with the fluctuating price of rice, the frequent clogging of the canal network, and the dubious discipline of the "transport braves" and hired hands who actually did the hauling, it was clearly beyond the capability of even provincial-level fiscal agents to establish regular currency quotas for the various administrative subdivisions under their authority.[24] In giving the district magistrate the right to adjust tribute rice commutation rates on a yearly basis, the Board of Revenue was merely recognizing in formal terms the impossibility of centralized budgeting of transport expenses under the current system.

Magisterial leeway in determining commutation rates had, however, another less desirable aspect. Forever solicitous of avoiding conflicts with influential or violent local rate-payers, district officials all too often used their authority over commutation rates to redistribute the *ts'ao-liang* (tribute rice) quotas along the lines of least resistance. Kept within limits, this was not necessarily disruptive. But from about the beginning of the Tao-kuang reign, magistrates in the lower Yangtze counties began to find that the expense of purchasing and forwarding rice to the capital was being annually inflated as a consequence of a growing scarcity of the silver currency with which government accounts were traditionally settled.[25] Inevitably they sought to collect the increment from those least able to protest, and the gap between commoner (*hsiao-hu*) and grandee (*ta-hu*) rate-payers soon reached enormous proportions.[26]

24. The stubbornly skeptical attitude displayed by local officials with regard to plans to commute and budget the tribute rice surcharge reflected, of course, personal as well as administrative interests. For example, see *HCTC*, 5:45b–46.

25. For an account of the origins and progress of the silver scarcity, see Sasaki Masaya, "Ahen Sensō izen no tsūka mondai" [The currency problem before the Opium War], *Tōhōgaku* [Oriental studies] 8.6:94–117.

26. For a discussion of the cause–effect relationship between the silver scarcity and the

From here the pattern will be familiar to any student of Chinese history. Once a certain critical level of disparity between privileged and nonprivileged rate-payers was reached, for whatever reason, a self-sustained snowballing effect could be expected to appear before long. The wider the gap between *ta-hu* and *hsiao-hu* commutation rates, the more irresistible became the logic of proxy remittance (*pao-lan*) of the tribute rice obligation through indigent junior gentrymen. But the more land that went into *ta-hu* registry, the greater the share that had to be absorbed by the remaining *hsiao-hu* rate-payers. Thus the process perpetuated itself.

The point of critical disparity was apparently reached in Soochow prefecture by the first year of the Tao-kuang reign. In 1826 the newly appointed provincial governor, T'ao Chu, was horrified to discover that *pao-lan* abuses had become endemic among the lower ranks of the gentry population; in spite of repeated punishment of offenders, neither he nor his successors before 1860 were able to remedy the situation.[27] But it was not merely the government which found the spread of proxy remittance threatening. Within the ranks of the gentry themselves there existed a group of literati of high academic station and metropolitan background whose particularly close ties to the bureaucracy set them apart from the majority of their fellows both in outlook and interest.

Because of frequent absence from their native communities and the careerist orientation imparted by their high rank and Peking experience, these metropolitan gentry did not themselves profit from the proceeds of proxy remittance. Although they were insulated from the rising pressure of the government fisc by virtue of their grandee status, the growing disparity in commutation rates affected their interests in a manner no less serious for being more roundabout. Appropriate to their status as upper gentry, most of them owned extensive though scattered holdings in the suburbs of Soochow. Prolonged insolvency reduced the value of these holdings in that it limited the state's capacity to maintain the irrigation and drainage canals necessary for agricultural production.[28] Increasing the tax burden of the commoner landlord tended to force more land into the market, thereby reinforcing the depressing effect upon land values of declining productivity.[29]

stratification of rate-payers in the lower Yangtze region, see Sasaki Masaya, "Kampō 2-nen In-ken no kōryō bōdō" [The 1852 tax boycott in Yin *hsien*], *Kindai Chūgoku kenkyū* 5:199–211.

27. For a catalogue of the major *pao-lan* scandals in Kiangsu between 1825 and 1860, see Ch'ü T'ung-tsu, *Local Government in China under the Ch'ing* (Cambridge: Harvard University Press, 1962), p. 334, nn. 142, 143; and Hsiao Kung-ch'üan, *Rural China: Imperial Control in the Nineteenth Century* (Seattle: University of Washington Press, 1960), p. 600, nn. 215–217.

28. For a contemporary discussion of the relationship between declining productivity and inadequate hydraulic resource maintenance, see Lin Tse-hsu, *Lin Wen-chung kung cheng-shu* [The memorials of Lin Tse-hsu], pt. 1, chüan 2 and 3.

29. P'an Tseng-i, *Kung-fu hsiao-chi* [An abridged collection of the poems of Mr. Kung-fu] (Soochow, 1854), 10:12, 13, and 11:4; P'an Tseng-i, "Feng-yü-chuang k'o-keng-hui chi" [Memoir of the agricultural improvement society at the Feng-yü estate], in *P'an Feng-yü-chuang pen-shu* [Basic documents of the P'an family's Feng-yü estate] (Soochow, 1882), p. 1.

But even more visible than such economic disruptions were the social consequences they engendered. As production slackened and commoner commutation rates soared, resentment against the magistrate and his agents inevitably mounted, and with it the frequency of tax strikes and violent demonstrations directed at government officials.[30] Though draconian remedies were not generally the stock-in-trade of late-Ch'ing officialdom, the gentry of nineteenth-century Soochow were well aware of the precedent that existed in the history of their own province for an indiscriminate crackdown on gentry landlords. In 1661, for example, a dilemma similar to that which local officials now faced had inspired Governor Chu Kuo-chih (d.1673) to order the summary arrest and imprisonment, *en masse*, of virtually the whole of Soochow's landlord-gentry community. The upper gentrymen who involved themselves in the Tao-kuang reform movement were above all determined that this sordid episode should not be repeated.[31]

The most visible consequence of this resolve was a new degree of local gentry involvement in the politics of reform during the Tao-kuang period. With this involvement came a renewed interest in the long-buried tradition of statecraft scholarship. Unfettered by direct official responsibilities, gentry activists of the 1820s and 1830s devoted much energy to developing a theory of reform, the foundation for which had already been laid by such late Ming thinkers as Ku Yen-wu (1612–1680) and Ch'en Tzu-lung (1603–1647). From these efforts emerged three major principles of reform. *Simplifying* the laws and administrative procedures was urged as a remedy for corruption; since everyone knew what the system expected of him, he would be less exposed to the whims of dishonest officials and clerks. *Shortening* the distances over which funds, communication, and personnel had to be shifted would be a useful way to reduce the cost of government. *Decentralizing* the functions of the state and turning them over, wherever possible, to natural units of social organization such as the lineage or village was universally counseled as the best means of removing pressure from local officials.[32]

Such then were the two major currents of concern which motivated re-

30. Wu Yun, *Wu hsu* [Wu's preface], pp. 2a-b, in *HCTC*; Kobayashi Kazuyoshi, "Taihei Tengoku zenya no nōmin tōsō" [Peasant disturbances on the eve of the Heavenly Kingdom], in Suzuki Tomō, *Kindai Chūgoku nōson kenkyū*, pp. 1–62; Wei Yuan, *Ku-wei-t'ang wai-chi* [Exoteric collection from Ku-wei hall], 4:35b, as cited in Hsiao Kung-ch'üan, *Rural China*, p. 136.

31. At least one family of metropolitan standing in the nineteenth century had suffered badly at the hands of Chu's subordinates. For details of the 1661 incident, see Hsu K'o, *Shun-chih hsin-ch'ou tsou-hsiao an* [The tax-clearance case of 1661], in *Ko-ming yuan-yuan* [Early origins of the Revolution of 1911] (Taipei: Kuomintang Commission to Commemorate the Revolution, 1964), I, 490–492. The misfortunes of the Weng family of Ch'ang-shou *hsien* are documented in Weng Shu-yuan, *Weng T'ieh-an nien-p'u* [Chronological biography of Weng Shu-yuan], 1663 entry, as cited in Koyama Masaaki, "Minmatsu Shinsho no daitochi shoyū" [Large landholding in the late Ming and early Ch'ing], *Shigaku zasshi* [Journal of historical studies] 67.1:53.

32. The most concise statement of these principles appears in *HCTC*, 1:10–11. Apparently the classic exposition is Ku Yen-wu's *Jih-chih lu*, chüan 8.

form in Kiangsu during the Tao-kuang period. Yet taking a closer look at
the history of the reforms themselves, it soon becomes apparent that progress
was made only after a new mode of official–gentry interaction came into
play, and that the mode of interaction in question, when it actually began to
operate, did so in a way which was only remotely compatible with the assumptions of the statecraft reformists. Though few direct polemics against
the implicitly radical approach of the statecraft school survive in their chronicles, it seems clear that the actual sponsors of reform in early Tao-kuang
Soochow were influenced only superficially by the devolutionary ideals of the
Ku Yen-wu tradition.[33] While the problem of bureaucratic corruption was
not overlooked, it was nevertheless with the upper levels of the provincial
bureaucracy, the very group most anathematized by the radicals of the early
Ch'ing, that they sought to cooperate. Moral rehabilitation of the ruling
classes was indeed intended. But its most likely medium was not regarded as
the "free" magistrate or the scholar so much as the concerned censor or conscientious provincial functionary. While acknowledging that the existing
gulf between bureaucratic and indigenous leadership was a serious problem,
the Soochow reformers of the 1820s and 1830s sought to bridge this gulf not so
much by attenuating the bureaucratic character of the local officer as by
bringing to bear their influence within Hanlin circles to widen the channels
of official/amateur contact in the capital and other principal administrative
centers.[34]

At least during the early Tao-kuang period, then, it was chiefly the metropolitan influence of its gentrymen and not statecraft dogma which provided
the leaven of reform in Soochow. Of the seven men who held the post of
Soochow governor between 1825 and 1841, five had been associated during
their apprentice years in Peking with a progressively minded poetry club
dominated by Soochow's influential P'an family.[35] The best known of these

33. P'eng Yun-chang (see below), for instance, while offering a vaguely approving opinion
on Ku Yen-wu's "Chün-hsien lun" [On the prefectural system], went on soon afterwards to a
career that saw him evolve into an extreme partisan of high bureaucratic privilege. See
P'eng Yun-chang, *Kuei-p'u-k'an ts'ung-kao* [Collected drafts of Kuei-p'u retreat] (Soochow,
1848), 10:10; and *Ch'ing-shih lieh-chuan*, 45:50a-b.

34. This, at any rate, is my personal impression of the character of the Hsuan-nan Club.
On the appearance of Kung Tzu-chen and Wei Yuan on the periphery of the Hsuan-nan
circle in the 1830s, see Hsieh Cheng-kuang, "Hsuan-nan shih-she k'ao" [On the Hsuan-nan
poetry club], in *Ta-lu tsa-chih* [Mainland magazine] 36.4:120; and Chu Chieh-ch'in, *Kung
Tzu-chen yen-chiu* [Studies on Kung Tzu-chen] (Taipei, 1971), p. 240. This association might
indeed suggest a close relationship between the Soochow reformers and statecraft thinking
but I do not believe such a relationship is reflected in the politics of the reformers themselves.

35. These were T'ao Chu (governor, 1825–1830); Ch'eng Tsu-lo (1830–1832); Lin Tse-hsu
(1832–1837); Ch'en Luan (1837–1839); and Liang Chang-chü (1830, 1831). For the Hsuan-
nan Club, see Chu Shou, *Hsuan-nan shih-hui t'u-chi* [Inscriptions for a picture at the Hsuan-nan
poetry club], in P'an Tseng-i, *Kung-fu hsiao-chi*, 8:16b–17. Properly speaking, Ch'eng Tsu-lo
seems to have made P'an's acquaintance through his *Landsmann* (and kinsman?) Ch'eng En-
tse, who was a prominent member of the poetry fraternity. See Chu Shou, *Hsuan-nan shih-hui*,
8:16b–17. For P'an's own views on the importance of these metropolitan connections, see P'an
Tseng-i, *Kung-fu hsiao-chi*, 9: 8b.

intendants, Lin Tse-hsu, enjoyed the advantage of a particularly close relationship with a Soochow literatus named P'an Tseng-i.[36] Until his retirement in 1824 to look after family interests at home, P'an Tseng-i had been one of the leading lights of the Hsuan-nan Club (as the reformist coterie was called); his unhurried and socially conscientious presence was to have a visible influence upon the character of the reforms attempted.[37]

Serious reform of tribute rice administration began in 1826. In that year the Kiangsu governor, T'ao Chu, and his advisor, Wei Yuan, took advantage of a temporary halt to traffic on the Grand Canal to deliver a large portion of the provincial tribute rice quota to Peking by sea.[38] Sea shipment (hai-yun), though far less costly than canal transport, had from Yuan times onward been associated with dynastic decline, which persistently discouraged its adoption. The logic of this association was presumably that, in abandoning the inland route, the throne would also be eliminating most of the incentive for adequate maintenance of the Yellow River and Huai drainage complex, with predictable consequences for north China's agriculture.[39] At the same time, opponents of any tampering with the status quo in ts'ao-liang administration could and did argue that the coastal shipping route around Shantung was too prone to pirate attack to offer a secure alternative to the Grand Canal. While this latter aspect of the conservative position was somewhat anachronistic in its emphasis of the experience of Yuan and Ming rulers with Wako marauders, the unsteady nature of China's diplomacy during the first half of the nineteenth century did indeed persuade against entrusting the capital's grain supply to a route easily interrupted by a maritime enemy.[40] For its conservatism on the sea shipment question, however, Peking was paying dearly by the second quarter of the nineteenth century, and reducing the cost of river conservancy and canal administration had become a major priority of the government.[41] Taking this as their cue, T'ao and Wei ap-

36. P'an Tseng-i, Chiang-shan feng-yueh chi [A collection of wind and moon in the rivers and mountains], pp. 6b, 14b; and his Kung-fu hsiao-chi, chuan 8.

37. P'an Tseng-i, P'an Feng-yü-chuang pen-shu, preface, pp. 1a-b; Kung-fu hsiao-chi, chüan 9; Su-chou fu-chih, 68:46b-49; Amano Motonosuke, Chūgoku nōgyōshi kenkyū [Studies in Chinese agricultural history] (Tokyo, 1962), pp. 340-341.

38. Harold C. Hinton, The Grain Tribute System of China (Cambridge: Harvard University Press, 1956), p. 8; Chu Ch'i, Chung-kuo yun-ho shih-liao hsuan-chi [Selected materials on the history of canals in China] (Peking, 1962), pp. 133-134, cited from Ch'ing-shih kao, Ho-ch'ü chih [Draft history of the Ch'ing dynasty, essay on waterways], chüan 2, Yun-ho [Grand Canal].

39. This was often conspicuously ignored by advocates of sea shipment during the Tao-kuang and Hsien-feng periods, many of whom persistently attacked the traditional policy of "borrowing the Yellow River to help canal transport" (chieh-Huang chi-yun). Until 1845, however, no major changes were made, perhaps because of the advice of an influential conservative group more aware than the reformers of the implications of disattaching river conservancy from tribute rice finance. See below, and the memorial of P'an Hsi-en (a distant collateral of the P'ans of Soochow) quoted in Chu Ch'i, Chung-kuo yun-ho, p. 133.

40. For an example of a diplomatically motivated argument against sea shipment, see Hinton, Grain Tribute, p. 22.

41. Hsiao I-shan, Ch'ing-tai t'ung-shih [Complete history of the Ch'ing period] (Shanghai; Commercial Press, 1927-1932), II, 890-891.

parently hoped that the sea shipment innovation would receive permanent sanction. In this hope they were disappointed, for the opposition of the canal transport lobby forced the reform to be abandoned in 1827. But the success of the sea shipment experiment was not forgotten. In 1848 sea transport was again ventured, soon thereafter to become a permanent practice.

The coldness of the initial reception given the sea shipment reform did not discourage further attempts at change. During Lin Tse-hsu's term in the Soochow governor's yamen (1832–1837), tribute rice reform continued to be a major priority. In collaboration with P'an Tseng-i and Feng Kuei-fen, Lin produced a plan for alleviating Peking's dependency on Yangtze rice by expanding irrigated acreage in the northern provinces.[42] Two benefits were seen as likely from such a scheme. The first was, of course, that a decreased reliance on southern rice for its food supply would put Peking in a better position to trim the tribute rice obligations of such overtaxed provinces as Kiangsu and Chekiang. The second was less ambitious; the improvements in land use and irrigation techniques necessary to make rice culture possible in the north were regarded as potentially advantageous to the hard pressed Kiangnan rice farmer, now struggling, after long years of government neglect, to maintain his traditionally high level of harvests with less water and inadequate drainage.[43]

But shorter term measures interested Lin as well. From the spring of 1833, Lin made it a practice to ask for annual discounts in the Kiangsu tribute rice quota on the grounds that natural disaster made it impossible to collect full taxes.[44] Using the fiscal leeway gained by this politically perilous device, he was able in the space of a few year's time to repair much of the damage suffered by hydraulic facilities in Su-Sung-T'ai over the preceding decades.[45] Equally important, he was able to divert the shrinking wealth of Soochow's agitated gentry class from largely ineffective and badly coordinated efforts at waterway maintenance to a more useful channel: the endowment of a new, publicly administered relief granary (the so-called ever-abundant welfare granary, *feng-pei i-ts'ang*).[46]

But perhaps most characteristic of the spirit of the 1830s reforms was the attitude taken with regard to rural control. Lin's memorials on the problems

42. Ts'ao Yun-yuan, *Fu-an lei-kao*, 3:3.

43. See P'an Tseng-i, *P'an Feng-yü-chuang pen-shu*, preface. For the details of the land-use techniques proposed, see Amano, *Chūgoku nōgyōshi*, pp. 364 ff.

44. For the memorial that initiated this practice, see Lin Tse-hsu, *Lin Wen-chung kung*, pt. 1, chüan 2. For the regularization of emergency relief petitions in the period 1833–1860, see *HCTC*, 9:3b–4.

45. *Su-chou fu-chih*, 11:23b–25.

46. For the generally ineffective character of nonofficial hydraulic projects in Soochow during the Tao-kuang years, see P'an Tseng-i, *Kung-fu hsiao-chi*; *Su-chou fu-chih*, 11:24a-b; T'ang Chi-shang, *P'an-k'o chi* [P'an-k'o collection] (Soochow, 1885), 1:21b; Wei Yuan, *Ku-wei-t'ang wai-chi*, 4:28b. For the ever-abundant granary, see P'an Tsun-ch'i, *Ch'ang-Yuan-Wu feng-pei i-ts'ang ch'üan-an* [Complete archives of the Ch'ang-chou/Yuan-ho/Wu-hsien ever-abundant relief granary] (Soochow, 1878), introductory chüan, pp. 4b–6.

of *ts'ao-liang* administration show him to have been very much in touch with opinion among the metropolitan gentrymen residing in the province he governed, and very much influenced by their tendency to view the evils in the system as the product of a conspiracy between corrupt junior degree-holders (*sheng-chien*) and local bosses (*t'u-hao*) on the one hand, and speculating yamen clerks (*hsu-li*) and tax agents (*ching-tsao*) on the other. Acting upon this analysis, he placed the major emphasis of his reform proposals upon a stricter disciplining of *pao-chia* functionaries and a minimalizing of the role of the sub-yamen bureaucracy in the handling of the tribute rice fleet's loading operations.[47]

Yet at the same time Lin exhibited a considerable reluctance to do away entirely with degree-holder privileges or yamen clerk bureaucracy. Junior academic ranks continued to be sold, and gentry intervention in the disciplining of constabulary (*ti-pao*) agents was kept within the framework of the slow moving formal legal system.[48] Nor did he show much enthusiasm for devolutionary government. Rejecting the advice of one local scholar who urged that kinship associations be given extraordinary legal powers, Lin not only refused to give clan patriarchs a role in local administration, but actually recommended that most lineage corporations be forced to return their property to the regular tax rolls.[49]

In sum, the tradition of fiscal reform inherited by Feng Kuei-fen from his apprenticeship in the 1830s was a socially conscientious and methodologically conservative one. Little faith was placed in Peking's willingness to depart from precedent; little in the way of harm resulted from its refusal to do so. Social justice preoccupied both official and gentry activists, even if for different reasons, and much importance was attached to reducing the inequities engendered by the prevailing system. The corrosive effect of junior gentry and junior official corruption was fully recognized, but no serious consideration was afforded the possibility of turning over state functions to indigenously constituted authority. The utopian inclinations of late Ming reformist thought lurked in the background, but they were not yet sufficiently pronounced to inspire impatience or despair.

47. Lin Tse-hsu, *Lin Wen-chung kung*, pt. 1, 2:35–38. The most comprehensive rendition of Lin's opinions on Kiangsu's fiscal administration appears in a memorial sent off from Canton in the autumn of 1839, evaluating several recently offered tribute rice reform proposals. See ibid., pt. 2, chüan 8. For a retrospective account of Lin's reforms, see Li Wen-chih, *Chin-tai nung-yeh*, I, 289.

48. For the continued (actually expanded) sale of brevet ranks, see Lin Tse-hsu, *Lin Wen-chung kung*, pt. 1, 2:34; and P'an Tsun-ch'i, *Feng-pei i-ts'ang*, introductory chüan, pp. 5b-11. For the disciplining of *ti-pao* (or *ching-pao*) agents, see Li Wen-chih, *Chung-kuo chin-tai nung-yeh*, I, 289.

49. For the proposal, see T'ang Chi-shang, *P'an-k'o chi*, 1:21b–22b; and *HCCSWP*, 38:1-3b. Characteristically, Lin did not oppose the establishment of lineage corporations when the endowment came from metropolitan gentrymen of high official reputation. For an example, see *WHC*, 31:24. But such cases were exceptional; the majority of existing foundations, according to Lin's analysis, functioned merely as tax havens for unscrupulous property owners. See Lin Tse-hsu, *Lin Wen-chung kung*, pt. 2, 8:229.

MAKING THE BREAK: 1848—1860

So much for the tradition from which the reforms of 1863 descended. What must be considered next is the thornier problem of how it was that the conscientious and optimistic spirit of the 1830s evolved into the much hastier and more cynical psychology of the 1860s. In 1837 Feng Kuei-fen was Lin Tse-hsu's secretary; in 1862, a quarter-century later, he was employed by Li Hung-chang. How did Feng himself account for the distance he had traveled?

In 1849, a year before his death, Lin Tse-hsu, then serving as Yunnan governor-general, received a disheartened letter from his erstwhile amanuensis. In the years since Lin's departure from Soochow, Feng explained, the situation there had gone from bad to worse. Commoner rate-payers were now charged as much as ten times what their betters had to pay. Bad harvests were practically a yearly event, while anti-government flare-ups in the countryside had become a regular part of the political landscape. The floods of the past autumn had been the worst since 1823, and only the area surrounding the Ch'ang-men gate to the west of the city had been spared water damage. More depressing still, government response to this year's adversities was not going to go beyond the temporary granting of additional tax relief.[50]

Feng's attribution of Soochow's troubles to official inertia was not altogether valid. Since the previous year most of Kiangsu's tribute rice had been arriving in Peking by sea, and there had been much talk of discontinuing a portion of the locally dispensed surcharge that up till now had been used to offset the cost of canal transport.[51] What evidently made Feng so particularly gloomy at the moment of writing his letter to Lin was the recent news that an influential group of ministers in the Council of State had memorialized to put the savings generated by the sea shipment reform to uses other than permanent tax relief. Under their proposed plan the surcharge was to be commuted into a regular, provincially budgeted tax obligation which would presumably subsidize such pressing projects as an expansion of the Kiangsu coastal fleet and disaster relief for the flood stricken Yangtze provinces.[52]

The party of Soochow literati who had given their steadfast support to the sea shipment project since 1825 saw this turn of events as nothing less than outright betrayal. Since the previous year, the Soochow reformers had been using their influence both in Peking and at home to urge that the opportunity not be wasted for reducing the tribute rice surcharge afforded by the conversion to sea shipment.[53] They had proceeded on the assumption, inherited

---

50. *HCTC*, 5:20b-21.

51. *HCTC*, 9:19.

52. *HCTC*, 5:31; *Su-chou fu-chih*, 84:13b; Li Hsing-yuan, *Li Wen-kung kung i-chih* [Posthumous public papers of Li Hsing-yuan] (Changsha, 1865), 20:44-48b; *CSL*:TK, 457:21b-22, 459:14a-b.

53. The two key memorials were submitted by P'eng Yun-chang and Wu Wen-jung. See *CSL*:TK, 456:2-4b and 463:8a-b, respectively.

from the 1820s and 1830s, that any change in Peking's hitherto conservative attitude concerning tribute rice reform would be for the better, and that provincial bureaucrats could usually be counted on to be solicitous of upper gentry opinion. The realization that neither of these assumptions continued to be automatically valid had a decisive impact upon the reformers' strategy.

From 1849 to 1860 the Soochow lobby in the capital gravitated toward a generally conservative position with regard to administrative reform or at least those reforms which might be imposed and supervised from Peking.[54] At the same time for the more dedicated members of the group, such as Feng Kuei-fen, the key to success in provincial level politics came increasingly to be seen as institutional rather than personal influence. More and more their energies were given over to the search for a mechanical and self-perpetuating form of gentry participation in local government.

A milestone in this latter quest was the raising of the militia in 1853, after Taiping armies had penetrated into the lower Yangtze environs. The delegation of paramilitary authority to local gentry leaders gave home based reformers a potentially greater toehold within the structure of government than they had previously enjoyed as informal assistants (mu-yu) to provincial functionaries.[55] But the t'uan-lien (militia) commissions were not constituted as offical government agencies. Their relationship to the formal bureaucratic state still depended very much upon the particular fashion in which gentry commissioners and their centrally appointed intendants agreed to share the powers of government. In the 1850s official–gentry interaction in Kiangsu generally lacked the lubricant of close metropolitan association which had expedited cooperation during the 1830s. As Feng Kuei-fen's own career so well illustrates, the continuity between the local and cosmopolitan roles of the literatus was growing ever harder to maintain during the 1850s, thanks both to the disruptive effects of the war and to the declining importance of the capital as a control center.

To someone of Feng's background, the new mode of gentry participation in government sparked by the issue of militia commissions was, accordingly, as much a source of frustration as it was of opportunity. The pressures of warfare and the atrophy of metropolitan connections made it inconceivable that the leisured and conscientious atmosphere of Lin Tse-hsu's antechambers, in which his career had begun, could be revived. But there was as yet no other modality of official–gentry interaction to take its place. Gentry class sympathies had ceased to provide a reliable basis for cooperation, but a consensus of opinion concerning policy options did not yet exist within China's ruling classes sufficient to motivate collaboration. It was not until the many

54. See below and *Su-chou fu-chih*, 84:12b; *Ch'ing-shih* [History of the Ch'ing dynasty] Kuo-fang yen-chiu-yuan ed. (Taipei, 1961), pp. 4623–4625.

55. For examples of local gentry participation in provincial politics in a secretarial capacity, see Momose Hiromu, "Hō Keibun to sono chōjutsu ni tsuite" [On Feng Kuei-fen and his writings], *Tōa ronsō* [East Asian studies] 2:100; Kung Tzu-chen, *Ting-an ch'üan-chi* [Complete works of Kung Tzu-chen], *SPPY* ed., supplementary collection, 3:9b–10; *HCTC*, 6:24–25.

reverses of the 1850s had created a common fund of experience for both gentry and officials that such a consensus could be proclaimed, and that Feng's *Chiao-pin-lu k'ang-i* (Inopportune proposals from Chiao-pin cottage) could be authored. What follows is a brief account of some of the experiences that went into this fund.

FENG KUEI-FEN AND THE REFORMS OF 1853

From the moment he learned of his appointment as head of the Soochow Militia Commission in the spring of 1853, Feng Kuei-fen let slip no opportunity to entangle military and political affairs in a way designed to promote the cause of fiscal reforms. Excuses were not lacking. The dismal performance of Lu Chien-ying's regulars during the preceding winter had made military reorganization a major priority. Funds had to be found immediately to keep up the pay of the Szechwanese mercenaries who alone barred the Taipings from moving upon Soochow from the west. The supply bureau (*hsieh-chi chü*) which had been set up in February 1853, ostensibly to raise subscriptions for a local self-defense force, was accordingly called upon from the moment its activities began to serve primarily as a fund raising station for Hsiang Jung's efforts to retake Nanking.[56]

If the truth be known, the transformation of his militia bureau into a paymaster's office suited Feng's inclinations perfectly. With a disdain that probably consisted largely of mistrust, the chief of the Soochow commission had already expressed little confidence in the fighting abilities of the Kiangsu peasant. The logistical assignment, by contrast, gave Feng adequate reason to meddle as he pleased in local fiscal administration. Until the summer of 1853, the lion's share of the subsidies remitted to Nanking from the Soochow station was produced by an ingenious innovation originally suggested by a friend and ex-colleague of Feng's named Ch'en Shih. Drawing upon his experience as a yamen secretary, Ch'en had earlier that year persuaded the Soochow governor and former militia expert, Hsu Nai-chao (*chin-shih*, 1835), to entrust the collection of the spring (*shang-mang*) portion of the land-and-capitation tax to the Soochow Supply Bureau, justifying the unorthodox measure on the grounds that the tax could not otherwise be raised. True to Ch'en's prophecy, the lure of subscriber status for those who paid in full proved sufficient to fill the bureau's coffers and, thanks to a timely rebate order from Peking and the absence of normal clerical corruption, Hsiang Jung's troops actually received most of what had been collected.[57]

The overwhelming success of Ch'en's experiment had two consequences. The first was that the Soochow commissioners were able henceforth to take a direct hand in local military operations. Using the surplus revenues created

56. *HCTC*, 5:1–2.
57. *HCTC*, 5:33a-b, 6:26a-b.

by the bureau-remission scheme, Feng was able to take over the upkeep of a force of one thousand "superordinary" mercenaries attached to the Kiangnan cantonment.[58] The move soon proved a wise one. In September 1853, a Triad band in Shanghai took advantage of disturbances in nearby Ch'ing-p'u and Chia-ting to occupy the Chinese quarter, and several surrounding district seats as well. Under orders from its agitated overseers, the Soochow detachment was immediately sent to clear the rebels from their strongholds. Their success was prompt. By November loyalist forces were at the walls of the Shanghai citadel, and all of the adjoining towns were back in government hands.[59]

The other development encouraged by Ch'en Shih's experiment occurred later that fall. Fortified by the news that the current year's tribute rice quota for Kiangsu had been slashed to help restore the province's finances, Feng prevailed upon the by now much impressed Soochow governor to cooperate in an even bolder departure from fiscal orthodoxy. Collection of the autumn taxes (*hsia-mang*), including tribute rice, was likewise to be entrusted to a mixed gentry–official committee; all *ts'ao-liang* obligations were to be commuted at a rate set by the provincial finance office; and assessments were to be equalized for all rate-payers.[60] Needless to say, the plan evinced immediate and violent opposition from several quarters. Yamen clerks, angered by the loss of their perquisites, set up howls of protest. The Ch'ang-chou magistrate, claiming that Feng's budgeting had bankrupted his treasury, threatened appeal to Peking. Most dangerous of all, several belligerent local officials intentionally picked quarrels with gentry rate-payers, undoubtedly hoping that protest would rebound to the disadvantage of the reformers.[61]

Until the following spring Governor Hsu held firmly to the tiger's tail, probably unaware that a relation of one of Soochow's much-provoked junior gentryman had just made his mark in the capital and was waiting for a chance to revenge his kinsman by bringing down Feng's trusting ally. The opportunity was not long in presenting itself. On April 4, 1854, a skirmish between some of Hsu's troops besieging the Shanghai citadel and a party of British and American sailors precipitated a diplomatic crisis which was not resolved until June 29, when China was forced to acquiesce to having her customs revenues collected under foreign supervision. Though Hsu Nai-chao could not be directly blamed for this humiliation, the delays in the recapture of the Chinese quarter of Shanghai and in the departure of the tribute rice fleet to which these events gave rise distempered the emperor, making him receptive to stories describing Hsu's partnership in crime with the notoriously corrupt Shangtai taotai, Wu Chien-chang. On July 7 Hsu was removed from office,

58. *HCTC*, 6:20.
59. Shanghai she-hui k'o-hsueh yuan, comp., *Shang-hai hsiao-tao-hui ch'i-i shih-liao hui-pien* [Collected materials on the Shanghai Small Swords uprising] (Shanghai, 1964), pp. 12–13.
60. *HCTC*, 5:33–40, 10:1–6.
61. *HCTC*, 9:27b, 5:45b–46, 5:29b.

and with him disappeared the tax reforms for which Feng had labored with such sacrifice.[62]

As fate would have it, the incident which cost Hsu Nai-chao his position was the inspiration for a marked improvement in the diplomatic situation at Shanghai, and for a radical change of thinking vis-à-vis foreign policy on the part of Feng Kuei-fen. From the agreement of June 29 sprang the Maritime Customs Service, an organization whose foreign-instilled efficiency and honesty immediately won the respect of the waste-conscious Feng.[63] The fashionable xenophobia of his first term in Peking notwithstanding, Feng's regard for a well kept account book soon led him to break with the prevailing foreign policy doctrine of the day, according to which, as Feng was later to caricature it, China foolishly hoped to keep the foreigner at bay by a confusing alternation of hawkish and dovish posturings.[64]

In thus turning his back on the strategy of suspicion and disingenuousness (ts'ai-hsien i-chi), Feng was doing more than merely attacking the core dogma of Hsien-feng diplomacy. In pleading for a more rational and consistent government position on the foreign question, Feng clearly had in mind the fate of Hsu Nai-chao, and the disruptive effect that Peking's veering and tacking had upon the morals of provincial officials. Reform, even of a moderate variety, was bound to be politically risky for the man who initiated it, particularly with a fluid military situation offering metropolitan character assassins all the ammunition they could consume. Making local officials bear the consequences of a deliberately insincere diplomacy was not only unfair, but served to further aggravate the domestic crisis by inhibiting reformist initiative. If Prince Kung did not grasp the point, Li Hung-chang certainly did.

But the need for a more consistent and coordinated foreign policy was not the only lesson which Feng drew from the failure of the 1853 reforms. Reflecting upon the internal dissent that had undermined the tax equalization initiative, Feng was soon to conclude that the reformist sentiments of such local gentry groups as the one he led in Soochow could not be made effective without steps first being taken to remove the institutional binds which rendered their metropolitan influence so productive of schism. In the Chiao-pin-lu

62. For the relationship between the 1853 tribute rice equalization reforms and Hsu's cashiering, see HCTC, 6:26b. Unfortunately, Feng's writings on the subject nowhere reveal the name of the party causing all the trouble. For hints, see HCTC, 1:11b, contrasted with Wang T'ao's 1897 edition of Feng Kuei-fen, Chiao-pin-lu k'ang-i [Essays of protest from Feng Kuei-fen's studio], preface, p. 2b; and HCTC, 5:23b. For the "Battle of Muddy Flats," as the April 4 skirmish was subsequently known, see Shang-hai hsiao-tao-hui ch'i-i, p. 14. For the factors affecting Hsu Nai-chao's demise, see CSL:HF, 127:4–5, 9a-b, 129:32b–33, 130:15a–b, 133:2b.

63. Feng Kuei-fen, Chiao-pin-lu k'ang-i, pt. 1, p. 25.

64. Among the first friends Feng made in Peking was Yao Ying, whose name ranks along with that of Lin Tse-hsu at the head of the list of "hawkish" literati whose careers were ruined by the foreign policy volte-face of 1842. See Hsiao I-shan, Ch'ing-tai t'ung-shih, III, 405; Ch'ing-shih lieh-chuan, 73:43; HCTC, 12:5a-b. For Feng's later disaffection with the jingoist (jang-i) cause, see his Chiao-pin-lu k'ang-i, pt. 2, pp. 4b–5, 6, 8, 10.

k'ang-i essays, Feng was thereafter to include a suggestion for shunting the flow of local intelligence to the capital, not through the censorate, its traditional channel, but through local academies, which were presumably more susceptible to oligarchic control at the grassroots level.[65] Though the proposal was never acted upon, Feng's explanation of its intent is illustrative of the increasingly negative way in which China's ruling elite was coming to regard the traditional institutions of dynastic authority on the eve of the restoration.

> Under the prevailing system, appeal of grievances to the capital is, of course, allowed. But timorousness usually prevents the upright commoner (*yuan-min*), and ignorance the local despot (*ao-min*), from carrying his troubles to Peking. Only the treacherous (*chien-min*) make regular use of this resort, for which reason nine of ten metropolitan appeals are found [by the Board of Justice] to be without substance, and the remainder discovered groundless by provincial investigators. . . . Such suits are, at worst, protracted beyond the lifetime of the appellant. But should the grievance [be handled through the censorate], it immediately becomes the affair of an entire district. Whenever local despots take the lead, the treacherous are happy to follow along, and the upright commoners are forced, against their will, to participate. The disorders provoked by this kind of action are indeed a major cause of the prevailing lack of rapport between the capital and the provinces.[66]

In the 1830s the critique would doubtlessly have been regarded as eccentric; in the 1860s it was to become very nearly a platitude.

P'ENG YUN-CHANG AND THE LEES OF CONSERVATISM

In June 1856, the loyalist siege of Nanking was abandoned in the face of a Taiping offensive in the vicinity of Chinkiang and Yangchow, so that the organization of military operations in southern Kiangsu was significantly transformed the following year. Matters of strategy aside, the issue which most preoccupied the men who presided over this reorganization was that of bureaucratic control, particularly over funds.

In addition to intermittent extraprovincial subsidies, the loyalist forces now attempting to regroup at Tan-yang were for the most part dependent on two sources of revenue. The first was a kind of bureau-collected assessment upon landlords (usually called land donation, *mu-chüan*), whose relationship to the tribute rice tax was exactly similar to that of the contributions Feng Kuei-fen

65. Feng Kuei-fen, *Chiao-pin-lu k'ang-i*, pt. 1, pp. 32–33. I am indebted to Frederic Wakeman for the observation that Feng is here apparently borrowing from Huang Tsung-hsi, *Ming-i tai-fang lu* [A plan for the prince] (P'an-yü, 1847 ed.), pp. 10–15. It is perhaps indicative of Feng's considerable distance from the political atmosphere of late Ming and early Ch'ing times that he envisages academies functioning not merely as centers of nonofficial opinion, but as an institutionalized part of the empire's intelligence system.

66. Feng Kuei-fen, *Chiao-pin-lu k'ang-i*, pt. 1, p. 33.

and Ch'en Shih had raised in 1853. Predictably, the Soochow bureau played a central role in handling and dispensing this subsidy. Though Feng and another of the original commission members had been promoted out of the action in 1855, the presence on that bureau of his friends Wu Yun and P'an Tseng-wei (the younger brother of P'an Tseng-i) insured that the Soochow gentry continued to exercise considerable influence in the structure of local government.[67]

The channel through which this influence was exerted was the likin apparatus near Yangchow, which was the other principal source of intraprovincial subsidies. Wu Yun's immediate superior in the Kiangsu support system was Lei I-hsien (chin-shih, 1823), to whose adroitly imposed tax upon northern Kiangsu's rice trade the likin actually owed its beginnings three years before.[68] The connection was not a fortunate one. The proliferation of likin stations in Hunan and Kiangsi in 1855, while doubtless facilitating Hu Lin-i's successes in Hupei the following year, also gave the Hsiang Army's many metropolitan critics the proof they needed to support their claims that Tseng Kuo-fan was fast becoming another Wu San-kuei (1612–1678).[69] Until 1856 the New Conservatism had been without either a scapegoat or a champion in the field. All that was changed, however, in the wake of Hsiang Jung's retreat to Tan-yang.

The scapegoat proved, not surprisingly, to be Lei I-hsien and the Soochow commission. Absorbing the blame for the reverses at Yangchow, Lei and his staff were stripped of their commissions, and the unfortunate Wu Yun cited for negligence in supervising commissary accounts and for his role in levying the "illegal" land donation surtax.[70] Early the following spring the conservatives found their champion as well, and Ho Kuei-ch'ing (1816–1862) was given the key office of Nanking viceroy, ex officio commander-in-chief of the lower Yangtze front.

Ho's principal metropolitan sponsor, ironically enough, was a highly conscientious Soochow literatus named P'eng Yun-chang (1792–1862).[71] In 1848 it had been a memorial of P'eng's which first sparked debate on reducing the tribute rice surcharge in Kiangsu.[72] But since his appointment to the Grand Council in 1852, P'eng had become increasingly conservative, not just in his intense distrust of the Hsiang Army, but in regard to tribute rice reform and

67. For the mu-chüan and Wu Yun, see CSL:HF, 192:28–29, 194:9, 197:6–7b, 201:14b, 206:12b–13b; also Ch'ing-shih, p. 4624. For P'an Tseng-wei, see HCTC, 5:45.

68. For Wu Yun's role as an agent of Lei I-hsien, see Chih Wei-ch'eng, Ch'ing-tai p'u-hsueh ta-shih lieh-chuan [Biographies of great masters of essential learning in the Ch'ing period] (Shanghai, 1925), 18:19. For Lei I-hsien and the beginnings of the likin, see Lo Yü-tung, Chung-kuo li-chin shih [A history of likin in China] (Shanghai, 1936), p. 14.

69. For likin in Hunan and Kiangsi, see Lo Yü-tung, Chung-kuo li-chin shih, pp. 20–21. For the accusations against Tseng and the Hunan Army actuated by the spread of likin stations in the upper Yangtze provinces, see Hsiao I-shan, Ch'ing-tai t'ung-shih, III, 412.

70. The progress of the impeachment of Lei and Wu is charted in CSL:HF, 192:28–29, 194:9, 197:6–7b, 201:14b, 206:12b–13b; see also Ch'ing-shih, p. 4624.

71. Hsiao I-shan, Ch'ing-tai t'ung-shih, III, 452–453.

72. CSL:TK, 456:2–4b.

foreign policy as well. His conservatism seems to have been motivated partly by a concern for the erosion of literati influence within the bureaucracy owing to the wartime promotion of staff adjutants and militia activists into high offices. Partly it reflected antipathy for the methods of Tseng Kuo-fan's chief patron, the Manchu statesman Su-shun (1815–1861), whose dictatorial tendencies were fast stirring up opposition in the capital.[73] P'eng's nomination of Ho Kuei-ch'ing for the Nanking post made perfect sense from the conservative point of view, according to which extraprovincial and bureaucratically controlled reinforcements were always preferable to intraprovincial and gentry controlled ones. During the two year stint as Chekiang governor which preceded his 1857 promotion, Ho had first built up an effective supply base at Hangchow for the Kiangnan cantonment, and then, after the latter's rout in the spring of 1856, rediverted the resources of the Hangchow supply facility to the support of a division of Chekiang mercenaries sent to forestall a Taiping penetration of southern Anhwei.[74] Though the success of the Anhwei foray was actually achieved by the deliberate sacrifice of the Kiangsu armies, the excellent impression it created in Peking, coinciding with the fact of Ho's access to an extraprovincial support system, made him in 1857 the only leader outside Hunanese circles with prospects sufficiently bright to recommend him as successor to the Kiangnan governor-generalship.

At first Ho's sponsor must have been pleased with his selection. By moving the headquarters of the Kiangnan cantonment downriver to Ch'ang-chou to be nearer his Chekiang base, Ho was able to expel the Taipings from Chinkiang before the first year of his appointment was out, and so gain the coveted title of grand guardian.[75] Though less spectacular, his efforts in the field continued to be effective until the spring of 1860. But beneath the veneer of strategic competence, Ho's actual power base remained dangerously shallow. Rendered complacent by the apparent sufficiency of his logistics apparatus, he made no attempt to revive the Soochow Supply Bureau from the apathy and corruption into which it had been plunged by the events of 1856, and rejected out-of-hand all talk of fiscal reform.[76] When a man known to be on good terms with Feng Kuei-fen was given the Soochow governorship early in 1859, Ho immediately ostracized the newcomer from his councils and passed him over for promotion in 1860.[77]

For this high-handedness, both Ho Kuei-ch'ing and his patron were to pay

73. Hsiao I-shan, *Ch'ing-tai t'ung-shih*, III, 412–413; *Su-chou fu-chih*, 89:29–30. For a summary of Su-shun's draconian fiscal policies and of the discontent they produced in Peking official circles, see Frank H. H. King, *Money and Monetary Policy in China* (Cambridge: Harvard University Press, 1965), pp. 156–158.

74. Tuan Kuang-ch'ing, *Ching-hu tzu-chuan nien-p'u* [The chronological autobiography of Ching-hu] (Peking, 1960), pp. 100, 103, 157; *CSL*:HF, 205:2a–b.

75. Hsiao I-shan, *Ch'ing-tai t'ung-shih*, III, 452–453.

76. For the decline of the Soochow Supply Bureau after 1856, see Jen Yu-wen, *T'ai-p'ing t'ien-kuo ch'üan-shih* [Comprehensive history of the Taiping Heavenly Kingdom] (Hong Kong, 1962), pt. 3, pp. 1768–1775. For Ho's attitude toward the reforms proposed by Feng et al., see *HCTC*, Wu Yün's preface, p. 2b.

77. Momose, "Hō Keibun," p. 104; *Su-chou fu-chih*, 68:50b.

a severe price. On May 6, 1860, taking advantage of a logistics dispute between the two Ch'ing commanders at the Nanking front, Taiping forces succeeded for the second time in lifting the siege of their capital city. By May 19, after a bloody day of fighting at Tan-yang, they had broken the back of the principal loyalist army in the area, leaving only the Ch'ang-chou garrison between them and the rich Shanghai hinterland.[78] Informed that rations and funds sufficient for a long siege were being stockpiled in Soochow, Ho Kuei-ch'ing chose that latter city to make his stand. On May 21, over the tearful protests of the local gentry, the beleaguered viceroy abandoned his former base camp, leaving the Ch'ang-chou militia to fend for itself. The response of the Soochow governor to this act of treachery was to close the portals of his walled city to the troops that began to trickle down the Grand Canal several days later. Faced with this hostile reception, Ho had no choice but to fall back upon Ch'ang-chou, fifty miles to the east, in a retreat that could no longer be represented as strategic. On June 8 an imperial order stripped Ho Kuei-ch'ing of his rank and office; on July 27 P'eng Yun-chang received permission to be relieved of his duties as councillor.[79]

But the triumph of righteousness was not to endure. The silver that lured Ho Kuei-ch'ing's troops to their ill-starred rendezvous at the walls of Soochow was ironically to prove the undoing of its tight-fisted gentry wardens as well. The problem was time. Until early May when news arrived of the disasters upstream, the Soochow commission had been largely inert. Whatever hopes had been raised by the appointment of a new governor in January 1859 were extinct before the end of his first year of tenure; by November 1859, P'an Tseng-wei was back in Peking, and Feng was secluded in his mountain retreat overlooking Lake T'ai.[80] The two remaining commissioners, Wang Ts'ao and Han Ch'ung, were not unaware of the menace that loomed upriver, but the bureau they headed, having been stripped of its taxing powers in 1856, was reduced to peddling nearly worthless patents of rank and (so some said) running opium to make ends meet.[81] Efforts initiated in May 1860 to raise a new land-donation subsidy on the model of Wu Yun's controversial undertaking four years earlier were immediately effective. But reliable mercenaries were not at once available to supplement the small force of Ch'ao-chou guards maintained by Governor Hsu out of his own pocket.

To remedy this defect, Han Ch'ung set out late in May for the suburban town of Chou-chung *chen*, where a gang of local rowdies had been reported willing to serve as a garrison force. The negotiations went well.[82] But on June 1, before any of the supplies and cash hoarded in the supply bureau's vaults

78. Jen Yu-wen, *T'ai-p'ing t'ien-kuo*, pt. 3, pp. 1739–1746.
79. Ibid., pp. 1751–1761; P'eng Yun-chang, *I-ku lao-jen shou-ting nien-p'u* [Chronological autobiography of I-ku lao-jen] (Soochow, n.d.), p. 43.
80. P'an Tseng-shou, *P'an Fu-t'ing tzu-ting nien-p'u* [Autobiography of P'an Fu-t'ing] (Soochow, n.d.), p. 21; *HCTC*, 5:23.
81. Wang Ping-hsieh, *Wu-tzu-ch'i shih wen-chi*, 10:4–7.
82. T'ao Hsu, *Chen-feng-li keng-shen chien-wen-lu* [Chronicle of the events of 1860 at Chou-

could be dispensed to the new recruits, an advance party of Taiping infantry reached the walls of Soochow. The next morning the Ch'ao-chou guards, disgruntled by rumors that the lucre they guarded was about to be turned over to a force of local braves, spiked the cannons on the city's parapets and opened its gates to a waiting contingent of long-haired marauders.[83]

After the Taiping occupation of Soochow, the better part of a year slipped by before Feng was again united with his fellow gentrymen exiled in Shanghai. In that time much else occurred to confirm the perspicacity of his judgments, for a failure to grasp the necessity of shortening lines of supply was not the only weakness in the position to which his colleagues in Peking had become committed. Uncertainty about the seriousness of British demands for treaty revision, and China's ability to resist them; the failure of the Yangtze military situation to take a visible turn for the better; repeated breakdowns in the capital's food supply system; and the spectacular inflation generated by several ill-conceived currency reforms—all these things and more made late Hsien-feng Peking at best a poor place to be urging institutionally conservative palliatives, or fretting about such intangibles as bureaucratic normalcy.

Yet it was into precisely this sort of behavior that the aging statesman P'eng Yun-chang found himself pressured as a result of both his reluctance to acknowledge the decline of literocratic influence, and his distaste for the methodologically cynical manner in which Su-shun's clique went about the business of enforcing its will upon the bureaucracy. In the spring of 1858, a growing sense of impotence had already pushed one of his particularly headstrong younger associates, Yin Chao-yung, into open confrontation with the ruling cabal over the handling of the Tientsin negotiations. By early 1861 not only had the precipitous Mr. Yin been dismissed, but four other fellow provincials were disgraced as well, including the grand secretary Weng Hsin-ts'un (1791–1862; father of Weng T'ung-ho), P'an Tsu-t'ung (nephew of P'an Tseng-i and P'an Tseng-wei), and Feng Kuei-fen himself.[84]

The break, so long postponed, had now at last become unavoidable. With men of Su-shun's character in power, as Feng was soon afterwards to tell Li Hung-chang, it was only a matter of time before the tragedy of 1661 would

---

chuang *chen*], appendix to T'ao Hsu, *Chou-chuang chen-chih* [Gazetteer of Chou-chuang], pt. 1, p. 3.

83. Jen Yu-wen, *T'ai-p'ing t'ien-kuo*, pt. 3, pp. 1772–1773.

84. For Yin Chao-yung's adventure, see his *Yin P'u-ching shih-lang tzu-ting nien-p'u* [Autobiography of Vice-President Yin P'u-ching] (Soochow, n.d.), pp. 32–33, 65. For the anti-compromise position of Weng Hsin-ts'un and P'an Tsu-in during the Tientsin parleys of 1858, see *Ch'ing-shih*, p. 4624; and P'an Tsu-nien, *P'an Wen-ch'in kung nien-p'u* [Biography of P'an Tsu-nien] (Soochow, n.d.), p. 16b. For the demise of Weng Hsin-ts'un, P'an Tsu-t'ung, Feng Kuei-fen, et al., see Hsiao I-shan, *Ch'ing-tai t'ung-shih*, III, 416–420; and Chang Ping-lin, *T'ai-yen wen-lu hsu-kao* [Further drafts and literary records of Chang T'ai-yen] (Taipei, 1956), chüan 5, *hsia*, p. 23. Feng Kuei-fen's involvement in the purges of 1858–1860 seems to have resulted from a friendship with Ch'eng T'ing-kuei, a former member of the Soochow militia commission and a prominent culprit in the 1858 examination scandal. See *HCTC*, 2:50b; and Hsiao I-shan, *Ch'ing-tai t'ung-shih*, III, 417.

again be repeated.[85] True or not, such was at any rate the kind of thinking which prevailed among the exiled gentrymen who in the autumn of 1861 determined to bring Li to Shanghai at the head of a new army. Having paid the maximum price for their tenacious conservatism, the gentry of Soochow were soon to emerge at the very vanguard of the new politics.

THE TAX REFORM OF 1863 AND THE NEW POLITICS

The depth of the disaffection stirred up by the purges and general vindictiveness of the late Hsien-feng period was nowhere more in evidence than in the political methods used to negotiate the 1863 fiscal reforms. On the surface, the prominence of the role played by the gentry metropolitan connections in coordinating the T'ung-chih reforms invites a comparison with the 1830s. In reality, however, the structure of politics upon which these reforms were built was much more akin to that of the Hsien-feng period. Peking in the 1860s, no less than in the preceding decade, was a hostile and uncertain presence. The difference was that by 1863 the gentry of Soochow had learned to manage their situation with almost perfect *sang-froid*. Literocratic prestige still counted, as it had in the early Tao-kuang years. But now it counted only insofar as it tended to reinforce the network of allegiances upon which the Hsiang command depended for its political clout.

The pivotal figure in this network of allegiances was a Soochow literatus named P'an Tsu-in (1830–1890), a man qualified by several circumstances for his role. Like the indignant Yin Chao-yung, P'an was young and willing to gamble. Like the legalistically inclined Feng Kuei-fen, he was intent more on success than gesture. Like the venerable statesman P'eng Yun-chang, he was aware that his appeal had to have a Ciceronian flavor if it was to excite response. But in contradistinction to these more illustrious associates, P'an Tsu-in could profit from extensive and immediate family influence.

Like his cousin P'an Tsu-t'ung, P'an Tsu-in owed his precocious advancement to high metropolitan office (at age twenty-six he was already a palace examiner) largely to the prestige of his late grandfather, the grand secretary P'an Shih-en.[86] But this was by no means the sole advantage afforded by the P'an pedigree. As a child in Soochow, Tsu-in had been the particular favorite of his distinguished uncle, P'an Tseng-i, who will be remembered as a confidant of Lin Tse-hsu during the latter's busy incumbency as Kiangsu governor.[87] Through this close relationship with his uncle, the younger P'an appears to have absorbed quite early in life some of that elusive sense of self-

85. *HCTC*, 5:8b–9.

86. Upon P'an Shih-en's death in 1854, his eldest grandchild Tsu-t'ung was granted the *chin-shih* degree, while P'an Tsu-in, who had already gained the metropolitan degree, was promoted to the post of sub-reader in the Hanlin Academy. See P'an Tseng-shou, *P'an Fu-t'ing tzu-ting nien-p'u*, p. 18.

87. P'an Tsu-nien, *P'an Wen-ch'in kung nien-p'u*, p. 6.

confident literary graciousness that was a prerequisite for popularity among the excessively leisured lower tiers of official society in the capital.[88] In his father, P'an Tseng-shou, the young man possessed, in addition, a mentor wise in the ways of Peking politics, as well as a powerful ally.[89]

In tandem, these several features of his patrimony put P'an Tsu-in in an excellent position to play a major role in late Hsien-feng and early T'ung-chih politics. By the last year of the Hsien-feng reign, rapid promotion had gained him the vice-presidency of the Imperial Clan Court, an office by no means comparable to that of board president or grand secretary in overt prestige, but actually a good deal more advantageously situated for safe reconnaissance of the inner processes of Peking politics.[90] In the years immediately preceding the restoration, only one Soochow literatus outranked P'an Tsu-in within what might be termed the palace bureaucracy. But that person, the palace tutor Yin Chao-yung, had been since 1858 too closely associated with Prince Kung (1833–1898) and those out of power to assert much influence within the government. Until Yin's star again rose, together with Prince Kung's, in 1862, P'an Tsu-in had the field of palace politics pretty much to himself.

But situation and *savoir faire* were not P'an's only advantages. During his years as a senior Hanlin official (1857–1860), P'an had gained numerous friends among the discontented younger element in the capital. Two of these in particular were destined to exercise a special influence upon his thinking— and later upon his actions. One was Weng T'ung-ho, embittered son of the recently purged grand secretary. The other was Kuo Sung-t'ao (1818–1891), a Hunanese literatus later to become famous as China's first ambassador to England.

P'an's celebrated friendship with Weng T'ung-ho had begun in 1858, when the two young men found themselves serving jointly as examination officials in Sian.[91] Ironically, it was probably only because of this provincial assignment that either of them escaped involvement in the examination scandal that rocked the capital that same year, giving Su-shun's government the excuse for its first massive crackdown on the metropolitan bureaucracy. This good fortune was not, however, shared by their senior kinsmen. The cashiering of P'an's elder cousin, P'an Tsu-t'ung (then a junior official in the

88. For P'an's lifelong popularity in Peking circles, see Chih Wei-ch'eng, *Ch'ing-tai p'u-hsueh ta-shih lieh-chuan*, 25:11.

89. P'an Tseng-shou rode out the political storms preceding Su-shun's downfall in the comfortable seclusion of his Western Hills retreat outside the capital. While it would be overstating the case to represent his lodgings as a conspirator's lair, several poems surviving from this period (c.1859–1861) suggest a degree of stubbornness and desperation entirely out of keeping with the predictable anchorite facade. See in particular *Kai-lan shu-ya erh-chi* [Kai-lan studio anthology, series 2], 2:20a–b, 3:1b–3b.

90. P'an Tsu-nien, *P'an Wen-ch'in kung nien-p'u*, p. 20b.

91. Ibid., p. 17. Chao Chung-fu, ed., *Weng T'ung-ho jih-chi p'ai-yin-pen* [Typeset edition of the diary of Weng T'ung-ho] (Taipei, 1970), 1:1, 6.

Board of Rites) in 1858, and of Weng's father the next year, inspired in
P'an a combination of resentment and revanchist determination that was
doubtless responsible for his becoming the first of Soochow's metropolitan
placement to depart openly from the course set by P'eng Yun-chang.

The occasion for this break came in the spring of 1860. Early in May of
that year, P'an was approached by Kuo Sung-t'ao, until recently a fellow
Hanlin officer, with a request to submit a memorial in defense of a Hunanese
named Tso Tsung-t'ang, currently under investigation on charges of misconduct as a member of Hu Lin-i's staff (mu-fu). In spite of has knowledge
that the man behind the request was none other than the terrible Su-shun
himself, P'an promptly agreed not only to submit the desired character reference, but to secure the services of a Landsmann (Ku Wen-pin) known to
be on good terms with the Hu-Kuang governor-general to intercede on Tso's
behalf.[92]

The motive behind P'an's puzzling readiness to collaborate with the
Hunanese contingent of military specialists did not long remain obscure.
Though Tseng Kuo-fan's formal appointment to the coveted Liang-Kiang
viceroyship was not announced until June 8, the May 2 collapse of loyalist
siege operations at Nanking had virtually guaranteed that one or another of
the Hunanese commanders would be named to the post.[93] Ho Kuei-ch'ing's
demise thus ironically put P'an in an awkward position. Given the legacy
of bad will that had accrued from the anti-Hunanese prejudices of his senior,
P'an had little reason to expect anything but hostility from the new appointee,
whoever he might prove to be. Given time, of course, things might improve;
but the descriptions he had heard from his uncle, P'an Tseng-wei (only
recently returned from the family seat), did not suggest that any time could
be spared.[94]

Accordingly, on May 20, P'an Tsu-in submitted the first of a series of
memorials on strategy designed to appease the Hsiang command. The Hunan
Army was to be given a free hand in turning Szechwan into a supply base,
while the militia (t'uan-lien) commissions in Kiangsu were to be reformed so
as to free their resources from pointless expenditure on locally recruited
condottieri.[95] In the last of these memorials, dated June 14, the object toward
which P'an's efforts were aimed surfaced in unmistakable form. Soochow and
Ch'ang-chou could not be held, P'an informed the throne, with their present
supply of troops. It was imperative, if the vital Shanghai hinterland was to
be kept in loyalist hands, that Tseng Kuo-fan be induced to hurry his drive

92. Hsiao I-shan, Ch'ing-tai t'ung-shih, III, 415; Min Erh-ch'ang, Pei-chuan chi-pu [A collection of epitaphs] (Peking, 1932), 17:20.

93. According to Weng T'ung-ho's diary, despair over the situation on the Kiangnan front
began to appear in Peking after the arrival in early April of news of the fall of Hangchow. See
Chao Chung-fu, Weng T'ung-ho jih-chi, 1:33–34.

94. For more on this point, see the memorial submitted by P'an on June 14, 1860, in P'an
Tsu-nien, P'an Wen-ch'in kung nien-p'u. p. 19b.

95. Ibid., p. 19.

on Anhwei from the west, and to dispatch the Hui-chou garrison to the immediate aid of Soochow.[96]

The advice was not only too late (Soochow having fallen to the Taipings on June 2), but in a sense premature as well. As the events of the next several years were to show, Tseng could not afford to shift troops out of southern Anhwei without opening a gaping hole in the net he was trying to close over Nanking, thereby exposing Chekiang to Taiping penetration from the west as well.[97] Even before Taiping troops overran the Shanghai hinterland in the summer of 1860, Tseng's commitment to keeping a secure rear dictated against dividing his armies in an attempt to hold southern Kiangsu. Now that the latter region was in rebel hands and its riches scattered to the winds, there was even less reason for an eastern front. With Tseng so obviously unenthused, P'an Tsu-in had little choice but to seek help from other quarters.

The opportunity came soon enough. On August 22, 1861, the Hsien-feng emperor died in exile in Jehol. A violent struggle over the make-up of the Council of Regency ensued, climaxed by the two empresses dowager overthrowing Su-shun and his princely allies and seizing power for themselves. Making expert use of his own and Weng Hsin-ts'un's credentials as victims of the late usurper, P'an Tsu-in was able to secure for himself a privileged place at the banquet that convened in November to dine upon the spoils afforded by Su-shun's demise.[98] In the following weeks as Weng, now tutor to the underaged monarch, reminded his charge of the importance of the Shanghai hinterland to the economic welfare of the state, P'an eagerly renewed his crusade for military reorganization, proposing to Prince Kung that the t'uan-lien commissions be discontinued, and the likin resources, which they consumed in so wasteful a fashion, be put under the control of the regular bureaucracy.[99]

How these apparently unrelated recommendations fit together became clear early in the following year. But to understand what happened in the spring of 1862, it will be necessary to review briefly the situation in Shanghai, which now functioned as a home for the Kiangsu provincial government in exile. Since the diplomatic crisis of 1854, both of the dynasty's principal sources of revenue in the Shanghai environs had come, to varying degrees, under foreign influence. The Shanghai customs were, of course, now collected

96. Ibid., p. 19b.

97. In fact, Taiping troops fleeing from western Kiangsu crossed through southern Anhwei into Chekiang no less than three times between 1860 and 1864. See Tuan Kuang-ch'ing, Ching-hu tzu-chuan nien-p'u, p. 156; and Jen Yu-wen, T'ai-p'ing t'ien-kuo, pt. 3, pp. 2013, 2117.

98. For P'an's role in the 1861 coup, and the positive effect of its success upon his career, see Liu Feng-han, comp., Li Hung-tsao hsien-sheng nien-p'u [Biography of Mr. Li Hung-tsao] (Taipei, 1969), pt. 1, pp. 109, 131, 133; and Hsiao I-shan, Ch'ing-tai t'ung-shih, III, 433.

99. Spector, Li Hung-chang, pp. 45–46, citing CSL:TC, 12:1a–b, 17:35; Chang Shou-yung, Huang-ch'ao chang-ku hui-pien [Compilation of snatches from the past of the Ch'ing dynasty], nei-pien, 53:21a–b, as summarized in Hsiao Kung-ch'üan, Rural China, p. 656, n. 148; and P'an Tsu-nien, P'an Wen-ch'in kung nien-p'u, p. 20b.

and remitted by a foreign-run organization. But even the likin stations in the area had felt the pressure of British concern about trade-obstructing inland transit imposts, and were in 1860 exposed to an indirect form of control through the mediations of Shanghai's famous duo of comprador-commissioners, Wu Hsu and Yang Fang.[100]

Until 1861 only a small part of the generous revenues produced by these two sources had been available to F. T. Ward's mercenaries; the rest was consumed by a slovenly army of some 500,000 locally enlisted "braves," nominally under the command of the Shanghai militia commissioner, P'ang Chung-lu, but in fact, as Feng complained, under nobody's command but their own.[101] Attempting to redress this absurd situation, a group of Soochow gentry headed by the indignant Feng himself had begun, in the autumn of 1861, to bring pressure upon the local Chinese authorities to seek a formal agreement with Rutherford Alcock guaranteeing British assistance in the event of renewed Taiping pressure on Shanghai. For their cooperation the petitioners proposed to reward the British with a regular monthly subsidy from the customs service's revenues; the likin funds, plus whatever was left of the customs, could then (P'ang's braves having in the meanwhile been disbanded) be quietly appropriated from their compradorial custodians and transformed into a tidy little nest egg for financing the reconquest of the interior.[102]

Naturally, the claque of Ning-po and Shao-hsing businessmen who had dominated Shanghai's fiscal bureaucracy since 1854 was not expected to acquiesce in its own demise, or to endorse the diversion of Shanghai's revenues to the support of Kiangsu gentry aspirations. But for this difficulty the ever-resourceful Feng had an answer as well. By a wonderful coincidence, one of the Soochow group's charter members, Wu Yun (1811–1883), happened to be a cousin of the man who held, along with Yang Fang, supreme influence within the Chekiang commercial establishment, the customs taotai Wu Hsu.[103] The uses to which the intelligence provided by this contact could be put had already been suggested by an unflattering description, in P'an Tsu-in's recent memorial on military reorganization, of the behavior of a Shanghai likin commissioner named Chin An-ch'ing.[104] To no one's surprise, Wu Hsu was glad to lend his support to the reorganization project.

Still, not all of the arrangements could be made in Shanghai. To begin with, Feng's impatient remonstrances notwithstanding, the hire of foreign

100. For an instance of foreign involvement in likin planning, see Tuan Kuang-ch'ing, *Ching-hu tzu-chuang nien-p'u*, p. 202.

101. *HCTC*, 4:15b, 5:5.

102. Ch'en Chin, *Sung-Hu ts'ung-jung chi-lueh* [Account of a military career in Sung-chiang and Shanghai], in *T'ai-p'ing t'ien-kuo shih-liao tsung-pien chien-chi* [Abridged compendium of materials on the Taiping Heavenly Kingdom] (Peking, 1961), II, 209.

103. Wu Yun, *Liang-lei hsuan ch'ih-tu* [Letters of Liang-lei studio] (Soochow, 1884), 2:22.

104. P'an Tsu-nien, *P'an Wen-ch'in kung nien-p'u*, p. 20b. It is quite possible that the information on Chin An-ch'ing was supplied with the latter's consent, for Chin was a good friend of Wu as well as of P'an Tseng-wei. See Wu Yun, *Liang-lei hsuan ch'ih-tu*, 7:39b.

guns to defend Chinese territory was a highly unorthodox and dangerous expedient.[105] Pending Peking's explicit sanction for such an accommodation, acting governor Hsueh Huan (1815-1880) could scarcely be blamed if he hesitated to give his consent. Then, too, a new army could not be organized in Shanghai until its commander had first been approved by each of the three parties whose interests would be affected: Tseng Kuo-fan, Hsueh Huan and, of course, the British. Aware by November that Feng and his cohorts intended to offer the job in question to a P'an family protege named Li Hung-chang, the acting governor was showing considerable reluctance to proceed even with the initial phase of the proposed reform.[106] And, though Li Hung-chang himself seemed to be the kind of man who could be persuaded to come to an understanding with Shanghai's foreign masters, Tseng had yet to give his consent either to the idea of a second front or to the notion of collaborating with the British.

It was to the solution of these problems that P'an Tsu-in's efforts had been directed in the autumn of 1861. This time they bore immediate fruit. On the day after a delegation of Shanghai gentry arrived at Tseng's bivouac near Anking (November 18) to finalize an agreement regarding Li's dispatch, an imperial edict was hurried off instructing the Liang-Kiang viceroy to investigate rumors of corruption in Hsueh Huan's likin apparatus.[107] On December 31 another edict told Tseng that the throne had lately been advised, by certain persons, to press for the recapture of Soochow and Ch'ang-chou at the earliest possible opportunity.[108]

By early 1862 the time was at hand to draw these leads together. Sometime in January, P'an Tseng-wei set out for Peking in the company of another prominent Shanghai emigre named Kung Ch'eng, son of the celebrated Hangchow poet and social critic Kung Tzu-chen (1792–1841), and a long-time friend of Thomas Francis Wade.[109] In late March P'an Tsu-in's introduction brought the visitors into the presence of Prince Kung, where news of recent developments in Shanghai was duly passed on, and the prince's approval was solicited for the formalization of the "joint defense" arrangement.[110]

If an accord was actually reached during this first encounter, it came

105. For Feng's case, as well as a summary of the opposing position, see *HCTC*, 10:16–17b.

106. For Li's connection with the ubiquitous P'an family patronage network in the capital, see Ho-ch'iao chü-shih (anon.), *Sheng-ch'uan pai-sheng* [An unofficial history of events at Sheng-tse *chen* during the Taiping occupation], in *T'ai-p'ing t'ien-kuo shih-liao*, II, 194; and Chang Ping-lin, *T'ai-yen wen-lu hsu-kao*, chüan 5, *hsia*, p. 23.

107. Spector, *Li Hung-chang*, p. 36.

108. Ibid., pp. 45–46, citing *CSL*:TC, 12:1a–b, 17:35.

109. Ch'en Chin, *Sung-hu ts'ung-jung chi-lueh*, II, 209. Kung Ch'eng is rumored to have inspired the sacking of the Yuan-ming Gardens in October 1860, in revenge for his father's alleged poisoning by agents of a Manchu prince. See Tanaka Kenji, *Kyō Jichin* [Kung Tzu-chen] (Tokyo, 1962), preface, p. 6.

110. *Ch'ou-pan i-wu shih-mo* [A complete account of our management of barbarian affairs], TC, 4:54.

barely in time. On January 21 a Taiping thrust from Hangchow had cut off Shanghai from the east, and only a British naval bombardment the next day prevented an assault upon the citadel. Even with the help of reinforcements dispatched immediately from Tientsin by Frederick Bruce, the interlopers were not persuaded to retreat from their positions on the east bank of the Whampoa until the end of February.[111] Not waiting to see the outcome of these skirmishes, Wu Hsu had meanwhile completed the outfitting of a fleet of steamers supplied by Mackenzie, Richardson and Co., for the staggering sum of 205,000 taels. Late in March the first of these arrived in Anking, its strongbox bursting with an additional 100,000 taels from the Shanghai customs that was to serve as a loan for the new commander. On April 8 Li Hung-chang arrived in Shanghai.[112]

Of the exploits of the Huai Army that grew from these humble beginnings, nothing need here be remarked. More to the point are the doings of Li's eager new hosts during the months that followed, doings which had a considerable bearing on the character of the 1863 reforms.

The first hint of things to come occurred soon after Li Hung-chang's disembarkment. Though an unsympathetic report on the charges against Hsueh Huan had, by April 25, already eliminated the foremost of Li Hung-chang's rivals in the Shanghai bureaucracy, the ends to which both Li and his gentry collaborators intended to mobilize the city's immense revenues were not compatible with only superficial control of the local power structure.[113] On June 6, 1862, a secret memorial was presented to the throne alleging the misconduct of Lin Fu-hsiang, Yang Fang, and Wu Hsu, respectively comptrollers of the Shanghai likin bureaucracy, Su-Sung tribute rice intendancy, and Shanghai customs. The immediate purpose of this memorial was realized over the course of the next several weeks as Feng Kuei-fen took over the supervision of likin administration, Kuo Sung-t'ao became the tribute rice intendant, and another Hunanese, Huang Fang, replaced the ill-used Wu Hsu as customs taotai.[114]

111. Jen Yu-wen, *T'ai-p'ing t'ien-kuo*, pt. 3, pp. 1965–1980. According to Li Hung-chang, P'an returned from Peking under the impression that Prince Kung was now fully prepared to endorse the use of foreign forces against the Taipings both at Shanghai and in the interior, and that only Tseng Kuo-fan's reservations prevented him from so doing. Li to Tseng, April 4, 1862, as cited (in translation) in Lillian Li, "The Ever Victorious Army," *Harvard University Papers on China* no. 21 (1968): 34, n. 27. For the British abandonment of passive for "armed" neutrality in the Shanghai environs early in 1862, see ibid., pp. 9–11.

112. Jen Yu-wen, *T'ai-p'ing t'ien-kuo*, pt. 3, p. 2007; Spector, *Li Hung-chang*, pp. 48–49, 55.

113. For Hsueh's cashiering, see Wright, *The Last Stand of Chinese Conservatism*, p. 88; and *CSL*:TC, 22:9–10, as cited in Wright, p. 333, n. 132. The heavy-handedness of Li's operations to dislodge Hsueh Huan—extraordinary even for the early 1860s—was later to boomerang with almost lethal consequences. See Liu Feng-han, *Li Hung-tsao hsien-sheng nien-p'u*, pt. 1, p. 139.

114. For the memorial, see Yin Chao-yung, *Yin P'u-ching nien-p'u*, p. 43b; and *Ch'ing shih-kao* [Draft history of the Ch'ing] (Peiking, 1942), *hsia*, p. 1390. For the appointments, see Spector, *Li Hung-chang*, p. 60; and K. C. Liu, "The Confucian as Patriot and Pragmatist," p. 23.

But the clandestine memorialist responsible for this shake-up, Yin Chao-yung, did not confine his attentions solely to matters of personnel. Concluding his review of the Shanghai fiscal situation, the restored palace pedagogue appended a slightly more elaborate version of the argument that had been presented by P'an Tsu-in the preceding winter. The land tax in the four principal prefectures of the Shanghai hinterland was the most severe in the realm. For the past thirty years the quotas had not once been fulfilled. Their retention had led only to official malfeasance. Now, thanks to the war, "the land lay everywhere fallow and deserted." It would be no great departure from precedent if, following the end of hostilities, the provincial executives having jurisdiction were allowed to reduce the land assessment quotas. Shortages in the provincial budget could be made up by permitting local governments to appropriate the revenues from such commercial imposts (*shang-shui*) as were now being levied in Shanghai.[115]

On the surface Yin's plea must have seemed reasonable enough, notwithstanding the somewhat novel use of commercial imposts. The imperial edict, noting the memorial's disposition, proposed no immediate action on tax reform, but ventured that Yin's recommendations were "not without value."[116] Had the throne the benefit of Yin Chao-yung's own recent experience in Shanghai, however, it might have reconsidered the verdict. During the last days of October 1861, a few days before he had appended his name to a letter beseeching Tseng Kuo-fan to rescue the beleaguered people of Kiangnan, Yin had crossed behind Taiping lines to visit his stepmother's tomb to the south of Soochow. To his astonishment, as he reports in his diary, he had found the nearby countryside, at least as far south as the Chekiang border, relatively undisturbed by the Taiping occupation. Even the family gravesite was in order.[117] Why then was Yin so anxious the following spring to impress upon Prince Kung the "fallow and deserted" condition of the farms in the Shanghai hinterland?

The answer was not to become apparent until almost a year later. On June 8 and June 11, 1863, P'an Tsu-in and Ting Shou-ch'ang presented the prince counsellor with petitions for a one-third reduction of the tribute rice quotas of five of the most heavily assessed prefectures of Kiangsu and Chekiang provinces.[118] An immediate announcement of tax relief, both men argued,

115. *Ch'ing shih-kao, hsia*, p. 1390.

116. For a summary by a critic of the orthodox position against regular market imposts other than those collected through state monopolies, see Feng Kuei-fen, *Chiao-pin-lu k'ang-i*, pt. 1. p. 26. For the imperial rescript, see *Ch'ing shih-kao, hsia*, p. 1390.

117. Yin Chao-yung, *Yin P'u-ching nien-p'u*, pp. 41b–42b. For more on the condition of the southern and southeastern suburbs of Soochow, see Yang Yin-ch'uan, *Yeh-yen lu* [Chronicle of wild smoke], in *T'ai-p'ing t'ien-kuo shih-liao*, II, 175–177; and Ho-ch'iao chü-shih, *Sheng-ch'uan pai-sheng*, II, 183.

118. Hsia Nai, "Ch'ang-chiang ko-sheng chih t'ien-fu wen-t'i," p. 454. Most of Hsia's data are cited from the archives of the Kiangsu Tax Reduction Bureau (*Chiang-su sheng chien-fu tsung-chü*). Ironically, it was P'an Tsu-in, and not Li Hung-chang (or Feng Kuei-fen), who was popularly credited with having secured imperial approval for the quota reduction. See

would be instrumental in regaining the loyalties of the Kiangnan peasantry and might well hasten the expulsion of the Taipings from the area. A few weeks later yet a third exhortation for tribute rice reform came into the hands of the government, this bearing the name of the Kiangsu governor, Li Hung-chang, though its actual authors were Feng Kuei-fen and Kuo Sung-t'ao. Comparing the havoc wrought by the callous long-hairs upon the recently recaptured Sung-chiang prefecture to that visited upon the same area by the Chin tartars in 1130, the supplicants warned ominously that "if Sung-chiang and T'ai-ts'ang, already recaptured, have been thus dismally ravaged, one can imagine the condition of Soochow, still in rebel hands."[119]

Presumably convinced of the need for immediate action, Prince Kung ordered the news of the Board of Revenue's acquiescence to the petition, as well as an announcement of interim suspension of all land taxes for two years, to be relayed to Shanghai by military courier. Li received the notification on July 24, apparently simultaneously with instructions for an advance upon Soochow.[120] On July 28 a well-armed flotilla under the command of Charles Gordon drove the Taipings from T'ung-li *chen*, the primary marketing town for the rich agricultural area directly south of the provincial capital. In the next few days of fighting, the rebel garrison occupying Soochow was cut off from reinforcement from the south, and all of the paddy land in the eastern and southern suburbs (Yuan-ho, Wu-chiang, and Chen-tse districts) passed into loyalist hands, free of tax claims until 1865.[121]

Satisfied for the moment with this initial success, Li Hung-chang did not attempt the recapture of his provincial seat until the following autumn. In the interim he had other more pressing problems to attend to, notably the question of how to raise additional subsidies for the final drive on Nanking, now not very far off. Also, funds had to be found for rehabilitation and refugee relief projects in the areas already restored to government control. Fortunately Li's gentry allies had an answer for both of these difficulties. Now that a paring down of the tribute rice quota had been promised, and popular enthusiasm for the dynasty regained, surely there could be little adverse reaction if a committee of Yuan-ho gentrymen were empowered to collect a small donation (*tsu-chüan*) from their tenants. If Li would agree to give the committee authority to punish the inevitable troublemaker or two who refused payment, and to mediate title disputes in the affected area, the committee would in turn volunteer two-thirds of all receipts to help offset logistics and reconstruction expenses, keeping but one-third for distribution among the actual owners of the taxed property. Understandably Li agreed,

Ts'ang-lang-tiao-t'u (anon.), *Chieh-yü huei lu* [Recollections of a survivor], in *T'ai-p'ing t'ien-kuo shih-liao*, II, 149.

119. For a summary of the contents of the various memorials, see Wright, *The Last Stand of Chinese Conservatism*, p. 165. For Feng's remarks, see *HCTC*, 9:5.

120. Wright, *The Last Stand of Chinese Conservatism*, p. 165; Hsia Nai, "T'ai-p'ing t'ien-kuo ch'ien-hou Ch'ang-chiang ko-sheng chih t'ien-fu wen-t'i," p. 460.

121. Jen Yu-wen, *T'ai-p'ing t'ien-kuo*, pt. 3, pp. 2137–2138.

and in the two years that followed, the Yuan-ho Rent Bureau (*shou-tsu chü*) 收租局
contributed more than a million taels to Li's war chest, and an equally impressive amount to local philanthropies.[122]

The self-proclaimed architect of this happy strategem was an otherwise
undistinguished scholar of Yuan-ho ancestry named Wu Pao-shu (1832–
1890), whose principal motivation seems to have been to gain a measure of
relief for the multitude of impoverished landowners, himself included, whose
land had been sequestered or abandoned during the Taiping occupation.[123]
But behind Wu Pao-shu's plan can be discerned the play of more powerful
local influences, including that of Wu's kinsman, the ubiquitous Wu Yun.
According to the latter's own account, it was upon Wu Yun's advice that
Feng Kuei-fen and Kuo Sung-t'ao had decided to press Li Hung-chang for
an early disposition of the quota reduction initiative.[124] Feng's retrospective
description of the circumstances surrounding Wu's intervention is revealing.

One day early in 1863 Kuo Sung-t'ao had called upon Wu Yun to solicit
an opinion concerning the feasibility of a plan to impose "registration" fees
upon the squatters occupying alluvial land in the Yangtze estuary. Wu had
rejected the plan out of hand as being too likely to provoke popular unrest,
and had promptly shifted the conversation to the matter of tax reduction, a
matter in which Kuo, as tribute rice comptroller, had some say. Perhaps
annoyed at the old man's importunity, Kuo had countered that no action
could be taken on the reduction proposal until Soochow was back in government hands, and that Tseng Kuo-fan had recently stipulated that Li Hung-
chang was not to move upon Soochow until Tseng had readied his forces for
a coordinated assault upon Nanking. It was, in fact, in the hope of expediting
Tseng's preparations that Kuo was now engaged in his hunt for hitherto
untapped sources of revenue. Tax reform was, after all, a sensitive issue, and
Tseng Kuo-fan preferred to confront the highly conservative Board of Revenue with the *fait accompli* of surcharge reduction, rather than follow Feng's
scheme for a frontal assault upon the quota question.[125]

But Wu had not been deterred by Kuo's explanation. Elaborating his own
reasons for seeking a rapid settlement of the tax question, he analogized the
government's position on quota reduction to that of a refugee landlord on
rent reform. Once matters had returned to normal, the force of inertia would
most likely be sufficient to prevent any further changes. What was important
was that the status quo be adjusted before normal revenue flows resumed.[126]

Here was an argument well calculated to appeal to Kuo's passion for fiscal

122. T'ao Hsu, *Tsu-ho*, p. 12; Yü Yueh, *Ch'un-tsai-t'ang tsa-wen* [Random prose from Ch'un-
tsai hall], pt. 6, 3:14.
123. Ibid.
124. *HCTC*, Wu Yun's preface, pp. 3a–b; Wu Yun, *Liang-lei hsuan ch'ih-tu*, 5:14b.
125. *HCTC*, 4:3b; Kuo T'ing-i, *Kuo Sung-t'ao hsien-sheng nien-p'u* [A biography of Kuo
Sung-t'ao] (Taipei, 1971), pp. 235–239, entries for TC 2/3/29 and 2/3/21 (May 6 and May
8, 1863), including citations from Wu Yun, *Liang-lei hsuan ch'ih-tu*, 5:12–18.
126. *HCTC*, 4:8b.

efficiency. If, as Kuo himself had been by now persuaded, quota reduction was a valid reform to seek, the question of apportioning the discount among the district rate-payers could not be tabled until regular bureaucratic control had been restored. No matter how well intentioned, the local magistrate in normal times was certain to be cowed by the disruptive potential of the same ancient conspiracy of junior gentry and junior official interests that had undermined fiscal administration in the prewar period. The consequences of this intimidation for the state's fiscal health during the antebellum decades was too well known to require elucidation. To permit the benefits of quota reduction to be corrupted from below (*chung-yung*) would not only defeat the purpose of the reform itself, but would provoke a drain of resources altogether intolerable at a moment when, as Feng's earlier memorial had observed, military expenditures were so enormous and Peking's food supplies were running so dangerously low. Moreover, tax rebates would not be the only subject of local controversy in the years ahead. Some action on the long postponed question of surcharge reform was obviously imminent. And new tax registers would have to be prepared *in extenso*, most of the prewar rolls having been lost or destroyed during the spring of 1860.[127]

In the eyes of its original sponsors, in other words, the Kiangnan tax reform package of 1863 was but one in a series of measures designed to achieve a more efficient transfer of resources from civilian to military hands. As such, its success was predicated on the formal cooperation of a politically cohesive gentry coalition. This imperative notwithstanding, there existed at the time nothing like a consensus of opinion regarding the extent to which such collaboration deserved formal recognition, and still less one concerning the question of the desirability of its prolongation. Indeed expectations differed almost as much in 1865 as during the days of the first experiments with militia bureaus and gentry assessments, if only because the future of the Yangtze military infrastructure created to deal with the Taipings was in itself problematic once the Yangtze provinces had finally been cleared of rebel forces.[128]

In contrast to his earlier ideal of government by a self-elected gentry magistracy,[129] Feng had evidently become reconciled by 1865 to the notion of gentry oligarchy within a framework of superficial bureaucratic control. Concession on the matter of appearances was, however, by no means synonymous for Feng with defeat. If he or his confreres had been so naive as to imagine that the Yuan-ho Rent Bureau would be perpetuated as an omni-

---

127. For Feng's remarks on military expenditures and the supply crisis in Peking, see *HCTC*, 9:5b. For the loss of the tax rolls and land registers in 1860, see Yao Kuang-fa, *Sung-chiang-fu hsu chih* [Revised gazetteer of Sung-chiang prefecture] (Hua-t'ing, 1883), 13:24; memorial of Li Hung-chang, as cited in Li Wen-chih, *Chin-tai nung-yeh*, I, 162.

128. Kenneth E. Folsom, *Friends, Guests, and Colleagues* (Berkeley and Los Angeles: University of California Press, 1968), pp. 89–93, contains an account of the political uncertainties that surrounded the inception of Li's Huai campaign.

129. Feng Kuei-fen, *Chiao-pin-lu k'ang-i*, pp. 13–15b.

competent and permanent nest of gentry self-rule, they must indeed have been disappointed. Indeed, the Yuan-ho Bureau was formally authorized only to collect a yearly assessment from tenants equal to half their normal rent obligations, and to initiate disciplinary proceedings against those who resisted the new levy.[130] By contrast, at least until 1865 disputes over property rights were handled through the semi-official Reconstruction and Relief Commission (*shan-hou fu-hsu chü*); compilation of new tax registers through a network of census bureaus (*yü-t'u chü*), administered largely by *pao-chia* functionaries; and planning of the details of tax reform by a bureaucrat-dominated Tax Reduction Bureau (*chien-fu chü*).[131]

減 賦 局

Mitigating these apparent setbacks, however, were a number of subtler political considerations. One of these had to do with the rather unusual nature of local government responsibilities and resources in the immediate aftermath of pacification. Coaxing philanthropic subscriptions from the impoverished gentrymen just back from three years of marginal existence in Shanghai was obviously out of the question. For the immediate present, the rent bureau arrangement was probably sufficient. But as far back as 1860, Feng had foreseen the need for a gentry-directed rationalization of local welfare facilities.[132] During his last year in Shanghai, in fact, Feng had already launched this venture by marrying one of his sons (Fang-chih) to the daughter of a fellow refugee known to have amassed a fortune as purchasing agent for the Taipings, and now extremely eager to buy his way back into the good grace of the authorities.[133] By the time Li Hung-chang was ready for his march inland, Feng had already wheedled a comptroller's post on the newly created Reconstruction and Relief Commission for his new in-law (Wang Heng-ch'ien), while at the same time insuring that two veterans of his Shanghai diplomatic secretariat (one of them, predictably, a P'an) held positions in the tax reduction commission.[134] Reinforced by his own and P'an family influence in the directorate of the reconstituted (i.e., gentry-controlled) public granary,[135] these moves gave Feng by 1865 a very nearly uniform control over welfare functions in the Soochow vicinity. This circumstance tended, of course, to strengthen the bargaining position of the gentry coalition in the following year, when flooding in northern Kiangsu sent hordes of refugees streaming across the Yangtze in search of food and lodging.[136]

130. T'ao Hsu, *Tsu-ho*, p. 12.

131. For the first, see Ho-ch'iao chü-shih, *Sheng-ch'uan pai-sheng*, II, 193, For the compilation of new tax rolls, see *HCTC*, 5:61 ff; and Kojima Yoshio, "Shinmatsu no kyōson tōchi ni tsuite" [On rural control in the late Ch'ing], *Shichō* [Historical investigations] 88:18. For the Tax Reduction Bureau, see Hsia Nai, "T'ai-p'ing tien-kuo ch'ien-hou Ch'ang-chiang ko-sheng chih t'ien-fu wen-t'i," p. 460.

132. Feng Kuei-fen, *Chiao-pin-lu k'ang-i*, pp. 91–92b.

133. Ho-ch'iao chü-shih, *Sheng-ch'uan pai-sheng*, II, 179–206 passim.

134. *HCTC*, 4:116–12, and 8:14; *Su-chou fu-chih*, 107:33b–34.

135. P'an Tsun-ch'i, *Chang-Yuan-Wu feng-pei i-ts'ang*, chüan 1, *shang*, pp. 1, 6, 10, *hsia*, p. 13, provides materials on the role of Feng and P'an Tsun-ch'i in the public granary directorate.

136. Yü Yueh, *Ch'un-tsai-t'ang tsa-wen*, pt. 6, 3:14.

But perhaps even more telling than this hegemony over welfare institutions was a factor singled out by T'ao Hsu in the work quoted at the outset of this essay. The Yuan-ho Rent Bureau did not, of course, outlast the two year moratorium on regular land tax collection promised by the throne in July 1863; and its contribution to local philanthropies was, T'ao conceded, enormous.

> But the fact of the matter was that [the architects of the plan] had been motivated chiefly by the fear that they would not be able to collect more than a small amount of the rents owed to them. . . . [Even after the bureau was discontinued], they now had the authority of the government behind them when rent collecting season came around. In the bringing of charges against defaulting tenants, and the collection of back rents, the landlord was now no longer required to go through the expensive process of formal litigation. And government agents could henceforth be mobilized [for debt collection] without the landlord having to apply each time for a warrant.[137]

In theory, there was nothing to prevent Li Hung-chang and his successors from rescinding the extraordinary privileges that had been granted, once conditions had stabilized. In practice, however, Li Hung-chang continued, until 1868, to have military obligations to discharge, and was accordingly in no position to chance gentry-inspired breakdowns in the flow of provincial revenues. Much as Wu Yun had foreseen, the need to keep funds moving put considerable limits on what even the most idealistic of Kiangsu's provincial intendants could do to reverse the encroachments of the Soochow patriciate.[138]

137. T'ao Hsu, *Tsu-ho*, p. 12. For one instance of the *shou-tsu chü's* funds being used for welfare work, see *Su-chou fu-chih*, 11:25b–26.

138. Wright, in *The Last Stand of Chinese Conservatism*, pp. 141, 166, has singled out Ting Jih-ch'ang (1823–1882; governor, 1867–1870) as the exemplar of bureaucratic idealism in Restoration Soochow, as indeed has Feng Kuei-fen himself in *Meng-nai shih-kao* [Poetic drafts of Meng-nai] (Soochow, 1875), pp. 34b ff. The choice is no doubt apt, since the only other incumbent to pit himself against the will of the Soochow patriciate during the T'ung-chih period was harried out of office and into a coffin within scarcely more than a year of his appointment as Kiangsu governor. For Feng's confrontation with Liu Hsun-kao (incumbent 1865–1866), see *HCTC*, 5:10–20. But it is by no means clear from the record that Ting actually viewed the concept of gentry oligarchy as itself the source of the inequities of which his complaints were so stirring. See Ting Jih-ch'ang, *Fu-Wu kung-tu* [Official documents while governor of Kiangsu] (Tientsin, 1877). Mere privileges vis-à-vis commoner households at assessment time was never the aim of Feng or his associates. Rather, the structural routinization of their political influence in provincial fiscal administration and treaty-port diplomacy—on terms circumventing the vagaries of Manchu despotism as well as Hanlin fanaticism—was the most consistent motivational element in Soochow gentry activity in the postwar years. Moreover, Ting, like his sponsor Li Hung-chang, was above all a specialist in logistics administration. Whatever his sentiments might have been concerning social justice, his role in Kiangsu province was, from the start (1863), bound up with the management of the Kiangnan Arsenal and the diplomacy upon which its success depended. See K. C. Liu, "The Confucian as Patriot and Pragmatist," p. 32. Seen from this angle, Feng's correspondence with

The exact nature of the compact that ushered in the 1863 reforms was, in sum, by no means entirely clear to all the interested parties, even by the time the reforms themselves had become history. As "un-Confucian" as Li Hung-chang's methods might have been, his position nevertheless depended, particularly after 1870, largely on his ability to control bureaucratic patronage. Conversely, however broad the arena in which the Soochow gentry were active in the post-1863 period, the preservation of the system of local, cliquish control that had brought them safely through the last years of the Taiping disorders continued to be a major preoccupation. Clashes were thus unavoidable. Yet both parties had much to gain from cooperation, and much to lose from protracted confrontation. An eventual accommodation was therefore as much a likelihood as the flare-ups that preceded it. How this accommodation was reached remains almost as obscure as the terms upon which it was founded. Given the importance of the problem, however, a hasty presentation of the few clues at hand would seem preferable to a bleak enjoinder for further research. Once again, therefore, our discussion must resume the anecdotal format with which it began.

AFTERMATH

Two episodes in particular appear to be most suggestive of the issues involved in the rapprochement we have postulated. The first survives in the diary of Yin Chao-yung (1805–1883), who will be remembered as one of Li Hung-chang's more outspoken lobbyists in 1862. Not surprisingly, Yin's enthusiasm for the Huai Army's commander did not long outlast the end of the Taiping legions. In the spring of 1865, provoked by a disagreement with Li on the subject of the tribute rice surcharge, Yin presented the throne with a memorial calling for the termination of likin collection in Kiangsu province.[139] From the timing of this first assault, it would appear that the impulse behind it was largely vindictive. But as the years went by and likin retrenchment continued to be postponed, Yin's position gradually assumed a note of genuine concern for the rural economy of his native province. Most likely this concern derived from an awareness of the deteriorating condition of the cocoon raising industry in the Shanghai hinterland. Hurt by neglect and excessive taxation under the Taiping occupation, the raw silk trade in Soochow and adjoining prefectures in northern Chekiang had been prevented from making a recovery by the especially stiff assessments imposed on "Huchow" thread between its place of origin and the Shanghai wharves.[140] By

Ting (c. 1870) suggests that the latter was no more capable than Li Hung-chang of defying the Soochow oligarchy as a matter of political principle. See Feng Kuei-fen, *Meng-nai shih-kao*, pp. 346 ff.

139. Yin Chao-yung, *Yin P'u-ching nien-p'u*, p. 54.

140. For the slacking of silk production in the Shanghai hinterland during the postwar period, see Wu Yun, *Liang-lei hsuan ch'ih-tu*, 5:24b, 6:33; and Wang Yeh-chien, "The Impact of the Taiping Rebellion," pp. 137–138.

the end of the 1860s, foreign and Chinese buyers alike were often bypassing Soochow's famous silk markets to do their purchasing in Nanking, where sales and transit taxes were lower.[141] In 1868, with the Nien Rebellion at last crushed, Yin and a co-provincial named Wang Hsien-ch'eng accordingly stepped up their efforts at likin curtailment. This time they were more successful, at least in enlisting Peking's verbal support for reductions.[142]

But the victory was short-lived. In October 1872, Yin paid a call upon a friend living in a town north of Tientsin. The friend was not at home, and so the task of entertaining fell to the family tutor, who happened to be ignorant of the caller's name, but well informed about the latest developments in Kiangsu. "The likin problem is back with us again, isn't it?" he led off amiably. "Last time, of course, there was this fellow Yin Chao-yung to help us out with a memorial or two. But lately he seems to have disappeared."[143] Though a hasty introduction soon cleared up the question of Yin's whereabouts, the puzzle of his post-1870 reticence on the likin issue cannot be so simply resolved. At stake were considerations which emerge in the second episode.

In August of 1888, a Soochow official named Wu Ta-ch'eng (1835–1902) was ordered to quit his post as governor of Kwangtung province, and to make his way posthaste to Chi-ning in Shantung, where he was to serve as acting director-general of river conservancy. The reason for Wu's hurried reappointment was the disastrous flood that had resulted from the Yellow River's overflowing its banks at Cheng-chou (Honan) the previous year. Inspired partly by Feng Kuei-fen, Wu had developed an early interest in hydraulic management problems. Until success at the metropolitan examinations removed him to the capital in 1867, he had, according to Wu Yun, been the most knowledgeable man in the Soochow area on the subject of local drainage and irrigation facilities.[144] Given the urgency of the situation, his transfer to the Honan-Shantung conservancy post was long overdue.

Reaching Chi-ning later that autumn, Wu at once took over the difficult work of restoring the errant Yellow River to its northern course. A few months later the project was completed, and Wu duly took his place among the ranks of the great river tamers. But his efforts produced only a temporary improvement in the situation. Although the river did not again overflow at

141. See Kiangsu Provincial Museum, comp., *Chiang-su sheng Ming-Ch'ing i-lai pei-k'o tzu-liao hsuan-chi* [Selected inscription materials from Kiangsu province during the Ming, Ch'ing, and republican periods] (Peking, 1959), pp. 462–464.

142. Yin Chao-yung, *Yin P'u-ching nien-p'u*, p. 61; *Su-chou fu-chih*, 101:16; Wright, *The Last Stand of Chinese Conservatism*, p. 169. Evidence that some reduction in likin taxation was achieved in Soochow by 1873 appears in *Chiang-su sheng pei-k'o tzu-liao hsuan-chi*, p. 16. It should be noted that the reduction was not very great (approximately 20 percent) and came nearly a decade after Li Hung-chang had promised to reduce the rates in the Soochow area by 30 percent. See Spector, *Li Hung-chang*, p. 97.

143. Yin Chao-yung, *Yin P'u-ching nien-p'u*, p. 69b.

144. Hsiao I-shan, *Ch'ing-tai t'ung-shih*, V, 254; Wu Yun, *Liang-lei hsuan ch'ih-tu*, 4:9b; Samuel Chu, *Reformer in Modern China* (New York: Columbia University Press, 1965), pp. 144–145.

Cheng-chou, almost yearly flooding in the vicinity of its estuary continued to bedevil the peasants of Shantung; and not a few of the desperate refugees who first raised the standard of the Boxers in 1898 appear to have been victims of a particularly catastrophic rupture of the river's dikes near Tung-a (Shantung) in the summer of that year.[145]

In point of fact, the problem of the Yellow River's increasing disruptiveness simply defied solution under the prevailing system of river conservancy, according to which, in the hyperbole of the contemporary novelist Liu O, the authorities regarded the squandering of huge sums for intermittent emergency repairs more "economical" than a systematic attempt at coming to grips with the problem of the river's "new" course.[146] As Liu was later to point out, the key to the success of the conservancy scheme operative in the early part of the century was the provision for a deep and fast-moving channel to carry the loess-clogged waters of the river beyond the coastal flats (because of the accumulation of sediment actually upland of the North China plain) and into the sea.[147] Since the 1852 northward migration of the Yellow River, however, such a channel had been lacking, and plans to create one foundered repeatedly over the question of the size of the initial outlay required for a relocation of the embankments.[148] With this history of government dilatoriness very much in mind, a group of officials had actually proposed that the 1887 catastrophe be made the occasion for abandoning the Shantung channel altogether, and that the funds earmarked for repairing the dikes at Cheng-chou be used instead for refurbishing the "old" riverbed, which debouched along the north Kiangsu coastline.[149]

To be sure, the restoration of the Kiangsu embankments would have been an expensive venture—though less expensive, in all likelihood, than the repairs effected by Wu in 1888.[150] Decades of disuse had reduced the old

145. Muramatsu Yūji, "The Boxers of 1898–1899," *Annals of the Hitotsubashi Academy* 3.2: 257–258.

146. Liu O, *Chih-ho wu-shuo* [Five essays on river conservancy] (1889), p. 12.

147. Ibid., p. 6b.

148. Liu O himself believed that the northern channel could be adequately improved for as little as 2.7 million taels, a rather trivial sum in comparison with the "tens of millions" regularly absorbed by the Huai embankments earlier in the century. See ibid., p. 14; and *HCTC*, 12:23b. What Liu's plan overlooked was that the Board of Revenue of the Kuang-hsu period no longer had the authority to appropriate even such a reasonable outlay without first consulting the affected provincial administrators—a requirement which effectively blocked all initiative, given the intense competition for revenues between the self-strengtheners and the central government. For an example of this kind of consultation and its predictably negative outcome, see Chao Chung-fu, *Weng T'ung-ho jih-chi*, 3:1116, entry for KHS 7/6/23. As far as I have been able to discover, the only significant effort undertaken during this period to improve the Yellow River's channel (Sheng Hsuan-huai's dredging of the Hsiao-ch'ing River) was financed by private subscription and accounted for a mere 700,000 taels. See Albert Feuerwerker, *China's Early Industrialization: Sheng Hsuan-huai and Mandarin Enterprise* (Cambridge: Harvard University Press, 1958), p. 64.

149. Chao Chung-fu, *Weng T'ung-ho jih-chi*, 3:1506, 1516, entries for KHS 13/9/25 and 13/11/25.

150. By using cement in place of the traditional stone, and by strict supervision of his work force, Wu managed to complete the repairs at a cost of approximately three million taels, or

dikes to a very poor condition, and they would have to be patched extensively. But the old course, which had carried the Yellow River's waters to the sea in confluence with the relatively cleaner but more sluggish current of the Huai, had several distinct advantages over the newer, northern one. The first was that, if properly maintained, it gave both rivers a fast-moving and relatively sediment-free passageway to the sea, something which neither enjoyed under the present arrangement. The second was that, thanks to the scouring effect of an accelerated Huai current, the cost of maintaining the Grand Canal could again be brought within reasonable limits, and the inland waterway system could be made available to increased traffic.[151]

Himself a competent hydraulic engineer, Wu Ta-ch'eng must have realized the validity of his critics' opinions. But as an experienced Peiyang bureaucrat,[152] Wu must have known also that the southern channel plan had been ruled out nearly two decades earlier, and that the decision was not likely to be reconsidered. Doubtless he was also aware of the identity of the man whose arguments had crushed the southern channel scheme: none other than the late Feng Kuei-fen.

The superiority of the Huai outlet had not escaped the notice of all the restoration's leaders. In 1867 Tseng Kuo-fan had put forward a detailed blueprint for reviving the southern course, including plans for its financing through a canal transport surcharge (ho-yun chin-t'ieh) to be levied on the tribute-rice provinces.[153] Undecided on whether or not to attempt the re-dredging of the old channel, the government had eventually referred the

about half the original estimate supplied by the Honan governor, Ni Wen-wei. See Ku T'ing-lung, Wu K'o-chai hsien-sheng nien-p'u [Biography of Mr. Wu K'o-chai], Yen-ching hsueh-pao [Yen-ching monograph series] no. 10, p. 168, as cited from Wu's telegram to Li Hung-chang, KHS 14/8/20; and Chao Chung-fu, Weng T'ung-ho jih-chi, 2:1504, entry for KHS 13/9/11. By contrast, Tseng Kuo-fan had estimated the cost of repairing the Huai (Kiangsu) channel at a bit more than one million taels. See his Tseng Wen-cheng kung ch'üan-chi [The complete works of Tseng Kuo-fan] (1876 ed., Shanghai, 1917), tsou-kao [draft memorial] 26:3 (memorial dated TC 6/7/29).

151. For the congested condition of the eastern extremities of the northern channel, see Liu O, Lao-ts'an yu-chi ch'üan-pien [Complete edition of Lao Ts'an's Travels] (Taipei, 1972), p. 161. For that of the "old" Huai channel (between Ch'ing-k'ou and the East China Sea), see Samuel Chu, Reformer in Modern China, p. 148. Since the reversion of the Yellow River to the Shantung channel, the Huai had ceased to have access to the sea, and had become a tributary of the Yangtze. For the use of the Huai to maintain the Grand Canal, see Chu Ch'i, Chung-kuo yun-ho, cited from Ch'ing-shih kao, Ho-ch'ü chih, chüan 2, Yun-ho, abstract from memorial of P'an Hsi-en.

152. For Wu Ta-ch'eng as a protege of the Peiyang establishment, see Chih Wei-ch'eng, Ch'ing-tai p'u-hsueh ta-shih lieh-chuan, pp. 515–516. In this connection it is interesting to note that, reflecting a pattern common to many successful bureaucratic careers in the late Ch'ing period, Wu began his service in Tientsin in 1870 with considerable misgivings about the policies of his superior, Li Hung-chang. See Chao Chung-fu, Weng T'ung-ho jih-chi, 2:564, entry for TC 9/9/5.

153. Wright, The Last Stand of Chinese Conservatism, p. 162. Apparently Li's opinion was not solicited, or at least not offered in final form until the summer of 1873. See Li Hung-chang, Li Wen-chung kung ch'üan-chi [The complete works of Li Hung-chang] (Nanking, 1908), tsou-kao [draft memorial] 22:9 (memorial dated TC 12/intercalary 6/3).

decision to Li Hung-chang, whose interests as commander-in-chief of the Huai Army were obviously affected.

The news of Li's consultation concerning the southern channel project had aroused Feng Kuei-fen to immediate action. In a long and eloquent letter to his former associate, Feng had spelled out the reasons for his violent opposition to the proposed scheme. To begin with, Feng had explained, the ultimate purpose of the "old channel" lobbyists was the reinstatement of the canal transport system of the prewar years. To Feng that purpose was an unworthy one, not only because it threatened to be ruinously expensive, but because it was technically unsound, and would inevitably complicate tribute rice logistics.

> In recent years, river conservancy has been consistently entangled with tribute rice administration. In this way harm has been done to both. . . . Whether or not the Yellow River is restored to its old channel, the eastern extremities of the Huai network will never afford a draft sufficient to carry [more than half of the tribute rice]. No matter how much effort is made [to improve the dikes], I fear that eventually we shall revert to the present system of "river conservancy for the sake of river conservancy; tribute rice administration for the sake of tribute rice administration." Matters will improve only once it is realized that the point of river conservancy is merely to prevent floods.[154]

But more than administrative logic lay behind Feng's antagonism to the "mixing of water and rice," as he put it. In a second letter on the same problem (this one to Tseng Kuo-fan), Feng attacked the other major argument of the "southern channel school": that the stream of incidental revenues generated by increased traffic on the Grand Canal would act as an economic stimulus for the badly depressed and war-ravaged Huai region. This was hardly likely, Feng asserted. Much more likely was that the greater part of the transit revenues would go to line the pockets of corrupt waterway officials, as they had before 1850. The northern provinces would probably reap little benefit from the plan. But it was a certainty that the southeast (i.e., Kiangsu and Chekiang) would suffer through increased surcharge assessment. Even without the added burden of canal transport costs, the Kiangsu landowner was paying at present a fleet money (pang-fei) surcharge of over one thousand cash for every picul of "quota" tribute rice assessed. Reviving inland waterway shipment would be certain to drive that surcharge up to its prewar level of six thousand cash per picul.[155]

154. *HCTC*, 5:59
155. *HCTC*, 5:60a-b. That Feng's position represented a regional and not merely personal perspective is confirmed by the equally loud trumpetings against the southern channel alternative sounded by Weng T'ung-ho and P'an Tsu-in during the debates that followed the rupture of the Cheng-chou dikes in 1887. See Ko Shih-hsun, comp., supplement to the *HC-CSWP* (Shanghai, 1898), 91:6.

Li Hung-chang was not likely to have missed the point. In 1865 he had provoked the anger of the Soochow gentry by attempting to collect a two thousand cash surcharge.[156] Feng had, of course, abided by his promise not to make difficulties over the tribute rice settlement.[157] But Feng's associate, Yin Chao-yung, had not been so well behaved, and the latter's slashing attacks on Li's fiscal policies had been very nearly disastrous.[158] If anything, Li was now even more vulnerable to attack than in 1865, since a sizable portion of the "fleet money" fund was being used to meet Huai Army expenses. The prisoner of his purse strings, Li had no alternative but to veto the southern-course proposal.[159]

But Li Hung-chang was not the only high official preoccupied with the Kiangsu surcharge rates in the late 1860s. In the spring of 1868, the Nanking governor-general, Tseng Kuo-fan, sent out an infuriated directive to the Soochow prefect ordering an immediate investigation into reports that local magistrates under his jurisdiction were again collecting an unauthorized land tax surcharge. Although the immediate cause of Tseng's intervention was the complaint of a French missionary about church property being assessed to finance the rebuilding of a local Confucian shrine, the peevish tone of Tseng's circular suggests his concerns were more than diplomatic. Not very long ago, Tseng noted tersely, he had specifically commanded that all such land donations (*mu-chüan*) and rent donations (*tsu-chüan*) be prohibited. Upon what excuse, then, had the magistrates in question seen fit to proceed with the collection of the new surcharge?[160]

The answer Tseng received could not have much improved his temper. According to the prefect's report, the shrine assessment (*wen-miao kung-fei ch'ien*) had originally been proposed by the gentry managers of the Soochow public granary. Magisterial cooperation had been gained only after the granary commissioners reported themselves unable to collect the levy without the law enforcement services of the local government.[161]

The theme was a familiar one to restoration administrators. For the past few years, gentry activists like Feng Kuei-fen had been using the pretext of surcharge collection to meddle ever more boldly in local judicial and police practices. Sub-magisterial personnel were now regularly taking bribes to

156. For Li's confrontation with the Soochow gentry in 1865, see *HCTC*, 4:11b–12; Yin Chao-yung, *Yin P'u-ching nien-p'u*, p. 54; Hsia Nai, "Ch'ang-chiang ko-sheng chih t'ien-fu wen-t'i," pp. 464–466; Spector, *Li Hung-chang*, p. 114, cited from Li Hung-chang, *Li Wen-chung kung ch'üan-chi, tsou-kao* [draft memorial], 9:1–7.

157. *HCTC*, 4:11b.

158. Yin Chao-yung, *Yin P'u-ching nien-p'u*, p. 54.

159. For the influence of Feng's arguments in persuading Li to take a negative attitude with regard to the southern-channel position, see Li Hung-chang, *Mu-chih ming* [Epitaph for Feng Kuei-fen], p. 3b, in *HCTC*, introductory chüan; and Li's 1873 memorial in Li Hung-chang, *Li Wen-chung kung ch'üan-chi, tsou-kao* [draft memorial], 22:9.

160. P'an Tsun-ch'i, *Ch'ang-Yuan-Wu feng-pei i-ts'ang*, 5:17–18b.

161. Ibid., 5:18b.

short-circuit the legal system at the market-town level.[162] The benefits of
"gentry" government, most significantly, a curtailment of magisterial and
clerical corruption, were being offset by a visible slackening in the morale of
the primary producer, occasioned (as T'ao Hsu later complained) by the
facility with which landlords could now shift their financial obligations onto
the shoulders of the tenant farmer.[163] As a committed physiocrat,[164] Tseng
could not but be appalled at a state of affairs in which the costs of local
government had come to be extracted directly from rural rents. Yet in thus
challenging the activities of the Soochow directorate, he was ironically
helping to dispose gentry opinion more favorably toward a development
equally distasteful to him.

Upon assuming office at Soochow early in 1871, Governor Chang Chih-
wan found himself under considerable pressure to expedite the dredging of
several key waterways in the vicinity of the provincial capital, last repaired
in the Tao-kuang period under the supervision of T'ao Chu and Lin Tse-
hsu. Evidently reluctant to entrust his gentry associates with the task of raising
the necessary funds, Chang decided instead to implement a plan endorsed
by Wu Yun and the former chief of the Shanghai Joint Defense Bureau, Ying
Pao-shih.[165] Having first coordinated his appeal with a memorial provided
by a high ranking local gentryman then active in Peking, Chang asked for
and received Board of Revenue authorization to divert a portion of the receipts of the Soochow likin bureau for the dredging of the Woosung River.[166]
From 1871 to 1873, over one hundred thousand taels of local likin revenues
went to finance hydraulic projects in the Soochow vicinity.[167] But that was
not all. In the same year that the Woosung project was initiated, the Soochow authorities acceded to the request of Feng Fang-chih and agreed to
allocate a tenth part of the locally collected tea donation (ch'a-chüan) as a
regular subsidy for a local reformatory.[168] By the end of the nineteenth
century, most of Soochow's public foundations were on the likin payroll,
including even the "ever-abundant" public granary.[169] In Wu Yun's native

162. Ting Jih-ch'ang, Fu-Wu kung-tu, 8:3a–b, 9:8b–10. For a specific instance at Kuang-
fu chen, one of the sites of operation of the Feng bursary, see Chiang-su sheng-li [Kiangsu provincial statutes], 2nd ser. (Shanghai: Chiang-su shu-chü, 1875), TC 12, Judicial Commissioner's Statutes, "Tso-tsa hsun-pien pu-chun shan-shou min-tz'u."

163. T'ao Hsu, Tsu-ho, p. 19b.

164. Ibid., p. 25a-b.

165. For the projects organized by T'ao and Lin, see T'ao Chu, T'ao Wen-i kung ch'üan-chi
[The complete works of T'ao Chu] (Yangchow, 1840), 28:8–11; Lin Tse-hsu, Lin Won-chung
kung ch'üan-chi [The complete works of Lin Tse-hsu] (Taipei, 1963), 1:3b; and Lin Tse-hsu,
Lin Wen-chung kung, chüan 3. For the role of Wu Yun and Ying Pao-shih in the 1871 operations, see Wu Yun, Liang-lei hsuan ch'ih-tu, 6:19 ff, and 7:28.

166. The "high-ranking local gentryman" was Chung P'ei-fu, a Landsmann of Wu's, at the
time serving as subchancellor of the Grand Secretariat (rank 2b). See Wu Yen, Liang-lei
hsuan ch'ih-tu, 7:28. For the likin appropriations, see Su-chou fu-chih, 11:27.

167. Ibid., 11:27–28b.

168. WHC, 30:9.

169. WHC, 30:9–13; Wu Ta-ken, Ch'ang-Yuan-Wu feng-pei i-ts'ang ch'üan-an hsu pien [Com-

Huchow (Chekiang), even educational expenses were covered by 1870 with a regular donation from local silk merchants, though Wu himself had once shared Yin Chao-yung's misgivings about the wisdom of commercial imposts being prolonged into the postwar period.[170] Thus isolated from the trend of the times, there was little that Yin Chao-yung could hope to accomplish by continued resistance.

Returning, then, to the question which these fragments were intended to help us answer, perhaps the most appropriate verdict would be that the quasi-conspiratorial terms of Li Hung-chang's initial pact with the Soochow gentry proved too convenient to both parties to be renounced upon the return of normalcy. In the eyes of some of its architects, at least, the T'ung-chih "restoration" was not designed to resuscitate the *ancien régime*. Rather, it was covertly intended to be the first step toward dismantling the old order, in conformity with the desires of a political constituency *narrower* than that active before the Taiping period. Seizing upon the evidence with which its master was most familiar, T'ao Hsu's jaundiced eye naturally picked out the irregularities of the 1863 tax reforms as most symptomatic of the flagrant hypocrisy of the age. But other charges might have been pressed with equal persuasiveness, for many of Feng Kuei-fen's other designs for dynastic regeneration betrayed a similarly conspiratorial and cliquish intent, however disinterested the language in which they were couched. Just what sort of limitations Feng's intrigues implied for "self-strengtheners" such as Li Hung-chang remains, of course, an open question. But surely the patent insufficiency of Professor Wright's portrait of the age should in itself encourage us to consider the possibility that these limitations were considerable. For if the agrarian policy of the restoration was, in Professor Wright's words, "epitomized in the reduction of the Kiangsu land tax,"[171] one can only marvel that there was a restoration at all.

---

plete archives of the Ch'ang-chou/Yuan-ho/Wu-*hsien* ever-abundant relief granary], 2nd ser. (Soochow, 1898), audits for KHS 8–9 (1882–1883).

170. For Fu's anti-likin stance in the early 1860s, see Wu Yun, *Liang-lei hsuan ch'ih-tu*, 5:24 7:1b. His approval of Yin Chao-yung's remonstrances against continuing the tax into the postwar period is recorded in ibid., 5:1. For the use of likin revenues to meet educational and examination expenses in Chekiang, see ibid., 6:10a-b.

171. Wright, *The Last Stand of Chinese Conservatism*, p. 164.

Local Self-Government
Under the Republic

PROBLEMS OF CONTROL, AUTONOMY, AND MOBILIZATION[1]

Philip A. Kuhn

For Chinese who lived through the republican period, the mention of local self-government (*ti-fang tzu-chih*) is an occasion for cynical smiles; and with 地方 自治 good reason. Local self-government was invariably connected with political programs that promised more than they delivered. It was a universally discussed component of twentieth-century political theory; but in practice was associated with all the evils of the age: the arbitrary exercise of power by rapacious local elites and petty functionaries; the ambitions of provincial warlords; and the preachments of a political party that promised democracy but delivered dictatorship.

Our own view of this subject must be conditioned by two mental operations. First we shall have to dissociate the historical reality of local self-government from the heterogeneous body of ideas that became attached to it, particularly that of political democracy. The roots of the theory had little to do with democracy, and the importance of the local self-government concept in twentieth-century political thought can only be appreciated if we refrain from judging it by an irrelevant standard. Second, our assessment of this theme in republican political history requires a more self-conscious view of the republican period as a whole. The republic was begun by one revolution and ended by another. This abrupt demarcation from the surrounding historical context has fostered a certain unconscious assumption that the institutional history of the republican years is somehow irrelevant to the really important questions we should be asking, whether about the decline of traditional Chinese society or about the origins of present-day China.

1. The generous assistance of the American Council of Learned Societies made possible the research for this study.

But recent trends of research have widened the context in which the great changes of modern Chinese history are presumed to have occurred: the mutation of political forms in the late Ch'ing period and the unabated revolutionary process in the People's Republic have both tended to reduce the significance of 1911 and 1949 as lines of historical demarcation. Accordingly the institutions of the republic will take their place in a continuum of change; for these institutions represented attempts to solve fundamental political and social problems which both preceded and outlasted the republic itself. In this respect local self-government can be seen as an attempt to cope with a set of internal conditions which were inherited from Ch'ing times and which in some respects persist today. Though local self-government can be considered something of a blind alley in China's political evolution, the techniques and assumptions that underlie it form vital components of the larger process whereby the relations between China's local society and government have been modernized.

CONTROL, AUTONOMY, AND MOBILIZATION

The central analytic categories in this study are obviously not unique to the Chinese case. Control here represents the efforts of the state bureaucracy to secure its share of society's resources and to insure that its conception of social order is maintained. By autonomy I mean not independence from the larger polity in any sovereign sense, but rather the ability of a social unit to govern certain spheres of its internal affairs according to its own procedures and using its own people. Mobilization I shall discuss later. In late imperial China local control was of necessity intimately linked to institutions in which no bureaucratic personnel took part and which were essentially autonomous in their internal affairs. The lowest link of the regular bureaucratic system was the county (*hsien*) seat; and below it local government largely depended on enlisting the energies of local people and organizations for attaining state purposes and carrying out state functions. The basic administrative problem was how to achieve effective taxation and internal security within a given limit of bureaucratic density. This is not the place to tackle the question of why China's bureaucratic density was restricted to the particular value it had reached in late imperial times, though that problem must ultimately face any student of Chinese government. But the net result was that the line of cleavage between state and society ran through the county yamen. The magistrate was an outsider imposed upon local society: selected, evaluated, and rotated by powers exogenous to the local scene. But the control requirements of the state dictated that his control reach somehow into village society. To accomplish its purposes, therefore, the state had to draw local people into its service. Thereby was established the characteristic interaction between state control and local autonomy that marked the government of Ch'ing China. The control–autonomy interaction operated through three principal channels: the formation of decimal hierarchies, the penetration of indigenous social groups, and the delegation of powers to the local elite. In none of these enterprises was autonomy permitted to remain a mere residual category of social action, a designation of those areas of life not directly controlled by the bureaucracy. Instead, a positive value was placed upon local people doing "necessary" tasks for themselves, as an essential adjunct to bureaucracy. For if local administration were to function, it was not enough that the people submit; they also had to act.

Decimal hierarchies known as *li-chia* (taxing) and *pao-chia* (police and census) were channels through which the state attempted to use local people for local administrative jobs. These systems posed delicate problems. Their headmen had to have sufficient community standing for effective action, yet not so much influence as to be uncontrollable by county authorities. The fact that the degree-holding elite ordinarily played no part in such decimal systems meant that the headmen had little social weight or political leverage. As an ordinary commoner, a *pao-chia* or *li-chia* headman might be beaten at the magistrate's pleasure; he stood in a distinctly disadvantageous position in relation to the real power structure of his community. That is certainly one reason these systems were generally weak in Ch'ing times. Their weakness makes it hard to take seriously the claim by early twentieth-century proponents of local self-government that China had been operating "self-government" for centuries in the form of such decimal systems.[2]

Nevertheless, the idea that such sub-county control systems somehow represented self-government, as opposed to a purely bureaucratic imposition from above, seems somewhat less spurious when we consider the close and continuing interaction between decimal hierarchies and the natural divisions of Chinese society such as village, intervillage association, lineage, and market community. Bureaucratic units might spring from natural ones or might realign themselves to conform to natural ones.[3] The realities of the local scene dictated that administrators often had to rely on indigenous forms of coordination as the basis for their control systems if those systems were to stand any chance of performing their functions. Thus to base a *pao-chia* unit on a natural village rather than on a group of 100 households was in one sense to admit that local society could not be satisfactorily bureaucratized. Yet, seen in another way, it was a method of enlisting indigenous social organs in the task of local control in hopes that they might further official purposes. It was this interaction between natural and bureaucratic units of coordination that produced the characteristic ambiguity of sub-county administrative systems: the principles of control and autonomy were not entirely separable, either in theory or in practice.

2. "Chung-kuo ti-fang tzu-chih-chih k'ao" [China's local self-government system], *Tung-fang tsa-chih* [Eastern miscellany] 4.10:429–440.

3. See Philip A. Kuhn, *Rebellion and Its Enemies in Late Imperial China: Militarization and Social Structure, 1796–1864* (Cambridge: Harvard University Press, 1970), pp. 93–96.

The lineage furnishes another example of this situation. In areas where many lineages were large and wealthy (principally in the south and southeast, but also to some extent in central China), they commonly formed the backbone of villages and multivillage associations. Through income from common property, a rich lineage could afford its members such vital services as education and local defense. Its ritual links and intergenerational cohesion made the lineage a natural node of social solidarity, an autonomous local unit of formidable powers. It was the state's policy in Ch'ing times to try to use the lineages for its own purposes. This it sought to do by identifying itself with the principles of kinship obligation and generational obedience on which the lineages themselves depended, and generalizing them into a vigorous ideological campaign. The lineage, it was hoped, would thereby become a bastion of conservative social doctrine and a major element in the system of local control. Besides ideological cooptation, the state attempted to penetrate the lineage more directly by making it an adjunct to the *pao-chia* system. Special posts called lineage headman (*tsu-cheng*) were created in areas where lineages were important, in hopes of capitalizing on existing frameworks of social cohesion and authority. This was another way of using local people for state tasks in sub-county administration.[4]

The effort to bring control and autonomy into a mutually supportive relationship was largely dependent on how well the local elite could be made amenable to state purposes. With a social identity as both a community leader and a participant in a political-academic system that transcended particular communities, the local degree-holder was in a complex position. His role was simultaneously one of furthering local interests and of maintaining the larger political system upon which his own formal prerogatives rested. Thus he was both an object and an agent of control. As agent, he was counted on to perform services that were essential to the economic and political stability of local society: supervising public works, famine relief, dispute resolution, and local defense. As object, he was a man who could use his considerable local influence in opposition to the state, either in his own or in his community's interest. In no other area, perhaps, was the success of local government as dependent on a fruitful relationship between control and autonomy. And to the extent that such a relationship existed, it was largely because of the elite's own view of itself as a group belonging to both a small and a large community, as native sons as well as members of a nationwide governing class.

The resulting interdependence of control and autonomy in the minds of the literati can be illustrated by the evolution of the *hsiang-yueh* (local covenant), a system in which the two principles tended historically to merge. Long before it became a formal instrument of state indoctrination in Ch'ing times,

---

4. See the discussion in Maurice Freedman, *Chinese Lineage and Society: Fukien and Kwangtung* (London: Athlone Press, 1966), p. 80–81.

the local covenant was proposed as a genuinely autonomous association for promoting good behavior in the villages. Chu Hsi's influential redaction of Lü Ta-chün's eleventh-century *hsiang-yueh* proposals envisaged the rectification of village life through group criticism sessions under the supervision of a locally-selected headman. Both public and private behavior were covered by the provisions of the *yueh*, or covenant, to which members of the community were voluntarily to pledge adherence. Self-cultivation, social conduct, dispute resolution, generational deference, and basic community functions such as poor relief, health care, and local defense were included in the covenant; and in all this, scarcely a reference to officialdom.[5]

In one sense this system can be seen as machinery for implementing Neo-Confucian moral revivalism. Yet it was also linked to desiderata of political control and social stability. The connection between the autonomous regulation of group mores and the maintenance of the imperial political system is suggested by the subsequent history of *hsiang-yueh*, in which the autonomous covenant became explicitly identified with the control apparatus of *pao-chia*. The sixteenth-century scholar-official Lü K'un proposed a version of *hsiang-yueh* in which the covenant was treated as an aspect of the *pao-chia* police and mutual surveillance system. Both were to be organized on the same decimal units ("administered as a single whip"—*i-t'iao-pien*). Thereby "litigation will naturally diminish; tax collection will naturally be fulfilled; paperwork will naturally become more economical. Exhorting to good conduct and punishing evil conduct are basically complementary. Thus *hsiang-yueh* and *pao-chia* are basically not two different things."[6] Chu Hsi's vision of *hsiang-yueh* had made no reference whatever to decimal systems of control; it relied wholly on natural settlement patterns and the initiative of indigenous leadership. Yet I suggest that Lü K'un's connection of *hsiang-yueh* and *pao-chia* may not have deviated substantially from the real spirit of Chu Hsi's prescriptions. It simply made explicit what Chu had left implicit: that local autonomy could not be considered apart from the general problem of control, and that the only way to achieve a system of control on the sub-county level was to enlist the efforts of the villagers themselves in administering it.

LOCAL REFORMISM AND THE FENG-CHIEN TRADITION

I have suggested ways in which the principles of control and autonomy, while in constant tension, yet remained closely interdependent in the local governance of imperial China. The trouble with this formulation, in brief, was that it did not work. That is, in the view of many among the reformist

5. Chu Hsi, *Tseng-sun Lü-shih hsiang-yueh* [Edited version of Mr. Lü's *hsiang-yueh* proposals] in Shen Chieh-fu, ed., *Yu-ch'un lu* [Texts whereby may be sought unspoiled simplicity] (Ming Wan-li ed.), 1:1–7b.

6. Lü K'un, "Shih-cheng Lu" [On making government effective] in *Ch'ü-wei-chai ch'üan-chi* [Collected works from the Expunge-error Studio] (1827 ed.), 3:5, 5:2b.

elite, it did not produce decent government for rural China. Control and autonomy could not play their complementary roles in local government because of certain institutional weaknesses of the bureaucratic system. The major difficulty was the outsider–insider relationship at the county level. The magistrate's role as outsider was supposed to preclude the dispersion of power, since there would always be a built-in tension between him and the county elite. The rule of avoidance, whereby no man might hold office within a designated distance of his home or in areas where certain of his kin were serving, formed the bedrock of imperial control in Ch'ing times. Locked into his controlling function, certain of imminent transfer, the magistrate might easily grow heedless of the welfare of those under his jurisdiction. The magistracy inevitably led most ordinary men toward irresponsibility, sloth, and rapacity. If the county were to remain bureaucratically detached from the magistrate's personal concerns, it could hardly engender the urge toward good government.

As for the sub-county control apparatus, although the clerks of the county offices were insiders, they could be effectively disciplined neither by bureaucratic accountability (since they did not have regular bureaucratic status) nor by any intimate and regular relationship to the natural units of local society. Hence they formed in effect a local interest group oriented solely toward its own enrichment. And the decimal-group headmen were too lowly in social status to exercise the kind of authority that would be needed to extend an infrastructure of effective government to the village level. In all, those elements of the state which could wield effective authority—the magistrate and his immediate underlings—seemed sometimes like a man-made plague, a disaster hitting society from the outside; more often destructive than protective, more often exploitative than supportive. As for the local elite, the vacuum of effective bureaucratic authority below the county level did not necessarily mean that society's natural leaders would govern local communities in the public interest rather than in their own. Advocates of the *feng-chien* (feudal decentralization of authority) approach sought a solution to these problems through fusing the control and autonomy principles in a new way: by denying certain social and psychological postulates of the imperial bureaucratic system. Control had somehow to emerge from the body of local society itself, rather than impinge upon it from outside.

The controversy between advocates of *feng-chien* and *chün-hsien* (bureaucratic centralization) was already at least a millenium old by the time of the Ch'ing conquest.[7] For imperial governments, as for the scholar-elite, the central question had generally been which system could contribute most toward the longevity and stability of dynastic regimes. By late Ming times,

---

7. For a historical resumé of this question, see Yang Lien-sheng, "Ming Local Administration," in Charles O. Hucker, ed., *Chinese Government in Ming Times* (New York: Columbia University Press, 1969), pp. 1–21.

however, two further considerations had emerged: the legitimacy of the imperial monarchy itself; and the corruption and ineffectiveness of local government. It is the latter that will concern us here.

Like so many aspects of Ch'ing thought, a discussion of this question must begin with Ku Yen-wu (1613–1682). The outlines of Ku's prescriptions for the reform of local government are generally well-known: his proposals for inheritable magistracies, his conviction that stable government required a greater density of officials at the bottom of the hierarchy than at the top, and his concern to bridle the undisciplined county clerkdom. My particular concerns here are the assumptions underlying his critical assessment of the quality of local government and his treatment of the principles of control and autonomy. It was characteristic of Ku's hard-headed approach to politics and history to forswear any return to the imagined glories of a golden "feudal" age. The *chün-hsien* system of centralized imperial bureaucracy had replaced feudalism because the political and social realities of late antiquity required that it do so.[8] But the realities of the late imperial age—his own day—ordained that the centralized monarchy, in its turn, become fundamentally transformed in some way if Chinese society were to survive.

What these realities were does not appear explicitly in Ku's nine-part treatise, "On Centralized Bureaucracy" (*Chün-hsien lun*). Their symptoms appear, however, as the inability of the bureaucratic system to maintain order or insure an adequate standard of living. Ku's formulations are perceptive hints about a general socio-political problem, phrased in terms of a specific administrative dilemma: how can you achieve decent local government in a situation where the very structure of the bureaucracy seems to militate against effectiveness and honesty on the part of local administrators? (Had this structural problem always existed within the *chün-hsien* system? And if not, what were the peculiar conditions of late Ming–early Ch'ing society that brought it forth?) The structural problem Ku was referring to—and this is really the core of the *feng-chien* argument—was reducible to a psychological one. The magistrate's role as outsider, enforced by the rule of avoidance, naturally gave him the wrong attitude toward his job. The security obsession of the monarchy meant that the separation between a magistrate and the society under his charge was too abrupt, with inevitable effects on the way he behaved. Far from engendering feelings of concern and responsibility, the avoidance system generated callous disregard. Instead of cherishing his subjects, he exploited or neglected them. What was needed was a system that would enlist the natural feelings of a man toward that which is his—his family, his property—instead of stifling and repressing such feelings. This was to be the role of certain aspects of the old feudal system: the granting of permanent and hereditary rights to a magistrate who, after a period of

---

8. Ku Yen-wu, "Chün-hsien lun" [On the prefectural system], pt. 1, pp. 1–2. in *Ku Yen-wu wen* [Ku Yen-wu's prose writings] (Shanghai: Commercial Press, 1934).

probation, performed his job well. With his ties to local society affirmed and his own future assured, all his energies would be turned to promoting the economic welfare and political security of his county.[9]

This stress on the ultimate social value of natural human feelings, and the determination to turn them to collective ends, seem to belong within that stream of Ch'ing thought, represented most prominently by Tai Chen (1724–1777), which saw in orthodox Neo-Confucianism a certain self-defeating repression of human nature. Ku's symbolic use of *feng-chien* (meaning, in essence, those aspects of the feudal system that exemplified the positive effects of a link between private property and political power) was a political expression of the same anti-dualistic impulses that Tai later expressed more abstractly in respect to the human personality. Ku's proposal of heritable magistracies meant abandoning the idea that local government could be reformed through such petty structural expedients as more rigorous codes or more elaborate control mechanisms. Instead, the solution was to achieve a new relationship between control and autonomy by infusing the autonomy principle into the very bones of local administration. Ku's faith in the ultimate collective benefits to be gained from the workings of enlightened self-interest in politics stands at the core of his effort to reorient the psychology of Chinese government.

Note that Ku Yen-wu and his followers envisioned, not a return to political decentralization, but rather an infusion into the centralized state of certain "feudal" principles. Ku belonged to what the Korean scholar Min Tu-gi perceives as a dominant mainstream group of *feng-chien* advocates who sought an accommodation between centralized and decentralized models of the state.[10] The centralized monarchy would remain; Ku thought it would even be strengthened by the introduction of hereditary county posts. His *feng-chien* proposals were not conceived in support of local autonomy for its own sake, but rather as a guarantee of stability and prosperity within the monarchic structure. Indeed the supreme authority of the monarch was indispensable to Ku's system, for it was through the monarchy that the myriad private interests throughout the empire would somehow be transformed into the public interest, as represented by the monarch himself. The sum of enlightened magisterial self-interests was only expressible as a collective phenomenon (and thereby made public rather than private) in the person of the ruler.[11] The musings of Ch'ing thinkers about *feng-chien* never lost sight

9. Ibid., pt. 5, pp. 7–9.

10. Min Tu-gi, "Ch'öngdae pongkon ron ui kundae jok pyonmo: Ch'öngmal chipang chach'i ron u ro ui kyongsa rul chungsim u ro" [The modernization of the *feng-chien* theory of local self-government in the late Ch'ing], with English summary, *Asea yon'gu* [Journal of Asiatic studies] 10:62. This important monograph has opened up the whole subject of the character of Ch'ing *feng-chien* theories and their relationship to the development of constitutionalism.

11. In Ku Yen-wu's expression: "Use the private interests of all within the empire to produce the public interest of one man [i.e., the emperor]." Ku Yen-wu, "Chün-hsien lun," pt. 5, p. 8.

of the larger collectivity. Local autonomy remained dependent on the principle of control, albeit in a new way; and beyond control, it was dependent on the survival of the unified Chinese state. This fact should be borne in mind as we approach the problem of how *feng-chien* theory was linked to the political concerns of the late Ch'ing period.

The pivotal figure in the adaptation of traditional political theory to modern conditions was Feng Kuei-fen (1809–1874), the Soochow magnate whose role in Kiangnan politics has been discussed by James Polachek in this volume. Feng's interest here lies particularly in his application of Ku Yen-wu's variety of *feng-chien* thinking to the problems of local government in his own time. Nobody has yet proven that he actually achieved a conceptual link between traditional reformist thought and Western ideas of representative government. That was the task of the succeeding generation. Unfortunately we have no conclusive evidence as to the extent of Feng's acquaintance with Western ideas. By his own account, his reform essays of 1862 "unsystematically included some barbarian ideas" (*ch'an-i i-shuo*); yet as he correctly points out, every proposal in them can reasonably be deduced from China's own traditions of political reformism.[12]

Feng was an early proponent of the *t'i-yung* idea of grafting Western technology onto Chinese values (and a reminder that *t'i* need not be conservative!). His essays suggest that what China had to learn from the West was limited to mathematics, science, and engineering.[13] At this point we can but speculate that his exposure to what passed for Western culture in Shanghai made him aware of the rudiments of Western liberal and constitutional ideas—ideas which, in a context of Western technological superiority and military power, excited resonances with his own *feng-chien* inheritance. But this remains still wholly unproven. The fact that Feng's essays were later drawn upon by much more explicit proponents of Western-style constitutionalism should not obscure the fact that his theoretical inheritance was entirely capable of generating the kind of solutions he offered for the reshaping of local government.

Feng, like his revered master of the early Ch'ing, was concerned to mitigate the effects of the rule of avoidance in county government. Like Ku, he believed that the constraints of a man's own integrity and self-respect (*tzu-ai tzu-chung*) would be ample guarantee against misconduct in office, were he serving in his home area; for the most fearsome criticism would be from his own kinsmen and neighbors. The rule of avoidance he saw as essentially a Ming–Ch'ing phenomenon, one which had gravely damaged local government. Though his prescription did not extend to hereditary magistracies, he urged the advantages of drawing local officials from within a reasonable

12. Feng Kuei-fen, *Chiao-pin-lu k'ang-i* [Essays of protest from Feng Kuei-fen's studio] (Taipei: Wen-hai ch'u-pan she, 1967), p. iii.

13. Feng Kuei-fen, "Ts'ai hsi-hsueh i" [Proposal to adopt Western learning], in *Chiao-pin-lu k'ang-i*, pp. 67–70.

distance of their native areas and posting them irrespective of family connections.[14] But his most distinctive offering was a new system of sub-county
officials.[15]

Like others of the *feng-chien* persuasion, Feng considered it axiomatic that
a magistrate was incapable of governing a county effectively, given the size of
the jurisdiction and the conditions (including the rule of avoidance) under
which he worked. A new sub-county infrastructure was required. Feng's
solution was a two-layered system beneath the magistrate and his immediate
assistants, of which all the functionaries were to be drawn from the locality.
At the lower rungs was a modified *pao-chia* system in which headmen of 100
and 1,000 household groups were to be chosen by popular election using
paper ballots. These were to be below the status of lower degree-holders
(*sheng-yuan*), yet the method of their selection would presumably give them
the prestige that the old *pao-chia* headmen lacked. Though salaried, these
headmen (like their *pao-chia* predecessors) were not to be considered officials.
Their functions were to be primarily the resolution of disputes and minor
law enforcement. Above them, however, was a layer of true minor officials.
Each in charge of 5,000 households, these *hsun-chien* or sub-district heads
were to be appointed from among lower degree-holders who had demonstrated
competence as members of regular officials' staffs. They were to be local
people (from within thirty to fifty miles, though not necessarily of that county)
and were apparently to have appellate jurisdiction and more substantial law
enforcement powers.

Feng thought it impossible that a network of true officials (full-time,
salaried functionaries appointed through bureaucratic channels) could be
extended to the village level. Though ancient codes such as the utopian
Rites of Chou were much admired for the fineness of their control networks, the
population density of Ch'ing times meant that such fineness could never be
achieved on a bureaucratic basis. Yet somehow the vacuum of control at the
village level had to be filled. Feng's solution was to install part-time officers,
essentially nonprofessional (like *pao-chia* functionaries), but to insure their
intimate connection to the real power structure of local society by having
them elected. And the next layer up, though actually within the official
system, would be able to function effectively within rural society by virtue of
its local origins. Though less so than the elected decimal headmen, they would
still be insiders, rather than outsiders superimposed upon local society by the
state. The whole proposal rested upon the idea that enlisting the energies and
community consciousness of local people in government was the only way to
make local government effective.

The historical significance of Feng's outlook can be appreciated only by

14. Feng Kuei-fen, "Mien hui-pi i" [Proposal to abolish the rule of avoidance], in *Chiao-
pin-lu k'ang-i*, pp. 6–7.
15. Feng Kuei-fen, "Fu hsiang-chih i" [Proposal for a restoration of local offices], in
Chiao-pin-lu k'ang-i, pp. 10–12b.

examining the social circumstances surrounding it. His period is rightly assumed to be one of power devolution from the official system into the hands of the local elite, as James Polachek has demonstrated with respect to Feng's own Kiangnan region. Yet it is doubtful whether Feng Kuei-fen's prescriptions for the reform of local government were really an unalloyed justification of gentry oligarchy. The underlying message in Feng's "Proposal for a Restoration of Local Offices" (*Fu hsiang-chih i*), with respect to the actual conditions of his native area, was that the system of gentry-managers was an unacceptable innovation in local government. Feng points out that the network of local power-wielders that had grown out of the militarization of the rebellion years was in certain ways superior to the old *pao-chia* system. The managers (*tung*) were of formal elite status, and thus (though not actually officials) were "near to officialdom" and could accordingly exercise some influence over local affairs. But his own proposals quite clearly would do away with the gentry-manager system in favor of a more highly bureaucratized and codified system of local rule. Feng was concerned to gather up dispersed power, to regularize and control it, not to celebrate its dispersal.

This does not exactly mean that Feng was in effect siding with the bureaucracy against the devolution of power into elite hands. He was an exponent of what we have come to call the "statecraft" approach to administrative reform. Though we have yet to see a systematic study of statecraft as a political-social-intellectual phenomenon, I suggest that neither statecraft, nor men like Feng Kuei-fen, can be understood without careful study of the competition for power and status within the scholar-elite. A fixture of the upper elite himself, Feng seems to have had little use for the petty power-brokers and local bullies who filled gentry-manager posts in the countryside. Urbanized, rich in official connections, a man like Feng had nothing to gain from accretions of power and wealth at the gentry-manager level. He was instead concerned to consolidate the power of urbanized rentiers like himself, whose close official connections and elaborate rent collection machinery placed them well above the sordid hustle in the market towns and villages. The solution to rural disorder and tenant unpredictability was not less control from the cities, but more control, on the basis of close collaboration between the upper elite and local bureaucrats.

Feng's prescriptions for a new kind of control–autonomy alignment in village government were entirely consistent with this kind of thinking. His efforts were to control local power by making it public rather than private—a favorite maxim of *feng-chien* theorists. Local energies were to be enlisted in rural government, but only in ways compatible with the control of the countryside by the city. Here are palpable resonances with Jerry Dennerline's "local bureaucratic elite" of late Ming and early Ch'ing times.[16] Reformers of this type were concerned to maintain the power of the imperial

16. See the article in this volume by Jerry Dennerline, "Fiscal Reform and Local Control: The Gentry–Bureaucratic Alliance Survives the Conquest."

state, which was in turn the firmest guarantee of their own position. To do this, they were quite prepared to sacrifice the interests of other branches of the elite who did not partake in their official connections. Writers in the *feng-chien* tradition certainly wanted to promote the power of local people to solve their own local problems. But this was not to be the unchecked, informal power of local elites, for local elites might themselves become predatory, disorderly, and a threat to the bureaucratic elite. In this concern, the *feng-chien* and statecraft outlooks seem to overlap.

The bursary system, so important to the economic position of Feng and others like him in late Ch'ing times, was an expression of this close collaboration between officialdom and one segment of the elite. It should not be forgotten that the bursary system, in one aspect, was a mechanism for making sure that landlords were able to pay their taxes—by insuring that their rents were paid. As a way of preserving the agrarian system and at the same time serving the state, it was in its own way a typical statecraft phenomenon.[17] For such a system to work, it was essential that local order be preserved and that rural resources not be siphoned off by local middlemen before they could reach the rentier stratum in the urban centers. And to this end the interests of rural gentry-manager types were expendable. Thus Feng's adaptation of Ku Yen-wu's *feng-chien* proposals meant, in essence, that the system that perpetuated the unchecked exercise of power by petty local elites—the system of avoidance, thin local infrastructure, and weak bonds between city and countryside—had to go.

LOCAL SELF-GOVERNMENT AND CONSTITUTIONALISM

It is time now to discuss in preliminary fashion our third theme, mobilization, and to suggest its relationship to the other two. I have pointed out that control and autonomy were intimately related in Ch'ing local government, as the bureaucracy sought to enlist the services of natural local groups for its own purposes. This system was not overwhelmingly successful, perhaps in part because it was vitiated by the social conditions of late imperial times in ways that we do not yet fully understand. Reformist political programs therefore sought to alter the control–autonomy relationship, either through new control schemes to bring the activities of local elites into line with state requirements; or, as in the *feng-chien* tradition, to relate the control and autonomy principles in new ways. Feng Kuei-fen can be seen as a representa-

17. It seems apparent, for instance, that the kind of *pao-lan* (engrossment of tax-paying functions) practiced by big landlord bursaries (such as the Wu bursary described by Muramatsu Yūji) was of quite a different character, from the point of view of officialdom, from that of the petty tax engrossers whose misdeeds punctuate nineteenth-century documents. Muramatsu Yūji, *Kindai Kōnan no sosan: Chūgoku jinushi seido no kenkyū* [Landlord bursaries of the lower Yangtze delta region in recent times: studies of the Chinese landlord system] (Tokyo: Kindai Chūgoku kenkyū iinkai, 1970), pp. 681–747.

tive of both approaches. But the requirements of the new age, dimly perceptible to Feng but abundantly clear to his successors, were to render both these reformist approaches inadequate. The modernizing nation requires, not the maintenance of a stable social and economic system, but rather the promotion of economic growth, national power, and the new relationships between governors and governed that new technologies and new political theories have made possible. Local energies have to be enlisted in a new way: one which will call forth the required amount of willing involvement, and at the same time weld local energies into national programs. New techniques are required to generate—and discipline—the higher intensities of local political energy required for a modern nation. Those techniques, and the public responses they engender, are what I mean by "mobilization."

Now it is apparent that the relationship between control and autonomy— that is, the dynamic interplay between bureaucratic organs and natural local units of action—is substantially transformed in a context of mobilization. Somehow individuals and organizations must be stimulated to higher levels of activity in their own spheres of life and yet be more amenable than before to the interests of the larger society. The psychological assumption that men can be induced to fuse their own particular interests with the general collective interest if only they are given a greater stake in running their own community affairs is, as I have already suggested, an article of faith in *feng-chien* thinking. Therefore it is not surprising that the *feng-chien* outlook was an important transitional vehicle in the development of Chinese ideas about mobilization. The local self-government movement that emerged as part of late Ch'ing and early republican constitutionalism relied heavily on this kind of conceptual mediation. And in its turn, local self-government may prove to have been an important precursor of more successful mobilization techniques in Chinese local administration.

By the time Feng Kuei-fen's writings were resurrected as an inspirational text for the reform movement of 1898, a number of thinkers had already moved well beyond him toward a basic reorientation of Chinese political theory. The constitutionalist movement, spurred by Cheng Kuan-ying, Ho K'ai, Ch'en Ch'iu, and others, drew to a considerable extent upon the *feng-chien* tradition, as Min Tu-gi has pointed out.[18] The thought of the early constitutionalists was heavily influenced by such familiar themes as improving communication between the rank-and-file literati and the monarch, as expressed in traditional injunctions to open up *yen-lu* (avenues of communication). Feng Kuei-fen had also promoted ideas of this sort, but the specific importance of *yen-lu* to the building of a strong modern state became a widespread reformist assumption only after Feng's day.

An equally important development was the rapid transformation of reformist views about local government and its relationship to the national

18. Min Tu-gi, "Ch'ŏngdae pongkon ron ui kundae jok pyonmo," pp. 62–74.

polity. By the late 1890s it was already apparent that the essentials of the *feng-chien* approach—antipathy toward the avoidance system, the conviction that private ends could be transmuted into public good—were serving as vehicles for the introduction of new conceptions about economic and political development.

Apparently it was Huang Tsun-hsien (1848–1905), the Cantonese diplomat and foremost Chinese interpreter of Meiji Japan, who introduced the term self-government (*tzu-chih*) to Chinese politics. While serving as judicial commissioner in Hunan during 1897, Huang was associated with Liang Ch'i-ch'ao and T'an Ssu-t'ung in the Changsha-based Southern Study Society (Nan-hsueh hui). There his appeal was to the Hunanese local elite on grounds which seem, at first sight, quite familiar. The rule of avoidance and rapid rotation in office had made Ch'ing bureaucrats strangers to their jurisdictions and incapable of solving their problems. The prefectural (*chün-hsien*) system, which had been established to insure the public interest, in reality catered to the private interests of the predatory underlings to whom local bureaucrats entrusted the business of government. The bureaucrats themselves either ignored their subjects or exploited them. On its face, Huang's solution seems entirely appropriate to the power dispersion that had resulted from the turmoil of the rebellions. It was only the local people themselves (presumably the literate elite who attended the lectures of the Southern Study Society) who could solve their own problems by assuming responsibility for the needs of their home districts. This was not a call to replace officials, but rather to attend actively to the manifold functions that the bureaucratic system ignored.

Yet Huang was actually seeking not the dispersal of power but rather the building of nationhood. It was only a new kind of localism, based on new kinds of local activism, that could serve as a basis for a powerful and unified state. Local activism was important, not for its decentralizing effects on the political structure, but for its invigorating effects upon the individual. Entrusting essential public functions to officials had left local people deficient in will and ability, like sons and grandsons who left all vital family business in the hands of a patriarch. "What I demand of you is to govern your own persons; and to govern your own localities" (*tzu-chih ch'i shen, tzu-chih ch'i* *hsiang*). And this injunction is clearly aimed toward economic development and ultimately toward national strength. The new activism was to be directed not only at traditional elite concerns such as water control and public security, but also at the promotion of commerce and industry. From a foundation in self-governing localities, a new order could be constructed in ascending stages—from the county, to the province, to the empire as a whole. Huang's message is replete with traditional imagery. Yet we would be unjustified, I believe, in assuming that he was simply exploiting the *feng-chien* vision as a convenient rhetorical tool to achieve institutional change.

His argument suggests rather that he saw the *feng-chien* tradition as a peculiar asset to China in her struggle to achieve modern nationhood.[19]

Huang must have become acquainted with the term *tzu-chih* through his studies of Japan, which had begun during his diplomatic service in that country from 1877 to 1882. The Japanese term *jichi* (*tzu-chih*—self-government) is curiously enough a second-hand inheritance from a German borrowing of the English word "self-government." This concept was central to the constitutional thought of the Prussian legal scholar Rudolf Gneist (1816–1895), who exercised a major influence upon Yamagata Aritomo, the founder of the Japanese local self-government system.[20] In his massive treatise on the history of the English constitution, Gneist simply uses the word "self-government" without translation, thus emphasizing its unique and culturally specific nature.[21] Gneist considered the genius of the English system to lie in the infrastructure of honorary (unpaid) appointive public service posts which mediated the interests of society (the propertied classes) and the state. By appointing local notables as lords lieutenant, justices of the peace, parish tax officers, and the like, the state was able to raise these elites above their own parochial and class interests and imbue them with "practical knowledge of the state and the right feeling for it."[22] In essence, self-government was a mechanism for socializing the dominant classes, who otherwise would pursue their interests in ways incompatible with the needs of society at large, oppressing the lower orders and crippling the liberal functions of the state.

Gneist, a moderate liberal in German politics, had inherited the views of Lorenz Stein (1815–1890), who believed that the state must promote the free development of all its subjects if its own power and freedom were to flourish. Therefore social interests must be made to transcend class interests. For Gneist, self-government was the educational device by which this might be accomplished. Another consideration for Gneist (and one which appealed to his Japanese admirers) was that self-government would insulate the realm of

19. Huang Tsun-hsien's first speech at the Nan-hsueh hui (probably in 1897), reprinted in Liang Ch'i-ch'ao, *Wu-hsu cheng-pien chi* [Record of the 1898 reform movement] (Peking, 1954), pp. 138–141. I am indebted to the recent study by Amy Ma, "Japan and the Political Thought of Huang Tsun-hsien" (unpublished seminar paper, University of Chicago, 1974). A study of the Nan-hsueh hui is found in Wang Erh-min, *Wan-Ch'ing cheng-chih ssu-hsiang shih lun* [Studies in late Ch'ing political thought] (Taipei, 1969), pp. 101–133.

20. For my understanding of Gneist's role, I am mainly indebted to Richard Staubitz' excellent study, "The Establishment of the Local Government System in Meiji Japan," (unpublished M.A. paper, University of Chicago, 1969). The principal Japanese work on this subject is Kikegawa Hiroshi, *Meiji chihō seido seiritsu shi* [History of the establishment of local administration in the Meiji period] (Tokyo, 1967). On Gneist, see Munroe Smith, *A General View of European Legal History* (New York: Columbia University Press, 1967), pp. 215–255. Gneist's major work has been translated as *The History of the English Constitution*, 2 vols. (New York: G. P. Putnam, 1886).

21. Rudolf Gneist, *Geschichte und heutige Gestalt der englischen Communalverfassung, oder des Selfgovernment* (Berlin: J. Springer, 1863).

22. Gneist, *The English Constitution*, II, 438.

local administration from the disturbances of party strife, and even on the
national level would condition the governing classes to pursue the interests of
the nation in a relatively independent and nonpartisan spirit.²³ Note that
Gneist never referred to the English system as "local" self-government. The
local administration was bound into a unified national system of law (local
units exercised only administrative and not legislative powers) and was thus
inseparable from the higher functions of the state. The nexus between local
service and societal consciousness was the main point of Gneist's idealized
conception of English government. Evidently the prefix "local" (the *ti-fang*
of the phrase *ti-fang tzu-chih*) was added in Japan.

Yamagata Aritomo was exposed to Gneist's views through Gneist's student
Albert Mosse and through his own agent Ōmori Shōichi, who was sent to
Germany in 1885 and became Mosse's student. Mosse himself, invited by
Yamagata to serve as advisor in the drafting of a local self-government code,
arrived in Japan in 1886; and the resulting code was promulgated by
imperial edict in 1888. It was essential, Yamagata thought, to establish a
local self-government system before the constitution itself was implemented,
for local self-government was the bedrock of stability upon which constitutional government must rest. This conviction was primarily conditioned by
Gneist's views.²⁴ The nation's future could be made secure, argued Yamagata, only through an essentially apolitical system that could generate devotion
to national service. Such a system, which could stand unmoved amid the
turbulent eddies of party politics, would bear the nation unscathed through
the inevitable factionalism of parliamentary government.²⁵ Thus Yamagata's
conception of local self-government faithfully mirrored the strong control
and indoctrinational elements present in the Meiji oligarchs' approach to
political modernization.

It is not certain how widespread was the influence of Huang Tsun-hsien's
introduction of the *tzu-chih* concept to China in the hopeful days of 1897.
But following the political catastrophe of 1898, the popularization of *tzu-
chih* began with K'ang Yu-wei. K'ang's important treatise of 1902, "On
 Citizen Self-Government" (*Kung-min tzu-chih*), seems in some respects an
elaboration of some of the basic concepts of Huang's 1897 appeal to the
Hunan literati. Yet it is far more systematic and explicit. It is an impressive,
if at times bewildering, amalgam of *feng-chien* concepts, traditional views of
elite roles, statecraft reformism, and a thoroughly modern awareness of the
necessity of popular mobilization for national survival.²⁶

23. Munroe Smith, *European Legal History*, p. 237; Gneist, *The English Constitution*, II, 357.
24. Staubitz, "Local Government System," pp. 19–22.
25. Yamagata Aritomo, in a speech to local administrators, 1890, in Tokutomi Iichirō,
Koshaku Yamagata Aritomo den [Biography of Duke Yamagata Aritomo] (Tokyo: Yamagata
Aritomo-kō kinen jigyōkai, 1933), II, 1097–1098.
26. K'ang Yu-wei's "Kung-min tzu-chih" [On citizen self-government] occurs in *Hsin-min
ts'ung-pao* [New people's miscellany] as a three-part serialization in 1.5:37–46; 1.6:17–24;
and 1.7:27–38 (April 8, April 22, and May 8, 1902). Also see Richard C. Howard, "Japan's

At the basis of K'ang's argument lie familiar *feng-chien* themes. On the one hand, anti-avoidance: under the *chün-hsien* system, not even the most able and honest official can gain adequate control over his county or generate the feelings of sympathy necessary to govern it decently. On the other, fineness of infrastructure: the tasks of local government are far too complex to be carried out by a thin layer of officials at the county level. But it is clear that K'ang is using *feng-chien* ideas in an utterly new way: linking them first to the social-Darwinist conception that only a "fit" people can survive; and second, to the idea of economic development for national strength. The psychological assumptions of *feng-chien* thinking are turned to the task of building the psychological substructure of modern nationalism.

K'ang begins with his favorite "three ages" theory of historical development: the modern system of local self-government (*ti-fang tzu-chih*) is really no different in principle from the ancient feudal (*feng-chien*) system. But the ancient world floundered in the era of disorder (*luan-shih*), and enfeoffment of individual nobles inevitably led to civil war for private ends. The present day, by contrast, is in the era of approaching peace (*sheng-p'ing*); if you "enfeoff the masses" by allowing them self-government and participation in public debate, then the natural workings of enlightened self-interest will bring about vigorous economic development and human improvement.[27]

The key concept behind K'ang's idea of local self-government is the release of energies. In the assumption that the pursuit of private advantage will ultimately tend to produce public advantage there is a probable line of influence from the laissez-faire economists. But there is also a conscious elaboration of the psychological assumptions of the *feng-chien* school: that properly channeled, man's natural feelings and ambitions will tend toward the public good and will thereby enable control and autonomy to be combined in a new way in local government. What has been added is the dynamic ingredient of development: the mobilization of energies for open-ended economic expansion. A network of bureaucratic government by outsiders cannot but stifle the latent energies of the people; self-government cannot but release them. K'ang cites the differential in what might be called social energy output between China and the industrial nations, and lays it solely to the fact that those nations have instituted self-government, while China has not.[28]

Besides releasing their energies, self-government would have other desirable effects upon the people. K'ang poses the basic antithesis of surrogate government (*tai-chih*—rule by officials in place of the people) and self-government. Only the latter can generate advances in learning, mechanical skills, mental acuity, and hardening of the will. Self-government is therefore prerequisite

Role in the Reform Program of K'ang Yu-wei," in Lo Jung-pang, ed., *K'ang Yu-wei: A Biography and a Symposium* (Tucson: University of Arizona Press, 1967), pp. 280–312.

27. K'ang Yu-wei, "Kung-min tzu-chih," 1.7:29.

28. Ibid., 1.7:29–30.

文佳 化 to evolutionary development (*chin-hua*), the prime desideratum of national survival in the modern world. The quality of the local political infrastructure is thus closely related to both the fitness of the people and the needs of economic development. No *chün-hsien* type of infrastructure—exogenous to local society and of low density—could accomplish these modernizing tasks. However, a finer infrastructure, composed of local men, could develop such needful appurtenances of modernity as railroads, banks, and public health, along with a host of traditional functions such as registration, police, and schools. It could also provide a new kind of psychological impetus by stirring up the patriotism and enthusiasm of the locals, something the old *chün-hsien* system was quite incapable of. Thus the traditional reformist proposition that a fine net of sub-county government was the key to good administration is turned to modern ends: popular mobilization and grass-roots economic development.[29]

K'ang's scheme for achieving all this is a rather sketchily-drawn hierarchy of self-governing units, from a basic bloc of 10,000 people up through the regular divisions of county administration and above. Each level is furnished with its elected deliberative assembly, operating under the benevolent supervision of the regular officials. The assumptions, however, remain elitist in a traditional sense. The franchise is to be restricted to citizens (*kung-min*) who have paid a fee for the honor and whose "citizenship" bears unmistakable resemblances to purchased civil service degrees. Citizenship is supposed to generate, for those who hold it, ardent feelings of identification with the nation; for those who do not, healthy feelings of ambition and emulation; and for the government, a substantial revenue. Members of provincial assemblies are to be selected from among the wealthiest stratum of landlords, merchants, and industrialists, as well as from returned students, university graduates, writers, and eminent traditional-style scholars.[30]

It is hardly surprising that K'ang's views on local self-government were influenced by the actual conditions of that segment of local society with which he was most familiar: the Canton delta region. Here, he felt, already existed the main elements of local self-government, in the gentry-led associations that had grown out of the civil warfare of the 1850s. In the delta region, he wrote, some of the counties rivaled whole nations in their vast populations. How could such a county be governed by the magistrate and his few assistants? It was essential that such tasks as dispute resolution, militia defense, schools, and bridge maintenance be carried out by local people. These jobs were managed by gentry, elders, and lineage headmen working through the headquarters bureaus (*chü*) of multiplex and extended-multiplex associations (*t'uan*).[31] Elsewhere in Kwangtung the situation was similar: local

---

29. Ibid., 1.6:19–20.
30. Ibid., 1.7:37.
31. Ibid., 1.6:23. For the origin and structure of these associations, see Frederic Wakeman, Jr., *Strangers at the Gate: Social Disorder in South China, 1839–1861* (Berkeley and Los Angeles:

notables had long been in de facto charge of the multifarious business of local government. In times of trouble, these local satraps would gather and deliberate, and were thus "very similar to the parliamentary delegates of the various nations." With this well-established background, Kwangtung should obviously be the first province to try instituting regular sub-county officials and deliberative assemblies of the modern sort.[32]

But here is the unmistakable link with Feng Kuei-fen and the statecraft tradition: K'ang was far from satisfied with the local self-government he observed in his home region, for there was no way of regulating the conduct of the local elite who staffed the system. There existed no formal system of selection by popular participation, no codes to govern their actions. Thus there were "hereditary houses and powerful gentry" who kept a tight grip on authority, throwing their weight around and oppressing the people, who had no recourse. Such was the baneful heritage of a system which "honored the elite" rather than the people, a system in which lawful political authority was restricted to the county level and above, and the people had no formal role in public affairs. To set up a constitutional government was to regularize the exercise of local power, to bring it within the scope of a national system of rules rather than simply to ratify its existence. Like Feng Kuei-fen, K'ang had no use for the rapacious local headmen of the *t'uan* associations. Their private power must be controlled: not repressed, but tamed and harnessed to public purposes. If K'ang's representative system was elitist in conception, it was oriented toward the upper elite, the cosmopolitan statecraft types rather than the local bosses.[33]

It cannot be emphasized too strongly that throughout K'ang's discussion of local self-government, his foremost concern remained the nation. If China were to compete successfully among the powers, her inner structure must be drastically changed. This would inevitably involve a new relationship between local society and the national entity. Here *feng-chien* ideas were peculiarly useful. Localism, far from being a danger to the collectivity, was really essential to it. The fundamental compatibility of particular interests and the general good, a *feng-chien* axiom, was made the basis for mass involvement in politics. By harnessing such local interests within a constitutional framework, the nation could both reap the benefits of local activism (autonomy) and bring local leadership within the reach of the law (control). But under the Ch'ing system, both autonomy and control were oriented toward the relatively stable, closed world of pre-industrial society. K'ang's system sought their modern counterpart: mobilization, in which localism and private energies were stimulated and then disciplined to the service of economic development and national vigor.[34]

University of California Press, 1966); and Kuhn, *Rebellion and Its Enemies*, pp. 69–75.

32. K'ang Yu-wei, "Kung-min tzu-chih," 1.6:23–24.

33. Ibid.

34. Besides the doctrines of the laissez-faire radicals, K'ang was evidently apprised of the

LOCAL SELF-GOVERNMENT AND THE LATE CH'ING ELITE

K'ang's treatise of 1902 was the progenitor of a considerable body of literature on the subject of local self-government between 1902 and 1911. The phrase *ti-fang tzu-chih* had become something of a catchword of the constitutionalist movement by the time of the revolution; and like most other catchwords, its meaning had become broad and ill-defined. By 1911 it embraced the elements of traditional anti-autocratic thought of the Huang Tsung-hsi variety; it formed the lower scaffolding of constitutional schemes; it embodied *feng-chien* and statecraft views on the reform of local government; and it was linked to the idea of local free enterprise and the mobilization of China's natural and human resources. What it did not contain, however, was any explicitly democratic component, in the sense of a natural-rights theory of participation or a well-articulated view of popular sovereignty. For that matter, none of the preeminent goals of local self-government proponents really required a democratic theoretical basis. The development of wealth and power, the modernization of the local economy, and statecraft programs for bridling the power of local elites could all proceed very well without any basis in democratic theory. And it was essentially devoid of such a body of theory that the idea of local self-government entered twentieth-century politics.

The Ch'ing government embraced the idea of local self-government in its constitutional program of 1908, but in a highly restrictive sense. The concept of self-government embedded in the government's decrees hardly went beyond the traditional idea of leaving a category of residual functions for local elites to perform. Self-government simply performed those administrative jobs on the local level which official government (*kuan-chih*) was unable to carry out. This purely supplementary role of self-government as envisioned by official Ch'ing constitutionalism was of course entirely different in spirit from the kind of mobilizational force envisioned by K'ang Yu-wei and others; and it was certainly designed to prevent, rather than to facilitate, the formation of a genuine counterweight to the regular bureaucracy on the local level.[35] The Ch'ing model of 1908 was based in part on a local self-government scheme adopted in Tientsin in 1907, sponsored by Yuan Shih-k'ai, the Chihli governor-general. The Tientsin model called for a deliberative assembly (*i-shih hui*) and executive council (*tung-shih hui*) on the county level. On lower levels there were similar bodies in municipalities (*ch'eng*), market towns (*chen*), and rural townships (*hsiang*).[36]

organic analogies of the Spencerians, which he used to show the basic compatibility of the interests of individual and public, locality and nation (as healthy cells were necessary to a healthy body, healthy organs to a healthy brain). Ibid., 1.7:27–28.

35. The 1908 decree on local self-government can be found in *CSL*:HT, 5:35–36.

36. For the Tientsin *hsien* regulations, see *Chihli Tientsin-hsien ti-fang tzu-chih kung-chueh ts'ao-an* [Draft public regulations for local self-government in Tientsin county, Chihli province], *Tung-fang tsa-chih* [Eastern miscellany] 4.5:208–222.

The national program of 1908 set forth an overall preparatory schedule for constitutional government, in which provincial assemblies (*tzu-i-chü*) and ultimately a national parliament were to emerge after several years.[37] In January 1909 there followed specific regulations for the institution of self-government on county and sub-county levels. A flurry of election activity on the eve of the 1911 revolution produced deliberative assemblies and administrative councils in many counties, the membership of which was duly reported in local gazetteers. For purposes of this study, the activities and personnel of these county self-government bodies can be treated separately from the problem of the provincial assemblies, which John Fincher has analyzed so ably. These lower-level bodies were not conduits for the formation of provincial and national-level assemblies, but represent rather the home-rule aspect of the self-government movement. They thus fall most clearly within the problem area I outlined earlier, and I shall confine my attention to them here. It is clear, though, that as research draws us closer to an understanding of local politics in this period, an integrated multi-level analysis will be required.

The actual workings of county government during the first two decades of the twentieth century is a large subject on which research has barely begun. Among other difficulties, one is constantly confronted with the question of whether the inception of local self-government really represents the continuing devolution of power from the bureaucracy into the hands of the local elite, an old process simply dressed up with new names; or whether this is an emerging local political system of a new sort. It is natural to hypothesize that the entrenchment of gentry-managers in sub-county administrative posts was simply legitimized by local self-government codes, with new titles and functions grafted onto old power realities. There is indeed considerable evidence for this, as I have suggested elsewhere.[38] Yet to make sense of this process in the context of twentieth-century politics, we may need something more substantial than an image of self-government as a mere facade for purely traditional social realities.

A valuable article by Teraki Tokuko, based on local gazetteers from a number of areas, opens up some important questions about the status of self-government activists at the county level and the nature of their interests.[39] First, it is apparent that the deliberative and managerial bodies at the county level had a large complement of lower degree-holders (*sheng-yuan* and

---

37. See the important study of the self-government movement in this period by John Fincher, "The Chinese Self-Government Movement, 1900–1912" (Ph.D. thesis, University of Washington, 1969), especially pp. 65–114; and John Fincher, "Political Provincialism and the National Revolution," in Mary C. Wright, ed., *China in Revolution: The First Phase, 1900–1913* (New Haven: Yale University Press, 1968), pp. 185–226.

38. Kuhn, *Rebellion and Its Enemies*, pp. 219–220.

39. Teraki Tokuko, "Shin matsu minkoku shonen no chihō jichi" [Local self-government in the late Ch'ing and early republic], *Ochanomizu shigaku* [Ochanomizu University historical studies] 5:14–30.

chien-sheng), along with holders of minor purchased titles. Though we may expect that the presence of even a moderate proportion of former and expectant officials in these bodies proved a strong influence on their political orientation, the crowds of lower and purchased degree-holders was a new and significant feature of local Chinese politics.[40] It must be remembered that the *sheng-yuan–chien-sheng* stratum had never held a really influential and respected place in Ch'ing local government. On the contrary, the influence of this group was relegated in the main to informal and often illegal channels. The meddlesome role played by these lower literati was a common theme of Ch'ing official documents. Interference in litigation, influence-peddling, engrossment of tax collection (*pao-lan*) were all hallmarks of this group, a situation that grew naturally from their relegation to a marginal place in the Ch'ing economic and political system. Such a large, literate, but politically powerless group was a natural and perennial source of disorder and disaffection. The inclusion of many such people in the gentry-manager apparatus of the late nineteenth century represented a partial recognition of their capacities and influence. The local assemblies of the self-government system represented another step in the same direction. The prominence of the lower elite in the formal apparatus of local government during the period 1909–1913 is a symptom of their ambition to achieve a more prominent place in the management of county-level affairs. Though much detailed work remains to be done before we can evaluate Ichiko Chūzō's statement that the lower elite monopolized all the important posts in local self-government,[41] the significance of their breakthrough into county government during this period is incontestable. The old gentry-manager system can have satisfied the political vocations of only a minor proportion of this stratum.

Though the official sponsors of local self-government in the waning years of the dynasty really thought that the new system would bring local elites under better control through a more formal delineation of their role (purely managerial, at the sufferance of local officials and under their supervision), the actual relations between the assemblies and magistrates turned out to be quite antagonistic. The major contest was over control of finances. Though the self-government assemblies were prohibited by their charters from interfering with the regular government tax revenues, being restricted to the management of purely local fiscal affairs, yet the administrative chaos surrounding the 1911 revolution brought some self-government bodies into

40. See ibid., pp. 16–18, 22. Teraki is concerned to show the dominance of these bodies by local gentry (*hsiang-shen*), in which she lumps together former and expectant officials, degree-holders of all strata, and holders of purchased brevet rank. This may have led her to overlook one of the more interesting features of county assemblies, namely the high proportion of what we have been used to calling "lower gentry." For instance, her chart (p. 16) of membership in eleven municipal assemblies in Hupei shows 98.6 percent *hsiang-shen*, whereas the more significant figure is the proportion of lower and purchased degree-holders to known official and higher degree-holders (nearly three to one).

41. Ichiko Chūzō, "The Role of the Gentry: An Hypothesis," in Wright, *China in Revolution*, p. 302.

direct competition with the county bureaucracy over the general management of finance. And a particularly prominent target of the local elite was the customary fees (*lou-kuei*) that were an entrenched perquisite of the county clerkdom.[42] Thus the familiar struggle between the local elite and the clerk-runner group over the control of local resources was played out in the new context of self-government. But now the self-government assemblies provided a new instrument whereby the financial powers of the magistrate himself could be challenged. This challenge could not be ignored by the provincial authorities, who were having similar troubles on the provincial level, and it was soon apparent that local self-government was doomed. In 1913 a barrage of telegrams from provincial authorities spelled out the outrages of provincial and local elites working through self-government bodies: "usurping financial power, resisting both national and local taxes, meddling in litigation, impeding administration." This, declared Premier Hsiung Hsi-ling in response, was certainly not what self-government should be up to. A decree of February 3, 1914, simply abolished local self-government throughout the country.[43] This was of course only part of Yuan Shih-k'ai's larger campaign to destroy the parliamentary system.

The sequel to this episode reveals important trends of official thinking in the early republic. Later in 1914 Yuan Shih-k'ai's government in effect admitted that local government could not be left in a constitutional limbo, nor could a respectable constitutional code on the local level be completely without the trappings of self-government. The new code issued December 30, 1914, called "Experimental Regulations for Local Self-Government," envisaged a restricted form of popular participation, closely hedged about with franchise limitations and official prerogatives, based on a unit called the "self-governing ward" (*tzu-chih ch'ü*). These wards were to manage essentially the traditional categories of locally-administered activity: education, road maintenance, promotion of agriculture, plus such modern amenities as public health. Their main significance, however, is in their intended level of co-ordination. These were to be large units, four to six per county, which might easily mean a population per ward of over 50,000. This clearly distinguishes the proposed ward divisions of 1914 from the earlier version of the ward (*ch'ü*) which had emerged from the fragmented gentry-manager system of the late Ch'ing.

Preparatory steps for local self-government under the 1908–1909 regulations had sometimes been carried out by "wards" that were simply a guise of the *li-chia* or multiplex defense associations (*tu* or *t'uan*) which had been under the control of local managers since the post-rebellion decades of the late

42. Teraki Tokuko, Shin matsu minkoku shonen no chihō jichi," pp. 25–26.
43. "T'ing-pan tzu-chih chi-kuan" [Order to stop the operation of self-government organs], in Lei Chin, ed., *Chung-hua min-kuo cheng-fu kung-pao fen-lei hui-pien* [Categorized collection of material from the government gazette of the republic] (Shanghai: Sao-hua shu-fang, 1915), vol. 25, *tzu-chih*, p. 1.

nineteenth century. These old wards showed great variation in size according
to local conditions, but could be quite small in some cases. In one Kiangsu
county, for instance, there were forty such wards before the revolution, mostly settlements or small multiplex clusters. It was apparently against this kind
of fragmentation that the 1914 self-government code was aimed. It should
be understood, however, that this code was not reflected in general practice
except in Shansi (a case I shall discuss shortly), and that in most areas the old
dispersed gentry-manager type of ward remained in operation at least until
1929. What the 1914 code really represents is a trend in administrative
thought toward the formal imposition of a level of coordination between
county and villages, a level only weakly reflected in the old Ch'ing system, but
which was now a clear necessity if rural China were to be controlled, or
modernized, or both.[44]

Looking back over the self-government experience in the late Ch'ing and
early republic, it must be recognized that the effort to bridle the local elite by
formalizing its power had been a failure. The happy blending of public and
private interests envisioned by the more optimistic of the constitutionalists
had not occurred. Neither the political and military bosses of the early
republic, nor the local elites themselves, were able to envision the relationship
between central and local power in other than traditional terms, and local
self-government became enmeshed in power struggles of a traditional nature.
It seemed for a time as if the control–autonomy relationship in local government was going to be left at the point it had reached by the empire's end: a
substantial ramification of the infrastructure of sub-county government by
means of formal control of wards and ward-like units by the lower elite, but
without a workable system whereby that elite might be disciplined in the
public interest, much less brought into a system of mobilization appropriate
to a modernizing nation.

LOCAL SELF-GOVERNMENT AND ADMINISTRATIVE MODERNIZATION:
THE KUOMINTANG EXPERIENCE

The effort by Yuan Shih-k'ai and his provincial allies to curb the powers of
county elites by nullifying their self-government charters was symptomatic of

44. The 1914 ward regulations are in Lei Chin, *Chung-hua hui-pien*, vol. 25, pp. 3–9. For the
Kiangsu case mentioned, see *Yen-ch'eng hsien-chih* [Gazetteer of Yen-ch'eng county] (1936),
1:7–10 and map, and 4:6b. On the insignificance of sub-county administrative divisions in
Ch'ing times, see Ch'ü T'ung-tsu, *Local Government in China under the Ch'ing* (Cambridge:
Harvard University Press, 1962), p. 10. In the first year of the republic, a post known as
hsien-tso (sub-county magistrate) was established as a substitute for the ineffective Ch'ing sub-
county officials (*hsun-chien*). This new system amounted to a dead letter in most provinces, but
survived to some degree in Szechwan, Shensi, Yunnan, Kweichow, Heilungkiang, and
Sinkiang. The Nanking government ordered these divisions abolished in 1930 when the new
self-government system was promulgated. Ch'en Po-hsin, *Chung-kuo hsien-chih kai-tsao* [The
reconstruction of China's county system] (Chungking: Kuo-min t'u-shu ch'u-pan-she, 1942),
p. 155.

the administrative dilemma that would face every Chinese government in modern times. If Chinese politics were to be rebuilt on the basis of a strong national government, some way would have to be found to reverse the process of power devolution into the hands of local elites that were essentially uncontrollable by existing bureaucratic organs. But to abolish county self-government was to meet only a segment of the total problem. There remained the question of how sub-county politics were to be brought within the purview of national control. Seen in another way, this problem was part of the larger problem of the regulation of urban–rural relationships. The ineffectuality of urban control over the rural hinterland was not new in republican times. It had stood in the background of much of the reformist literature of Ch'ing times, including of course the arguments of the *feng-chien* theorists. By the twentieth century, however, the problem had swollen disastrously. The disintegration of control mechanisms in the countryside had led to virtual anarchy in some areas, a collapse of local security, and rampant banditry. From the standpoint of the bureaucracy on all levels, an equally serious difficulty was sequestering the rural economic surplus for state purposes, because so much of it was being siphoned off by sub-county functionaries, local elites long out of control.

These problems could no longer be solved in traditional ways; and republican literature on local control seems generally to reflect this fact.[45] It is likely that this was already the case by mid-Ch'ing times, if not even earlier. Increased population density and economic competition, and local elites with growing numbers but declining social mobility, were hallmarks of late Ch'ing society. Added now were the disruptive effects of modern economic influences, changes in military and communications technology, and the new awareness that national strength and economic development required tighter local organization. In other words, the old control–autonomy proportion, in which regular bureaucratic control stopped at county level, was essentially

45. For a sampling of the enormous literature on local self-government in republican times, see the bibliography in Tung Hsiu-chia, *Chung-kuo ti-fang tzu-chih wen-t'i* [The problem of local self-government in China] (Shanghai, 1936). One compendium of such material is Chou Ch'eng, ed., *Ti-fang tzu-chih chiang-i* [Lectures in local self-government], 12 vols. (Shanghai, 1925). Development of this concept in practice by regional regimes in Kwangtung, Kwangsi, Hunan, and Shansi is an important research area. During the warlord period, local self-government became a popular slogan, with manifestations at virtually all points of the political spectrum. These ranged from Ch'en Tu-hsiu's call for mass participatory democracy through small residential and occupational cells, to the militarist Chao Heng-t'i's effort to bolster his Hunan domain with provincial autonomy and a provincial constitution.

The development of the Hunanese self-government movement is explored in an important article by Angus McDonald, "Konan jichi undō ni kansuru Mō Taku-tō no gohen no chosaku" [Five writings by Mao Tse-tung on the Hunan self-government movement], *Hōgaku kenkyū* [Journal of law, politics, and sociology] 46.2:90–107. This article explores a little-known aspect of Mao Tse-tung's career in 1920 and reprints some important early writing. Further material on Hunan can be found in *Hunan ch'ou-pei tzu-chih chou-k'an* [Hunan self-government preparation weekly] (Changsha, February to July 1921). For Ch'en Tu-hsiu's views, see 'Shih-hsing min-chih ti chi-ch'u" [Effectuating the foundation of popular government], *Hsin ch'ing-nien* [New youth] 7.1 (December 1, 1919):13–21.

unsuited to modern conditions. And autonomous control by local elites—
whether of the old informal sort or of the semi-formalized gentry-manager
sort—was by now generally discredited, both in traditional statecraft terms
and in the modernized vocabulary of local self-government. What were the
alternatives? They were either a more thorough bureaucratization of the
countryside, an expansion of the regular bureaucratic system to the lower
interstices of rural society; or some form of popular mobilization that would
involve local people in regulating their own affairs in a new way—one that
would enlist their energies at the same time that it integrated them into larger
mechanisms of national control. The local administrative program of the
Nationalist government after 1927 began with a commitment to achieve
mobilization through a transition to democracy. It ended with a highly
bureaucratic formula which embodied certain features of traditional statecraft outlooks.

The Kuomintang's interest in local self-government dates from the days of
the T'ung-meng-hui. The editors of the revolutionary organ *Min-pao* could
hardly afford to make local self-government a major plank in their platform,
since the issue was already preempted by the constitutionalists. Yet we find
that as influential a writer as Wang Ching-wei was quite ready to endorse the
idea as an instrumentality of revolution. It seemed an excellent weapon
against absolutism, which for him was virtually synonymous with Manchu
rule. And since the Manchu constitutionalists were "using the name of local
self-government as a facade for increased central control," the revolutionaries
should proceed to use it as a facade for revolution. But there was more to it:
Wang pointed out that "enterprises not yet undertaken represent power not
yet generated." Since all the specifically modern sorts of governmental
activity (such as modern-type police and schools) fall naturally within the
competence of local organizations, it behooves such local organizations (all
run by Han Chinese, of course!) to steal a march on the Manchu monarchy
and initiate them, thus in effect creating new instruments of power. But the
struggle for central authority remained paramount for Wang; and he never
integrated the idea of local self-government into a general view of national
political organization.[46] That became the hallmark of Sun Yat-sen's ambitious program for national reconstruction.

There is evidence that Sun had conceived local self-government to be the
bedrock of republicanism as early as 1897,[47] but it was not until fifteen years

46. Wang Ching-wei, "Man-chou li-hsien yü kuo-min ko-ming" [Manchu constitutionalism and the national revolution], *Min-pao* [The people's journal], vol. 8, October 8, 1906
(facsimile reprint, Peking: K'o-hsueh ch'u-pan she, 1957), pp. 46–51.

47. "Chung-kuo pi ko-ming erh hou neng ta kung-ho chu-i" [China must have a revolution before she can attain republicanism], conversation with Miyazaki Torazō and others, in
Kuo-fu ch'üan-chi [Collected works of Sun Yat-sen] (Taipei: Chung-yang wen-wu kung-ying-
she, 1965), II, "Conversations," p. 1. This version is evidently loosely translated from Miyazaki's *Sanjū sannen no yume* [A thirty-three year dream] (Tokyo: Bungeishunjūsha, 1943), pp.
145–146. It is not entirely clear from Miyazaki's version whether Sun actually used the
term "self-government" (*tzu-chih*) in its nominal form, but it looks that way. See ibid., p. 145.

later that he forged the characteristic link between local self-government and national integration that was to become the organizing principle of his *Outline of National Reconstruction* (1924). "As local self-government develops," he declared in 1912, "the politics of a whole province will advance according-ly; and this process will expand to the whole nation in like manner. Thus China will naturally grow strong and prosperous, able to compete with the great powers on the world stage."[48] This marked the beginning of Sun's public commitment to the idea that constitutional government must be built from the bottom up. As developed in the *Outline of National Reconstruction*, democracy is to be instituted first at the county level. Only when all the counties within a province are practicing democratic self-government does that province become democratically self-governing. And when half the provinces in the nation reach this condition, the organs of national demo-cratic government are established.

It is clear that Sun viewed both democracy and local self-government not as independent values, but as essential prerequisites to the supreme goal of national integration and strength. Self-government was to inculcate national consciousness, not local separatism. The distribution of power in his *Outline of National Reconstruction* leaves no residual enclaves of sovereignty to prov-inces or counties; and in all his writings on this subject, the national con-stitutional government toward which local self-government was ultimately directed had the main purpose of achieving a secure and independent place for China in world affairs. Sun's insistence that constitutional government be constructed from the bottom up can of course be traced in part to the disil-lusionment everyone felt toward the paper constitutions and sham parliamen-tarianism of China's central government since 1912. But it is also wholly consistent with the premises of the *feng-chien* tradition out of which contem-porary local self-government theories had emerged. Sun's program embodied that mainstream concept of political modernization which had emerged from the late Ch'ing and early republic: that the infrastructure of local government must mobilize the energies of the public in ways that would render local initiative compatible with national purposes.[49]

The Nationalist government came to power in 1927 committed to the implementation of Sun's *Outline of National Reconstruction*, the cornerstone of the Kuomintang program since 1924. The direction of Kuomintang policy on local government during the decade preceding the Sino-Japanese War can be illustrated by its handling of the problem of sub-county administrative units and its efforts to control the power of local elites. In both spheres, the Kuomintang program veered decisively away from the mobilization concept and toward more rigorous bureaucratic control.

48. "Ti-fang tzu-chih" [Local self-government], speech delivered in Ch'ao-chou, May 5, 1912, in *Kuo-fu ch'üan-chi*, II, "Speeches," pp. 16–17.
49. *Kuo-min cheng-fu chien-kuo ta-kang* [The national government's outline of national recon-struction], promulgated in April 1924, in *Kuo-fu ch'üan-chi*, I, "Programs," pp. 369–371.

THE WARD DIVISIONS UNDER KUOMINTANG TUTELAGE

Shortly after the establishment of the Nanking regime, it was decided to model sub-county administration upon the system which Yen Hsi-shan, governor of Shansi, had been operating in that province since 1917. Both the structure and the spirit of Yen's system were largely incompatible with the stated program of the Kuomintang; we do not yet know whether the decision to imitate it was made in full knowledge of this incompatibility, or whether it simply seemed attractive as the only such system in operation. The Shansi system was essentially in accord with the 1914 self-government directive, but went further in the fineness of its control mechanisms. It was based on a four-level hierarchy of units below the county; the *lin*, a five-family group, and the *lü*, of twenty-five households, which were obviously akin to the lower echelons of the old *pao-chia* system. Above them stood the village (*ts'un*), most often an administrative or linked village consisting of several small adjoining settlements, though the natural village was also an accepted division on this level. Higher still were the wards (*ch'ü*), three to six per county, depending on local conditions. The ward head was really a kind of sub-magistrate, appointed directly by the province chief, with purely administrative rather than representative functions. Ward heads were appointed according to a modified avoidance system, in which each was to serve within his own sector of the province though not within his own or an adjoining county. They held wide-ranging powers, serving concurrently as police superintendents and commanders of the ward militia.[50] The performance of the ward heads was seen by provincial authorities as crucial to the success of the system. In effect they had become the lowest level of regular bureaucratic administration.[51] Further research will reveal the degree to which this extension of bureaucratic administration was actually able to supplant or balance off the power of indigenous elites on the ward level. There are abundant indications that it was only marginally successful in this respect.

The system's bureaucratic structure was a faithful reflection of its spirit. As Yen Hsi-shan pointed out in 1918, the problem of the age was that modern influences and economic development exacerbated problems of local control. The more prosperous the people, the more grievous their vices. More purchasing power meant more opium addiction. Improved communications made it easier for opium to penetrate rural areas. Better schooling led to the deterioration of wholesome customs and values. Economic develop-

50. A fairly complete description of the Shansi structure can be found in Chou Ch'eng, *Shansi ti-fang tzu-chih kang-yao* [Outline of local self-government in Shansi] (Shanghai: T'ai-tung t'u-shu chü, 1922), pp. 1–10. Documents generated by this system are collected in *Shansi ts'un-cheng hui-pien* [Collected documents on Shansi local administration] (Shansi ts'un-cheng ch'u, 1928), consisting mostly of orders sent down from province to county.
51. *Shansi ts'un-cheng hui-pien*, 2:18b.

ment in itself was obviously desirable, but how could it be achieved and social order still be maintained? The answer was, first, a finer infrastructure of local control; and second, a "spiritual self-government" that could only be attained by involving local people in the very process of their own control. This was "the politics of using the people" (*yung-min cheng-chih*). Though the fundamentals of the system were clearly in the category of official government (*kuan-chih*) rather than self-government, Yen went on, yet self-government would somehow emerge from it all—a faith in the ability of official control systems ultimately to transform themselves into a more popular form of government, not unlike the ill-founded faith underlying the Kuomintang's tutelage concept.[52]

The Shansi system represented an amalgam of the old control–autonomy interaction with a more bureaucratic format. The control component had been moved a major step closer to the villages by means of the new ward offices and a multiplication of purely managerial personnel. The autonomy component had been dressed up in a spurious new vocabulary but was kept free of the more volatile contemporary concepts of popular mobilization. This was in short a conservative system with a heavily bureaucratic emphasis. And this was the system that in 1927 was recommended by the Kiangsu provincial Department of Civil Affairs (*Min-cheng-t'ing*) for adoption as the basic format of local tutelage government under the new Nanking regime.[53]

Nevertheless, the series of ordinances that emanated from Nanking during 1928 and 1929 seemed to be aimed at an accommodation between the Shansi system and the principles of self-government laid down by Sun Yat-sen. A slightly modified version of the Shansi system was in fact adopted, including the highly important wards as sub-county administrative units. Ward headmen, though appointed rather than elected, were not subject to a rule of avoidance. In accord with the tutelage principle, they were to be local men, serving as an integral part of the process whereby local communities were to gain their initial experience in self-government. The wards themselves, like the ones in Shansi, were substantially larger entities than the old wards that had emerged from late Ch'ing times, though the levels involved were very flexible. Regulations called for a ward to encompass between ten and fifty rural townships or market towns (*hsiang* or *chen*), which normally produced as many as a dozen or so, or as few as three or four wards per county. The old wards, which had represented the ultimate in power fragmentation, were now used as the bases of the new townships. Thus Nanking seemed determined to institutionalize the intermediate level of coordination between the county seat and the villages. The social importance of this consolidation has yet to be studied in detail; the displacement of power upwards to the level of the new ward cannot have been without effects on the network of local

52. Chou Ch'eng, *Shansi ti-fang tzu-chih kang-yao*, pp. 78–79 and appendix p. 33.
53. *Kiangsu SCKP* 1 (September 15, 1927):5–7, and 2 (September 22, 1927): 36–38.

influence and dependency which had grown out of the disintegrating Ch'ing system.[54]

Initially the Nanking regime seemed ready to infuse the inherited Shansi format with the principles of local democracy to which it was so deeply committed. Detailed plans were issued for the implementation of democratic self-government in all local units, with an ambitious timetable that would lead to full self-government by 1934. It was not long, however, before the timetable was interrupted. By early 1933 central and provincial administrators were conducting a basic reassessment of the future of local government, the result of which was a decision to put off the election of local officials indefinitely and, at the same time, to transform the wards into purely administrative arms of county government. By early 1934 this decision was embodied in a revised local government code, in which the wards were either to be abolished or bureaucratized, according to local circumstances. The actual process of bureaucratization had begun even earlier (1932) in the "bandit-extermination" (anti-communist) regions under the control of Chiang Kai-shek's military headquarters. In its final version, the plan in these areas made the ward heads subject to a rule of avoidance and to a term of office limited to three years. At the same time the wards were given a more extensive role in local security as regular units of a reinstituted *pao-chia* system. As an indication of the ward's changed status, the name of the ward offices in bandit-extermination areas was ordered changed from *kung-so* (a traditional appellation for the headquarters of an elite-managed multiplex association) to *shu* (meaning a regular government office). All this may actually have been a formalization of a trend already well underway in administrative practice, whereby ward and township offices were treated by county authorities not as self-government headquarters, but as administrative bureaus (*hsing-cheng-chü*).[55]

Nanking's growing determination to bureaucratize local self-government can in one sense be seen as an outgrowth of its obsession with internal security. This was of course occasioned by the struggle to exterminate the Communists through local purges (*ch'ing-hsiang*), an effort which colored the Kuomin-

54. Ch'ien Tuan-sheng, *Min-kuo cheng-chih shih* [History of governmental institutions in republican China], rev. ed. (Shanghai: Chung-hua shu-chü, 1946), II, 286–287. On the stages of ward consolidation, see *Yen-ch'eng hsien-chih*, 1:7–10, and map, also 4:6b; and *Kiangsu SCKP* 62 (December 3, 1928):15.

55. Ch'ien Tuan-sheng, *Min-kuo cheng-chih shih*, II, 285–297; Ch'en Po-hsin, *Chung-kuo ti ti-fang chih-tu chi ch'i kai-ko* [China's local institutions and their modifications] (Changsha: Kwangsi chien-she yen-chiu-hui, 1939), pp. 65–76; Matsumoto Yoshimi, "Chūgoku ni okeru chihō jichi seido kindaika no katei" [The stages of modernization of the local self-government system in China], in Niida Noboru, ed., *Kindai Chūgoku no shakai to keizai* [Modern China's society and economy] (Tokyo, 1951), pp. 51–81; Ch'eng Mao-hsing, *Chiao-fei ti-fang hsing-cheng chih-tu* [The local administrative system in bandit extermination areas] (Shanghai: Chung-hua shu-chü, 1936), pp. 124–128; also *Kiangsu SCKP* 62 (December 3, 1928):15, and 69 (January 21, 1929):15–18. For a survey of local self-government from an authoritative Kuomintang source see Li Tsung-huang, *Chung-kuo ti-fang tzu-chih tsung-lun* [General discussion of China's local self-government], fourth ed. (Taipei, 1954).

tang's whole approach toward rural administration during the early 1930s. In a broader context, however, the Nationalists' program was an outgrowth of the historical role they had inherited: as centralizers of authority, as a national regime concerned to reassert control over rural China and redress the centuries-old imbalance between bureaucratic and extrabureaucratic power. The trouble was that the means at hand were severely limited. Popular mobilization seemed a dangerous expedient, even had the Nationalists possessed the political technology to undertake it. But why could they not rely on the indigenous rural elite operating through the wards? If the local elite were the natural allies of the Kuomintang, as has so often been suggested, how can we account for the effort to replace this stratum of community leadership with a purely bureaucratic system, as we have seen taking place in the early 1930s?

WHO WERE THE "LOCAL BULLIES AND EVIL GENTRY?"

A 1934 directive from Chiang Kai-shek's military headquarters pointed out that the bureaucratization of the wards was necessitated by the disastrously low caliber of their headmen. "The people view ward headmen as no different from the *t'uan* heads and *chuang* heads of the old days,[56] and therefore have no respect for them." And since decent people shunned the job and rascals competed for it, "the post of ward head is everywhere monopolized by corrupt local bullies and evil gentry (*t'u-[hao] lieh-[shen]*). Such types have no administrative ability, but ample ability to oppress the people."[57] The identification of sub-county self-government personnel as "local bullies and evil gentry" (*t'u-hao lieh-shen*)—especially the ward heads—was ubiquitous in the 1920s and 1930s, and there is more than sufficient evidence that this characterization represented the common view not only of reform-minded administrators, but also of ordinary citizens.[58]

The trouble is that the term *t'u-hao lieh-shen* is neither a formal status designation nor a rigorously defined category of social analysis, but a popular term of opprobrium which hardened into a political slogan. What we are dealing with is a general popular conception which bore a definite relation to reality; but the actual social referent of which has yet to be explored systematically. The terms *t'u-hao* (local bully) and *lieh-shen* (evil gentry) can both be found in nineteenth-century literature. Not surprisingly, *t'u-hao* is the more abundant. In Ch'ing usage it meant a man of wealth, usually landed

56. The *chuang* heads were local leaders of the *lien-chuang* or linked-village system, a multiplex form of local defense association; the term *lien-chuang* prevailed in Shantung, Hopei, parts of Honan, and the Kiangpei area as a regional designation of the *t'uan-lien* local defense system. On the *t'uan*, see Kuhn, *Rebellion and Its Enemies*, esp. pp. 102–104.

57. Ch'eng Mao-hsing, *Chiao-fei ti-fang hsing-cheng chih-tu*, p. 125.

58. For instance, see Ch'en Po-hsin, *Chung-kuo ti ti-fang chih-tu*, pp. 62, 235. Also see *Kiangsu SCKP* 5 (October 13, 1927):7, and 68 (January 14, 1929):21–25.

wealth, generally but not necessarily literate, but with no formal degree status, whose community power was exercised in coercive and illegal ways. Although *lieh-shen* is also found, the term's relative rarity in Ch'ing times is easily explainable by the ability of gentry types to control the written language in ways favorable to themselves. A *lieh-shen* in an official document was a local degree-holder who broke the law so flagrantly and consistently that he could not cover it up. With the abolition of formal gentry status in the last years of the Ch'ing and the advent of a popular press, *lieh-shen* must have been attached to many men who would otherwise have shown up in historical records as perfectly respectable elite types. Whereas both *t'u-hao* and *lieh-shen* had been targets of conscientious Ch'ing officials, the twentieth-century flux of formal social distinctions and the eruption of social revolution brought the two terms together in a generalized attack on holders of power and wealth in the rural scene. Thus to define the social reality behind *t'u-hao lieh-shen* is at the same time to define the social status and activities of a sizable portion of the rural elite. Following contemporary descriptions and government documents, it is possible to arrive at a tentative estimate of their social position and character.

To begin with, it is clear that persons described as local bullies and evil gentry were widely spread through local self-government posts on various levels of sub-county administration. Though ward heads were most commonly so described, even lower level *pao-chia* headmen and village headmen (*ts'un-chang*) are occasionally included.[59] It is possible, of course, that this wide variation in political status can be accounted for by regional differences and loose social survey techniques; but it also suggests that we are dealing with a rather versatile social group that was able to dominate rural administrative structures on a number of levels. It is also apparent, however, that contemporary observers distinguished the local bullies and evil gentry from the more cultivated and leisured stratum of urban elite, variously referred to as *shen-shih* or *shih-shen* (terms which under the empire referred to scholar-officials or higher degree-holders). A 1933 survey in rural Honan found that although the power of the ward heads was formidable in the village setting, yet the real "hidden" power lay with the upper elite, evidently residing in the county seat, whose dictates even the magistrate could not contravene.[60] A Kiangsu magistrate's report of 1928 illustrates the clear functional differences between local self-government personnel and the scholar-elite (*shih-shen*). The latter,

59. Ts'ui Chieh-hsun, *Hsin-hsien chih* [The new county system] (n.p., June 1946), p. 62; Chang Yu-i, ed., *Chung-kuo chin-tai nung-yeh shih tzu-liao* [Materials on China's modern agricultural history] (Peking: San-lien shu-tien, 1957), III, 383. The data used for the following discussion come mainly from Kiangsu and Honan, with lesser amounts from various other provinces. There are many indications of similar conditions in areas farther from Nanking's control, though the actual range of regional variation remains to be determined systematically.

60. Hsing-cheng yuan, Nung-ts'un fu-hsing wei-yuan-hui [Executive Yuan, Rural Reconstruction Committee], comp., *Honan sheng nung-ts'un tiao-ch'a* [Investigation of Honan villages] (Shanghai, 1934), p. 87.

operating through an informal scholar-elite assembly (*shih-shen hui-i*) along with the merchants of the merchants' association (*shang-hui*), were the groups to which the magistrate turned for important policy advice and for major fund-raising enterprises. This upper elite was almost certainly an urban group, on which the magistrate had to rely for support in county-wide projects.

The local *hsiang-tung* (managers of the rural township divisions) were left with routine administrative tasks; their knowledge was considered inferior, and their administration undisciplined. The magistrate was determined to transform such local managers into more efficient and responsive organs of county government, though he admitted the job could not be done overnight.[61] In some areas an analogous distinction existed in the rural credit system between big absentee landlords, who made no direct loans to poor peasants, and the local *lieh-shen* who divided the rural usury business with the rich peasantry.[62]

Notwithstanding the social distinction between these rural *t'u-hao lieh-shen* and the urbanized upper elite, those who sought to maintain rural power had inevitably to seek official and elite patronage at the county level. During the warlord period, a clique of wealthy bullies (*fu-hao*) in Sui-ning, Kiangsu, were said to have exercised powerful influence over the magistrate. One of them, a certain Chu Heng-hao, was able to secure the title of county militia captain (*hsien ching-pei-ying-chang*) and to use this position to solidify his own power as local manager (*tung-shih*), apparently displacing older elite families in the process. Although Chu's county connections seem to have been shaken by the ouster of the warlord authorities in 1927, his local power remained considerable. The new magistrate reported that while on an inspection tour he had been barred from entering Chu's walled settlement by a party of armed men. And we know that this man, whom the magistrate denounced as a reactionary leader and an enemy of the Kuomintang, was able to stand off government power right through the Nanking period; for he is still listed as the local militia commander under the puppet regime in 1939.[63] Kinship and pseudo-kinship relations might also serve a *t'u-hao lieh-shen* as guarantees of local status. One unsavory character in Fu-p'ing county, Shensi, known to the local peasants as "poisonous black beetle," was a man of some education and leisured background who got his start as a pettifogger (*sung-kun*) and local enforcer (*tao-k'o*) and rose to a lucrative post as local irrigation supervisor and thence to platoon leader in the militia and *pao-chia* headman. Beetle's

61. *Kiangsu SCKP* 63 (December 10, 1928):21–24.
62. Mao Tse-tung, ed., *Nung-ts'un tiao-ch'a* [Village investigations] (Harbin: Tung-pei shu-tien, 1948), p. 23.
63. *Kiangsu SCKP* 45 (August 6, 1928):15–18, and 53 (October 1, 1928):25; *Sui-ning hsien-chih* [Gazetteer of Sui-ning county] (1887 ed.), 16:11–12; Su-pei hsing-cheng chuan-yuan kung-shu min-cheng-k'o [Civil affairs division, northern Kiangsu administrative supervisory office], comp., *Su-pei ko-hsien chih kai-k'uang* [The situation in northern Kiangsu counties] (n.p., 1939), p. 83.

authority seems to have depended on a skein of connections leading to the county seat: he betrothed his child into the family of a local landlord who was the sworn brother of the head of the merchant association in the city and was known to consort with "official" types. Though he was able to accumulate a modest parcel of land, the social position of such a man was clearly not high; but through appropriate patronage connections he was able to exercise immense local power in his rural setting.[64]

The educational level of local headmen and *t'u-hao lieh-shen* was invariably described as low, no doubt by comparison with the upper elite. Yet this group, though not highly educated, was generally at least literate. A 1933 survey of eighty-seven ward heads in Honan revealed that 16 percent had at least a middle–school education (one had a university degree!); another 16 percent included primary school graduates, products of teacher training schools, and holders of lower level imperial degrees. About 67 percent had graduated from a provincial training course for self-government leaders, which probably reveals literacy if little more.[65] On the whole, it seems likely that the educational level of this stratum of rural headmen can be roughly compared with the lower fringes of the local literati a generation earlier, which would have included not only holders of lower degrees, but also that more extensive pool of literate men who were kept off government student rolls by restrictive quotas.

The nearly universal association of these local self-government posts with landlordism raises the usual problem of the relationship between landowning and political power in China. In the Honan sample cited above, 59 percent held between sixteen and fifty acres each; 27 percent held less than sixteen acres; and only 13 percent held more than fifty acres. These were huge holdings in an environment of overpopulation and land shortage. Yet this was clearly not a class that could subsist comfortably on its rents. Self-government posts were themselves important sources of income, perhaps more important than rents themselves. The main income of such posts came generally from miscellaneous surtaxes (*chüan*), over which the regular bureaucracy had little control. In Shensi it was reported that in a single collection period one village head could make more than ¥1,000, and a ward head more than ¥10,000. Such profits made these posts attractive investments, worth substantial bribes to obtain. In a rice-growing region (Wu-chiang, Kiangsu), usury took the place of *chüan* levies as the main source of profit for local functionaries. And income from administrative posts was supplemented by a host of subsidiary occupations, including commerce and the kind of pettifogging interference in county judicial affairs that had long been a sideline of China's local elite.[66]

64. Shensi-sheng Fu-p'ing hsien Ch'eng-kuan kung-she Chi-ku-ts'un ts'un-shih p'ien-hsieh-tsu [Village history compilation group of Chi-ku village, Ch'eng-kuan commune, Fu-p'ing county, Shensi province], comp., *Chi-ku-ts'un en-ch'ou chi* [Record of loves and hatreds in Chi-ku village] (Peking: Chung-kuo ch'ing-nien ch'u-pan-she, 1964), pp. 13–19, 20–23.

65. *Honan sheng nung-ts'un tiao-ch'a*, pp. 75–76.

66. Ibid.; Chang Yu-i, *Chung-kuo chin-tai nung-yeh shih*, II, 380, 382; *Kiangsu SCKP* 45 (August 6, 1928):17. All figures have been converted from *mou* to acres.

The image of these headmen as a big rentier class is further blurred when we compare them with the really big absentee landlords. These were typically urban-based, wholly separated from the rural scene, and dependent upon agents to manage their huge but fragmented holdings. A Japanese field study of Shantung in 1941 revealed that absentee landlords in county seats commonly owned land investments of some 160 acres, and the richest might own more than 500. Their business ventures in urban centers were ramified, as were presumably their political connections on the county level and higher. Apparently this class enjoyed wealth and influence on a distinctly grander scale than that of the local self-government functionaries we have been describing.[67]

As a wealthy group that lacked the kind of direct access to official circles enjoyed by the urban absentee landlords, the rural self-government headmen had to wield political power in very direct ways. In view of local government's rapacity toward the rural inhabitants, landholders without political power were unlikely to hold onto wealth for long. A 1933 survey of Yen-ling county, Honan, discovered that although a decade earlier there had been ten-odd landlords with holdings of over 160 acres, the local surtaxes had ruined them all. In such an environment, a local self-government post could have the same protective force as an academic degree under the empire. Further, such posts could reinforce the economic enterprises of their incumbents. In the Wu-chiang case, the usury business was solidly backed by political power. The resident gentry-managers in this area, according to a 1927 report, were able to get away with interest rates of 40 percent per season (three times a year, as determined by the cropping schedule) by means of the enforcement powers built into their administrative posts. They could supervise government runners themselves, locking up defaulters and detaining them indefinitely. Foreclosures were effectively destroying local society ("the strong emigrated, the weak begged"), banditry was rampant, and whole villages were depopulated.[68] It would be interesting to discover how this kind of local anarchy affected the bursary system, which sought to rationalize the rent-collection process in the interest of the urban rentier class and which was supposedly well established in this area (Soochow prefecture). It is hard to believe that the orderly flow of agricultural surplus from country peasant to city elite—which the bursary system was supposed to effect—could long continue in such an environment.

Local self-government could absorb only the most successful of the local

67. Cited in Ramon Myers, *The Chinese Peasant Economy: Agricultural Development in Hopei and Shantung, 1890–1949* (Cambridge: Harvard University Press, 1970), p. 232. This excellent study is the first to make systematic use of Japanese field surveys of the North China economy.

68. *Honan sheng nung-ts'un tiao-ch'a*, p. 123; *Kiangsu SCKP* 7 (October 27, 1927): 15–16. Usury based on local political power was a common phenomenon and took many forms. In Szechwan, for example, local militia headmen (described as *t'uan* lords—*t'uan-fa*) used militia funds (obtained from surtaxes) as capital for pawnbroking businesses, which relied on the militiamen themselves as collection and enforcement agents! Lü P'ing-teng, *Szechwan nung-ts'un ching-chi* [Szechwan's village economy] (Shanghai, 1936), p. 453.

elite, who became in effect their upper stratum. Yet income from local administration was typically only part of a diversified economic position, as the
examples above suggest. And data in Chang Yu-i's source compilation show
that commercial capitalism also accounted for a share of the income of self-
government functionaries.[69] How new economic patterns were affecting the
social and political position of these headmen, and particularly how they
affected their relationship to urban elites, remains to be determined through
study of individual cases. Yet it appears that administrative posts were the
direct source of much of their wealth and without question provided the
necessary political underpinning for the rest.

Others of the rural elite had to rely on a miscellaneous array of enterprises,
some in the category of ordinary criminality, but most well within the
traditional range of rural elite activities. Here the evidence suggests significant differences in the styles of local bullies (*t'u-hao*) and evil gentry (*lieh-
shen*), the latter shunning the more blatant forms of illegal behavior and
seeking a more genteel route to economic survival. An outright *t'u-hao*, for
example, might be involved in armed resistance to authority and plain
thuggery.[70] But a *lieh-shen* was more likely to subsist quietly in traditional
employments like usury, pettifogging (*pao-sung*), and engrossment of taxes
(*pao-ts'ao* or *pao-lan*). The *lieh-shen* are for this reason more interesting, for
they represent the persistence of the kind of struggle for survival that characterized the old licentiate group (*sheng-yuan* and *chien-sheng*) under the empire.
Mao Tse-tung's field studies from the Kiangsi Soviet period contain a revealing description of the *lieh-shen's* economic position. Most of them owned some
land, but not enough to support them as rentiers. Therefore they relied on
pawnshops to support a leisured life-style. Mao points out that, realistically,
they could hardly be called landlords; nor were they rich peasants, obviously
because their life-style was not that of peasants. They were just *lieh-shen*—a
piece of awkward Marxism but effective social analysis.[71] *Lieh-shen* are elsewhere described as involved in other traditional economic enterprises.
Engrossment of taxes (collection of other people's taxes for commission), for
example, a common illegal business among lower degree-holders in the old
days, is mentioned in a 1927 edict from the Kiangsu provincial finance
department in terms that would seem quite familiar in the pronouncements of
a Ch'ing governor-general.[72]

A tentative conclusion about *t'u-hao lieh-shen*—and their upper crust, the
headmen of local self-government posts—is that this was a class of rather low
social position vis-à-vis the urban elite and of decidedly precarious economic

69. Chang Yu-i, *Chung-kuo chin-tai nung-yeh shih*, III, 379.

70. See the case in Hai-men county, Kiangsu, in *Kiangsu SCKP* 53 (October 1, 1928):31–33.

71. Mao Tse-tung, *Nung-ts'un tiao-ch'a*, p. 23.

72. *Kiangsu SCKP* 4 (October 6, 1927):22–23. The difference between *t'u-hao* and *lieh-shen*
is pointed out here also: the former resist taxation (*k'ang-liang*), but the latter engross taxes
(*pao-ts'ao*). These closely related activities represented notorious threats to government control
of rural tax revenues.

prospects. Any description of them as a landlord class must be hedged with important qualifications: even those who owned substantial amounts of land were clearly to be distinguished from urban-dwelling rentiers, who inhabited quite another culture and were socially a long way from the rural scene. Their economic position was dependent upon success in various kinds of local enterprise, of which self-government administration was the most rewarding. To survive amidst the rural insecurity and economic chaos of the republican decades, they had to fit themselves into whatever environmental niches they could. Many of these were of traditional sorts, and others—including local self-government—were the result of the changing technology and politics of the age. A reasonable hypothesis, I suggest, is that the *t'u-hao lieh-shen* represented the remnant of the lower rural elite of imperial days, marooned by the closing of traditional mobility channels, relatively unsuccessful in adapting to the requirements of the times, and with deteriorating social links to the higher elites of the cities.

We may well ask whether there were not important changes going on within this rural entrepreneurial class: changing outlooks and new social configurations stemming from a generation of political and cultural turmoil. Much study will be necessary before we can penetrate this problem. There are plenteous hints of change. A 1932 impeachment proceeding, for instance, lists various old-style elite (*chiu-p'ai shen-shih*) who had been connected with the county self-government organs of the early republic, along with one prominent member of the new-style elite (*hsin-p'ai shen-shih*) who was formerly a Kuomintang county committeeman and was now "a meddler in legal suits and a gambler."[73] A Kiangsu provincial official, back from an inspection tour, warned that despite vigorous efforts during the 1925–1927 revolution to "overthrow the *t'u-hao lieh-shen*," there was now arising a "fearful new force: the new *t'u-hao lieh-shen*" who were impeding all aspects of local administration.[74] The problem is to find out precisely what is meant in each such case in terms of social background, economic base, and interpersonal connections. Such matters can be approached only through detailed research in local sources covering a span of several generations.

Signs of continuity are also abundant. Kinship ties seem to have been successful in penetrating new forms of local organization. A survey in Wu-hsi county revealed a remarkable situation in which persons of the Hsueh surname, who may have formed an actual lineage, controlled virtually every local organization in and around the town of Li-she, including the township self-government office, the Kuomintang party branch, the merchant militia (*shang-t'uan*), and the local peasants' association. And the hereditary transmission of ward headships is visible in some areas as late as the mid-1930s.[75]

---

73. *Chien-ch'a-yuan kung-pao* [Gazette of the Control Yuan] (Nanking: Kuo-min cheng-fu chien-ch'aen yuan pi-shu ch'u), nos. 13–14 (May–June 1932): 35–42.

74. *Kiangsu SCKP* 34 (May 21, 1928):36–37.

75. *Wu-hsi Chin-kuei hsien-chih* [Gazetteer of Wu-hsi and Chin-kuei counties] (1881 ed.),

Old gentry-manager types, tenacious and politically adaptable, might dominate the headmen of the new, larger ward organizations by obtaining posts as their deputies.[76]

The efforts of the Nationalist government to bureaucratize and finally to abolish the ward divisions during the 1930s can only be understood in the light of the larger problem of controlling the *t'u-hao lieh-shen*, the larger group from which the self-government system drew so many of its personnel. Efforts to deal with the local bullies and evil gentry began in the earliest days of the Nanking regime. In Kiangsu a special penal code issued in August 1927 covered practically every misdeed of which the local elite had ever been accused, including not only outright violence and criminality but a host of traditional business and political activities such as usury, litigiousness and pettifogging, and dominating public organizations. Such a code offered carte blanche to the local drumhead courts (*t'e-pieh hsing-shih ti-fang lin-shih fa-t'ing*), which were the rough-and-ready local judiciary of the new regime (and which handled communist cases as well as *t'u-hao lieh-shen*).[77] These "temporary local courts" were kept busy during the single year in which they operated, and their standards of justice were probably impossible to control. They were abolished in January 1929, and all pending cases were to be turned over to the regular organs of the Judicial Yuan.[78]

It is not clear whether the abolition of these courts meant a slackening of the drive against the *t'u-hao lieh-shen*, but government efforts continued through other channels. Irregular local military power was one area in which the Nanking authorities and their provincial subordinates sought to displace local satraps. The Kiangsu provincial government, for example, made repeated efforts to break up old militia corps, many of which were controlled either by *t'u-hao lieh-shen* or by illicit popular societies such as the Red Spears, and to prevent the formation of new ones. Local security was declared to be the responsibility of the regular armed police (*kung-an-chü*) under provincial control, seconded by a nonprofessional militia based on the *pao-chia*-like lower echelons (*lü* and *ts'un*) of the self-government units. The problem of insuring that local militia units were either completely bureaucratized or completely nonprofessional was one that the Nationalists had inherited from the nineteenth century. And even in provinces such as Kiangsu, most directly under Nanking's control, the problem was not easily solved. Even the vigorous promotion of the militarized *pao-chia* system in the mid-1930s often meant that indigenous local militia systems, with their customary and personalistic power structure, were simply absorbed into the new system without changing their inner character.[79]

30:12; Chang Yu-i, *Chung-kuo chin-tai nung-yeh shih*, III, 380; Feng Ho-fa, *Chung-kuo nung-ts'un ching-chi tzu-liao* [Materials on China's village economy] (Shanghai, 1935), II, 330.

76. *Hopei SCKP* 1460 (September 10, 1932):4–5.

77. For the *t'u-hao lieh-shen* penal regulations, see *Kiangsu SCKP* 6 (October 20, 1927):46–47.

78. *Kiangsu SCKP* 67 (January 7, 1929):50–51.

79. *Kiangsu SCKP* 8–9 (November 10, 1972):26–30; 60 (November 19, 1928): 15–17; and

The struggle against the *t'u-hao lieh-shen* for control of local resources was another inescapable one for the Nationalist authorities. Surtaxes of a traditional sort were diverting sizable amounts of revenue out of regular tax channels into the hands of ward functionaries. Such revenues did not even reach the county office, much less the provincial. Many of the judicial prosecutions of the *t'u-hao lieh-shen* seem to have been aimed at this aspect of their activities; and of course much irregular local taxation was connected with support of militia corps, another good reason for militia reforms.[80] But the struggle spread into many other spheres of economic life. For example, the huge profits to be made from polder lands (*sha-t'ien*) pitted the government against tenacious and well connected local interests. Unscrupulous land developers were able to resist the government for years by naked coercion as well as through connections with highly placed front-men among the urban elite. Powerful "polder-rascals" (*sha-kun*) were among the most indomitable of *t'u-hao lieh-shen*. Since they stood in the way of the Kiangsu provincial government's effort to cash in on the rich polder land business, the conflict with them was sharp and unremitting.[81]

The government's attack on the *t'u-hao lieh-shen* culminated in the effort to strip them of their control of self-government posts, principally the ward headships. Efforts to set up standards for the appointment of ward heads were naturally a first step, and we can find elaborate paper schemes for the testing and training of ward personnel.[82] Whether these were conscientiously applied or not, it is evident that they were unsuccessful in controlling the quality of ward heads. Not until the suspension of self-government in the bandit-extermination areas was the problem attacked with vigor. The scope of the government's difficulty can be sensed from the 1933–1934 purges of ward heads in Honan, in which many scores were fired or criminally prosecuted, but with inconclusive results.[83]

The question of the character of the Nationalist government—what classes, outlooks, and historical forces it represented—has been much discussed but little studied. The Kuomintang was of course dealing with problems unique to its own area. But like many other "unique" historical phenomena, the problems of the 1930s were often new manifestations of old realities.

---

68 (January 14, 1929):52. Also see Hopei Min-cheng-t'ing [Department of civil affairs, Hopei], comp., *Hopei sheng-cheng-fu min-cheng-t'ing pan-nien kung-tso yeh-yao* [Semi-annual report of the Department of Civil Affairs, Hopei] (Peking, 1929), p. 120. Also see Yao Yung, *Yü-tung hsiang-ts'un tsu-chih chih yen-chiu* [Village organization in eastern Honan] (Nanking: Chin-ling ta-hsueh nung-hsueh-yuan nung-yeh ching-chi hsi, 1935), p. 10.

80. See, for instance, *Kiangsu SCKP* 59 (November 12, 1928):5–52.

81. Documents on the immensely complicated polder land question are plentiful in the *Kiangsu SCKP*. This was a problem that dated from Ch'ing times and will repay detailed study. See, for example, *Kiangsu SCKP* 31 (April 30, 1928):15–16; 32 (May 7, 1928):13–14; and 36 (June 4, 1928):18–22.

82. See *Kiangsu SCKP* 69 (January 21, 1929):9–10 for the Kiangsu regulations.

83. Honan sheng-cheng-fu pi-shu-ch'u [Honan provincial secretariat], comp., *Wu-nien-lai Honan cheng-chih tsung-pao-kao* [Quinquennial report on political work in Honan] (Kaifeng, 1935), pp. 22, 35, 65.

Though the outward texture was that of the social, technological, and conceptual world of the 1930s, the inner structure had a time dimension that linked it to the world of the late empires. With respect to local government, the central problem can be stated as follows: how can local power be made to serve social ends? The alternatives seem, in retrospect, quite clear. Local power had either to be disciplined directly by the state (a bureaucratic solution) or to embody a more substantial measure of discipline by local society itself.

By Ch'ing times, none of the more creative political thinkers was satisfied with the prevailing relationship between control and autonomy on the county level. Ku Yen-wu sought a fundamental change in the magistrate's position by linking him organically to the society he governed. Feng Kuei-fen sought a finer infrastructure on the sub-county level that would simultaneously curb the arbitrary powers of the gentry-managers and allow a network of control to emerge from indigenous social agencies. The statecraft and *feng-chien* side of K'ang Yu-wei's formulation would have brought the power of local elites into a constitutional framework, thus disciplining it and linking it to the nation's larger purposes. But K'ang also emerges as the first truly modern thinker in the tradition of local reformism: his concern to energize local society, as well as control it, makes him the first to envisage a solution based upon mobilization. The local self-government idea—not in the restrictive version of the official Ch'ing code, but in the mobilizational sense infused into it by K'ang—was a potent influence on the thought of Sun Yat-sen, and thereby entered the mainstream of Kuomintang political theory.

By 1927 it was abundantly clear that a purely traditional control–autonomy relationship on the county level was no longer viable. This point had been clear even to Yen Hsi-shan, who understood that modernity, whether one liked it or not—and perhaps all the more if one did not—required new institutional departures in local government. Nanking's desperate internal security problem, along with Chiang's ambivalence toward modernity, made the Shansi pattern very attractive. It did not take long for the self-government aspects of the Kuomintang's heritage to be shelved in favor of a purely bureaucratic solution: the intensification of control through the proliferation of bureaucratic infrastructure in local society. In this respect Nanking inherited the statecraft determination to curb the undisciplined powers of local elites with agencies more responsive to the bureaucratic state. Thus Nanking was on a collision course with sub-county satraps who could neither insure local security nor transmit sufficient revenues upward. Just as Feng Kuei-fen was concerned to order the chaotic world of rural government in the interest of urbanized rentiers and the bureaucratic order on which they depended, the Kuomintang found itself in the position of attacking the position of indigenous rural elites in the interest of urban classes: classes whose interests, whether as rentiers, as modernizers, or as nationalists, were ill served by the *t'u-hao lieh-shen* in the hinterland.

Yet Chiang Kai-shek remained well aware that national strength and modernization could not be achieved on a purely bureaucratic basis. He was enough a man of his time to be affected by the prevailing conviction that popular mobilization was an essential ingredient of modern nationhood. This view had been part of the local self-government movement since its beginnings. And as heir to Sun Yat-sen's leadership, Chiang could not afford to abandon the mobilization component of the Tsung-li's program. Accordingly, the war of resistance precipitated the highly touted "new county system" (*hsin-hsien-chih*). Promulgated in 1939, this ambitious but vaguely phrased program seemed to be aimed at mobilizing the Chinese people by reinstituting certain aspects of local self-government. This was to be done through the unlikely expedient of investing the *pao-chia* system—which of course retained all its old police functions—with representative and self-governing functions. A number of other features, including special *pao-chia* indoctrination schools, were aimed at widening the circle of political participation and arousing national consciousness. The county itself was to be reinvigorated as an agent of economic development.[84] This project, though apparently of high importance to Chiang, remained largely on paper. Yet it is evidence of the general recognition that a purely bureaucratic solution to local government-society relations had no future.

Yet formidable problems stood in the way of a program that would mobilize the countryside and widen political participation through a self-government system. One of the persistent themes running through the thought of men like Feng Kuei-fen and K'ang Yu-wei is that local self-government is a sham—and a potentially destructive social force—unless some means be found to control its class character. By this I mean that "self"-government, like "self"-determination, leaves open the question of precisely who is to do the governing or determining. It makes no assumptions about the organization of power within the autonomous unit; and contains no safeguards against arbitrary, anti-social, and exploitative behavior by the indigenous elites who are best prepared to control local society. This recalls the German jurist Hermann Roesler's (1834–1894) critique of Gneist: that far from training local elites to the service of state and society, self-government would simply become a license for the dominant social classes to exploit and mistreat everybody else.[85]

In this respect the Kuomintang was confronted with a social situation long in the making. The stratum of lower degree-holders and of lettered but untitled commoners was the group which the Ch'ing regime was perhaps least successful in controlling. Restrictive *sheng-yuan* quotas and declining

84. Chang Yuan-mou, *Hsin-hsien-chih chih li-lun yü shih-chi* [The theory and actuality of the new county system], fifth ed. (Chungking, 1944), pp. 4–9.

85. Joseph Pittau, S.J., *Political Thought in Early Meiji Japan* (Cambridge: Harvard University Press, 1967), pp. 131–157. Also see Johannes Siemes, S.J., *Hermann Roesler and the Making of the Meiji State* (Tokyo: Sophia University Press, 1966).

opportunities for mobility into official careers meant that very few such men could be integrated into the national polity and thereby brought within the system of rewards and sanctions that controlled the upper elite. Their struggle to survive in a leisured life style often meant involvement in local political affairs in ways that the bureaucracy found either meddlesome or illegal, or both. The abolition of the examination system after 1905 stimulated a search for new ways of involvement in public affairs, culminating in the brief efflorescence of county self-government around the time of the Revolution of 1911. But during the first two decades of the republic the rural elite were left to survive on the basis of more traditional devices. By 1927 they stand forth as the group least able to adapt to the new opportunity structure and increasingly isolated from urban elites living in a different cultural and economic world. In this situation local self-government became only the most lucrative of many local enterprises, and presumably the most satisfying to this group's political vocation.

The Kuomintang, as I have suggested, partook of the contemporary assumption that modern conditions required new approaches to local government. But turning rural self-government over to existing local elites was tantamount to putting local society at their mercy. The shift toward a purely bureaucratic solution was the inevitable result. But a new local system based on mobilization rather than a mere intensification of bureaucracy would face essentially the same problem. Political power that was both community-based and nationally controllable could not be generated through existing social relationships. Those relationships—or what was left of them after the war's devastation—were destroyed in the course of land reform, along with the local elite that dominated them.

Glossary

This glossary does not include proper names in Arthur Hummel, *Eminent Chinese of the Ch'ing Period* (Washington, D.C.: U.S. Government Printing Office, 1943–1944); Howard L. Boorman, *Biographical Dictionary of Republican China* (New York: Columbia University Press, 1967); or Donald W. Klein, *Biographic Dictionary of Chinese Communism, 1921–1965* (Cambridge: Harvard University Press, 1971). Well-known figures of Chinese history (e.g., An Lu-shan, Han Wu-ti) are also omitted; as are well-known cities, reign names, and common terms readily identifiable to a Chinese expert (e.g., *chin* [catty], *chin-shih* [metropolitan degree-holder], etc.).

a-fu-yung 阿芙蓉
A-ssu-ha 阿思哈
ao-min 鶩民

ch'a-chüan 茶捐
ch'a-i 插翼
ch'ai-i 差役
ch'ai-yin 差銀
ch'an-i i-shuo 羼以夷說
Chang Ching-shih 張經世(章)
Chang Chü-cheng 張居正
Chang Hsun 張巡
Chang Shih-ch'eng 張士誠
Chang Su 張宿
Chang Ta 張達
Chang Tiao-ting 張調鼎
Chang Ting-t'ai 張鼎泰
Chang Tuan-ying 張端英
Chang Yun-chang 張雲章
ch'ang-ch'iang 長鎗
chao-fu 招撫
chen 鎮
Ch'en Chao-hsiang 陳兆相
Ch'en Ch'i-hsin 陳啓新
Ch'en Jui-chih 陳瑞之
Ch'en Ming-shih 陳明時

Ch'en Ming-yü 陳明遇
Ch'en Shih 陳時
Ch'en Yü-chi 陳玉瑛
ch'eng 城
ch'eng-huang ti 城隍帝
Ch'eng Pi 程璧
chi 稷
chi-hou-so 羈候所
Chi-she 幾社
Chi Shih-mei 季世美
chi-t'ien 寄田
Chi Ts'ung-hsiao 季從孝
Ch'i Chi-kuang 戚繼光
Ch'i Fan 戚藩
Ch'i-hsi (Teng Ta-lin) 起西 (鄧大臨)
Ch'i Hsun (Po-p'ing) 戚勲 (伯屏)
chia 甲
Chia-pien lu 家變錄
chia-shou 甲首
chia-ting 家丁
Chiang Ying-chia 姜應甲
chiao 剿
Chiao-pin-lu k'ang-i 校邠廬抗議
chieh 解
chieh-chih 介之
chien-Huang chi-yun 借黃濟運
Chieh-tzu (Huang Yü-ch'i) 介子 (黃毓棋)
ch'ieh-tao 竊盜
ch'ieh-tao san-fan 竊盜三犯
chieh-ch'a yü-shih 監察御史
chien-fu 減賦
Chien-fu chü 減賦局
chien-min 奸民
chien-min 賤民 ?mean people
Ch'ien Chi-teng 錢繼登
Ch'ien Mo 錢默
Ch'ien Shih-chin 錢士晉
Ch'ien Shih-sheng 圖士升
Chin An-ch'ing 金安清
chin-hua 進化
ch'in-wang 勤王
ching-chi 警跡 (迹)
ching-chi 經濟
ching-pao 經保

ching-shih 經世 *statecraft*
ching-shih chi-min 經世濟民
Ching-shih wen-pien 經世文編 *Selected Essays on Statecraft*
ching-tsao 經造
ching-ying 京營
Ching-yueh ch'üan-shu 景岳全書
ch'ing-hsiang 清鄉
Ch'ing-men lu-kao 青門簏稿
chiu-p'ai shen-shih 舊派紳士
Ch'iu Yang-wen 邱仰文
Chou Ch'en 周忱
Chou Ch'i 周岐
Chou Chih-k'uei 周之夔
Chou Jui-lung 周瑞隆
Chou Shou-ch'ang 周壽昌
Chu Chih-pi 朱之弼
Chu Heng-hao 朱恆顥
Chu Kuo-ch'ang 朱國昌
chu-pu 主簿
chu-shih 主事
chü 局
chü-pao 具保
Ch'u-wang 楚王
chüan 捐
chuang-shih 壯士
chuang-t'ou 莊頭
chün-chia 均甲
chün-fu 均賦
chün-hsien 郡縣
Chün-hsien lun 郡縣論
chün-i 均役
chün-kuo ping 君國兵
chün-pan 均辦
chün-t'ien 均田
chün-t'ien chün-i 均田均役
chün-t'u 均圖
chün-yao 均徭
chung-i chih pang 忠義之邦
chung-i tz'u 忠義祠
chung-yung 中鏞

fan-Ch'ing fu-Ming 反清復明
fang 坊
Fang Heng 方亨

Fei-fang 匪房
feng-chien 封建
Feng Hou-tun 馮厚敦
feng-kuo 封國
feng-su 風俗
fu 賦 *land tax*
fu-hao 富豪
Fu hsiang-chih i 復鄉治議
fu-hu 富戶
Fu-i ch'üan-shu 賦役全書
fu-ku 復古
Fu-li-hun 富勒渾
fu-ping 府兵
Fu-she 復社

Hai-ch'eng 海成
hai-yun 海運
han-chien 漢奸
Han Shih-ch'i 韓世琦
hao-hsieh 豪傑
hao-yu 豪友
Hei-ch'ien ti-hsiung 黑錢弟兄
Ho Ch'ang 何常
Ho Hsien-ch'ih 何獻墀
Ho Kang 何剛
Ho-lan Chin-ming 賀蘭進明
Ho T'ai 何泰
ho-yun 河運
ho-yun chin-t'ieh 河運津貼
Hou Chih-tseng 侯岐曾
hsi 吸
Hsi Chin chih hsiao lu 錫金識小錄
Hsi-liang 錫良
Hsi-yuan lu 洗冤錄
hsia 俠
Hsia Ch'i-lung 夏起隆
Hsia Kung-yu 夏供祐
hsia-mang 下忙
Hsia Wei-hsin 夏維新
hsiang-chia 鄉甲
Hsiang-fu ssu 祥符寺
hsiang-ping 鄉兵
hsiang-tung 鄉董
hsiang-yueh 鄉約 *local covenant*

hsiao-hu 小戶

hsiao yao-k'ou 小窰口

Hsiao-yu hsien shih yuan chung ts'ao 小遊仙詩園中草

hsieh-chi chü 協濟局

hsien-tso 縣佐

hsin-hsien-chih 新縣制

hsin-p'ai shen-shih 新派紳士

hsing-cheng-chü 行政局

hsing-shu 刑書

Hsiung Hsi-ling 熊布齡

Hsiung Hsueh-p'eng 熊學鵬

Hsu Chieh 徐階

Hsu Chih 徐陟

Hsu Chin 許晉

Hsu Ch'ü 徐趣

Hsu Erh-hsuan 徐爾鉉

Hsu Erh-sui 徐爾邃

Hsu Erh-yung 徐爾鎔

Hsu Fu-yuan 徐孚遠

hsu-li 胥吏

Hsu Nai-chao 許乃釗

Hsu Nai-chi 徐乃濟

Hsu Shih-ch'i 徐石麒

Hsu Ta-tso 徐達左

Hsu T'ing-t'ui 徐廷退

Hsu Tu 許都

Hsu Yuan 許遠

Hsu Yun-chen 徐允貞

Hsu Yung-chen 徐永貞

Hsu Yung (-te) 許用(德)

Hsuan 宣

Hsueh Wang 薛王

Hseuh Yen 薛顏

hsun-an 巡按

hsun-chien 巡檢

hsun-ching 巡警

hsun-tao 訓導

Hu Shou-heng 胡守恆

Hu T'ing-tung 胡廷棟

Huang Ang 黃卬

Huang Chen-lin 黃貞麟

Huang Liu-hung 黃六鴻

Huang Ming-chiang 黃明江

Huang-shan-cha 黃山閘

Huang T'ing-hu 黃廷鵠

huang-ts'e 黃冊

Huang Yü-ch'i (Chieh-tzu) 黃毓棋(介子)

hui 會

hui-kuan 會館

Hung-ch'ien ti-hsiung 紅錢弟兄

huo-hao 火耗

i 役 *corvee*

i-ch'uan 驛傳

i-fa 役法

i-min 義民

i-shih-hui 議事會

i-t'iao-pien 一條鞭 *single whip tax*

i-yung 義勇 *village braves*

jang-i 攘夷

Jih-chih lu 日知錄

ju 儒

kan 桿

kan 贛

kan-ch'ing 感情 *rapport*

kang-yin 綱銀

k'ang 炕

k'ang-liang ts'e 抗糧冊

Kindai Kōnan no Sosan 近代江南の租棧

ko 葛

k'o 客

K'o Sung 柯聳

kou-t'ung t'u-kun 勾通土棍

Ku Hsien-ch'eng 顧憲成

ku-i 雇役

Ku San-ma-tzu 顧三麻子

Ku Wen-pin 顧文彬

Ku Yuan-pi 顧元泌

k'u-miao an 哭廟案

kuan-chih 官治

kuan-shou kuan-chieh 官收官解

kuan-shu 管束

kuan-t'ien 官田

kuang-kun 光棍

K'uang Chung 況鐘

kuei-chi 詭計

kung-an-chü 公安局
kung-min 公民
Kung-min tzu-chih 公民自治
Kung Shih 龔氏
kung-so 公所
kung-t'ang 公堂
k'ung-le ch'ü-ts'ai 恐嚇取材
kuo-chi 國計
Kuo Shih-ying 郭士璟

li 例
li-chang 里長
li-chia 里甲
Li Chih 李贄
Li Chin 李進
Li Fu-hsing 李復興
Li-hsiang 麗享
Li Hung-pin 李鴻賓
li-i 里役
Li Sheng 酈生
liang-chang 糧長
liang-chia tzu-ti 良家子弟
liang ssu-ma 良司馬
lieh-shen 劣紳
lien-chuang 聯莊
lien-pu 廉捕
likin (li-chin) 釐金
lin 鄰
Lin Chih-chi (See: Lin Mu-kua) 林之驥 (林木瓜)
Lin Liang-tso 林良佐
Lin Mu-kua 林木瓜
Liu Han-ju 劉漢儒
Liu Hsiang-k'o 劉湘客
Liu Ju-shih 劉如是
Liu Kuang-tou 劉光斗
Liu O 劉鶚
Liu Shih-tou 劉士斗
liu t'ou, pu liu fa; liu fa, pu liu t'ou 留頭不留髮, 留髮不留頭
Lo-tung tsa-chu 甚東雜著
lou kuei 陋規
Lu Chien 陸束
Lu Sung 盧松
lü 閭
lü 律

Lü K'un 呂坤
Lü Ta-chün 呂大鈞
luan-shih 亂世

ma 麻
Ma-p'i-ch'iao 麻皮橋
Ma San 馬三
Ma T'ien-ch'i 馬天麒
mai-t'u mai-yen 買土賣烟
min-cheng-t'ing 民政廳
min-chuang 民壯
Min-pao 民報
min-sheng 民生
min-t'ien 民田
min-tsu 民族
min-t'uan 民團   *private militia*
Ming-i tai-fang lu 明夷待訪錄
Ming Ling 明令
mo-ming 沒命
Mo-ming she 沒命社
Mo Shih-ying 莫士英
mu-chüan 畝捐
mu-fu 幕府
mu-i 募役
Mu-lu shih 慕廬氏
mu-ping 募兵
mu-yu 幕友

nan yü te-li 難於得力
nei-wu fu 內務府
nei-ying 內應   *traitors within*
nei-yu wai-huan 內憂外患   *internal anxiety + external calamity*
nien 捻
Ning Shih 甯氏

pa-wang she 覇王社
pai-hsing 百姓
p'ai chia 排甲
p'ai t'ou 牌頭
pan 板
pang 邦
pang-fei 幫費
P'ang Chung-lu 龐鍾璐
pao-chang 保障

pao-chia 保甲

pao-chuang 保狀

pao-hsiang ping 保鄉兵

pao-i 包衣

pao-lan 包攬 *proxy remittance*

Pao Shih-ch'en 包世臣

pao-sung 包松

pao-ts'ao 包漕

P'ei-yuan-t'ang o-ts'un kao 培遠堂偶存稿

Pen-ts'ao kang-mu 本草綱目

pien-tan-she 扁擔社

p'ing-mi 平米

po-ch'uan 駁船

Po-ping (Ch'i Hsun) 伯屏（戚勲）

pu-an-fen 不安份

pu-i 捕役

pu-k'uei 捕快

pu-wang 捕亡

Sa-tsai 薩載

san-fan 三藩

san-kung tz'u 三公祠

san-wang chih-lueh 三岡識略

sha-kun 沙棍

sha-ping 沙兵

sha-t'ien 沙田 *polder fields*

shan-hou fu-shu chü 善後撫恤局

shang-hu 上戶

shang-hui 商會

shang-mang 上忙

shang-shui 商稅

shang-t'uan 商團

Shao K'ang-kung 郡康公

she-chi 社稷

she-meng 社盟

she-ts'ang 社倉

shen-shih 紳士

shen-tung 紳董

Shen Yueh-ching 沈曰敬

Sheng (shih) 盛氏

sheng-chien 生監

sheng-p'ing 升平

Sheng-wu chi 聖武紀

shih 勢

shih-chia-p'ai-fa 十甲牌法
shih-jen 士人
Shih Kung-pi 石公弼
shih-shen (see *shen-shih*) 士紳
shih-shen hui-i 士紳會議
shou 收
shou-tsu chü 收租局
shu 署
shu-she 書社
shu-t'ien 熟田
shuai 率
shun-min 順民 *surrendering people*
ssu-ch'ai 四差
Ssu-i t'ang jih cha 思益堂日札
ssu-shih 司史
Su Erh-te 蘇爾德
Sui-yang wang 睢陽王
Sun (Shih) 孫(氏)
Sun T'ing-ch'üan 孫廷銓
Sung Cheng-pi 宋徵璧
sung-kun 訟棍

ta-chia 大家
ta-chü 大衆
ta-hu 大戶
Ta-tzu Hu-erh 韃子胡兒
ta yao-k'ou 大窰口
tai 袋
tai-chih 代治 *surrogate government*
tang 黨
T'ang Ch'eng-hsin 湯澄心
tao-k'o 刀客
tao-kuan-yin 盜官銀
T'ao Hsu 陶煦
t'e-pieh hsing-shih ti-fang lin-shih fa-t'ing 特別刑事地方臨時法庭
Teng Ta-lin (Ch'i-hsi) 鄧大臨(起西)
ti-chi 遞籍
ti-chieh yuan-chi 遞解原籍
ti-fang tzu-chih 地方自治 *local self gov.*
ti-pao 地保
ti-ting-yin 地丁銀 *land + capitation tax*
t'i-yung 體用
t'ieh-kan 鐵桿
tien-shih 典史

T'ien-hsia chün-kuo li-ping shu 天下郡國利病書

ting 丁

t'ing 廳

t'ou-hsien 投獻

t'ou-k'ao 投靠

t'ou-shen 投身 *gentry*

tsa-fan 雜泛

ts'ai-hsien i-chi 猜嫌疑忌

Ts'ang 蒼

Ts'ao Ch'i 曹溪

ts'ao-liang 漕糧 *tribute rice*

ts'ao-mi 漕米 *tribute rice*

ts'e 冊

Tseng Hua-lung 曾化龍

tsou-hsiao an 奏銷案

tsou-hsiao ts'e 奏銷冊

tsu-chan 租棧 *landlord bursaries*

tsu-cheng 族正

tsu-chih 租制

tsu-chüan 租捐

tsui-jen 罪人

ts'ui 催

ts'un-chang 村長

Tsung Hao 宗灝

tsung-hsiao-chia 總小甲

ts'ung-su 從俗

Tu Chi-ch'un 杜及春

Tu Chia-ch'un 杜甲春

Tu Heng-ch'un 杜恆春

Tu Lin-cheng 杜麟徵

tu-ssu 都可

Tu Teng-ch'un 杜登春

t'u 圖

t'u-hao lieh-shen 土豪劣紳 *local bullies + evil gentry*

t'u-pang 土帮

t'u-ping 士兵 *mercenary soldiers*

t'u-shen 土神

t'u-tien 土店

t'uan 團

t'uan-lien 團練 *militia*

tung 董

Tung Han 董含

Tung-lin 東林

Tung-p'ing wang 東平王

tung-shih 董事
tung-shih-hui 董事會
Tung-yang 東陽
t'ung-hsiang hui 同鄉會
T'ung-meng-hui 同盟會
tzu-ai tzu-chung 自愛自重
tzu-chih 自治
tzu-chih ch'i shen, tzu-chih ch'i hsiang, 自治其身，自治其鄉
tzu-chih ch'ü 自治區
tzu-i-chü 諮議局
tzu-ts'ui tzu-chieh 自催自解
tz'u-hsueh yu 刺血友

wang-fa 枉法
Wang Hua 王華
Wang Hung-tso 王宏祚
Wang Kung-lueh 王公略
wang-ming she 亡命社
Wang Shih 王試
Wang Ts'ao 汪藻
wang tz'u ta pang 王此大邦
wei-so 衛所
wen-jen 文人
wen-miao kung-fei ch'ien 文廟工費錢
Wu Chia-ying 吳嘉贏
Wu Chih-k'uei 吳志葵
Wu Ch'in-chang 吳欽章
Wu-chung i-kuei 五種遺規
Wu Pao-shu 吳寶恕
wu-t'u 烏土
Wu Yu-hsueh 吳幼學

ya-i 衙役
ya-p'ien 鴉片
ya-p'ien-yen 鴉片烟
Yang Fang 楊坊
yang-lien 養廉
yao 猺
Yao Ch'i-yin 姚奉胤
Yao Hsi-meng 姚希孟
yao-k'ou 窖口
yao-ts'ao 妖草
Yao Wen-jan 姚文然
yen-ch'a 煙茶

yen-chiu 煙酒
yen-kuan 烟舘
yen-lu 言路
Yen Ssu-sheng 晏斯盛
Yen-t'ang chien-wen tsa-chi 研堂見聞雜記
Yen-tzu ch'un-chiu 晏子春秋
Ying-su 罌粟
yu-hsiao-pi 右小臂
yu-tsui chih jen 有罪之人
yü 圩
yü-lin t'u-ts'e 魚鱗圖册
yü-men 虞門
yü-t'u chü 與圖局
yuan-chi 原籍
yuan-min 愿民
yuan-pao 元寶
yueh 約
yueh-cheng 約正
yueh-shih 約史
yueh-shu 約束
Yun-chien chü-mu ch'ao 云間据目抄
yung-min cheng-chih 用民政治

Index

Abahai, 13n, 154 f.
Abbasid caliphate, 32 ff.
Abel, Clarke, 148
Aborigines, 189, 192, 194, 198
Absolutism, 282
Academia Sinica, 174n
Academies, 231
Actors, 17, 124, 139
Adams, Leonard, 143
Administration. *See* Local administration
Administrative centers, 186 ff.
Administrative sanctions, 129, 132
Adultery, 131n
Agriculture, 44 f., 116, 153, 173, 189, 223, 279, 291; and cash crops, 105, 147, 153; festivals, 138; production of, 168, 220, 224, 225; failure, 178
Ahee, 167
Alawite Muslims, 37
Alcock, Rutherford, 240
Algiers, 35
Allen, Young J., 166
Alumni groups, 198
America, 229
American opium dealers, 167
Amherst mission, 19
Amnesty, 138
Amoy, 148, 162, 163; gazetteer of, 145
Ancestral tablets, 48
Anhwei, 51n, 61, 64, 64n, 65, 134n, 159, 215, 233, 239
"An Inquiry into Rents," 215
Anking, 241, 242
An Lu-shan, 50, 78n
Anti-Christian movements, 192, 204
Antiforeignism, 84, 193, 230
Anti-Manchuism. *See* Manchu-Chinese conflict
Anti-Opium Society, 170
Anti-taxation violence, 189. *See also* Riots
Arab, 33
"Arboricultural foundation," 212
Aristocracy, 14. *See also* Nobility
Army, 33 ff., 63, 65 f., 156, 179, 181, 192, 200 ff., 209, 214, 246, 267, 286; expense of, 9, 193, 198, 200, 244 f.; logistics of, 52n, 116n, 233 f., 248n; colonies of, 71n;

opium addiction in, 150 f., 155 f., 160 f.; deserters from, 164; suppression of mass movements by, 206 ff.; operations of, 231 ff.; reorganization of, 240; technology of, 281. *See also* Arsenals; Banners; Military households; Military institutions; Military specialists; Militia
Arsenals, 161, 171, 248n
Artillery, 75n, 76 ff., 82, 235
Artisans, 34, 67n, 75
Arts, 41
Assemblies: at provincial level, 85, 274, 277; at local level, 278 f.
Assistant magistrate, 49 ff., 284
Associations, 3, 9, 23, 34, 44, 51n, 52n, 69, 72 ff., 88 f., 96 ff., 100 f., 103, 109, 115, 116n, 118, 198, 260, 270 f., 274, 289 f.
Atlas mountains, 35

Bailiffs, 14, 23
Bambooing, 121, 128n, 129 ff., 138 f., 141, 158 f.
"Bandit-extermination" region, 286, 295
Bandit house (*fei-fang*), 138
Banditry, 29–31, 43, 46–47, 52–53, 55, 64, 73, 75, 102, 135n, 181, 183, 189, 192, 193, 194, 196, 200 ff., 204, 208, 281, 291,
Banishment, 121 ff., 130, 134n, 156 f.
Banks, 33, 143, 274
Bannermen, 56 ff., 84, 110, 110n, 130, 144, 200
Banners, 13 f., 19
Banqueting court, 160
Baraka, 36 f.
Barbarians, 71n, 145, 147, 265
Batavia, 147, 161 f.
Beattie, Hilary, 95
Bedouin, 34, 35, 37
Beggars, 124, 134n, 136 ff., 139, 192
Bengal, 151, 152
Board of Civil Appointments, 9, 11, 53, 67n, 109n, 112, 125n; Office of Scrutiny of, 76n
Board of Justice, 11, 53, 125n, 127, 128n, 129, 131, 133, 134n, 135n, 150, 158, 159, 231
Board of Personnel, 111

313